D0623318

TRICKSTERS & ESTATES

Tricksters & Estates

On the Ideology
of Restoration Comedy

J. DOUGLAS CANFIELD

THE UNIVERSITY PRESS OF KENTUCKY

Publication of this volume was made possible in part
by a grant from the National Endowment for the Humanities.

Copyright © 1997 by The University Press of Kentucky

Scholarly publisher for the Commonwealth,
serving Bellarmine College, Berea College, Centre
College of Kentucky, Eastern Kentucky University,
The Filson Club Historical Society, Georgetown College,
Kentucky Historical Society, Kentucky State University,
Morehead State University, Murray State University,
Northern Kentucky University, Transylvania University,
University of Kentucky, University of Louisville,
and Western Kentucky University.

Editorial and Sales Offices: The University Press of Kentucky
663 South Limestone Street, Lexington, Kentucky 40508-4008

01 00 99 98 97 1 2 3 4 5

Frontispiece: Portrait of Anthony Leigh in trickster role
by Sir Godfrey Kneller. Courtesy National Portrait Gallery, London

Library of Congress Cataloging-in-Publication Data

Canfield, J. Douglas (John Douglas), 1941-
    Tricksters and estates: on the ideology of Restoration comedy /
J. Douglas Canfield.
        p.   cm.
    Includes bibliographical references and index.
    ISBN 0-8131-2012-8 (cloth: alk. paper)
    1. English drama—Restoration, 1660-1700—History and criticism.
2. Literature and society—Great Britain—History—17th century.
3. English drama (Comedy)—History and criticism. 4. Inheritance
and succession in literature. 5. Rogues and vagabonds in literature.
6. Deception in literature. 7. Trickster in literature. I. Title.
PR698.C6C36 1997
822'.05230904—dc21   96-48626

This book is printed on acid-free recycled paper
meeting the requirements of the American National Standard
for Permanence of Paper for Printed Library Materials.

Manufactured in the United States of America

For Jack Cope

Contents

Preface

I attempt in this book to write a small chapter of the cultural history of English Restoration drama. Because I want to preserve the integrity of the plays and to draw attention to some noncanonical but nevertheless interesting, exciting, and even brilliant jewels, my procedure has been, in the main, play-by-play analysis within subsets. Because of considerations of space and the patience of readers, I have submerged the treatment of several plays into notes, from brief to extended references. In the face of the latter, readers can choose to be gluttons for punishment or simply return to the main text. But cultural history requires density, and I have attempted to supply it one way or another (though with one or two exceptions I have had to eschew comparison of these comedies with their sources).

For the making of this book I owe a significant debt of gratitude to the University of Arizona: to Carla Stoffle, dean of the University Library, Lois Olsrud of its Reference staff, and the staff of its Special Collections for the materials, conditions, and support necessary for primary and secondary research; to Rudy Troike, former head of the Department of English, for professional surroundings and atmosphere; to Charles (Chuck) Tatum, dean of the College of Humanities, for funds for a research assistant; to Provosts Nils Hasselmo (now president of the University of Minnesota) and Paul Sypherd for sabbaticals that proved the bookends of this project; to President Manuel Pacheco for nominating me for, and to the Arizona Board of Regents for granting me, a Regents' professorship, with its attendant research account; to friends among colleagues for lending ears (Meg Lota Brown, L.D. Clark, Homer Pettey, Brian McKnight) and among graduate students for lending not only ears but assistance (Lori Snook [now assistant professor at Stetson University], Maja-Lisa von Sneidern, Yuxuf Abana).

All of us who work in Restoration comedy today are indebted to the scholarship and interpretive work of colleagues from previous generations; some of my debts are acknowledged through citations, but many have gone unacknowledged because I have kept my references to work that specifically impinges upon mine. I want, however, to single out the new generation of revisionist critics of Restoration and eighteenth-century drama, especially the comedy, from whose work and conversation I have benefited enormously: Richard Braverman, Laura Brown, Helen Burke, Jill Campbell, Stephan Flores, Pat Gill, Susan Green, Heidi Hutner, Richard Kroll, Elizabeth Kubek, Cynthia Lowenthal, Robert Markley, Jean Marsden, Jessica Munns, Cheryl Nixon, Deborah Payne, J.S. Peters, Laura Rosenthal, Judith Slagle, Kristina Straub, James Thompson, Peggy Thompson, Harold Weber, and Chris Wheatley. Among them, Pat Gill, Deborah Payne, and James Thompson have been especially supportive. I am also endebted to scholars working on comedy and satire who (along with others mentioned above) were kind enough to comment on an early version of the discrimination between subversive comedy and comical satire: Kirk Combe, Brian Connery, Brian Corman, DeAnn De Luna, Peter Holland, Howard Weinbrot, and Rose Zimbardo. Corman was also one of my readers for the University Press of Kentucky, Marsden the other, and I have tried to respond to their concerns. I am grateful to both.

Derek Hughes's *English Drama, 1660-1700* (Oxford: Clarendon, 1996) arrived too late for me to refer to it seriatim. While we have genuine disagreements about tragedy, we have few about comedy, though he is more interested in language as mediation between self and systems of social order, while I am more interested in action as mediation between the two. His is a more psychological if not metaphysical meditation on the progressive inadequacy of language through the 1670s to negotiate identity in relation to a destabilized hierarchy and even ontology. Mine focuses on the mostly successful ways in which tricksters of various stripes negotiate personal stability within an economic order that is enormously fluid, elastic, and, yes, sometimes radically destabilized—often by subversive tricksters themselves. Despite our different approaches we are in general agreement about several of the major playwrights (Wycherley, Otway, Shadwell, Durfey, Southerne), about the early comedy of the 1660s, and about the development of comedy in the 1690s, at which I only gesture. If we are in less agreement about other major authors (Dryden, Etherege, Behn) and about the import and function of what Hughes calls "farcical" comedies, that is what makes criticism dialogic and interesting. I welcome and honor Hughes's contribution to the dialogue.

I am tremendously indebted to a few scholars and friends who do not toil so much in the field of Restoration drama, though they have done so occasionally and with distinction: Lincoln Faller, Paul Hunter, and Michael McKeon, whose conversation over the phone, at dinner, in corners of lobbies, in nooks and crannies of our houses has sustained me for more years than I care to count. One of my greatest debts is to my own son, Rob Canfield, whose passion, planning, and insights helped me create a prizewinning course, in which he was one of my assistants, and whose mind-bending conversation has intensified my intellectual life these past few years. And now there's the new kid on the block, Bret Canfield, who has joined the family intellectual confab. Can brother Colin be far behind?

But this book is dedicated to the teacher who taught me about tricksters when Claude Lévi-Strauss's and Victor Turner's epigones were in short pants and pigtails. In the 1960s Jack Cope appreciated more than any scholar of seventeenth-century comedy after C.L. Barber what its great energy figures signify and where they come from. And he communicated to his students in both undergraduate and graduate classes an infectious passion for the study of that comedy not just as it comes down to us on the page but as it must have disrupted audiences from the stage. I am deeply grateful to him for initially sharing that passion, for extending it over the years to the great comedies of France and particularly Italy, and for, especially recently, engaging with me in a dialogue about the daemonic and the democratic. *Grazie, maestro.*

Adumbrations of my argument have appeared elsewhere. Part of the Introduction has appeared as "Shadwell at the Crossroads of Power: Spa as Microcosm in *Epsom Wells,*" in a special issue of *Restoration: Studies in English Literary Culture, 1660-1700,* edited by Judith Bailey Slagle (fall 1996). A short version of chapter 5 has appeared as "Tupping Your Rival's Women: Cit-Cuckolding as Class Warfare in Restoration Comedy," in *Broken Boundaries: Women and Feminism in Restoration Drama,* edited by Katherine Quinsey (Lexington: Univ. Press of Kentucky, 1996). A much different version of chapter 8 will appear virtually simultaneously as "Woman's Wit: Subversive Women Tricksters in Restoration Comedy," in *The Restoration Mind,* edited by W. Gerald Marshall (Newark: Univ. of Delaware Press, 1997). And part of chapter 12 appeared as part of "Poetical Injustice in Some Neglected Masterpieces of Restoration Drama," in *Rhetorics of Order/Ordering Rhetorics in English Neoclassical Literature,* edited by myself and J. Paul Hunter (Newark: Univ. of Delaware Press, 1989).

A Note on Texts

I have mainly used first editions, except where a reliable modern edition was readily available. In some of these instances I have used the more readily available Regents Restoration Drama Series volumes instead of a modern edition less available. In the instance of Shadwell, since Montagu Summers was not so reliable yet his edition is readily available, I have employed it except for the individual texts where it has been superseded.

Introduction

This is a book about the ideology of Restoration comedy. By ideology I mean the set of cultural ideas, values, and especially power relations it propounds as if they were natural but are, in reality, socially constructed to serve the interests of the hegemonic class.[1] By Restoration I mean the period of the Stuart monarchy's last attempt at absolutism, from the Restoration of Charles II to the defeat of James II's forces at the Battle of the Boyne. Absolutism is, of course, too strong a term, but I am thinking of the arrogance of these Stuarts in their repeated attempts to rule by prerogative alone without Parliament and with clandestine financial aid from Louis XIV of France, as well as with actual Catholic priests eventually in the councils of power. And on a more abstract level, I am thinking of Michael McKeon's use of the term *absolutism* to signify the effort, even as monarchial theory was most threatened, to assert its naturalness, as if its cause lay outside social construction (*Origins of the English Novel,* ch. 5).

In my series of articles on Restoration "serious" drama—heroic and tragicomic romance, political tragedy ("Significance," "Ideology," "Royalism")—I have argued over the last two decades that this drama generally reinscribes Stuart ideology in the teeth of challenges it caricatures as at best oligarchic and at worst anarchic. And the competing oligarchies of power are portrayed as having none of the legitimacy of Stuart de jure ideology but as being based upon mere will to power. A master trope of that ideology, as it forms the twilight instance of English if not generally European feudal culture, I have argued at length elsewhere is *word-as-bond,* the bond of loyalty and fealty between men (with emphasis on male bonding), between husbands and wives, subjects and king, man and God (*Word as Bond*).

Restoration comedy, in the main, is part of this same *official discourse,* to borrow a concept central to the work of the great Russian critic Mikhail Bakhtin. That is, it underwrites the same ideology, the same natural right of the English aristocracy—from peers to the gentry—to rule because they are superior in intelligence (wit) and natural parts, and because they have been bred to rule. But the comedy differs from the more serious genres of romance and tragedy in that more of the material reality of Restoration economy manifests itself, however opaquely. The bulk of Restoration comedy is what I call *social comedy,* comedy that socializes threats to the ruling class,[2] threats that are explicit (like a competing class and its attendant ideology) or implicit (like resistance to its control of the transmission of power and property through genealogy). Most social comedy is of the latter type and brings attractive young couples together for the preservation of this superior ruling class. This social comedy includes some of the best known and most cherished Restoration comedies, like Sir George Etherege's *The Man of Mode* (1676) or Aphra Behn's *The Rover* (1677).[3]

But from the beginning exist comedies in which the threat to be socialized is explicitly political, the Good Old Cause of the Commonwealth, from John Tatham's *The Rump; or, The Mirrour of the Late Times* (1660) to Abraham Cowley's *The Cutter of Coleman Street* (1661) and Sir Robert Howard's *The Committee* (1662). What is at stake in these plays is *estate*, from a Cavalier's lost estate[4] to a younger brother's absent one, to the contested land of England itself. The anti-Puritan stream of Restoration social comedy might be said to run underground after the early 1660s, echoing in various satiric caricatures, but it resurfaces with whitewater in the Cit-cuckolding plays of the late 1670s and early 1680s. These plays simply peel back the civilized veneer to reveal the naked power politics of class warfare beneath. They reinscribe Stuart ideology, in Michel Foucault's terms, not only through *language* but through the *body-language* of stage performance, and indeed, through *bodies* themselves (see *Power/-Knowledge*, ch. 5), where the perfect, potent bodies of Cavalier rakes dominate over the imperfect, impotent bodies of Cits and where the bodies of women become the contested ground for class dominance and, ultimately, symbols of the contested land of England. But whether the threat to society is explicit or implicit, the endings of Restoration social comedy reunite the beautiful people with landed estates and the political hegemony they symbolize.

Not all Restoration comedy is thus social. Some of it is subversive. That is, some of it shows the seams of Stuart ideology, seams through which one can see elements of Restoration society that resist being stitched into one fabric. Cavalier-cuckolding plays, for example in comedies by William Wycherley and Thomas Otway, reveal obliquely that the warfare is not really inter- but intraclass—that while it is to the benefit of Stuart ideology to portray the enemy as Puritan Cits, in reality the English Civil War, as Christopher Hill has perhaps best shown,[5] pitted parts of the ruling class against each other. The hidden implication is that no class has a natural right to dominate another, but each oligarchy rules in turn because it can, because like the sword and the phallus of the male protagonists, it has the power to dominate.

Although most women protagonists of these comedies are not really subversive of the established order but, at their best, simply insist on their choices within it, some comic playwrights of the Restoration—most notably Behn, Thomas Shadwell, and Thomas Southerne—do indeed give us truly subversive heroine tricksters who succeed by their wits in destabilizing, particularly through sexual promiscuity, that order's patriarchal, patrilineal genealogical power structure of inheritance. Unfortunately, these protagonists end up, in the main, simply inhabiting the margins of patriarchal society as parasites unable to establish their own order of counter-estates. That is, the radical nature of their subversion is limited by the imaginative prospects (or discursive formations) open to the playwrights. Their radicalism consists more in a Bakhtinian than a Foucaultian sense, more in the carnivalesque undercutting of official discourse than in any shift in epistemes or social structures and paradigms. Nevertheless, these protagonists obtain space of their own on those margins in which to maintain a combination of agency and (subversive) integrity.

Finally, there is a set of plays—or better, an element within several of these plays—containing a folk energy that is so boisterous that it refuses to be contained in the hegemonic system but constitutes perhaps a daemonic, as Jackson Cope would argue, but certainly a democratic force that the official discourse of the age continually portrayed as the fickleness of the mob, the rabble. This force was enormously abetted by the brilliance of great comic actors, John Lacy in the early years, then James "Nurse" Nokes and Edward Angel and Cave Underhill and Jo Haines, joined finally by Anthony Leigh. These actors (not quite like the Ruzante and Joey the Clown figures Cope so capably analyzes, because they don't become just one role) become instead embodiments of an English comic spirit, not in some ethereal, mythic, transcendent sense but in a Bakhtinian sense of the grotesque, the bodily excessive, the irrepressibly vulgar and voluble (see especially *Rabelais and His World*). These great male actors played the likes of Howard's Teg in *The Committee* or Lacy's Monsieur Raggou in *The Old Troop* (1664) or Behn's False Count in her play of that name (1681) or Nahum Tate's Trappolin in *A Duke and No Duke* (1684)—characters that stole the show not in our trivial sense but in the profound sense of overwhelming class hierarchy with the sheer folk energy of the Third Estate.

Since Leo Hughes's fine study of farce, we have focused on these male actors. But there were great women comic actors too, most notably Katherine Corey, who played countless landladies and older women, like Strega, the amorous old woman in Thomas Duffet's play of that name (1674), who today would need a Jim Henson to create: that pile of fetid, excessive flesh whom her servant, Sanco panco, disassembles in front of her suitors to see if they can stomach her—all the way down to a *lazzo* of folk humor still alive at least in Flannery O'Connor, the unscrewing of her leg. It must have been an amazing final hymeneal scene, which one character calls "a rare Comedy of Mirth" (V.vii, 70)[6] and which included not just the marriages of all the troubled young couples but the marriage of the blind old man Cicco with the amorous old woman herself. The wealth that she adds to the estate that Cicco's daughter and son-in-law will eventually inherit is symbolically the wealth of mud—of the very folk base upon which those estates are built.

Besides this distinction between social and subversive comedy, it seems to me useful also to distinguish a separate genre of comical satire. A generation or two ago, scholars like Oscar James Campbell and Alvin B. Kernan tried to make a case that there was such a thing as comical satire on the English stage. Kernan in particular seemed to infer that the generic clue lay in the sense of an ending. Most of us would agree that we can recognize objects of satire in Restoration comedy: Cits, Country bumpkins, fops, parvenus, termagants; superannuated amorousness, cowardice, parsimoniousness, affectation—to name a few major ones. The question whether a comic play with satiric elements remains a comedy or becomes a satire per se, however, depends entirely on the ending. Comedies end in closure, celebration, centripety, even if subversive elements spin off centrifugally. Satires end sometimes in draconian or apocalyptic closure but more often in nonclosure.

There seem to me to be two kinds of comical satire worth discriminating: corrective and absurdist—the one with at least an implicit standard of judgment, the other pulling the ground out from under any certain standard. Several of Durfey's early plays, Shadwell's *The Woman-Captain* (1679), and Behn's *The Luckey Chance* (1686) are all examples of the former, while Durfey's *A Fond Husband* (1677), Tatham's *The Rump* (1660), and Dryden's *Amphitryon* (1690) are examples of the latter. These last two, the greatest comical satires of the Restoration, frame the period at its alpha and omega. *The Rump* ends with poetical justice for the supporters of the Good Old Cause but in a manner that is astonishingly existential, and *Amphitryon* ends not only without poetic justice but without the providential justice it was supposed to mirror because the very god of supposed justice in the play, Jupiter, is merely a Nietzschean god of sheer power. And if at some level, as James Garrison has suggested, Alcmena, Amphitryon's adulterated wife, stands for an England Jupiter/-William III has appropriated with impunity, then Dryden's indictment of a *deus* he portrays not as *absconditus* but as Ultimate Trickster gains poignancy. But the ludic of the Sosia subplot allows us to play the delightful, opportunistic, unidealistic, pragmatic Mercury of the ending off against the ponderous, prudish, moralistic Apollo of the beginning—not to escape the satiric implications of the play but perhaps to escape the madness of Otwavian tragical satire. Unlike social and even subversive comedy, then, Restoration comical satires end in no real restoration: neither of the estate nor of England itself. They may, at their most conservative, end in poetical justice or warn against the destruction of the old order from its own internal threats. But they may also, at their most radical, playfully portray that order as empty rhetoric.

A Theoretical Word about Generic Distinctions

Why bother with generic mapping at all in this age of deconstructive slippage? Generic criticism seems to me nevertheless an ineluctable modality of our professional practice. However much we may want to have moved beyond genre, at least as a system of ontological categories, we continue to attempt to map out the territory, to bring it under manageable control. And if we have less faith in the structuralist enterprise to define genres in synchronic fashion, thanks to recent books like Thomas Beebee's *The Ideology of Genre* and, more appropriate to my purposes here, Brian Corman's *Genre and Generic Change in English Comedy, 1660-1710,* we seem to understand at least the diachronic importance of genres, especially as they become institutionalized and as both authors and critics negotiate the burden of the past.

First, authors: Restoration dramatists were conscious of a received generic tradition that included such broad categories as tragedy and comedy, categories its period attempted to rigidify in its neoclassicism. Yet it is a commonplace of criticism that authors were notoriously sloppy about generic categories; moreover, they consciously mixed and matched, creating hybrids like the many variations on the already existing Renaissance hybrid, tragicomedy, or like the dramas they simply called "plays."[7] Corman is consequently wise to suggest that we consider Restoration comedy generally to be of a "mixt way" (Dryden's phrase), combining the Fletcherian romance lovers of "sympathetic" comedy with the Jonsonian satirical humors characters of "punitive" comedy (4–11).

Second, critics: Just as an author's generic choice is a historically interactive modality, so also is a critic's choice of categories. We inevitably interact with other critics from Aristotle to Frye to Derrida and, in my case, less familiar names like Corman and Kernan and, later, Dustin Griffin and Deborah Payne. I am less concerned, for example, whether Dryden called *Amphitryon* a comedy than whether it is more useful for us, heuristically, to distinguish it as a comical satire.[8] Furthermore—and I cannot stress this enough to ward off protests by traditional, formal essentialists—*my distinction between social and subversive comedy is based not on traditional, literary categories but on my own critical, functional categories. I am finally not so interested in genre theory per se as I am in a taxonomy that allows us to understand the cultural work that comical drama performs in the Restoration.*

I present my taxonomy as enabling that task, as a set of categories that best reveal the three main functions of this subset of Restoration plays: to underwrite Stuart ideology (social comedy), to undercut it (subversive comedy), and to challenge it as fundamentally immoral or amoral (comical satire). Moreover, I hope to situate some of the Restoration's most attractive comedies, whose function remains problematic to late-twentieth-century criticism. For example, however subversive may appear Etherege's *The Man of Mode,* it is finally a social comedy; however satiric may appear Wycherley's *The Plain Dealer* (1676), it is finally a subversive comedy; however similar Durfey's *A Fond Husband* (1677) may seem to other subversive comedies, it is finally a comical satire. My use of the copulative *is* and of the adverb *finally* here is obviously polemical, for again my categories are not ontological but heuristic. I hope they are nevertheless as useful to others as they have been to me. I unabashedly put a good deal of emphasis in generic classification on the sense of an ending, for I believe endings alter generic categorization. Shakespeare's *King Lear* is a tragedy; Tate's a heroic romance (there's that copulative again). As I will demonstrate below, the ending of Ravenscroft's *Careless Lovers* renders it categorically different from Etherege's *The Man of Mode.*

Tricksters and Estates

The contested ground in Restoration comedy is the estate,[9] both the emblem and the reality of power in late feudal England, and this comedy features nothing so much as tricksters who contend for that ground, from romantic lovers who want to marry as they will but do not want to be disinherited (the young men) or dis-portioned (the young women) in the process, to younger brothers who desperately need estates, to witty women who need to outtrick male sexual tricksters in order to socialize and possess their extraordinarily valuable energy; from dispossessed Cavaliers, in early, more political comedy, to latter-day Cavaliers, who fear being once again dispossessed, in comedy around the time of the Popish Plot and the Exclusion Crisis; from witty women who are by gender to humble folk who are by class dispossessed.

Since its debut, Restoration comedy was about tricksters and estates. Royalists, having been deprived of their estates or having had to compound for them (that is, in effect, buy them back) or mortgage and even sell them off (see Hill, 146–47), either become tricksters themselves or co-operate with other tricksters to get their estates back. Cowley's *The Cutter of Coleman Street* (originally entitled *The Guardian* when produced in 1641) features a Royalist colonel whose estate has been confiscated in the Civil War and who is forced to scheme to retrieve it by marrying the fanatical Puritan widow of the man who bought it. Furthermore, this Colonel Jolly has become guardian of his absent and presumed dead brother's daughter, Lucia, whose portion of £5000 will diminish to a mere £1000 if she fail to marry with Jolly's approval. So the desperate Jolly schemes against her too in order to get the moiety of her portion for himself and for his own daughter, Aurelia. And Lucia's lover, Truman Jr., has been threatened by his father, Truman Sr., with disinheritance—at first because Senior wants Junior to marry the daughter of the same widow, whose husband also rifled the Truman estate. The play is thus triply concerned with the transmission of estates, figuring forth the destabilization during the Commonwealth (as Stuart ideology would have it) of the very basis of government, property.

If we see the play as displaced class warfare,[10] Jolly's trickery is understandable, and he is certainly sympathetic in his effort to redeem his own estate, if not in his effort to diminish his niece's portion (because he denies her emotional if not legal rights; see Nixon). Like a Jonsonian comic overreacher, he compounds his trickery, at first bribing the impostors Cutter and Worm to compete for her in an unapproved marriage, then conniving with Aurelia to marry Lucia to the witwoud Puny. But his trickery also begets other trickery: Lucia administers him a dose that makes him think he's dying so she can get him to sign an agreement to let her marry Truman Jr.; because she loved Junior as a young girl, Aurelia at first conspires with her father to trick Lucia into an unapproved marriage, then plans an outrageous trick—apparently for the sublimity of it more than the revenge—to marry Lucia's maid to Junior; after Jolly shuns Worm, the latter pretends to be the absent brother come to take back guardianship of his daughter, till Jolly is forced to play "trick for trick" (V.ii.104) and create a counterbrother.

Having turned Lucia's trick on him into another trick of his own, Jolly pretends to have converted to the Widow Barebottle's fanatical sect in order to trick her into marriage. Aurelia protests they won't be able to stand her ravings; moreover, she asks plaintively, "[S]uppose the King should come in again, (as I hope he will for all these Villains) and you have your own again o' course, you'd be very proud of a Soap-boyler's Widow then in Hide-park, Sir" (III.i.36-39). Jolly responds with wonderful aplomb, "Oh! Then the Bishops will come in too, and she'l away to New-England" (40-41). In a mirrored trick, Cutter changes his name to Abed-nego and pretends to be as fanatical as the Widow Barebottle in order to court her daughter Tabitha. In comic foreplay on their wedding night, Cutter delightfully reverts to his Cavalier mode—complete with sword, hat, feather—gets Tabitha drunk, and asks her what she thinks now of her mother. Tabitha blurts, "A fig for my Mother; I'l be a Mother my self shortly" (V.vi.84). If the play was revised in 1658, these developments manifest Royalist wish-fulfillment and must have delighted the audience with their barbs when it was finally performed after the king really did return. Symbolically, they portray restoration as the reappropriation of women, as the reconversion of land-as-woman to its rightful lord.

The other Cavalier tricksters triumph as well. By accident Lucia is re-warded for her long-suffering by a clandestine marriage to Truman Jr. Au-relia shows herself her father's daughter by substituting for her sister in a clandestine marriage to Puny, who had already bribed her with five hun-dred gold pieces and who is worth fifteen hundred per year. Finally living up to the full potential of his name and overcoming his erstwhile meanness to his niece, Jolly blesses both unions and, by bestowing the entire portion upon Lucia, appeases the froward Truman Sr. The sense of the ending, then, is that estates are restored and secured—in anticipation of the restoration of the king prophesied in the song sung by Cutter and Worm:

> *Worm:* Now a Pox on the Poll, of old Politique Noll.
> *Both:* Wee'l drink till we bring,
>   In Triumph back the King.
> [*Cutter*]: May he live till he see
>   Old Noll upon a Tree.
> *Worm:* And many such as he. [II.viii.208-13]

As the Restoration audience knew, Charles II indeed lived to see the disin-terred body of Cromwell hanged upon the "tree" at Tyburn (see Back-scheider, 7).

Robert Howard's *The Committee* features *two* Royalist colonels whose es-tates have been sequestered and *two* wards whose guardians are trying either to usurp or appropriate their property rights. Colonels Blunt and Careless have returned from exile with their king to compound for their estates before the infamous Committee of Sequestration, but they are told they must swear an oath of allegiance to the Commonwealth—the "Covenant" (passim)—or "You must have no Land then" (I, 77). Both nobly refuse the terms:

Blunt: Then farewel acres, and may the dirt choak them. . . .
Careless: No, we will not take it, much good may it do them
   That have swallows large enough;
   'Twill work one day in their stomachs.
Blunt: The day may come, when those that suffer for their
   Consciences and honour may be rewarded. [I, 77; II, 93]

In short, the Cavaliers anticipate a retributive justice that will ensue with the restoration of the king, a prophecy the audience knows has already been fulfilled.

Chairman of the Committee is Mr. Day, who is in turn ruled by his wife (in another image of the topsy-turvy consequences of the overturning of de jure government). Together they attempt to manipulate the estates of their two quasi-wards—Anne Throughgood, whose deceased Royalist father's estate they have appropriated as well as appropriating her as their own daughter, to whom they have given the Puritanical name, Ruth; and Arbella, whose Royalist father has just died and whose estate the Days are attempting to secure to themselves, allowing her access only through marriage to their uncouth son Abel. Like the Cavaliers, Arbella nobly resists, demanding the land as her own and attacking the Committee for marriage jobbing. In a comment that can be extended to Arbella, one of the Committee members concludes of these resisters:

   It is well truly for the good people that they
   Are so obstinate, whereby their Estates may
   Of right fall into the hands of the Chosen, which
   Truly is a mercy. [II, 95]

At this point in the play it appears as if the Cavaliers' hope of justice is fond. Blunt's humorous comment about the legal papers carried by the comically litigious solicitor Obadiah—"Those are / The winding sheets to many a poor Gentlemans Estate" (II, 86)—would seem to spell their doom. And what makes the pill all the harder to swallow is the lack of worthiness of those who have succeeded to power, from the hypocritical Day, to the boorish Abel, to the tasteless Mrs. Day, who used to be Careless's father's scullery maid Gillian. But taking a page from Cowley's *Cutter,* Howard puts at the center of the play a woman trickster, Ruth, who takes matters into her own hands. Through her quick wit, she saves Careless, to whom she is spontaneously and irresistibly attracted (naturally, for he is a Cavalier, a natural aristocrat and ipso facto eminently desirable), from the clutches of Mrs. Day and then again from prison. More important, when Day's greed to obtain another estate causes him to depart in such a hurry that he drops his keys (poetic justice), Ruth uses them to unlock his papers, retrieve her and Arbella's deeds, and discover incriminating papers she uses to blackmail Day into not only accepting the loss of their estates but also cozening the Committee out of the colonels' estates. The play ends with all four Cavaliers—and all four estates—united two by two in impending marriage.

Ruth has been a trickster in another important action. Careless, as his name implies, is a libertine, to whom "Matrimony" is against "Conscience" (III, 106). Moreover, because he believes Ruth the Days' daughter, he thinks her an easy mark and is surprised when she tries to make him take the "Covenant" in another, witty sense—that is, a contractual oath. He protests, "'[T]is not fit a Committee/Mans Daughter shou'd be too honest, to the reproach/Of her Father and Mother." She leaves him with this cryptic admonition: "When the quarrel of the Nation is reconcil'd, you/And I shall agree: till when Sir—" (III, 107). They court throughout in witty, gay-couple fashion, but when he, like one of Robert Jordan's "extravagant rakes," tries to coax her into his very prison cell where it is so dark he will not be able to see the Day's daughter in her, she confesses her love but demands he pursue her virtuously. He insists he can never marry the daughter of his father's scullion, begging her to swear falsely she is not.[11] Ruth responds by swearing truly she is not, by letting him into the truth of her origins now that she has tried not only his constancy to her but his constancy to the nation, its rightful king, and its rightful order: "I have try'd you fully;/You are noble, and I hope you love me; be ever firm to/Virtuous principles. (V, 126)

Virtue is not merely sexual, it is political. Sexual loyalty is related to political loyalty. The restoration of the king—anticipated by the colonels' prophecy, the songs in the middle of the play, and the concluding "dance for the King" and the cry, which all are invited to utter in the very last line of the play, including the Days, "God bless the King" (V, 134)—means not only the restoration of estates to their proper aristocrats but also the very code of word-as-bond that solidifies the orderly transmission of power and property through marriage.[12]

Tricksters, Estates, and Scrambled Eggs: *The Man of Mode* in Its Context

The significance of estates in Restoration comedy, then, is central and obvious in these early political plays. It is less obvious but no less central in the rest of the comedy of the period. Two decades ago Raymond Williams called attention to that significance in comments that have been virtually overlooked by subsequent criticism (*Country and City,* 51-54). Restoration comedy generally celebrates Town sophistication over Country boor-ishness (and City parsimoniousness, I would add). But the counterpas-toral promulgated in the former dichotomy ignores the essential re-lationship between the two realms (as well as that between the Town and the City), between the fashionable, insouciant manners of the Town wits amid their ostentatious display of wealth and conspicuous consumption and "the country houses by which many of them were still maintained" (52)—and, I would add, those City lawyers who were increasingly in-volved in the traffic in estates. "There is then no simple contrast between wicked town and innocent country, for what happens in the town is gener-ated by the needs of the dominant rural class. The moral ratification of this drama is not marriage against an intrigue or an affair . . . , nor is it wit against folly, or virtue against vice," Williams sagely writes, summarily dis-missing the preoccupation of three hundred years of criticism of this drama. "It is the steering of the estate into the right hands" (53). Whereas at its most ironic Restoration comedy could portray "a committed love" as "'more dismal than the country,'" a place filled with the noise of rooks, "'what the birds cry is what the world cries in the end: that the settlement has to be made, into an estate and into a marriage" (52).

The play Williams quotes here is, of course, one of the most famous and beloved of all Restoration comedies, Etherege's *The Man of Mode*. Many critics see the relationship between Dorimant and Harriet at the end of the play as antithetical to the kind of "settlement" Williams infers, espe-cially because the language of "committed love" seems to them to have been too thoroughly compromised.[13] I agree with Williams and have argued (*Word as Bond*, 104-14) that the traditional language of "commit-ted love," however problematized throughout the play, especially because Dorimant's libertinism has been threatened to bankrupt it, is nevertheless restored—wittily—to its function of underwriting marriage and that Dori-mant, the sexual trickster whose promiscuity threatens the genealogy that continues estates, has been so socialized as to be willing to keep a Lent for Harriet in the unfashionable Country in expectation, we are to assume, of the Happy Easter of marriage. I shall not repeat that argument here. Suf-fice it to say for my present purposes that it is no accident that the wild and witty Harriet is an heiress of great fortune (however much she may threaten to exercise a freedom of choice that might separate "land" from "love" [III.i.67] and that Dorimant excuses to his cast mistress his immi-nent union with Harriet as repairing the "ruins" of his "estate" (V.ii.265). The import of these facts has less to do with the psychology of Dorimant's movement toward Harriet than with the ideology of their match: the best characters in the play in terms of sheer genetic energy represent the con-tinuing vitality of the dominant class, the *aristoi* who deserve to rule.

In order better to understand and corroborate William's thesis about Restoration comedy, let us examine a couple of plays nearly contemporary with *The Man of Mode,* plays that reveal clearly the function of estates in the reclaiming of a sexual trickster. In 1675, John Crowne brought forth his first comedy, *The Country Wit.* The play displays typical counter-pastoral satire on the Country for its lack of breeding, however much Lady Faddle may have attempted to educate the eponymous antihero, her nephew Sir Mannerly Shallow. But her description of Sir Mannerly's father ironically exposes the very rural economy upon which the status of Town gentlemen rests:

> you must know his father the old baronet was a man that had mortal en-
> mities to the town, and to all sorts of town-vanity, and would never
> suffer him to wear a gentile suit, to read any book, except a law-book
> [for the sake of the control of property, obviously], nor to stir from
> home, but in his company; and that was seldom any whither but to his
> farms, and tenants, to see his grounds, and woods, or over-look his quar-
> ries, and cole-mines[.] [I.i.394-401]

As Williams notes (52), in order to expand and solidify such estates, either through marriage or legal transaction, Country lords and ladies came to London, from Etherege's Lady Woodvil to Crowne's Sir Mannerly. And despite the fashionable satire on that rural base, the Town could not have existed without it.[14]

As critics from Smith (106 n. 7) to Hume (307) to Corman (45) have noted, Crowne's play is close to Etherege's in that its central protagonist is one Ramble, a sexual trickster who expounds the libertine ethic: "the order of Nature is to follow my appetite"; he won't eat just because it's the right time; "I will pay no such homage to the sun, and time, which are things below me: I am a superiour being to them, and will make 'em attend my pleasure"; "The world is Nature's house of entertainment, where men of wit and pleasure are her free guests, ty'd to no rules, and orders"; "I am for reducing Love to the state of Nature: I am for no propriety, but every man get what he can" (II.i.228 ff). But "propriety" or property in women involves the other property of estates, so Ramble's rambling threatens both. Yet, like Dorimant, he begins to contemplate abjuring his ethic for the witty woman of the play, who happens to be worth a £5000 portion,[15] a woman so desirable he's willing to put up with her foolish father. At a crucial moment in the play, when he seems to have lost her because of his confounded inconstancy, he debates with himself: "now I am discover'd in all my rogueries, and intrigues, and falshoods; and must never hope to enjoy the sweet pleasure of lying and forswearing any more; I must now either repent, and become a down-right plodding Lover to Christina, or in plain terms lose her: I must either forsake all the world for her, or her for all the world: well, if I do forsake her, she has this to boast, I do not forsake her for any one woman, I forsake her for ten thousand" (IV.iii.7-14). The real danger, he soon realizes, is that she will forsake him. He determines, "Well, I cannot bear the loss of Mrs. Christina, I had rather endure marriage with her, than injoy any other woman at pleasure—I must, and will repent, and reform, and now should an angel appear in female shape, he should not tempt me to revolt any more" (18-22). Of course immediately he is tempted by another woman. When at the end Ramble attempts to square things with Christina, she upbraids him with his courtship of the kept whore, Betty Frisque. Ramble declares his conversion in terms as filled with ironic awareness of human frailty as Harriet's responses to Dorimant's declarations:

> Oh, forgive me, I acknowledge my faults with grief and penitence; I am amazed how it was possible for me to think of any thing but you, but hopes of love are like the prospect of a fair street a great way off, and you cannot blame a poor thirsty traveller, if he takes a sip here and there by the way. [V.ii.439-444]

When Christina asks if he will give up drawing other people's portraits (his scam to gain access to Betty), he replies, "Now I am in heaven, and all my sins forgiven, upbraid me not with them; I will draw no pictures but my own, and those never without your help" (460-62). The pictures he means to draw are those replications of himself in the faces of his heirs, who will inherit his now enriched estate.

In order to understand what *The Man of Mode* would look like if it were a truly subversive play about tricksters and estates, let us examine Edward Ravenscroft's *The Careless Lovers,* performed three years earlier than Etherege's play (1673). It too has a pair of respectable but not very witty lovers who move toward a marriage finally blessed by a blocking father. It too has a foppish fool who is duped in the end. And it too has a gay couple who move joltingly toward marriage. When Lovell, the rather dull lover, tries to get Careless the rake to visit honorable women for once, the latter proclaims the typical libertine ethic: "[W]hilst I am in my right Witts, I will not leave Delightful Variety for the Unsavoury Insipid Bitts of Constancy" (I.33-35). Later he expands on the same ethic: "Give me Love as Nature made it, Free and Unconfin'd.—Observe but Mistress, and Gallant: How Brisk, how Gay, how Fierce they are in their Amours! Whil'st Marriage-love comes like a Slave loaden with Fetters, dull and out of humour" (II.438-42). After he meets the amazingly witty and dynamic

Hillaria, he suffers an immediate and overwhelming attraction, but insists (very much like Dorimant), "the Thoughts of her are Momentary": "I'le keep my Soul free as the Bird that flyes i'th Aire, / I'le ne'r love one, till I of all besides Despair" (I.277-79).

More than Etherege's Harriet, more than Behn's Hellena, Hillaria has a free spirit equal to her Town wit. When Muchworth, the old alderman and Hillaria's uncle, tries to marry his daughter Jacinta not to the Lovell she loves but to the foppish but titled lord, De Boastado, Hillaria takes him on, asking if he thinks Jacinta "han't as much wit to choose a Husband as you?" (III.41-42): "Uncle, it is not now as it was in your young days, Women then were poor sneaking sheepish Creatures. But in this Age, we know our own strength, and have wit enough to make use of our Talents. If I met with A Husband makes my Heart ake, I'le make his Head ake I'le warrant him" (45-49). After he leaves, she continues in her rebellious vein with Jacinta: "I'le have Women say and do what they will: Have not we Rational Souls as well as Men; what made Women Mopes in former Ages, but being rul'd by a company of old men and Women: Dotage then was counted Wisdom, and formerly call'd Gravity and good Behaviour" (60-64). Hillaria leads Jacinta in a spirited dissection of De Boastado to his face—and over his face, including his nose, which is at least an inch too short! When Muchworth threatens to cane Jacinta to her knees in submission, Hillaria brandishes her own cane and brings De Boastado to his knees in cowardly fear. Muchworth expels her from his presence and indeed his house, but she cheekily fights back: "[D]on't you think to Domineer when I am gone; if I hear you do, I'le have a bout too with you Uncle, as old a Cock of the Game as you are, I'le have a Sparring Blow too with you" (IV.i.20-23).

Hillaria's most hilarious action occurs when she puts on breeches to accompany Jacinta on a frolic to a play where she can hector the Cits but ends up dogging Careless into a tavern and stealing his whores from him and even fencing with him over them—shades of Dryden's Florimel in the tragicomedy *Secret Love,* but with more of the subversive energy of James Howard's Mirida in the tragicomedy *All Mistaken* or Southerne's eponymous heroine, Sir Anthony Love. When next she meets Careless, she allows him to feel he has gained the ascendant in his posturing against marriage. Then, she sighs, she will just have to be his mistress; she will retire to consider it. Pushing the advantage, he warns her not to let "vain Considerations of Virtue, Modesty, Honour, Chastity, Reputation and the like" get into her head, for "these are Bugg-Words that aw'd the Women in former Ages, and still fool a great many in this; and if once these idle Notions get into your Thoughts, I shall give you over for a lost Woman" (V.i.214-18).

The play is full of all those little signs, however, that indicate that the rake is going to be converted. Muchworth respects his father and his estate, though he has heard Careless is wild, and Careless justifies himself: "I have my Froliques as most young Men have—but I keep my Estate out of the Devil's Clutches; I have yet not sold one Foot of Land, or cut down one Stick of Wood" (III.173-75). So he is a proper aristocratic choice, and Hillaria has wealth as well as worth, so they are the perfect match to perpetuate the system. Lovell lectures his friend on the value of the conversion of the rake to marriage: "Why do the great Wenchers at last forsake all their Mistresses for a Wife? for, we find most of them Marry at the Long-run; Nay, generally they prove the best Husbands: And the reason is, they have experimented the Folly of that Lewd Course of Life" (V.i.132-35). Careless has worried throughout the play that Hillaria will get the ascendancy over him when she realizes how much he loves her.

So the audience sees the approaching proviso scene with expectations that this too will be a social comedy, libertine rake and rebellious witty woman joined in a centripetal union that energizes but continues the system. Such expectations are frustrated, however. Amidst the swirl of concluding marriages, listen to their most outrageous provisos:

> *Hillaria:* I will be your Wife, and since I can't have a Gallant before Marriage, I'le do like other Wives, and have one after; and, now I think on't too, a Husband is very necessary, if it is only to save the trouble of being ask'd questions o're and o're, as who's the Father, who got it? and besides, what Children the Gallant gets, the Husband must keep.
>
> *Careless:* I can be even with you there, for you can bring me none to keep, but what are your own at least; and if you expect I should be Father to all your Children, I expect you should be a Nurse to all mine, and I may have 'um brought home to me on all sides, from twenty several women; for I intend to be a great getter and Father of many.
>
> *Hillaria:* Well, I have but this thing more to say to you; whosoever I choose for my Gallant, you are not to quarrel, or fall out with him, but on the contrary, to make him your particular intimate Friend, to be always inviting him home to Dinner, and the like.
>
> *Careless:* And also, whosoever I like for A Mistress, be she Maid, Wife, or Widdow, you are to get acquainted with her, to Visit her often, to speak in my praise, and tell my good qualities, to commend my abilities; and in fine, to use the utmost of your power to bring us together, *gain us opportunity, and if need be, to watch at the Stair-head, and in case of necessity, to hold the door.* [V.ii.299-321]

Ravenscroft italicizes these last few lines to emphasize their outrageousness.

I submit that this ending is truly subversive, for instead of the control of sexual energy and reproductive capacity for the purposes of Restoration political economy it threatens scrambled eggs—a jumbled genealogy. Dorimant's movement toward Harriet is a downward centripetal spiral; Careless's toward Hillaria is an upward and outward gyre where the falcon cannot hear the falconer.

Shadwell at the Crossroads of Power: Spa as Microcosm in *Epsom Wells*

Let me conclude this introduction by examining in detail a play that can be read as a microcosm of the kinds of comedy I shall be examining in the body of this study. Shadwell's *Epsom Wells* (1672) has been appreciated over the years as one of the best plays of this generally unappreciated Restoration dramatist, his one, or at least his best, contribution to the Restoration comedy of manners or wit comedy.[16] The play straddles the border between *social* and *subversive* comedy. While it socializes the dangerous sexual energy of a pair of gallants through the agency of a pair of witty women, it also features a couple whose dangerous energy is not socialized. Moreover, while it satirizes typical butts of Restoration comedy— a Country squire, a pair of Cits and their wives, and a couple of lower-class pretenders—in order to portray the dominant class as naturally superior, at its deepest level it brings a microcosm of society together at the crossroads of the spa in a condition of apparent suspension of the order of that society precisely to reveal not their common human nature for morality's sake but their interdependence upon a political economy that serves to support the conspicuous consumption of that dominant class at the expense of the other classes in that society.

Shadwell's play socializes the eminently desirable energy of the sexual trickster into the hell of his libertine code, marriage. For Bevil and Rains, "Marriage is the worst of Prisons," an "Ecclesiastical Mouse-Trap" (I, 117), even if the nubile aristocratic bride bring with her £8000. Lucia, the very woman with the fortune, protests to the courting Rains, who since he has met her has talked of converting to constancy, "I am as hard to be fixt as you: I love liberty as well as any of ye" (III, 146). But she and her friend Carolina are just being *dangereuses*. They know the libertine ethic propounded by these Cavaliers—"Virtue and Chastity[?] unsociable foolish qualities!" (III, 147)—and at the same time they know the value of constancy in a monogamous system: when their gallants court for the second time in a day the masked witty women, Lucia exclaims in exasperation, "Oh, if witty men had but the constancy of Fools, what

Jewels were they?" (II, 133). Throughout the play the women exact promises of various kinds to test the men's sincerity, promises they repeatedly break. Rains wittily demurs, "The wilder we are, the more honour you'll have in reclaiming us" (II, 134). And anticipating Etherege's Dorimant, he rationalizes as he proves inconstant to Lucia, "I love *Lucia* even to the renouncing of Wine and good Company; but flesh and blood is not able to hold out her time without some refreshment by the bye" (IV, 152). When he is summoned to give advice to his Cavalier friend Woodly's wife, he wittily appropriates the religious language designed to enforce the system of monogamy: "Gad I believe she stands in need of something else than my Advice, she has a design on my Chastity[.] shall I go? good Devil, do not tempt me, I must be constant, I will be constant: nay, Gad, I can be constant when I resolve on't, and yet I am a Rogue. But I hope I shall have Grace, and yet I fear I shall not; but come what will, I must suffer this tryal of my Vertue. . . . What a Rogue am I to run into temptation; but Pox on't, *Lucia* will ne'er miss what I shall lose" (V, 171-72).

The wittiness of this last line, one that reaches back to Chaucer's Wife of Bath and beyond, underscores the politics of the sexual economy embodied in the system of monogamy. Ever since by analogy with animals men discovered the connection between intercourse and birth, they have madly developed a system of transition of power and property through patrilinearity. Accordingly, since it is far easier to determine maternity than paternity, they perforce invented religious and social sanctions to control their women's reproductive capacity and freedom. The vessel must be kept pure so that the seed it is supposed to carry is not contaminated and supplanted. And the women had to be duped into internalizing sexual discipline so they would feel incredible shame for transgression and the consequent loss of reputation that ruins them in the sexual exchange that builds estates. But the men had also to develop a backup system, a double standard, whereby they could safely bleed off excess sexual capital: thus prostitutes, farmers' daughters, and so on. In an aristocratic patriarchy, the dominant class claimed an implicit *droit du seigneur,* renamed in a stroke of ironic French humor *droit de cuissage* (the right of thighdom, or the right to one's lap), which allowed them to cuckold the lower classes, including middle-class Cits, with impunity. Thus Lucia will not lose the surplus capital Rains spends because nature will conveniently replace it. And whether Rains spends upon Mrs. Jilt or Mrs. Woodly makes no real difference, because the former is a whore by trade and the latter a whore by practice; that is, they are already damaged goods, cracked receptacles for his surplus. As for their husbands, past or future, caveat emptor.

Lucia and Carolina, if they do not understand the hidden rationale for the system, understand its rules. And they also understand what Christopher Wheatley nicely points to as male sexual narcissism (*Without God or Reason,* 133). That is why they are so *dangereuses,* so distrustful of the protestations of eternal constancy from men they know regularly use such rhetoric as the price of admission. And that is why they tease them at the end with the threat of years of courtship and "tryal." When Lucia asks with apparent indifference and insouciance, "If you should improve every day so [as they have just done], what would it come to in time?" the separate answers from Rains and Bevil reveal both the ideology and the reality of the monogamous system:

> *Rains:* To what it should come to, Madam.
> *Bevil:* 'Twill come to that, *Jack;* for one Fortnights conversing with us
> will lay such a scandal upon 'em, they'll be glad to repair to Marriage.
> [V, 181]

Rains's prediction is based on a theory of nature, one opposed to libertinism, that love leads naturally to marriage. In contrast with the libertine song earlier, taught Carolina's maid by the more radically libertine Woodly and celebrating a "*mutual Love*" free from the confines of marriages, especially of "convenience" (II, 124), the poetic tag that concludes the play reappropriates such mutuality precisely for monogamy: "Marriage that does the hearts and wills unite,/Is the best state of pleasure and delight" (V, 181). Bevil's comment, on the other hand, points to the sexual economy: the women cannot afford for their reputations' sake to keep company for long with such known libertines without marrying to preserve their value as exchange items. The epilogue wittily but pointedly demonstrates the need for marriage to preserve the patriarchal aristocratic genealogy and its concomitant dominance. Under the apparent guise of bourgeois morality, one of the cuckolded Cits (my guess would be Bisket the comfitmaker, played by the irrepressible Nokes) deplores the modern way of making plays wherein the authors

> please the wicked Wenchers of the Age,
> And scoff at civil Husbands on the Stage:
> To th'great decay of Children in the Nation,
> They laugh poor Matrimony out of fashion.
> A young man dares not marry now for shame,
> He is afraid of losing his good name.
> If they go on thus, in a short time we
> Shall but few Sons of honest Women see:

And when no virtuous Mothers there shall be,
Who is't will boast his ancient Family? [182]

Consequently, the epilogue calls for "Gallants" to "leave your lewd whoring and take Wives" and, I would argue in contrast to Wheatley (*Without God or Reason*, 135-36) and Michael Alssid before him (65), so does the ending of the play.[17] As in *The Man of Mode*, the powerful sexual energy of the Restoration rake is like a pharmakon, dangerous and desirable at the same time. His domestication requires a period of detoxification. *Mais ça vient.*

In its main action, then, *Epsom Wells* portrays the reaffirmation of the code of power of its dominant class even as, in its other actions, it reasserts that class's dominance per se. The play roundly satirizes the two main competitors to the power of the upper aristocracy from the Town: the Country and the City. The Country squire and magistrate Clodpate, who hates the London that cheated him as a youth, is constantly belittled by the Town wits; tricked, robbed, and hilariously transformed into a ghost by Suburban hectors; and finally tricked out of a good deal of his estate by a Suburban whore, Mrs. Jilt. Two Cits from London, Mr. Bisket the comfitmaker and Mr. Fribble the haberdasher, like Littlewit in Ben Jonson's *Bartholomew Fair*, reveal their lack of breeding by exposing their wives—and their wives' bodies literally—to the sexual rudeness not only of the same hectors who eventually seduce them but also to the Cavaliers who have already seduced them (Rains is a constant card partner to Mrs. Bisket). Moreover, the hectors Kick and Cuff, who ape the manners and morals of the Town by coming to the wells to seduce women as well as gamble and bowl with the men, are constantly exposed as cowards and bullies by the Cavaliers.

Yet even as Cavalier class dominance is thus reasserted, that dominance is subverted by the transgressive behavior of members of the Cavaliers' own class, who threaten their code of genealogical control, and by members of the Suburban class, who outrageously get away with their scams. In *Word as Bond* I argued that when a major figure stands out amidst the comic closure as unregenerate, his or her dangerous energy lurking within and still threatening society, "the effect is subversive to the code of the word" (117). Although the movement of Bevil and Rains toward marriage would seem to reaffirm patriarchal society's need for such a code to contain dangerous sexual energy that threatens its system for the orderly transmission of power and property, their prospects of marriage are juxtaposed at the end to their fellow Cavalier Woodly's divorce. Like Dryden's Rhodophil and Doralice from *Marriage A-la-Mode* (apparently produced in the fall of the previous season, ca. November 1671) and even more like Joseph Arrowsmith's Lysander and Juliana from the apparently contemporaneous *Reformation* (ca. 1672-73), Shadwell's Woodlys have grown bored with each other and seek other game, he with Carolina, she with Bevil first, then Rains. Mrs. Woodly is not so honest as Doralice but like Juliana masquerades behind a hypocritical vizard of virtue. Even as she sequesters Bevil in her closet, she protests to her husband who has surprised her: "If I were so perfidious and false to take pleasure in a Gallant in the absence of my Husband; but I am too honest, too virtuous for thee, thou ingrateful Wretch: besides, if my Conscience would give me leave, I love you too well for that, you barbarous base Fellow." He responds aside and ominously, "A Pox on her troublesom Vertue, would to Heaven she were a Whore, I should know then what to do with her" (II, 131).

The problem is that both Woodlys are indeed dangerous. By accident, they discover the growing relationship between Bevil and Carolina —and each other's intrigue, hers achieved with Bevil, his attempted with Carolina. Ironically forgetting that there is no honor among thieves, Mrs. Woodly rails against Bevil for inconstancy, calls him "perjur'd Man!" (IV, 158), and vows revenge. Despite Bevil's protestations that nothing has passed between them, Woodly determines to meet his wife's gallant in a duel. And Mrs. Woodly sets up an occasion for such a duel, proclaiming like a female Machiavel, "[I]f [Woodly] kills *Bevil*, I am reveng'd, if *Bevil* kills him, he rids me of the worst Husband for my humour in Christendom" (V, 173). When Woodly is disarmed by Bevil and discovers that his wife has set up their rendezvous, he invites the gallants back to his lodgings to observe how he will "behave [him] self like a man of honour" (V, 175). Like Rains ("Be not rash, consider 'till to morrow"), the audience fears violence. Instead, the Woodlys celebrate their "Divorce . . . like a Wedding" (V, 179). They can really only separate, but they stand out as a threat to the monogamous system and its code of constancy, for each obviously will continue a life of unlimited promiscuity. They exchange these among several items in their parody of the gay couple proviso scene:

> *Woodly:* Then, that I am to keep what Mistress I please, and how I please, after the laudable custom of other Husbands.
> *Mrs. W:* And that I am to have no Spies upon my company or actions, but may enjoy all Priviledges of other separate Ladies, without any lett, hindrance, or molestation whatsoever. [V, 180]

The tag at the end, celebrating mutual love and marriage, turns out to be recited by the Woodlys, a fact which is already subversive enough, but they conclude, "But—/ When Man and Wife no more each other please,/

They may at least like us each other ease" (V, 181). This easing of separation does not resolve but exacerbates the concern of the epilogue. With such egg scramblers still at large, "Who is't will boast his ancient Family?"

It could be argued that Mrs. Woodly is not really a member of the aristocracy. The play opens with her conversing at the wells with the city wives and sounding no different from them:

> *Mrs. Bisk:* How do the Waters agree with your Ladyship?
> *Mrs. W:* Oh Soveraignly; how many Cups are you arriv'd to? [I, 107]

Mr. Fribble sagely reads the lesson to his wife of the Woodlys divorce: "This 'tis to marry a Gentleman, forsooth; if you had marry'd one, you certainly had been turn'd away for the prank [i.e. adultery!] you plaid to night" (V, 180). One could read out the implication that Mrs. Woodly was a Cit's daughter who was married up to an aristocrat. But Woodly is certainly that aristocrat. His cousin Lucia has a portion of £8000, no mean sum in those days. So while Mrs. Woodly's subversion of the code designed to enforce monogamy may not be so much an intraclass transgression, Woodly's certainly is. Moreover, as in the few other Restoration comedies that feature intraclass cuckolding among the aristocrats, Woodly's relations with his fellow Cavaliers are even further destabilizing to the dominant class as is evidenced by the repeated threat of dueling. When overheard discussing their affair, Bevil tries to reassure Woodly that nothing has passed between him and Mrs. Woodly, and Rains tries to calm Woodly down with the same assurance. Lucia and Carolina try desperately to keep Bevil from fighting, and Rains gives his word that nothing will be done. But the code of honor between men prevails; they fight; luckily, Woodly is merely disarmed.

The importance of class solidarity on the issue of adultery—that is, adulteration or contamination of genealogy—is underscored in the play in a couple of key passages. When Bevil brags about how good a mistress Mrs. Woodly is, Rains invokes class morality, cloaked in terms of the ancient aristocratic code of friendship:

> *Rains:* Art not thou a Villain to Cuckold this honest fellow, and thy friend *Ned*?
> *Bevil:* Gad it's impossible to be a man of honour in these Ca[s]es. But my intrigue with her began before my Friendship with him, and so I made a friend of my Cuckold, and not a Cuckold of my friend.
> *Raines:* An admirable School distinction. [I, 109]

The point is not, as Wheatley would have it, that there is no morality in this play but that the morality is, from Machiavelli to Nietzsche, whatever the dominant class says it is: *virtù* and not *virtue*. Later, when Bevil and Rains meet Carolina and Lucia again in masks, they find upon removal of the masks that they are paired opposite to their earlier encounter. Bevil comments tellingly (and ironically, given his relationship with Mrs. Woodly), "I cannot invade the propriety of my Friend" (II, 134). When Woodly offers to introduce Rains to his rich cousin Lucia, who, he says, is already attracted to him, Rains responds as a libertine uninterested in marriage, but his response lays bare the realities of the sexual economy: "Prethee, *Woodly,* what should I do with her? I love thee and thy Family too well to lye with her, and my self too well to marry her; and I think a Man has no excuse for himself that visits a Woman without design of lying with her one way or other" (I, 117). Out of respect for Woodly and his *family*—that is, aristocratic genealogy in general as well as that set of kin in particular—Rains will not risk contaminating an aristocratic vessel. Or won't he? Those are Mrs. Woodly's arms he leaves to keep Bevil from dueling with Woodly over alleged adultery.

Thus the significance of Bevil's transgression against class is made clear—as well as that of the perpetual threat of a duel as the punishment for such a transgression. Unlike the burb bullies, Woodly is no coward, knows how to use a sword. When Rains tries to prevent the duel by protesting Mrs. Woodly's virtue and innocence, Woodly, suppressing any sign that he really thinks his wife unfaithful, insists nevertheless, "Sir, since I do not question her honour, do not you make bold with it, 'tis for his false accusation that I require satisfaction" (V, 165). Intraclass sexual rivalry is deadly rivalry. And while Bevil's dangerous sexual energy may have been socialized by the end of the play, Woodly's has not. He remains free to court not just City wives but Town wives as well.

Restoration comedies often end in some form of poetical justice, usually for the purpose of reaffirming dominant ideology. The fate of the Cits in the play is typical: they get what they deserve for not being able properly to value their wives. They lack breeding so much as to have no sense of shame, a sense of which the hectors even try to remind them. No, they will go so far as to sue the hectors in open court, thus broadcasting their cuckoldry and, as a sure sign that they do not understand the system for patriarchal control of women's reproductive powers, protesting that their (adulterated) wives will be "not one jot the worse" (V, 179). The hectors themselves appear to get poetical justice. Not only are they exposed as pretenders and consequently beaten by the Cavaliers as their natural, better-bred betters, they are also arrested and brought before Justice Clodpate for their adultery. He recognizes them as those who cheated him, robbed him, stole his horse, and left him tied up as a ghost. He orders the Constable, "[S]ecure 'em to night, and I'le send 'em in the morning to *Kingstone* Goal without Bail or Mainprize" (V, 178). The hectors are led off and do not reappear for the comic closure.

Yet Kick and Cuff announce a defiance of both their accusers and their judge that has a kind of chilling if still comic effect. Kick accuses Bisket and Fribble of being "Shameless Rascals, to publish thus [their] own disgraces"; Cuff goes further to actually threaten them with retribution: "Rogues! we shall meet with you." They then turn their threats to Clodpate:

> *Cuff:* Mr. Justice, you are a Coxcomb; and I shall find a time to cut your Nose.
> *Kick:* And I will make bold to piss upon your Worship.

However comic Kick's threat (a late twentieth-century critic cannot read it without thinking of Monty Python), Montague Summers's note reminds us that such noseslittings were indeed a real means of enforcing power relations (389n). Furthermore, to Clodpate's orders that they be remanded to Kingstone jail Cuff responds dismissively, "Pheu, our Party is too strong for that, here in Town" (V, 178). Because Clodpate has been so thoroughly satirized, we do not take him seriously as a figure for justice. I think we should take Cuff's prophecy seriously and expect that the hectors will be sprung by their party.

Meanwhile, the other lower-class figure from the Suburbs, Mrs. Jilt, succeeds handsomely in her and her sister Peg's scam to ostensibly marry Clodpate. Peg is Mrs. Woodly's maid, who helps her sister come off as "a greater person" than she really is (III, 138) so that, like Moll Flanders after her, she can ply the other side of the marriage market, where lower-class women trick men into marriage for security's sake. Mrs. Jilt's trick is to pretend to hate London as much as Clodpate, but as soon as they are married, she reveals her real affinities with the Town, threatening to hire a townhouse in Lincolns-Inn-Fields—a step up from her native "*Coven-Garden*" district—and to bring Clodpate into acquaintance with her former suitors and through them into favor at Court. Of course, the audience understands the real nature of her relations (Bevil himself calls her "Old Acquaintance" [V, 176]), that Clodpate's exaggerated identification of her as a "Strumpet" simply because she is from London is actually the truth (V, 177). She and Peg negotiate a "Divorce" with the desperate Clodpate in which Mrs. Jilt gets enough money so she can now marry not just one she "like[s] better" but one, presumably—since at one point she tries to land Rains—socially better as well (V, 179-80).

That Mrs. Jilt gets off with no punishment but instead thrives so well by means of her and Peg's wit contributes to the subversive atmosphere caused by the leaving at large of so many disruptive threats to aristocratic social order. These threats include not only the Woodlys and the hectors but Mrs. Fribble and Mrs. Bisket as well, for not all their posturing of penitence at the end can convince us that their husbands are truly in control of their sexuality. Bisket's triumphant "Why then this is the first day of my reign" (V, 179) would have to be undercut by a knowing smirk from Mrs. Bisket to the audience, which, after all, has observed his earlier failed attempts to control her. These petty bourgeois women, conjoined with Mrs. Woodly, Mrs. Jilt, and Peg, represent a formidable subversive agency of women's wit, an underground version, if you will, of the witty women of the "high" plot. In short, we seem in Epsom to be in a carnival world where the centripetal order of society, as Bakhtin might put it, is balanced by the centrifugal forces of subversion (see esp. *Rabelais*).

Half a century ago Richard H. Perkinson pointed to the importance of topographical site in seventeenth-century comedy, where it is part of the plot (271). Concerning *Epsom Wells* he argues that Shadwell accurately portrayed the clientele and manners of the wells (286) but then, perhaps under the influence of the New Criticism, backed off to insist that these plays "reveal in their topography, not a sociological interest, but one rather in effective theater" (290). Some years ago now, Alssid provocatively characterized Epsom as "symbolically, the site of freedom, where people unmask and where truths are revealed" (59). Alssid was quite right, although I believe the real truths revealed escaped him. For they are not the truths of some universal human nature or human condition that New Criticism taught us to look for. Nor are they truths purely aesthetic and free from "sociological interest." Nor are they the truths Bakhtin has unearthed for us in his studies of the carnivalesque, the grotesque, and their subversion of official discourse. Epsom Wells is not a place, as Shadwell portrays it, where relations are suspended. We are not in some cloud-cuckooland. What Peter Stallybrass and Allon White say about the fair, romanticized (albeit incredibly provocatively) by Bakhtin as a site of folk subversion, strikes me as applicable to Shadwell's spa. The fair, they write, is "a point of economic and cultural intersection": "Languages, images, symbols and objects met and clashed at the fair and it was their *interconnection* which made for their significance. One could even mount the precise contrary argument to Bakhtin: that the fair, far from being the privileged site of popular symbolic opposition to hierarchies, was in fact a kind of educative spectacle, a relay for the diffusion of the cosmopolitan values of the 'centre' (particularly the capital and the new urban centres of production) throughout the provinces and the lower orders" (38).

    In other words, while *Epsom Wells* takes place in a state of apparent suspension of the order of society and at least partial subversion of its official discourse, it serves at the same time to reveal the interconnectedness of the levels of society and to reaffirm the power of the class at the top of its hierarchy. Throughout this section I have referred constantly to Town, Country, City, and Suburbs. The site of Epsom Wells is a crossroads of those other locations and their real, material as well as symbolic connotations.[18]

Let us examine first the antithesis between Town and Country by way of Raymond Williams's brilliant analysis in *The Country and the City:*

> In Restoration comedy, the contrast between "country" and "town" is commonly made, but with some evident ambiguity. Written by and for the fashionable society of the town, the plays draw on evidently anxious feelings of rejection, or a necessary appearance of rejection, of the coarseness and clumsiness, or simply the dullness, of country life. Certain rural stereotypes are established: a Blackacre or a Hoyden or a Tunbelly Clumsey; as later a Lumpkin and the whole lineage of Mummerset and the village clodhopper. Such types are easily laughed at, in the small talk of fashionable society. Separated from the country houses by which many of them were still maintained, the members of town society composed the sourest kind of counter-pastoral that anyone could have imagined. [51-52]

The portrait of Clodpate is just such a sour counterpastoral. Others have shown (Coleman, Novak), with reference to pamphlet wars as well as the drama, that there was a rhetorical warfare being conducted between Town and Country at the time of Shadwell's play, but no one has analyzed, in the manner of Williams, that rhetoric as ideological obfuscation. Such obfuscation is most evident in the debate over Country versus Town especially as it is conducted between Clodpate and the Cavaliers. Clodpate gives an idealized pastoral portrait of the Country, defined against that "Sodom" of London (passim), by which he means both Town and City, which he constantly satirizes as a den of iniquity. The irony is that at the moment we meet him he is inquiring of his servant if he has found Clodpate's "Cozen" (the spelling conflates kinship with confidence game), one "*Spatter-Brain,*" and recovered from him "that Interest money due to me this Midsummer" (I, 110). Obviously, there is an interdependence between this Country squire and the City after all, a financial interdependence that, as Williams and Hill both demonstrate, was increasing as England moved toward agrarian as well as mercantile capitalism.

As Cavalier Woodly says, Clodpate is full of "dull Encomiums upon a Country life, and discourse of his serving the Nation with his Magistracy, popularity, and Housekeeping" (I, 110). He prides himself especially on this good housekeeping, this husbandry: "I serve my Country, and spend upon my Tenants what I get amongst them" (I, 111). When asked to specify what other service, he enumerates such responsibilities as causing "Rogues to be whipt for breaking fences or pilling trees, especially if they be my own"; swearing in "Constables, and the like"; calling "Over-seers for the Poor to an account"; assigning "Rates" (i.e. taxes); as a Game-keeper, confiscating "Guns and Grey-hounds" obviously from poachers; and generally keeping the peace (I, 112). What is omitted from this ideal-ized portrait, but is right beneath the surface, is the class on whose backs is supported his and the nation's agrarian economy, a class he supposedly benevolently invites to his board every now and then but who live gener-ally at the level of subsistence nourishment; a class against whom he brings the power of law for breaking fences or poaching. Now many of those fences were erected as part of the enclosure of common lands associated with what Williams calls throughout his study the supposed "improve-ment" of England by squeezing as much as possible out of both land and people. Just such engrossment and enclosure may have necessitated poaching for survival or pilling trees for necessary ingredients for folk remedies traditionally gathered free. It is also interesting to note that Clodpate is particularly exercised by the pilling of *his* trees. No benevolent altruist he. He invites tenants to his board for the same reason he attends that of the lord lieutenant in his shire: to maintain the relations of power and his particular position within them.

What about those "Poor" that must have overseers? As Williams re-minds us throughout, these landless must be kept in their own parish, for they will not be cared for elsewhere and instead will be forcibly returned to their own neighborhoods. But as we know, they increasingly made their way to London, where, like today's urban underclass, they had to make do as best they could. Many gathered in the Suburbs, the disreputable district Dryden describes in *MacFlecknoe* just outside the City, the locale of the-aters and nurseries for both actors and punks. Mrs. Jilt is more likely from this "*Coven-Garden*" district, not the real Covent Garden (though that district had its prostitutes as well). Are not also the hectors Kick and Cuff from the Suburbs? Are they not representatives of the landless dispos-sessed who must thrive by their wits? Protesting a Machiavellian ethic of survival, Cuff says with some wit, "We that are to live by vertuous indus-try, ought to stand out at nothing" (V, 164).

It is a grand irony that all three tricksters are of the class of "Cheating Knaves, and Jilting Whores" Clodpate fears so much in London, the ones who cheated him on his first trip up as a youth, for they are the ones dis-possessed by the system of engrossing agribusiness Clodpate represents (I, 111). He has feared losing his "Land to the Scriveners," as part of that steady interaction between Country and City wherein property, as well as daughters, was being traded to build estates. Ironically, he loses a significant part of it to one excluded from "society" by the increasing maldistribution of wealth. And when Lucia condescendingly characterizes the City wives at the wells as having "more trading with the youth of the Suburbs, than their Husbands with their Customers within the walls" (I, 113), beneath the ideology of her disdain is the fact that the dispossessed Suburban males as well as females often tried to enter the marriage market and move on up the class ladder. Not only does Mrs. Jilt reject Clodpate for a better, but Kick and Cuff, after all, parade as "persons of quality" with "money" and approach Lucia herself and Carolina, representatives of the highest, most privileged class (I, 114). That they are run off by their supposedly natural superiors (Rains opines that such hectors "are most violently bent upon the things they are least capable of, as if it were in spite of Nature" [II, 132]) is part of the ideology that posits a great gap between the highest and the lowest classes and masks their interconnectedness. Indeed, the absence of a poetic justice at the end which puts them back in their places suggests that the reality of the homeless may be obscured in capitalism, but it will not go away.

There is a further irony in Lucia's contempt for City and Suburb alike. When Clodpate comes courting, Lucia playfully but significantly taunts, "I have vow'd never to Marry one that cannot make me a Lady, and you are no Knight" (II, 120). She herself wants to marry up as high as she can, because up is where the power is. Indeed, as Williams says, "the moral ratification of this drama is . . . the steering of the estate into the right hands" (53). And yet the *rightness* of those hands is part of dominant class ideology, obfuscating the increasing (though always present) reality of class intermarriage in England, the reality Hogarth depicts in *Marriage à la Mode*. The Woodlys of the gentry often turned to the City for wives to repair their estates. Just as Lucia has commented on the Suburban youths who dally with the City wives, Mrs. Woodly comments on the trickery of the City wives themselves "that lye upon the snap for young Gentlemen, as Rooks and Bullies do for their Husbands when they come to Town" (II, 129). Epsom Wells is a microcosm for a world of cheaters, of lower classes that prey upon upper.

But of course, upper prey upon lower. Typical Cavaliers in Restoration comedy, Bevil and Rains believe in a kind of *droit de cuissage* with regard to all lower-class women, and the cuckolding of Cits, the seduction of City wives, is a special reaffirmation of class dominance. Why was Cit-cuckolding portrayed with such virulence if not actual violence in the Restoration? Because the middle class was increasingly threatening aristocratic hegemony. Yet ironically, not only is Clodpate dependent on the services of the City, so also are the gallants. Fribble is a haberdasher. Where else do their fashionable clothes come from if not from such petty bourgeois traders and merchants? When Clodpate is satirized for busying himself with the political and economic news of Europe, what is being obfuscated is England's reliance on that trade and its need for political stability in Europe to advance it. We are occasionally reminded subtly how global that trade is becoming, as in Rains's witty reference to the extension of English law to the *"East Indies"* (I, 117). Indeed, England's expanding empire supports a political economy that enables not only Country affluence but the Town's extravagant lifestyle.

Thus in its satire of the City, Restoration Town comedy obscures the Town's interdependent relationship with it. Moreover, in its satire of the Country, this comedy obscures the Town's interdependent relationship with it as well, because of that anxiety Williams mentions, that need to distance itself from its own real power base. Not surprisingly, Lucia has the most delightful satire on the Country. She caricatures the Country life of a Country wife:

> To see my Ducks and Geese fed, and cram my own Chickens. . . . To have my Closet stink, like a Pothecaries shop, with Drugs and Medicines, to administer to my sick Neighbours, and spoil the next Quack's practice with the receipt-book that belongs to the Family. . . . And then to have one approved Green-salve, and dress sore Legs with it, and all this to deserve the name of as good a neighbourly body as ever came into *Sussex*. . . . Never to hear a Fiddle, but such as sounds worse than the Tongs and Key, or a Gridiron; never to read better Poetry than *John Hopkins* or *Robert Wisdom*'s vile Metre; nor hear better singing than a company of Peasants praising God with doleful, untunable, hoarse voices, that are only fit to be heard under the Gallows. [II, 121]

This "sour counter-pastoral," Williams reminds us, evinces the Town's need to distance itself in its ideology from the very "country houses by which many of [the "members of town society"] were still maintained" (52). So when Mrs. Jilt mockingly portrays in song "the fluttering vain Gallant in" London who "consumes/His Estate in rich Cloaths and Perfumes" (III, 140), she reveals the conspicuous consumption of the dominant class that was the sign of its power, of its special relationship, in contrast to both Country and City, with the Court, with that "centre" of political power, as Stallybrass and White characterize it, around which circulated all the symbolic relationships of the nation. When Rains mocks Clodpate for spending "upon [his] Tenants what [he] get[s] amongst them," Rains's answer obliquely reveals the source of his subclass's conspicuous consumption: "And so, indeed, [you] are no better than their Sponge, which they moisten only to squeeze again" (I, 111). Rains's earlier metaphor for *husbanding* his health so he can lay it out again in debauchery (I, 108) contrasts his carpe diem philosophy of libertine hedonism explicitly with "sober" bourgeois morality but implicitly with Clodpate's husbandry. The exchange between Rains and Bevil that concludes the portrait of that husbandry is marvelously telling:

> *Rains:* That men should be such infinite Coxcombs to live scurvily to get reputation among thick-scull'd Peasants, and be at as great a distance with men of wit and sense, as if they were another sort of Animals.
> *Bevil:* 'Tis fit such Fools should govern and do the drudgery of the world, while reasonable men enjoy it. [I, 112]

Just as Shadwell, in a throwaway song of apparently no consequence, forces his Cits to praise "Cavaliers," condemn "old Belzebub, *Oliver*," and toast "a Health unto his Majesty" (V, 166; italics reversed), so also would it seem that the Court-dominated theater system forced Shadwell himself, despite his earlier, antilibertine plays, to celebrate the Cavalier ethos of his patrons Newcastle and Rochester, an ethos symbolically centered in the figure of Charles II himself (see Braverman, "Rake's Progress," and Weber, *Paper Bullets*), who sanctions this upper–upperclass's ostentatious display of wealth and its concomitant obfuscation of its real, material base—particularly that of the peasantry so condescendingly dismissed by both Lucia and Rains. In words that seem especially appropriate to the crossroads microcosm of the spa, Williams says of the gentry who come to town, "What they brought with them, and what they came to promote, rested on the brief and aching lives of the permanently cheated: the field labourers whom we never by any chance see; the dispossessed and the evicted; all the men and women whose land and work paid their fares and provided their spending money" (54). Charles also sanctions the theater and its contribution to his regnant ideology of what Williams calls "the 'town and country' fiction," which served "to promote superficial comparisons and to prevent real ones."

Thus Shadwell creates in *Epsom Wells* a site for the apparent suspension of reality as the audience revels in his pleasing fiction. But let critics no longer suspend their attention, for Shadwell unwittingly reveals not superficial but real power relations, as well as his art's complicity with that regnant ideology as if it were Stallybrass and White's relay for the diffusion of "the cosmopolitan values of the 'centre'" from the theater to the spa to "the provinces and the lower orders" (38).

Shadwell's play maps out some territory we will be examining: the meaning of the marriage of the wits as well as of the Cit-cuckolding in social comedy; of Cavalier buddy-cuckolding and lower-class resistance in subversive comedy. And although Shadwell writes more tragical than comical satire (as in *The Libertine* and *Timon of Athens*), his satiric spirit finds formal comic expression in his own *The Woman-Captain* (1679); in Durfey's surprising attacks on extravagant Cavalier tricksters at their apparent apogee; and ironically, in his nemesis Dryden's attack on the deus ex machina without principle who descends upon the stage even as the estate of England slips through the fingers of the Stuarts.

Part One
SOCIAL COMEDY

Restoration social comedy socializes threats to the dominant aristocracy and reaffirms its patriarchal order by absorbing the vital energy of its youth and satirizing those who stand in their way. Employing Corman's useful distinctions, let us analyze the *mixt way* of Restoration social comedy by artificially separating out *sympathetic* from *punitive* elements. Each subset performs its own cultural work. And let us begin with those sympathetic elements, the tricksters who obtain the lovers and the land, always at the expense of fools and knaves, sometimes at the expense of other tricksters. Chapters 1 to 4 focus on the implicit threat to Stuart hegemony, rebels against its sexual political economy. Most Restoration social comedy portrays such rebels, who resist the marriages necessary to sustain the system but conclude in those marriages after all—albeit with some freedom of choice within class.

Nevertheless, from the political plays by Cowley and Robert Howard I analyze in the Introduction to plays around the time of the Popish Plot and the Exclusion Crisis, several social comedies portray explicit threats to that Stuart hegemony in the form of a middle class that needs to be put in its place. Chapter 5 focuses on the aggressive cuckolding of Cits by Town wits.

Interpretation of Restoration comedy often excludes at least half of what actually occurs on the stage. That is, by focusing on the sympathetic elements and characters, as we do almost exclusively in the criticism of this drama, we generally neglect to analyze the significance of comic butts and farcical action. Chapter 6 thus turns from sympathetic to punitive elements and a representative sampling of the further disciplining of the emergent bourgeois counterculture.

1

Nubile Tricksters Land Their Men

In Restoration social comedy at its most familiar the threat to established order takes the form of promiscuous rakes and rebellious young women resisting—marriage itself, in the case of the libertine rakes, or enforced marriage, in the case of the witty women. At the end of these comedies, the centrifugal energy of rakes who insist on freedom to change and women who insist on freedom to choose is normally centripetalized in a marriage that finally presents no threat to status hierarchy and that guarantees the continuation of an aristocratic order in which power and property continue to be safely transmitted through genealogy.[1] Or to put Raymond Williams's spin on it, Restoration social comedy ends in the right couple set to inherit the estate, which is the center, at least symbolically, of late feudal political economy.

These resisting, nubile women, asserting their right to choose mates, defy society's guardians of their reproductive power. The guardians, from fathers to uncles to brothers to duennas, are intent either on building estates through arranged marriages and the male heirs produced through that power or on sequestering the power itself in a nunnery or just a locked room. The fear of the guardian is twofold: that he will lose the opportunity to extend his economic and political power through his enhanced prestige and that the goods he has to trade will become soiled, either by sexual contamination or, worse, class contamination. The point in the marriage market is to trade across or up, not down (though as we have seen that was a rule come to be honored in the breach as much as the observance in marriages increasingly designed to join the land of the Country with the wealth of the City). Thus these witty women threaten what Gayle Rubin in a classic article has called *the traffic in women*.

Often, as in *The Cutter of Coleman Street* and *The Committee*, as we saw in the Introduction, guardians tyrannize over not just the bodies and wills of women but over their wealth, not just a portion but in some instances an inherited estate. So the women become tricksters with doubled motivation.

And they mostly refuse to run away in the middle of the night but insist on obtaining both their choice and their portion. Constance and Isabelle in Dryden's *The Wild Gallant* and Otrante and Flora of Richard Rhodes's *Flora's Vagaries,* both of the next season (1663), manage to get choice and financial security despite tyrants. In the former play Constance maintains that it is only proper she who is a fortune should marry the penniless Loveby, while her fortuneless cousin should marry the rich Sir Timorous (who has the land in the country she mocks but needs). Their outrageous trick has been to convince their father/guardian Lord Nonsuch that by some miracle (it's the water!) they are all capable of parthenogenesis, men and women alike, and the lord watches as not only Constance's but his own belly grows apace.

The trick has symbolic import: the entire marriage game exists to produce heirs. When the trick has done its work, Isabelle appeals to her nonplussed uncle's sense of endings: "Come Nuncle 'tis in vain to hold out now 'tis past remedy: 'tis like the last Act of a Play when People must marry" (V.v.84-85). But it has the sense of an ending Williams sees in these plays as well: when Nonsuch worries about their great bellies, Lady Constance says hers has "vanish'd already" (91), but Loveby wittily ripostes, "I'll do my best, she shall not be long without another" (93-94). Nonsuch finally gives his blessing in these lines addressed to both couples: "To bed, to bed: 'tis late"; he adds to his new son-in-law and heir, "Son *Loveby* get me a boy to night, and I'll settle three thousand a year upon him the first day he calls me Grandsire" (147-49). Similarly, when Flora and Otrante get their men in Rhodes's play, they also get their money from their tyrant father, Grimani; some now, he says to the particularly rebellious but therefore energetic Flora, "more when you are a Mother" (V, 75).

Girls as young as fourteen-year-old Hippolita of Wycherley's *The Gentleman Dancing-Master* (1672) are forced to be resourceful, in this instance displaying her merchandize—her beauty, her wit, and her worth—right under a foolish father's nose. Desperate to escape her father's control and an arranged marriage, she tricks her French-fried fiancé into sending someone (anyone will serve her turn at this juncture, provided he is a "Gentleman" [I, 132]) up to her through her window—a kind of enfenestration—and announces to him, "I am an Heiress, and have twelve hundred pound a year, lately left me by my Mothers Brother, which my Father cannot meddle with, and which is the chiefest reason (I suppose) why he keeps me up so close" (II, 157). Living up to her amazonian name, when caught by her father with a man in her chambers, Hippolita takes matters into her own wits and passes her lover off as her dancing master. Moreover, she lets Gerrard know in no uncertain terms that she intends to remain a Town and not become a Country wife: "I know 'tis the trick of all you that spirit Women away to speak 'em mighty fair at first; but when you have got 'em in your Clutches: you carry 'em into *York-shire, Wales,* or *Cornwall,* which is as bad as to *Barbadoes,* and rather than be served so, I would be a Pris'ner in *London* still as I am" (II, 166). Her counterpastoral references are not casual, for such outlying counties and colonies—the latter increasingly so—are the basis of that London leisure life.

True, Hippolita, in order to test Gerrard's motives, pretends that she lied, she's no real heiress, and she exults in the triumph of his "love" over his "interest" (V, 220). Nevertheless, he is, after all, a gentleman—and worth enough to have a coach and six waiting for their elopement (passim). Moreover, though she may have inherited nobility from her mother's side of the family, her father's wonted pride in his heraldry is based upon origins, first, in petty manufacturing and trade (V, 224). Yet she succeeds through her wit in landing a gentleman she has come to love and in retaining not only her own inheritance, but her father's as well—the "most part" now, "the rest" at his death (V, 234). In other words, the play symbolically underwrites the appropriation of City wealth by the landed aristocracy, and the beautiful couple will become a fixture of the Town, even as Hippolita produces an heir. Hippolita's Aunt Caution capitulates to the young couple's trickery in mock sarcasm, pointing to the cultural sense of the ending: "Nay, Young-man, you have danc'd a fair Dance for your self royally, and now you may go jig it together till you are both weary; and though you were so eager to have him, Mrs. *Minx,* you'll soon have your belly-full of him, let me tell you, Mistress" (V, 233).[2]

In the typical romance ploy of Ravenscroft's Hillaria, appropriated from tragicomedy for comedy's less mystified purposes,[3] the eponymous heroine of the anonymous *The Woman Turn'd Bully* (1675), Betty Goodfeild, dons man's apparel to achieve her freedom of choice of a Town wit for a husband (her widowed mother, attempting to solidify estates with her neighbor, has arranged a marriage in the Country). Meanwhile, her brother has slipped down from Cambridge to pursue Lucia, "a Fortune" (I.ii, 4), who is niece and ward to the estate-consuming lawyer Docket. Docket has maintained that Lucia's obtaining of her portion is contingent upon his approval of her marriage choice, which he intends never to grant. Thus, he has already spent the value of her portion. Insisting he has money enough for both as heir to his deceased father's estate, Goodfeild tempts Lucia to elope, but she refuses to marry behind her uncle's back, much less let him have her money.

Goodfeild's best friend is one Truman, whose own estate was mortgaged by his deceased father and continues to be mortgaged in service to his conspicuous consumption—to the point that Docket attempts to purchase the rest of it for a mere £500 (apparently bringing Truman's indebtedness to a nice, cheap, round sum). Truman responds with indignant sarcasm: "So in effect, you will have an Estate of 500*l* a year in the best Lands in *Hartfordshire,* all improvable, with 100 Acres of Timber, and all this for 7000*l.* And so you and I shall continue good Friends" (I.iii, 14). Such details as the timber remind us again of the value in land and its resources, here the timber being sold off by lords needing ready cash, while the timber itself goes to support especially the maritime industry. Mrs. Goodfeild's old and faithful steward Trupenny introduces into the play more of this material reality, albeit now in a Country benevolent pastoral version: "I have the value of all their Estate to a penny, in my books at home. Besides this, their Tenants are able men, and special Paymasters; and indeed, my Lady does oblige 'em to it: For every *Christmas* she calls 'em all to dinner at the Hall: Then have we the Bagpipes, and are so passing merry" (II.ii, 26). Of course, Williams would remind us that this description is a self-serving mystification, part of the charity of consumption distributed at festival times to assuage the consciences of landlords who the rest of the year kept their tenants at subsistence level: "All uncharity at work, it was readily assumed, could be redeemed by the charity of the consequent feast" (31).

Out of sheer delight in trickster play, Betty bullies both gallants into duels. Revealing herself in the nick of each one, she is immediately attracted to the energy and wit of Truman. Her brother prophesies that Betty's "second Duel" with Truman, her amatory one, "will have a more bloudy conclusion than the first" (III.i, 36)—the naturally bloody conclusion of the courtship between the socially "right" inheritors of estates. But an unexpected hurdle arises: Docket is attracted to Mrs. Goodfeild's estate and through marriage, Goodfeild fears, could affect his and his sister's inheritances, as well as Lucia's. The real problem, however, is not Docket but Mrs. Goodfeild, who ought to have the good grace to retire from the marriage market. It is part of the ideology of these comedies that the older generation should not compete with the younger—for the quite logical reason that they thus complicate the transmission of power between generations.

So Truman becomes trickster, courts Mrs. Goodfeild for himself, and pawns Docket off onto Mrs. Goodfeild's superannuated but husband-starved maid, Loveal. Meanwhile, Betty disguises herself as a bully in the night to scare Docket out of marriage. But Loveal has secured him. Truman has married Betty. And Goodfeild has married Lucia, and they kneel for Docket's blessing. He refuses Lucia her portion, but Loveal, playing Mrs. Goodfeild still, refuses him hers, and he finally admits that Lucia never needed his approval. When Loveal unveils and Docket threatens to sue, Truman offers to pay his niece's portion in return for his mortgaged estate. Most important, as the play ends in hymeneal celebration of youth and love, Mrs. Goodfeild recovers her pride by pretending she never took Truman seriously; she pledges never to marry again but to live celibate and bequeath all her widow's jointure upon her death. She thus sets the stage for orderly transition to the wits.

A bizarre example of these nubile trickster plays is Lacy's *Sir Hercules Buffoon; or, The Poetical Squire* (1684), bizarre not only because it was produced posthumously (Lacy died in 1681) and seems closer to other Lacy plays of the 1660s, but because its guardian plot verges on tragicomedy and yet strangely looks back to Middletonian city comedy and at the same time forward to Gay's *The Beggar's Opera*. It is one of the most overtly class-conscious social comedies of the Restoration, for it is a play about the reappropriation of women, property, and prerogative by the upper class from an upstart middle class, represented by both City and Country versions.

Sir Marmaduke Seldin is guardian to two nieces worth a fabulous £300,000 between them, the inheritance from a wealthy merchant. Appearing at first a basically honest fellow who landed in debtors' prison because of pride, this impecunious City uncle soon manifests felonious greed, for he plans to murder his nieces, substituting his own daughters and marrying them to the highest bidders regardless of their inherent worth. So he deals with rich Alderman Buffoon, who has £100,000 of his own and wants to gain an additional fortune for his nephew, the booby poetical squire of the subtitle. When Sir Marmaduke pretends that Squire Buffoon is "of unrefined Clay, such as Bearwards and Tinkers were made up of," the alderman proposes to buy an even higher title than his brother Sir Hercules's knighthood and make his nephew a lord (III.ii, 26). Sir Marmaduke's response—"There are so many *Buffoons* stolen into Titles, that men wou'd judge they came not lawfully by them"—satirizes the erosion of the aristocracy it publicly decried even as it absorbed City money (not to mention genes) for increasing agrarian capitalism (see both Hill and Williams, passim). Of course, Sir Marmaduke merely mouths the rhetoric of class snobbery even as he leaves to draw up the writings for the "Estate."

Sounding like Peachum, Sir Marmaduke expresses astonishment at his daughter Mariana's resistance to fraud: "That ever we should bring our Children up to be religious! it onely teaches them to rebel against their Prince and Parents. Then Dame Nature, that cunning Gilt, commands and orders us to doat on them, when they return nothing but ingratitude. Wou'd Nature had let that subtil knack alone, for 'tis the chiefest curse that Mankind has, loving and providing for our Brats" (I, 5).[4] His younger daughter, the waggish Fidelia, appears to have inherited her father's morality (as well as his perverse sense of humor): "'[T]is time enough to think of virtue when ones Teeth are out: to be a virtuous young Woman, and a virtuous old Woman too, is too much; I think 'tis fair, Father, for a young Woman to resolve to be virtuous when she's old" (3). When Mariana employs euphemisms for the impending murder of her cousins, Sir Marmaduke insists on calling a spade a spade: "Throw by your fears, or I'll throw by your lives: bloudy words suit best with bloudy deeds, therefore I'll have no other phrase but Murder, startle that dares" (II.i, 9). When the nieces themselves balk at embarking on the ship that will carry them to the frozen coast of Norway and their death, Seaman exclaims, "I hate peevish people that will not be murdered quietly when 'tis their turn" (II.iii, 13).

Such humorous language keeps the high plot from the "melodrama" of which Hume accuses it (372-73), though Sir Marmaduke's stabbing of Mariana for betraying him is the stuff of tragicomedy. The daughters have secretly arranged through their maid, the lover of the rough seaman, to have the nieces safely ensconced in England. Meanwhile, Lord Arminger has fallen in love with Mariana, whom he takes as the heiress Belmaria. Mariana refuses to participate in fraud, even when the truth comes out and Arminger declares he loves her anyway. Mariana refuses to marry him, and he refuses to marry Belmaria. Fidelia comments wittily but accurately, "I thank Fate I am not in Love'[s] Lime twigs, for here's the Devil and all to do: In point of honour forsooth one will not marry, and the other will not marry; so that I find the Punctilio's of [H]onour will destroy Generation, and is't not pity such a Lord shou'd die, without leaving some of his Brood behind him?" (V.iv, 48). Arminger tricks Mariana into jealousy, then a commitment to marry. The nieces have offered to share their estates with their saviors, but Arminger is so rich, he can raise Mariana up himself. And the unromantic, pragmatic Fidelia has fended for herself, winning the booby, eminently manageable squire by hilariously imitating the younger, more country of these northern heiresses and her Yorkshire accent (she pretends outrage at the squire's offer of premarital copulation: "Marra out upon the Grisely Beast, wie wad ta make a Slut of me, and have me play at Bawdiness with thee" [III.ii, 26]). She has manipulated a settling of the entire Buffoon estate onto her.

In the comic subplot, three Town wits—Laton, Bowman, and Aimwell—have with the aid of Sir Hercules's epic mendacity manipulated a judge into signing over his estate to Laton. Laton, a young gentleman without means, justifies the trickery as turnabout fair play: "Your Conscience knows you cozen'd my Father grosly, and I have got it [the estate] again by a trick, so there's trick for your trick" (V.iii, 46). But when Aimwell at the end asks Lord Arminger, who has just been named by the dying Sir Marmaduke as the heiresses' new guardian, if he and the other wits may make their addresses, Arminger says no to his former comrades, for he will admit only "men of such Honour and Wealth, as shall deserve their Fortunes" (V.iv, 52), an answer even Laton accepts. For all its aristocratic triumph at the end, then, the play subtly absorbs into official discourse the economic reality that the late Stuart ruling class is no pure nobility but a plutocratic oligarchy.[5]

More mainstream writers like Dryden and Behn reveal other aspects of the power relations in Restoration society obscured by the veneer of official discourse. Dryden's witty heroines get their men and their fortunes in *An Evening's Love; or The Mock-Astrologer* (1668) and *The Assignation; or, Love in a Nunnery* (1672). In the latter, there is much delightful raillery against the unnaturalness of a nunnery, where younger daughters are often placed to reduce the financial burden on fathers and also the chances of bastards at family picnics. Laura and Violetta, wealthy heiresses, are, in addition, wards to Mario, who doesn't want to give up the revenue from their entrusted estates and so denies consent to all suitors till the prince promises his father's power to force compliance at the end.

Behn's heroines in *The Feign'd Curtzans; or, A Nights Intrigue* (1679) also escape a guardian's tyranny—one from an arranged marriage not with an old but an ugly nobleman, the other from a nunnery—by fleeing to an upscale brothel neighborhood and pretending to be high-class whores. Hamlet's famous pun reminds us of the way both kinds of *nunnery* exist as ancillary institutions to patriarchy: both siphoning off excess female fertility but prostitution serving to siphon off excess male fertility as well. Especially when Marcella and Cornelia role-play as courtesans, even as the audience is aware they are chaste, Behn points obliquely to the backstairs free love and its attendant erotic celebration of infinite variety that lurk behind the facade of official aristocratic ideology. Cornelia's waggish declaration that "Curtizan" is "a Noble title and has more *Votaries than Religion,* there's no Merchandize like . . . that of Love. . . . there are a thousand satisfactions to be found, more than in a dull virtuous life" (II.65-90) may seem to be just idle chatter from a young girl on a holiday, but it provides a counterdiscourse to the traditional code of sexual virtue, underwritten by religious language and underwriting the merchandizing of bodies for the perpetuation of estates and titles. This counterdiscourse is not merely swept out of memory as the play closes in marriages blest by the guardians but is co-opted into official discourse by Cornelia's converting her wild man lover to marriage by promising to be "the most Mistriss-like Wife," plying the tricks of her "trade" she never got to practice, including being "Inconstant" (V.709-11)—this last an impish but, given her strenuous preservation of chastity at the critical moment earlier, finally empty gesture. The import of the ending is that an ugly and therefore inappropriate suitor has withdrawn, and the beautiful people are married with the blessing of the guardians. Cornelia has left a nunnery and has brought her fertile body as well as her fertile wit and her "Fortune" (IV.446) into a marriage that redeems an obviously younger brother (Galliard satirizes elder brothers throughout as being, ipso facto, less sexually potent).[6]

Similarly, despite all her wild, libertine posturing about loving for no more than a fortnight or a month at best, the rich Jacinta in *An Evening's Love* insists upon marrying the poor but desirable Wilding during the last evening of carnival, wittily rationalizing her haste to her guardian father thus: "If I stay till after *Lent*, I shall be to marry when I have no love left: I'll not bate you an Ace of to night, Father: I mean to bury this man e're *Lent* be done, and get me another before *Easter*" (V.i.465-68). As Markley argues so well (*Two-Edg'd Weapons*, 93-99), the carnival atmosphere has licensed libertine discourse, but aristocratic necessity reinterprets Jacinta's double entendre to mean she will bury Wilding in her body in order to conceive a male heir in time for the Resurrection.

What has gone without saying in my treatment of these nubile tricksters is that often the men they land are sexual tricksters like Galliard and Wilding.[7] It is part of the mystique of Stuart ideology that these libertine rakes, whose ethos is the antithesis of traditional sexual morality, are so attractive, so vital that they are not only worth trying to *save* in a social if not a religious sense but indeed are necessary for the infusion of their energy into the very bloodlines of aristocratic families (even those alloyed with City genes). Their very *extravagance*, to employ Jordan's useful term, is the sign of their desirability. As Hellena puts it in *The Rover*, Willmore's inconstancy is an incredible turn-on: "how this unconstant humour makes me love him!" (IV.281).[8]

The greatest of these nubile trickster plays is *The Rover; or The Ban-ish't Cavaliers* (1677). Florinda, destined by her father for the old Count Vicentio and by her brother for the Viceroy's son Antonio, demands her own choice, the valiant and handsome English Cavalier, Belvile, who saved her from rape at the siege of Pamplona. Her sister Hellena, destined by both father and brother for a nunnery so that her "Fortune" might be used to enhance her sister's portion (I.42), rebels in the name of youth: "And dost thou think," she asks her sister, "that ever I'le be a Nun? or at least till I'm so Old, I'm fit for nothing else[?] . . . prithee tell me, what dost thou see about me that is unfit for Love—have I not a World of Youth? a humour gay? a Beauty passable? a Vigour desirable? Well Shap't? clean limb'd? sweet breath'd? and sense enough to know how all these ought to be employed to the best advantage[?]" (30-31, 38-42). Like Hippolita, she'll take nearly anyone, with only one qualification: "I'm re-solved to provide my self this Carnival, if there be eer a handsome proper fellow of my humour above ground, tho I ask first" (33-35).

The description of old Vincentio's estate reminds us what Florinda re-linquishes but also, once again, what undergirds the Town society of the beautiful people and its built-in necessity. Hellena and their brother Pedro banter a pastoral and counterpastoral contrapunto about its various props:

> *Pedro:* The Girl's mad—it is a confinement to be carri'd into the Coun-try, to an Ancient Villa belonging to the Family of the *Vincentio's* these five hundred Years, and have no other Prospect than that pleas-ing one of seeing all her own that meets her Eyes—a fine Ayr, large Fields and Gardens where she may walk and gather Flowers.
> *Hellena:* When, by Moon Light? For I am sure she dares not encounter with the heat of the Sun, that were a task only for *Don Vincentio* and his Indian breeding, who loves it in the Dog dayes.—and if these be her daily divertissements, what are those of the Night, to lye in a wide Moth-eaten Bed Chamber, with furniture in Fashion in the Reign of King *Sancho* the First [10th century?]; The Bed, that which his Fore fathers liv'd and di'd in. [I.89-99]

The bed is precisely what Florinda is destined for in order to continue that genealogical continuity and keep the estate—growing thanks to colonial trade with the Indies—all in the family.

The bed is also what Hellena opts for as she says she knows what to do with her youth, beauty, and wit. When, in masquerade as a gypsy, she informs the Cavalier wit she has randomly chosen during Carnival that she has vowed to "dye a Maid," he responds with wonderful exaggerated rhetoric, appropriating in typical libertine fashion religious language for his counterreligion of the natural, "Then thou art damn'd without redemption, and as I am a good Christian, I ought in Charity to divert so wicked a design" (I.ii.149-51). Her design is wicked because it subverts the function for which nature (according to patriarchal aristocracy) intended her: sex. But the consequences of sex are what the libertine male can ignore but the female cannot, and that fact is what Hellena uses finally to socialize Willmore's great energy into marriage.

Despite all her protestations that "I am as inconstant as you. . . . therefore, I declare, I'll allow but one year for Love, one year for indifference, and one year for hate—and then go hang yourself—for I profess my self . . . *Hellena the Inconstant*" (III.167, 171-73; V.461), Hellena defers the collation of their love till after grace; as with Harriet, there's no taking up with her without church security. Balking at the "Bugg words . . . Priest and *Hymen*" because such words are attendant upon such mercenary and therefore unnatural concerns as "Portion, and Joynture," Willmore offers Hellena only a morganatic marriage: "I cou'd be content to turn Gipsie, and become a left-handed bride-groom, to have the pleasure of working that great Miracle of making a Maid a Mother, if you durst venture; 'tis upse Gipsie that, and if I miss, I'll lose my Labour" (V.420-29). Her dazzling answer focuses upon the real biological labor and consequent economic slavery that would ensue without real church security: "And if you do not lose, what shall I get? a cradle full of noise and mischief, with a pack of repentance at my back? can you teach me to weave Incle to pass my time with? 'tis upse Gipsie that, too" (V.430-32). As an upper-class woman, Hellena would have to take her bastard and join some group of the dispossessed. Because he adores her "Humour" so much—because, as she herself had wished, they are "so of one Humour"—Willmore accedes (445).

The meaning of the union of the three couples at the end is complex. Florinda, Hellena, and their cousin Valeria have all abandoned their native country and the Country estates they might be mistresses of (it turns out that Hellena controls her own inheritance of 200,000 crowns) for the virtually penniless *banished cavaliers* of the subtitle. Pedro acquiesces in these marriages partly because he is upset with Antonio both for dishonoring his sister by pursuing another woman and for pursuing the woman he himself desires, partly because the Cavaliers are noble, as Belvile manifested in his courage at Pamplona, but especially because all three have remained loyal to their banished king. Belvile speaks for himself implicitly as well as his friends explicitly: "[M]y Friends are Gentlemen, and ought to be Esteem'd for their Misfortunes, since they have the Glory to suffer with the best of Men and Kings" (V.481-82). Therefore they may well get their estates back at the Restoration Behn's audience knows is imminent. More-

over, particularly Willmore seems invested with that special value of loyalty, for Belvile continues in words that are ambiguous in their reference:
"'[T]is true, he's a Rover of Fortune, / Yet a Prince, aboard his little
wooden World" (V. 511-12). Willmore is a captain aboard his majesty's
ship. This reference to Charles Stuart as "a Rover" links the two not so
much to criticize Charles's sexcapades but to raise Willmore's value to one
that transcends Vincentio's estate, for he represents briefly at this closing
moment the estate of England.[9]

The waggish Maria of James Carlile's *The Fortune-Hunters; or, Two
Fools Well Met* (1689) is no peer of Hellena, but her trickery to gain the
extravagant rake Frank Wealthy demonstrates, along with *Sir Hercules
Buffoon* (whenever it was written), that this subset of Restoration social
comedy persisted through the 1680s to the end of the period. Maria and
her more stately cousin Sophia are wards to Sir William Wealthy, who
plans to keep their money in the family by marrying Sophia to his eldest
son Tom and Maria to himself, however sexagenarian he be. Sophia's only
quarrel with Tom Wealthy is his intemperate jealousy, which she endeavors
to tame but which almost costs him her love when he duels with a foppish
rival. Maria refuses to return to the Country married to Sir William, but
rebelliously intends to stay in the Town and, like her soul sisters Hippolita
and Hellena, marry the first young gentleman she likes and make him
master of her £10,000 "rather then I'll dye of the Pip, to leave it to you
[Sophia] and your Heirs" (I.ii, 3). She yearns to meet young Frank
Wealthy, who by his reputation seems to her a potential kindred spirit. Instantly attracted to him at the moment of acquaintance, she discerns she
must wean him away from the Lady Sly, a wealthy widow who keeps him
and who becomes a termagant Mrs. Loveit when threatened with losing
him to Maria. Tricking Lady Sly with a feigned letter supposedly from
Frank to her, Maria turns the lady into her procuress, leading her to her
lover. But the widow countertricks.

Frank, who has been disinherited by his father for prodigality, has been
tentatively readmitted to the household upon the promise of repaying his
debt to his father. Once there, Frank in courtship dances with Maria while
his father hilariously paws at her skirts. By demonstrating how deeply Maria
is attracted to him, Lady Sly provokes Sir William to have Frank imprisoned
for debt. Both his rivals visit him in prison, Lady Sly offering him herself
and "all" she has in marriage (V.i, 52), Maria disguising herself as the
brother of one of the fools of the subtitle, whom Frank has bested in a duel
as his brother Tom's second, and issuing him a challenge to another duel
unless he relinquish his interest in Maria. Frank outrageously accedes to
both, taking the widow into an adjacent chamber to seal their bargain and
then meeting the disguised Maria on the dueling fields.

Maria screws the test up a notch, hiring ruffians to join her and offering Frank the choice of relinquishing Maria or dying. The don juan finally grows a spine, refuses despite the odds, and thus earns Maria's commitment to him. Frank convinces Sophia to forgive Tom and marry first so they can follow suit, saying Maria won't yield to him without church security: "[S]ince this young Niggard will be paid her price before she parts with any of her Goods, let the black fellow thunder in my Ears" (V, 60). The price is marriage; the goods monetary as well as sexual. Together they disappoint Lady Sly and Sir William, gaining the latter's grudging blessing only when Maria convinces him that in loving his son, she loves him—a position that gently persuades him to accept the necessity of successive generations. Maria's trope of mirrored images implicitly grants Sir William Wealthy the immortality he seeks as a superannuated lover and at the same time perpetuates both the Wealthy family and its combined estates.[10]

2

Mature Women Tricksters Man Their Land

Another group of Restoration social comedies features experienced women who either have estates or regain them in order to share them with men of their choice.[1] In James Howard's *The English Mounsieur* (1663), Lady Wealthy, a rich widow, is courted by Welbred, a wild younger brother whose vice is not promiscuity but gambling. When he proposes to her early in the play, she responds with composure and control:

> *Lady W:* Indeed it seems 'tis for my money then you would have me.
> *Welbred:* For that and something else you have.
> *Lady W:* Well, I'le lay a wager thou hast lost all thy money at Play, for then you'r alwaies in a marrying humor. But d'e hear Gentleman, d'e think to gain me with this careless way, or that I will marry one I don't think is in love with me. [I.i, 7]

The plot of the play in little, then, is both a test of his love beyond mere mercenary desire and a test of her power to tame his vice so that she can then bestow her wealth on one well-bred enough in manners as well as birth to deserve it.

One night when Welbred has lost heavily at the tables, he approaches Lady Wealthy with parson in tow. She protests that he would gamble her away if he could. But she agrees to marry him on the spot if he can produce a mere ten pieces of gold to pay the parson. Of course, he cannot. She then ups the ante: if he wants admission to her presence again, he must put up front money of £100. Borrowing from a scrivener he returns later in the play with the money, which opens the door to him, then slips the bag back to the lender—a transaction unfortunately espied by the lady's servant. So Lady Wealthy brings in a parson herself, says again she will marry him if he provide the ten pieces. Welbred departs a defeated ass. Finally he returns with a pistol, declaring that if she proclaims thrice that she does not love him, he will kill himself. She says it twice so quickly he begins to fear she'll call his bluff. Then she muses how pretty he will look in a winding sheet and predicts his epitaph. Finally, she admits she loves him and will marry him tomorrow, with his friend Comely giving her away because she does not trust herself to do so foolish a thing.

> *Welbred:* You shall ne're repent this Noble Act, for what I want in Fortune, i'le make up in Love.
> *Lady W:* I ne're consider'd, we'l exchange, you shall have one for t'other. [V.i, 60]

On the morrow, however, the widow waits in vain for Welbred. All she gets in response to her previous night's generosity is a note from him saying he's winning and can make another £500. She's understandably furious. Of course, he loses his winnings, is penniless again, slinks home to be married, and she spurns him. Comely asks her to excuse this fault of Welbred's youth, begging her to eavesdrop on one further test he will administer. Comely offers Welbred a cousin, completely at his disposal, who is worth £20,000. When Welbred refuses and declares the widow the only woman for him, she becomes convinced he is not mercenary, exacts from him a promise never to gamble again, and finally marries him. Amidst the happy ending it is important for us to realize that the widow has an implicit pragmatic reason for breaking him of his "humour" (II.ii, 27): gambling depletes estates.

Meanwhile, the play has a subplot that also concerns experienced women tricksters managing their affairs in order to end up with estates and malleable husbands. The Crafty sisters, cast mistresses of Welbred and Comely, dupe the foolish Frenchlove, the pretender to French fashions of the play's title, and the equally foolish Vaine, a pretender to fashionable libertinism, into marriages. The fools are constantly at each other's throat, and at one point the sisters conclude, "[W]e must pray for their health now, till we are married, and have our Joyntures setled; And then let the Bell tole for them both as soon as time pleases" (IV.iii, 50). The sense of this part of the ending is complicated. Aristocrats, exercising their *droit du seigneur,* can with impunity cast off their mistresses on elements of society less worthy than they. By association with these Town wits, the mistresses themselves acquire enough wit to dupe parvenus and pretenders who, however wealthy, lack the breeding—in both literal and metaphoric senses—to merit anything better than used goods.

The duke of Newcastle's *The Humorous Lovers* (1667) features two *dangereuses* women, an apparently rich gentlewoman named Emilia, who is beloved by Courtly and holds him at bay till she is sure of him, and a wealthy widow named Lady Pleasant, who toys with the notorious rake Colonel Boldman till she reduces him to a form of madness over the very love he professes to scorn. The opening exchange between the two Town wits ironically reveals economic realities. Courtly, dressed in black, mopes. Boldman, ignorant of the cause, asks waggishly, "How? in the Melancholy Garb, thy Father is not dead, thou wou'dst be glad of that, for the Land of Promise, an Heir is in the solitary Desert, and wilderness of wants till then; nor thy Mother, that wou'd save a Joynture; nor thy Sisters, nor Brothers, that would save portions; what's the cause?" (I.i, 1). As elder brother, Courtly might well not mourn any of these events. Sounding a bit like Leporello in Mozart-DaPonte's *Don Giovanni*, Boldman sings a catalogue of his various loves, then scorns marriage and brags of his bastards: "Faith I have a very hopeful Progeny some where; my Wife lies in, for the most part in some stately Cage, and hath Lady Beggars to visit her, and the whole Parish is so kind, I thank them, to take care of our Offspring, and prefer them to Charitable Hospitals, where they triumph with their Blew Coats and Horn Books" (3-4). Obviously, if the appellation "Wife" is accurate, this is one of those left-handed marriages Willmore wanted. Boldman's implicit *droit du seigneur* frees him from any responsibility toward her and his by-blows.

Lady Pleasant's offhand response to Emilia's pretended insouciance over Courtly's absence—"And you are as glad to be excused that trouble, as Landlords are (when the Tenants miss their quarter day) to be excused the telling of the money" (I.ii, 8)—also indirectly refers to economic realities. The two witty women resist the advances of Mistriss Hood the marriage matchmaker, who wants to marry one of them to the idiosyncratic Master Furrs (fortified against the cold in the warmest weather) to further his designs of engrossment of his already large estate. Instead, Emilia tests Courtly's resolve by telling him she is already in love—and revealing only at the end that he has been the object all along. Lady Pleasant strips Boldman of his cocksureness and causes him to be publicly and mercilessly mocked. In a strange masque of Cupid and Venus, an effigy of Boldman is stabbed with an arrow, and as a result he goes mad for love of the widow. She is sympathetic but doesn't want the others to know. So like Beatrice and Benedick, they become the humorous lovers of the title. Turnabout is fair play, and he causes her to be mocked for her tyranny, but she plays Beatrice till the end, forcing him to accept grace before the meal. Courtly's final speech is meant to be metaphoric, but constitutes the final reference to the underlying economic realities: "So, the Chaplain is ready, let us go in; we that have not yet enter'd into Bond, will Seal and Deliver, and then we will all fall to telling of the money" (V, 59).

Four women tricksters inhabit *The Debauchee; or, The Credulous Cuckold*
(1677), a comedy originally by Richard Brome and altered, probably, by
Behn. Clara is a slighted maid pursuing the perjured Lord Loveless
dressed as his man Bellamy. Mrs. Saleware is a City wife, first Sir Oliver
Thrivewell's then Lord Loveless's mistress, who now pursues Bellamy.
Mrs. Crostill is a rich widow whom Loveless pursues for her estate to
repair the mortgages of his to Sir Oliver but who is attracted to the rake
Careless's extravagance. Finally, Lady Thrivewell, whom Sir Oliver has
married in order to beget another male heir to supplant his prodigal son
Careless, seems to invite Careless to increase Sir Oliver's failing sperm
count and supplant himself by a bastard of his own begetting.

Clara is not much of a trickster. She manages to substitute Mrs. Saleware's own foolish husband for a tryst she was supposed to have with
Bellamy but gets outtricked by Mrs. Saleware, who convinces Loveless that Bellamy tried to seduce her and Lady Thrivewell too. With this
scam Mrs. Saleware revenges herself on Bellamy but also on Lady Thrive-
well, for the latter has discovered Mrs. Saleware's affair with her husband,
has forgiven him, but has conned Mrs. Saleware out of one hundred
guineas of fine lace, the value of Sir Oliver's payment for services rendered. Mrs. Saleware gets crossbit by Lady Thrivewell, who reveals that
Bellamy is a young woman. A better trickster, Mrs. Crostill senses Loveless
protests too much, parries him with widow's wisdom: "Impossible! I
wou'd not have you so degenerate from the true gallantry of your Sex,
and Age, to be a constant Husband. O how vile a sound it has! a young
Lord, and constant to his Wife! Not for the World, wou'd I be that
Woman, that shou'd be guilty of making you so strange a Monster"
(IV.18-22). Careless enters, brushes Loveless aside, and courts the widow
outrageously. She responds by mock-courting him in matching whining
tones. His affected insouciance actually pleases her, but she plays *dangereuse* by starting to retire with Loveless. Careless pushes him, they nearly
draw, but Mrs. Crostill controls the situation, telling his friend Saveall to
get Careless out of there lest her servants eject him "more indecently"
(43). Having decided she wants Careless despite, or rather because of, his
extravagances, including his pregnant mistress Phebe, who is suing for
breach of promise, the widow, worth £10,000, enters at the end to claim
the prodigal as her own, summons a parson, and marries him as he
announces his conversion from debauchery. Mrs. Crostill's attraction
throughout to Careless's outrageousness (the morning he awakens from a
bedtrick, ignorant his partner was not his aunt, he pursues the aunt almost
to the point of rape in front of his uncle) mystifies his in-your-face libertinism into the mark of the superior desirability of the aristocratic rake
because of the enormous energy he infuses into the bloodlines, thus maintaining their supposedly natural superiority.

Lady Thrivewell is the trickster par excellence, however. She manages everyone's affairs. Instead of outrage at Careless's presumption with her, she treats the returned prodigal gently, then out of sisterhood with Phebe works a bedtrick to reconcile them. When Careless's servant Watt reveals he too has had Phebe, thus discrediting her paternity claim, and says he will take her for a wife, Lady Thrivewell supplements the portion Mrs. Crostill offers with the one hundred guineas she owes Mrs. Saleware, with Sir Oliver's permission (as a final rebuke to her wayward husband). Having leverage through the mortgages, she brokers the reconciliation between Loveless and Clara/Bellamy, with Sir Oliver rendering back Loveless's mortgages as her portion. Amidst the hymeneal celebration of the ending, with only Mrs. Saleware and her credulous cuckold dismissed from participation, it is instructive to remember Lady Thrivewell's response not to her husband's adultery but to the price the Cit wife demands: "O unmerciful! how rich would the City be, were every kindness that their Wives granted, so return'd and pay'd! Why, twould begger the Court and Country" (I.ii, 11). Having already tricked Mrs. Saleware out of the lace but seeing Bellamy (whom at this point she does not know as Clara) enter Mrs. Saleware's shop, Lady Thrivewell returns to the shop herself to rub in her class scorn by congratulating Mrs. Saleware on taking a lover less dangerous than an old Country squire. No romantic she, but the guardian of the class power structure.

The subtitle of *The Counterfeit Bridegroom; or, The Defeated Widow* (1677), perhaps also by Behn, would seem to be a counterexample to the pattern I am discussing. But the Widow Landwell is defeated by a smarter woman trickster, Mrs. Hadland, who disguises herself as a counterfeit bridegroom in order to retrieve the estate the widow's late husband "by knavish practises, couzen'd my Father of just before he [too] died" (I.ii, 10). Assured by her husband that they cannot recover their lost estate through the courts, Mrs. defiantly proclaims her Machiavellian project before Mr. Hadland: "Wit now perform, what Justice could not do;/All ways are just, when we our Rights pursue" (14). Mrs. Hadland successfully defeats her rivals to the hand of the widow by playing an extravagant rake irresistibly. As the widow rudely dispatches some of her tenants come from her estate in Kent, Mrs. Hadland says aside, "Those were my Tenants once, but what relief now; yet e're we part, Widow, I shall have full revenge— Your heart is mine already, and when the whole Cargoe's in my power, I'le hoist my sailes, and with my streams playing in the Aire, make to the blest Harbour of repose" (III.i, 26). Her ultimate trick is rough: on their wedding night, she substitutes for herself in the wedding chamber her brother, significantly named Noble. Hugging the deed to her estate, Mrs. Hadland says puckishly to the audience, "I believe I am the first Bridegroom that ever procur'd for his Bride the first Night" (V.i, 47). As Noble slips into her place, Mrs. Hadland triumphs, "Widow, y'are caught at last—/Thy Husband's subtleties shall be repaid,/Thus Women are by Women best betray'd" (48). Noble does not downright debauch the widow; instead, Mrs. Hadland blackmails her into trading her estate for her reputation, threatened by the presence of another man in her bridal chamber, and into accepting Noble as her husband. Mrs. Hadland resumes her identity, promises to take only that part of the widow's estate her father had lost, and reconciles with the widow as now her "Sister" (V.iii, 56).

In another plot, though his father Sir Oliver has destined him for the Widow Landwell's daughter Eugenia, Peter Santloe has clandestinely married a gypsy encountered in a search for a missing sister. When his missing mother returns and identifies the gypsy as really his sister, Peter follows his "noble Savage" instincts in the face of "dull fantastick Law" (IV.i, 38) and is saved from incest only by the revelation that Eugenia and his sister had been switched at birth. Thus Peter remains married to the object of his desire, his friend gets Eugenia, and patriarchal genealogy is preserved pure for transmission of estates. The law, which has nothing to do with nature, by the trick of the playwright continues to protect property. Noble concludes the play not by congratulating the women for the trickery and resolution but by male bonding:

> [A]nd now, Gentlemen, let us in and congratulate each
> others good success and fortunes.
>> Thus in the Storms of Fortune you may find,
>> Where Justice is deficient, Wit proves kind. [58]

The male self-congratulation is actually appropriate, for Mrs. Hadland is just a trope in the hands of a playwright who, even if she is a woman, underwrites patriarchal aristocracy. The widow will send her lawyer the next morning to compound for the moiety of her estate with *Mr.* Hadland.

The more bizarre plays of this subset were written by that underrated experimentalist Thomas Durfey, who in *The Virtuous Wife; or, Good Luck at Last* (1679) and *Madam Fickle; or, The Witty False One* (1676), creates a couple of resourceful married women who take revenge on their men. Passing herself off as a rich widow, ward of her uncle, Mme. Fickle takes out on her suitors revenge for her husband's jealousy and desertion. She responds to patriarchal power with the only power she has. Witness this exchange with Lord Bellamour, an arrogant suitor:

> *Bellamour:* What woman but you durst provoke a lover thus? Nay, one
>   that is to marry you, and consequently to have power to tyrannize

over you; to lie with you but once a week, and then with an ill will
too; to send you into the country to look to your dairy; to keep a mis
in town, and live three times beyond my estate, according to custom.
Fickle: Is it not also in my power to be false? Is my beauty so mean, think
   you, that no one wou'd make addresses? Lies it not in my ability to
   wheedle you into a belief of love, and at last to forsake you? Assure
   your self it does[.] [II.ii.95-106]

The play is a whirlwind of plots and counterplots, as Mme. Fickle dan-
gles three men on a string and the virtuous women in the play try to
expose her (a motif Durfey will repeat in *A Fond Husband*). Calling herself "a second *Machiavil*," Madame articulates her motivation with all the
energy of a villainess in Restoration tragedy: "To betray in me's a virtue,
being first betray'd, the thought of which does like an eating canker prey
on my heart and vitals" (V.i.131-37). Earlier, she rhapsodizes in blank
verse and heroic couplets:

> I am resolv'd to work my sly deceipts,
> Till my revenge is perfect. Thus far I've done well,
> And I'll persevere in the mistery.
> Wheadle 'em to the snare with cunning plots;
> Then bring it off with quick designing wit,
> And quirks of dubious meaning. Turn and wind
> Like foxes in a storme; to prey on all,
> And yet be thought a saint. Thus Queen I'll sit,
> And Hell shall laugh to see a womans wit. [IV.ii.378-86]

Like so many of these women tricksters, her ultimate trick is to cross-dress
and outface her suitors, concluding with Madame's message that she has
left town in order "to be rid of your troublesom impertinences; she also
did me the favour to desire me to give you this assurance: that she hated
you all three, and her former proceedings with you have been only to
divert herself with your ceremonious addresses" (V.iii.134-38).

Lest we think this is a feminist play, however, let us note Durfey's patriarchal bias in Mme. Fickle's condemnation of "Silly men, that fetter'd
with a smile, forget the business of their creation, the motives of their
honour, and the safety of their countrey" (II.ii.246-48). Her sentiment
could have been uttered by as thoroughgoing a misogynist as Dryden's
Ventidius in *All for Love*. Moreover, when she is finally exposed, she declares herself "unworthy" of the "addresses" of her suitors (V.iii.192).
And in this instance, Durfey provides a spouse ex machina: her absent husband returns, convinced of her constancy and cured of his jealousy. He
promises to return all gifts of courtship, and anyone who is not satisfied
may meet him on the dueling fields. So Madame has her man back and,

she tells her maid, though she originally had thrown herself into the arms of "One of mean descent, and also slender Fortune" (II.ii.21), would appear to have redeemed her status, having become in the meantime, according to her guardian, "an heiress" (IV.i.42). Mme. Fickle is a rewarded trickster, then, but only by Durfey's bizarre logic has she merited her final estate.

The Virtuous Wife, though still bizarre, is more conventional. Beverly, described in the dramatis personae as "A wild extravagant Gentleman," has married the "witty high spirited" Olivia by impersonating her lover Beauford. What's worse, he has a mistress whom he courts in his wife's face. She threatens to treat him in kind: "[F]rom this moment, the duty of a Wife, and the reserved behaviour incident to that name, shall be as far from me, as Constancy from thee. . . . [Y]ou cancell'd your right in that ['bondage' he still thinks he holds over her], when you broke your Marriage vow, and let those frozen fools own it, whose souls are too narrow and spiritless to revenge their injuries, mine shall be free as thought: I'll plot the manner instantly, and my proceedings shall to after ages, prove a Law for all wrong'd Wives to plague their Husbands with" (II.ii, 24-25). Too virtuous to cuckold him with Beauford, instead she cross-dresses as a man and courts Beverly's mistress, Jenny Wheadle, in his face, winning her by promising her more attention and even marriage. Jenny responds almost pathetically, "Oh heaven! Shall I be marry'd at last?" (IV.iii, 47). Beverly calls this insolent young blade out to a duel, and Olivia does fool with his sword a bit but insists on first enjoying his mistress. Leaving him frustrated and furious, Olivia exults, "[T]his happens as I could wish—and now dear Wit I thank thee" (49). When he gets her back, because she has betrayed him with another man, Beverly reduces Jenny to the Country garb he found her in, sunburnt, working in her father's fields. Apologizing to Jenny for not being able to satisfy her, Olivia triumphantly reveals herself to be the blade who stole her, and Beverly is at last converted by his wife's wit.

Unlike Behn's tragicomedy, *The Town-Fop; or, Sir Timothy Tawdrey* (1676), this play invokes no deus ex machina of divorce or annulment to extricate Olivia from a fraudulent marriage in order to honor a previous commitment. Once married to Beverly, despite her affection for Beauford she remains constant to him and wins him back to preserve their family and estate intact. Obviously, that preservation is more important to patriarchal aristocracy than even her freedom of choice.

3

Eligible Male Tricksters Get into the Deed

From Sir Thomas St. Serfe's *Tarugo's Wiles; or, The Coffee-House* (1667) to John Crowne's *Sir Courtly Nice; or, It Cannot Be* (1685), both adapted from the same Spanish source (Augustín Moreto's *No puede ser*), male tricksters are, of course, a staple of Restoration comedy. Identified as a younger brother in the dramatis personae, Tarugo is described as "one whose greatest subsistence depends upon his wit" (I.ii, 5). The ubiquity of this character type in Restoration comedy has an economic cause: "The legal device of the 'strict settlement', evolved in the fifties in order to prevent heirs breaking up estates, enabled families to concentrate land and capital into large units. Younger sons now received their patrimony in the form of a capital sum, not in land: they were thus impelled to seek a career elsewhere, and turned to the expanding professions and the civil service" (Hill, 204). But playwrights, perhaps because many were younger sons themselves, created other, less mundane escapes for younger brothers, turning them into tricksters seeking estates by hook or crook. St. Serfe merely puts Tarugo in service of Liviana's resistance to a tyrant brother, and he abets the triumph of her "Womans will" (passim) in her escape to marry her lover Horatio and eventually in her securing her brother's blessing.

Between St. Serfe's and Crowne's plays crowd a host of male tricksters whose energy is socialized, from Plot-thrift in Thomas Thompson's *The English Rogue* (1668), who articulates the play's sense of comic necessity: "But hangh't handsome English Girls and good fortunes may tye us close to their tails in tyme. . . . Money and Beauty are two taking bates and must prevail" (III.ii, 29-30); to the generous Lovewell of Edward Revet's *The Town Shifts; or, The Suburb-Justice* (1671), who acts as a comic class avenger in one-upping the nouveau riche Leftwell by stealing his intended rich merchant's daughter as his wife; to the brother and sister team of tricksters, Peregrine and Phillis Airy, who manipulate themselves into desirable marriages, while their younger brother Dick falls into one by chance, in Peter Belon's *The Mock-Duellist; or, The French Vallet* (1675). Tricky Dick articulates one of Restoration comedy's trickster manifestos, as he contemplates spending his last guinea:

> I shall be throughly clear'd of that small stock
> Which never did me good since the first hour
> My Father left it me. How he came by't
> I know not; let that pass: then will I try
> What I can do of my own self to live:
> What know I but Fortune would prove more kinde
> Were this gone also?
> Unwilling peradventure I should owe
> My happiness to any thing but he[r].
> I'll try her once; Fortune, an't be thy will
> To have me loose this Gold, yet help me then,
> Meerly out of stark kindeness and pure love. [IV.i, 39]

Great insouciance for a younger brother! Fortune indeed helps him to a fortune, and the play concludes with all the youngsters married and well-heeled. Fortune is, after all, a dynamic inserted into the play by a Town playwright. Let me concentrate, however, on the greatest of these tricksters.

Francisco in the earl of Orrery's *Guzman* (1669) is the youngest of three brothers, "Gentlemen of decay'd Fortunes, left to shift by their Wits," as Orrery describes them in the dramatis personae. Orrery provides him with a scheme to get rich that is as unromantic as it is ingenious. First, the two older brothers, Guivarro and Alvares, become servants in the household of two rich fops in order to provide money enough for their two oldest sisters to set up in finery and eventually marry the fops. Guivarro explains to the sisters: "We do but wear the Names of Servants, and thereby Command their Purses, as we hope you Two shall soon their Hearts; your Births, your Educations, and your Beauties, joined with our Contrivances, must restore our withered Fortunes" (I.i.23-26). It is the fops who are the romantic puppies, arguing with their guardian uncles against arranged marriages. Oviedo, the young swaggerer, postures, "'Twould be an Injustice to all Humane Kind, if still the Rich should only Wed the Rich; the World would then consist only of Usurers and Beggars: But if Rich Men marry the poor and handsom Women, and the Rich Women the Poor and handsom Men, the Gifts of Nature, and of Fortune, will be equally distributed; Delight and Wealth so shar'd will restore to both the Sexes that Happiness, which the Old formal Ways of acting have so long deprived them of" (I.i.63-70).

In a sense, such income distribution occurs by the end of the play, but only within the ruling class. Oviedo and his companion fop Piracco are married to Maria and Lucia, the portionless sisters of Francisco and his brothers. Oviedo again postures: "[T]hey are of Noble Birth and Poor, all the Ingredients to compose fit Wives for us" (IV.vii.803-4).[1] Alvares justifies the match in terms of class, insisting to the fops that his sisters are "of equal Birth to yours, though the Frowns of Chance robb'd us of all our Fortunes; but we dare say, bating what the World calls Portions, you are not unequally married" (V.ii.221-23). Piracco's gallant romantic gesture now might seem appropriate: "Portions are but the Invention of Gown-men: a meer Trick to enhance the price of Drawing, and of Engrossing Settlements. I could never see a Reason why a Man should pay Mony to lie with a dishonest Woman, and receive Mony to lie with an honest One" (V.ii.228-32).

Yet the ending of the play dissolves the sham marriage of the foolish, superannuated uncles, who think they have married the sisters, with their maids. The uncles' patronizing rationale for pursuing the impoverished sisters—"So that to marry Men of our Estates and Degree, is a Happiness they could scarcely hope; but we are Rich enough, and they are prodigiously Handsom, and their Gay-humor pleases me as much as their Beauties" (IV.iv.398-402)—will not extend to the maids. Moreover, as superannuated lovers who scheme to supplant their nephews, they are explicitly not allowed to "disinherit" them "only to make your Wives Children your Heirs" (V.ii.302-4).

The trickster par excellence of this play is Francisco, who disguises himself as an astrologer to secure a rich widow and her two rich daughters for himself and his brothers. The widow, Leonora, understandably anxious about her family's fortune, goes to the fortune teller, Alcazar. He tells her she is still nubile, an asset with assets: "[Y]ou are on the right-side of Forty, . . . are Rich and Fair, and . . . carry so much Youth about you, that could you meet with one you liked, you could receive a second Wedding-Ring" (III.i.88-91). Francisco/Alcazar arranges for Maria, pretending to be a devil sorceress, to prophesy that the widow will not have good fortune till she marry, and she should marry the Cavalier who will rescue her from attempted rape. He arranges for Lucia to prophesy to the heiresses that they must marry two down-and-out Cavaliers, and not a couple of cowardly, foolish fops.

The mature Leonora responds to this prophecy in terms that reveal women's need to play the game of economic necessity wisely: "I do not like their being confin'd from Marrying of Rich Fools; for, Sir, to be Born to Petticoats, and yet to wear Embroider'd Breeches, is a pleasant thing: I speak, Sir, what I have Experienced" (207-10). Has the widow herself transcended class, with petticoats the sign of lower and embroidered underwear the sign of upper? Or does this remark simply refer to gender, to the widow's wearing her husband's embroidered breeches sexually before he died, then economically after? Howbeit, once Francisco qua Cavalier rescues Leonora from feigned rape, she considers the prophecy fulfilled and contracts to marry him, while he courts for his brothers in language that would have strong echoes of England's Cavaliers, dispossessed by the ravages of civil war, forced to fight in foreign wars: "Two of the bravest Youths that e'er were born in *Spain;* but brought to great Distress by the ill Fate of their Father, which made them follow the Wars, where they have got Immortal Fame. Their good Meens you see; I assure you, Madam, their Valours, Civilities, Friendships and Good-natures, are more than equal to it. . . . Oh, Madam, had these two Gentlemen Estates answerable to their Merits, how happy would your two Daughters be to have such Husbands: For they are now the Objects of my Care as much as yours" (IV.vi.703-8, 726-29). Of course, Francisco is merely playing into the prophecy he himself planted, and when Leonora complains at the end about their being cheated into the three marriages, Francisco assures her, "Finely Cheated, since 'tis into good Husbands: For such by all that's good, you shall still find us; you wanted Honest Proper Men, and we wanted Rich and Handsom Wives; Consider then, what in all Conscience could both Parties desire better than what my Astrology has brought about?" (V.ii.82-86).

Francisco has even provided for his youngest sister, the most economically vulnerable of all of them, by tricking the lovable old rich fool Guzman into marrying and providing her a jointure. When Julia complains about being sacrificed to a fool, her brother once again eschews romantic for realistic discourse: "[W]hat can be better than to have a Husband of 5000 Pistols Rent, and to be able to beat him out of Four of it annually when thou wilt?" Julia prudently responds, "I beg your Pardon, Brother Negromancer; I confess I did not think on that; I will leave all my Fortune to your Art" (IV.iii.212-16). At the end of the play Julia demonstrates that she can manage her fool by threatening to cuckold him if he doesn't shut up. She mimics his habit of swearing by classical gods and heroes, saying if he ever gets jealous, "I'll Cure you of it, by *Taurus*" (V.ii.186). Although there is some Platonic rhetoric among the highest group of characters in the play, mostly used by Francisco to seduce Leonora but also used by Leonora when she realizes it is not just the prophecy but loving attraction that drives her daughters toward the brothers, the economic basis of Stuart ideology shows through in this play as clearly as anywhere in Restoration comedy.[2]

While a woman trickster lands her man in Francis Fane's *Love in the Dark; or, The Man of Bus'ness* (1675), the male trickster Trivultio takes two-facedness to a higher level. Parhelia, the doge's daughter, employing the masquerade of a Venetian carnival to her advantage, wins the love of the Milanese Count Sforza and then tests his constancy. Like Maria in *The Fortune Hunters,* Parhelia screws this typical testing up a notch, has Sforza imprisoned, tortured by ghostly Turkish bassas, and offered the choice of inconstancy or death. Parhelia finally reveals herself to be the doge's daughter, and they plight troth, but their marriage is interrupted by her father.

Trivultio, troth breaker of legendary proportions, is supposed to be pursuing his "Legitimate pretensions to my rich Mistress *Aurana;* but a Pox; these Marriages in earnest come time enough, and spoil the others. The Oaths and Promises of Batchelors pass currant, and are not disproveable; but a marry'd Man, that swears Virtuous Love to others, is perjur'd in a Court of Record" (I.i, 1). So instead he pursues the wonderfully named Belinganna, wife to the Venetian banker Cornanti, whose horny name indicates the gift the beautiful trickstress his wife bestows upon him. Even when it is obvious that Aurana loves him not despite but because of his reputation, Trivultio still responds, "Here are Riches, but Marriage attends it: a Golden Trap. My free-born Genius moves for *Bellinganna.* Lying with another Man's Wife, is like invading an Enemies Country: there's both Love and Ambition in't; 'tis an enterprize fit for a great Spirit" (20). So he disguises himself as Belinganna's duenna Vigilia to gain access to her. But it turns out that Belinganna is actually working for Aurana and brings the two of them together. When Trivultio protests love and constancy, like Etherege's Harriet, Aurana has reasons to mistrust the first signs of repentance: "All sudden Converts are to be suspected. / Maintain your Character:/Be constant to your self, if not to me" (II, 36). Her desire for him to remain himself is based on her attraction to his great energy. At the same time, she desires to socialize that energy just enough for it to move from centrifugal to centripetal. So the playwright moves him, like Dorimant, to declare that he is willing to undergo the scorn for doing something so unfashionable: "Then, faith, dear *Aurana,* I love thee to that desperate extremity, that, if you'll take me in the humour, I am reslov'd to undergo the scorn of all wise Men, and my own repentance, and sneakingly submit to that solemn Conjuring Cheat call'd Marriage; though my Reason kecks at it, and I shall certainly swoon at the sight of a Priest" (37). But they, like Parhelia and Sforza, are interrupted by a patriarchal guardian, the procurator Hircanio, who takes his daughter home to protect her from matrimonial theft.

In order to gain credibility and needed credit with this banker, Trivultio puts on another face with Cornanti. He and Belinganna stage a scene in which she pretends to expose his rakishness to her husband, but

Trivultio mockingly rebukes her precisely in the language that underwrites the code of patriarchal sexual control: "You're very liberal of what's not your own./I'll ne'r grow rich by robberies: *Venetian* Commons/Are well stock'd; I'll never break inclosures. . . . No, no Madam, the Dignity of a Senator is not so cheaply to be valu'd. Were I dispos'd to those voluptuous sins, I'de quench my Flames in common Waters, and not corrupt the noble Streams, to viciate a Race of Princes" (III, 55). Coming from a don juan, this is funny. But it is the code of noninvasion that protects the concluding marriages and the property the couples both are and own, complete with "inclosures."

Before they can all consummate, however, they are interrupted once more by guardian fathers, and Trivultio is forced to don another face in his most outrageous trick. First, in the funniest escape from jail scene I've "seen," he tricks his guard into believing that just before you die when you hang yourself, you get a vision of paradise. Trivultio goes first, then the guard, who gets out of his garter only to see Trivultio on the other side of the bars. Then Trivultio masquerades as the pope's legate, Cardinal Colonna, and presides at the ecclesiastical court to which the fathers refer the Milanese seducers, whose crime is portrayed as sedition, then mitigated to seduction. Cardinal Trivultio sagely judges that marriage itself is sufficient punishment:

> I solemnly condemn 'em
> To the perpetual Prison of the Nuptial Sheets.
> Late Councils hold, Marriage from Heav'n was sent,
> Not the reward of Love, but punishment. [V, 82]

The doge accepts this judgment, but Hircanio balks at the uncertainty of Trivultio's estate. Cornanti reveals he has made this son of his old friend his heir.

At this moment the real cardinal arrives. Trivultio brazen-faces it out, and the doge orders Colonna clapped in irons. Cardinal Trivultio intervenes and forgives all "since this is a day/Of general jollity" that is "Carnival time too," as one of the senators puts it (88). Then Trivultio divests, runs to the cardinal, falls on his knees, and begs forgiveness, which the cardinal grants because of "his good Nature" (89). Despite Hircanio's protestations, the cardinal also ratifies the former sentence for the couples. The trickster has, in the spirit of carnival, worn many faces. But ultimately he has socialized himself.

Not tricksters in the same league with Trivultio, nevertheless Bruce and Longvil in Shadwell's *The Virtuoso* (1676) disguise themselves as fellow virtuosos in order to gain access to Sir Nicholas Gimcrack's wealthy nieces, Miranda and Clarinda. The latter are wisely aware that their Town wits have had "a correspondence with too many factories," that "most men" (at least of their type) "are apt to break in women's debts," and therefore "There's no trusting you, for though you seem to be taken off, as you call it, yet you'll stick fast to your good old cause" (II.i.85, 89, 220-22). Referring to their libertinism as their "good old cause," Clarinda deprives these Town wits of their major identifying distinction as free-spirited Cavaliers in opposition to niggardly Puritans. Indeed, Bruce and Longvil are brought down in the general leveling of the play to the point where their sexcapades with the tawdry Lady Gimcrack diminish their wit (they do not recognize her but are themselves tricked) and place them on the level of all the other dupes of whores in the play—and that includes three of the play's most satirized comic butts, all of lower status than these wealthy gentry. Like Dorimant, despite their protestations that they are converted to true love and marriage, they are flesh and blood yet. But Lady Gimcrack is no Bellinda.

So these Town wits, while tricksters, are not in control of the situation. Indeed, the nieces themselves conspire to escape their tyrant guardian and are present at the masquerade where their lovers seek them among the masks but encounter instead the omnivorous Lady Gimcrack. So much for their witty perspicacity. Lady Gimcrack, if she cannot have these desirable rakes herself permanently, out of envy of her nubile nieces tries to derail the progress of these four toward marriage by leaving both men postcoital messages ostensibly from each other's lover. They draw upon each other in the deadly rivalry that so threatens in these plays when the rivals are from the same ruling class. And they precipitately distrust their beloveds, who arrive to part them and then banish them for their distrust.

Why does Shadwell, who elsewhere satirizes libertines, fix the track and let these four marry? Wheatley (*Without God or Reason,* 140-44) rightly notes the fact that the women still love the rakes, as Miranda puts it, "almost to distraction" (V.v.68), and he points to the rakes' conversion to the need for mutual love (thus the motif of switching from the niece who doesn't love to the one who does). But Bruce uses a metaphor that can enable us to descend to a deeper level: "Since our affections will not thrive in the soil we had plac'd them in, we must transplant them" (86-87). The eminently desirable rakes must be socialized into cultivation. Without discussing the significance, Wheatley quotes the earlier exchange between the rakes where they only superficially understand that they must switch partners. But this passage reveals the Williamsesque necessity that provides the dynamic for the denouement:

> *Bruce:* 'Tis too evident we have plac'd our loves wrong. They are both
> handsome, rich, and honest—three qualities that seldom meet in
> women.
> *Longvil:* 'Tis true. And since 'twill be necessary after all our rambles to fix
> our unsettled lives to be grave, formal, very wise, and serve our coun-
> try, and propogate our species, let us think on't here. [IV.iii.64-70]

Despite their opening Epicurean insouciance about social responsibility, even as they decry the degeneration of the current ruling class, Bruce
and Longvil *must* by the comic necessity of the play accept their social responsibility. Their spontaneous leadership and bravery in quelling the rebellion of the workers displaced by newfangled scientific inventions is
designed to demonstrate their inherent nobility, their inherent right to
rule. Shadwell appropriates the motif of the conversion of the rake to
serve, even as he satirizes scientific virtuosos, the emerging alliance between Town, City, and Country in a new economic oligarchy that continues to dispossess the majority of the people, first from their land and
then from their industries (see Hill, 204-8).

Shadwell has not yet supplanted Stuart with bourgeois ideology, however, as in just a few short years he will. Amidst the general collapse of the
satiric butts at the end of the play, Shadwell provides his witty women and
converted rakes with an escape clause. As Rothstein and Kavenik rightly
note (179n), Shadwell ignores the change in the law concerning wards
(see Nixon) and has the nieces choose new guardians (which they could
do under the old law between the ages of fourteen and twenty-one)
to whom they entrust their fortunes, Bruce and Longvil. Their final exchange is instructive:

> *Longvil:* I hope, ladies, since you have put your estates into our hands,
> you'll let us dispose of your persons.
> *Miranda:* You must have time to leave off your old love before you put
> on new.
> *Clarinda:* Nothing but time can fit it to you.
> *Bruce:* You have given us hope, and we must live on that awhile. And
> sure 'twill not be long that we shall live upon that slender Diet: for—
> "If love can once a lady's outworks win,
> It soon will master all that is within." [V.vi.134-43][3]

Like Dorimant, they must keep a Lent in order to be weaned off "old
love" before putting on "new"—not just the switch between sisters they
have made, of course, but the switch from "rambles" to cultivating the soil
in their country's service. The "outworks" they have conquered are the
ladies' fortunes. Unlike tyrannical guardians, they are confident enough of

their attractiveness to trust that they will soon "master" the attendant "persons" in a perpetuation of the patriarchal aristocracy begun in England at least as early as the Norman, if not the Saxon or the Roman, conquest.

While performed as part of the Tory backlash over the Exclusion Crisis and while administering for his Whiggism serious punishment to the eponymous fool of the subtitle, the main action of Behn's *The City-Heiress; or, Sir Timothy Treat-All* (1682) is, as in its Middletonian source *'Tis a Mad World, My Masters,* the triumph of a prodigal rakehell, who is forced to preserve his inheritance by his wits. Resentful of his Tory politcs as well as his prodigality, Sir Timothy announces to his nephew Tom Wilding his intention to marry and "wipe your Nose with a Son and Heir of my own begetting" (I.102-3). In retaliation, Wilding threatens to cuckold his uncle and when chastised for being profane protests, "Profane! why he deni'd but now the having any share in me; and therefore 'tis lawful. I am to live by my wits, you say, and your old rich good-natur'd Cuckold is as sure a Revenue to a handsome young Cadet, as a thousand pound a year. Your tolerable face and shape is an Estate in the City, and a better Bank than your Six *per Cent.* at any time" (122-26). While the play celebrates his wit and "Face and Shape" and exuberance, however, it is not a Cit-cuckolding play. Unlike some of Behn's other rakehell heroes, Wilding becomes not a parasite but a successful trickster who regains his inheritance.

Wilding's first trick is to try to convince his uncle he has settled down with Charlot, the City heiress of the title, trusting that Sir Timothy will be so impressed as to not only reinstate him as heir but grant him settlement for an annuity till he dies. But his trust goes only so far; he disguises his low-class mistress Diana as Charlot. Meanwhile, Charlot has heard that Wilding is not the heir he pretended to be and is afraid if he lied about that he must think she has entrusted herself with him for mercenary reasons. So he needs to get the deed of inheritance from his uncle to prove he was not lying and thus keep her on a string. He is also in love with the rich widow, Lady Galliard. But he has no intention of marrying any of these women, hoping instead that his uncle will die so he can have the resources necessary to live a wildly profligate existence.

Sir Timothy, taken with Diana himself, puts off Wilding's request for the writings and determines to steal the City heiress from him. So Wilding is forced to take his trickery up another notch. Disguised as a lord come as emissary to offer him the throne of Poland (the hit at Shaftesbury is obvious, if heavy-handed), Wilding thus gains access to his uncle's household for the night, brings in his friends, steals not only the writings, but gold and valuables and enough seditious papers to blackmail him into submission. Sir Timothy, discovering the "Heiress" he has married to be his nephew's cast mistress, is doubly furious, both for the theft and the deceit, and he threatens to try to get him "hang'd, nay, drawn and quarter'd" (V.548, 568-69). But Wilding protests, "What, for obeying your Commands, and living on my Wits?" (570). Rather generously, he offers in exchange for pardon to "render your Estate back during Life" (576), for partly out of revenge on Lady Galliard for marrying someone else and partly out of appreciation for Charlot's devotion he has decided to marry his City heiress after all, and her "fortune" will sustain him "Without so much as wishing for [Sir Timothy's] death" (576-77).

Behn's play features another threat of disinheritance: the old Tory-rory Sir Anthony Merriwell is so frustrated with his nephew Sir Charles's whining, polite love that he swears Charles will inherit "Not an Acre, not a Shilling" of his estate (II.ii.316) unless he pursue Lady Galliard more aggressively—indeed to the point of near rape later in the play. To avoid the rape, Lady Galliard promises to marry Sir Charles on the morrow, not realizing that she has been overheard by witnesses. Her problem is that she loves Wilding, attracted by his great energy, and that moments before Sir Charles's drunken entrance she has yielded to her desire despite her concern for honor and reputation.

It would seem then that *The City-Heiress* is quite an anomaly in these Restoration comedies, for it appears to have joined the wrong couples together. Charlot's wit is no match for Wilding's. Only Lady Galliard has his intelligence and worldly wisdom. They would seem to be the gay couple destined for marriage, inheritance, children.[4] But Lady Galliard finally decides to honor her betrothal to Sir Charles because he, unlike Wilding, is chary of her beloved honor: "Ah, he has toucht my heart too sensibly" (V.418). Yielding to him, she proclaims, "[Y]our unwearied Love at last has vanquisht me," and she bids her "fond Love" for Wilding adieu (586-88). In the sense that they are both more conventional characters, then, perhaps Sir Charles and Lady Galliard are meant for each other. At another, harsher level, they deserve each other precisely because they are not able to play the game: Sir Charles can be a rake only when spurred by wine and his boisterous uncle; Lady Galliard, however attractive, in the moment she yields to Wilding, at least in the cruel world of Restoration social comedy, becomes merchandise untradable among the Town wits, as even Behn's sympathetic courtesan Angellica Bianca is forced to admit.

Wilding, on the other hand, feels betrayed by both his mistresses: Diana for marrying Sir Timothy and thus positioning herself to be the source of his being supplanted by a male heir (perhaps "of his own begetting," as Diana mischievously suggests [III.117]), Lady Galliard for contracting with his friend immediately after their tryst. He concludes, "How fickle is the Faith of common women" (V.473), a category into which now falls even Lady Galliard. Wilding takes up with Charlot because he concludes her to be, in contrast, the "truest of thy Sex, and dearest" (529). Moreover, the disguised Charlot who follows him to his uncle's manifests talents he did not know his Charlot had, like her delightful singing and dancing, not to mention her ability to masquerade behind a northern dialect. What is the ideological sense of the concluding symbolism? A highly valuable young Town rake is converted, after all, into marriage with a virgin, albeit from the City, and together they shall inherit the earth. They represent a restoration of the "Order" celebrated in the closing tag, a symbolic juxtaposition of couple with country, as "all *honest* Hearts as one agree / To bless the King, and Royal *Albanie*" (597-98, emphasis on *honest* is mine: for it, read *Tory*). That is, while the union of Wilding and Charlot at the end may be in violation of our twentieth-century, bourgeois desire for psychological verisimilitude, it is not necessarily in violation of the normal sense of an ending of Restoration social comedy.[5]

Unable to convince the insanely jealous (and misogynistic) guardian Bellguard that her virtue is its own guard and that she ought to have freedom of choice of a marriage partner instead of the foolish fop Sir Courtly Nice, Crowne's Leonora enlists the aid of Bellguard's beloved Violante, a lady of quality and fortune; her lover Farewel, a gentleman of "a fair and free estate" (I.i.34); Surly, a crank in love with Violante; and especially Crack, a trickster thrown out of Oxford for his shenanigans. Bellguard has set an old aunt and two humors characters—Hot-head, who cannot abide Puritan fanatics, and Testimony, who is precisely such a one—to guard his sister. Violante employs Surly to dun Sir Courtly, and Surly assaults his fastidiousness with a relish, trying to frighten him with a rival. Farewel employs Crack, who first impersonates a tailor to deliver to Leonora a billet-doux and picture from Farewel, which picture Bellguard unfortunately discovers, railing against his loose sister, Leonora.

Crack's far greater impersonation is as the crackbrained son of the president of the East India Company, who has taken a shine to Bellguard's uncle, Rich, a fellow merchant, and made him ward of his son, Sir Thomas Callico. Supposedly, Rich has sent Sir Thomas with his estate into Bellguard's protection. The first thing he does is to redeem the situation of the picture, pretending that he was sent to England also to arrange for the marriage of someone to his supposed sister, but lost his picture. Meanwhile, Violante rails at Bellguard for his tyranny, saying the only woman who would dare marry him would be one subject to transportation (who therefore might have her sentence reprieved or the system bribed).

Violante concludes, "I scorn the slavery, nor will marry a king to encrease his dominions, but to share 'em" (IV.i.77-79).

What is significant about these apparently inconsequential references to colonies, transportation, fabulous wealth acquired through trade, and a king's spreading dominions is that we are almost imperceptibly reminded that increasingly, especially since the passage of the Navigation Act of 1660, the wealth of England's ruling class was greatly enhanced by its expanding role in world trade and imperialism (Hill, 209-12). To scorn slavery was not a luxury for the growing labor force of the colonies, and the metaphoric enslavement of women in a misogynistic patriarchal system at home pales by comparison with the material reality of slavery abroad.

Such associations are obscured by Crack as Sir Thomas (probably played by Tony Leigh), with his Jonsonian rhetoric. An example is this passage where he sounds like a seventeenth-century version of W.C. Fields as he tries to conjure up the name Westminster in his attempt to locate the loss of the picture. He gropes for something with west in it; Bellguard offers West-Smithfield.

> *Crack:* That's not th'appellative. Is there no monster in the west, call'd *Westmonster*?
>
> *Bellguard: Westminster* I believe you mean.
>
> *Crack:* Y'ave nicked it. To Westminster I rode, to behold the glorious circumstances o' the dead; and diving into my pocket, to present the represser with a gratification, I am fully confirm'd I then lost it; for my eyes and the picture had never any rencounter since. [III.iii. 364-71]

This delightful trickster uses nonsensical loquacity to screen Farewel's entry into Bellguard's citadel, and he preens himself on his successful pimping. Farewel, however, the erstwhile rake, has been converted to unfashionable constancy: "Oh! let the wits keep the jilting rotten wenches, and leave the sweet virtuous ladies to us marrying fools, I can be as well pleas'd to keep a fine wife to my self as they can be to maintain fine wenches for all the town" (IV.ii.103-7). Though he spends the night with Leonora, he proceeds only so far as innocence will allow. Crack tricks the watchdogs Hot-head and Testimony into kicking Leonora, disguised as a whore, out of the house without seeing her face (because Sir Thomas goes crazy at the sight of women).

Curiously, though Farewel has enough of an estate for them to live and Leonora has eloped with him without concern for her portion, this play uncharacteristically ends without the normal comic resolution signaled by the guardian's blessing and bestowal of portion. Nor is Bellguard reconciled to his family rival Farewel. But the *sympathetic* elements of the play have been focused primarily on the issue of patriarchal tyranny, of which Bellguard seems to be cured, concluding, "Vertue is a womans only guard" (V.iv.214-15) and accepting Violante's terms: "Promise I shall enjoy all and singular the priviledges, liberties, and immunities of an English wife" (150-51). Crack has helped Farewel get his woman and abetted the cause of English women's freedom of choice—within a very narrow range and with no threat to the overall system of patriarchal political (and colonial) economy.

4

Some Tricksters Get Tricked

The trickster tricked is a leitmotif of trickster literature worldwide. In Restoration social comedy, the trickster who is so tricked may be simply an inept upstart. He or she may, however, be quite adept and must be defeated for the necessary purposes of this comedy to be obtained. The funniest of the inept tricksters is perhaps the title character of Dryden's *Sir Martin Mar-all; or, The Feigned Innocence* (1668), who, as his name implies, is a marplot figure. Every time his servant Warner has the situation ready to be exploited for Sir Martin's marriage to the heiress Millisent, Sir Martin shoots off his mouth and explodes everything. Millisent is intended by her father Mr. Moody for Sir John Swallow, for their estates in Canterbury lie cheek by jowl. On the other hand, Sir Martin, an upstart parvenu, can use the alliance to further his status ambitions. But proceedings move apace, and Warner must try not only to set up assignations but especially to steal the legal marriage writings establishing Millisent's "Joynture" (II.ii.23). Warner suborns Rose, Millisent's maid, and has the paper in hand when Sir Martin reveals it to Sir John.

Warner is forced to other stratagems, pretending to have been discharged by Sir Martin and offering himself in service to Moody and Sir John. Again and again he is on the verge of success only to be blown up by Sir Martin. One of his schemes is to try to convince Sir John that Millisent is not virtuous and to turn his affections toward the supposedly rich and innocent Country girl Mrs. Christian. Another is for Sir Martin and him to impersonate old Moody's bastard son Anthony and his servant newly arrived from the East Indies. When Sir Martin cannot remember his lines for this role, Warner, pretending to have just entered Anthony's service, joins Moody in beating him as a cheat. This scene has extraordinary implications. The audience is used to the Western tradition of clever servants. And it is obvious that Warner is the superior trickster in the play, "a kind of Mountebank" he calls himself (V.i.36). But for a servant to join in the beating of his master is a serious breach of decorum. Moody may think Anthony no master at all, but the audience knows Sir Martin is and must have been shocked. Just as the return of a rich bastard son from the Indies represents an implicit threat to status hierarchy, so also does this revolutionary behavior of a servant.

All's well. Restoration playwrights regularly, as we have seen, stimulated their audiences with such implicit threats to ruling class ideology by featuring witty women rebellious against the tyranny of sexual guardianship, only to have the threats disappear when the women marry men with not only the right stuff but the right class credentials. So Dryden retreats from the radical implications of Warner's rebellion by revealing in the last act that he is the true aristocrat, while Sir Martin is, after all, a middle-class pretender to upper-class status, taste, manners, breeding. In a carnivalesque masquerade, the blocking characters are tricked, and the masked tricksters steal their women. But when they unveil, Sir Martin is appropriately married to Rose of the servant class and the servant Warner incredibly married to Millisent. Yet the world has emphatically not been turned upside down, for Lord Dartmouth steps forth to acknowledge Warner as his "Kinsman, though his Father's sufferings in the late times have ruin'd his Fortunes" (V.ii.120-21). Warner acknowledges that his estate is mortgaged, and Moody promises to "bring it of [*sic*]" (126). Thus another banished cavalier is restored to his proper place and estate. The loyalist symbolically remarries the land.

Though the right couple inherits the earth, there is nothing sentimental about this ending. It reaffirms not only class superiority, but class—and Town—privilege. Lord Dartmouth, who steps forward thus at the end, appears throughout the play to be something of a fool himself. The clever Lady Dupe (since she is a landlady, her status is probably widow of a City knight) teaches her daughter Mrs. Christian those Wife of Bath tricks of women's sex trade in order to "distill" the married Lord Dartmouth, who desires a fashionable kept mistress, "into Gold my Girl" (II.i.6-8). The two women plan how to manipulate him until his passion for Mrs. Christian (who constantly mouths Christian phrases) is so strong that "when he sees no other thing will move you, hee'l sign a portion to you before hand." "Take hold of that," advises the earthy Lady Dupe, "and then of what you will" (112-14)!

After serious bloodletting in the form of monetary settlements with his now pregnant mistress, Lord Dartmouth appeals to Warner to relieve him of this parasite. Despite the demands on his time in scheming for his master, Warner accepts the lord's request "for the honour of my wit is ingag'd in it" (IV.i.197-98)—not to mention class solidarity. At the end of the play, the Town wit Warner fobs off Mrs. Christian (and her bastard) on the Country bumpkin Sir John Swallow, and the Town lord preserves his *droit du seigneur*.[1]

John Caryll's title character in *Sir Salomon; or, The Cautious Coxcomb* (1670) is inept in a different way from Sir Martin—a fool of a different order, meaner, more powerful, played not by a Nokes or a Leigh but by Thomas Betterton himself, a casting choice that automatically increased Sir Salomon's rhetorical register. Sir Salomon thinks he lives up to his name. He intends his rich ward, daughter of a long absent "Indy-Merchant" (dramatis personae), for himself and plans to beget on her heirs to displace his already disowned prodigal son Single. He has disguised himself as a Mr. Evans so that his quality and identity are unknown to his ward, Mrs. Betty; furthermore, he has had her raised as an ignorant Country wife, and he visits her to quiz her on the "catechism" he has compiled of protections against cuckoldry (II, opening scene passim). Despite his steward Timothy's advice, he has arranged for his lawyer to transfer ownership of his entire estate to Betty so that if they are unable to produce a supplanting heir, at least she will supplant his son.

Meanwhile, the Town wit Peregreen, impecunious son of Sir Salomon's old friend, the squire Woodland, asks Sir Salomon for room, board, and some ready cash till his father arrives in London, that father having summoned him home from Italy. Peregreen innocently but fatally divulges to Sir Salomon that he has fallen in love with an ingenue. Every time Peregreen manages an interview or actually escapes with Betty, he unwittingly informs this old family friend, and a great deal of the hilarity of the play resides in Betterton's quasi-heroic ravings at being defeated and potentially cuckolded. Comically, wonderfully, Sir Salomon finally calms himself with the rational understanding that to avenge himself makes no sense, that neither Betty nor Peregreen is guilty of any crime (yet), that his only recourse is to marry her instantly and hope to teach her her duty: if not, then he must be patient like other husbands!

A second plot has familiar outlines. The wealthy Cit Mr. Wary denies access to the disinherited Single, who is in love with his daughter Julia: "[S]ince your Father is resolv'd to make you a stranger to his Estate, I must entreat you henceforth to be a stranger to my House; for (to deal freely with you) no Deserts (though never so great) attended with poverty, can satisfie the care of a Parent in the disposal of his Daughter" (I, 11). Single himself doubts whether Julia can still love him without his estate, and she upbraids him: "Your want of Means, and Friends / My love can pardon, and (perhaps) supply; / But your Mistrusts I never will forgive" (10). But she refuses to marry without her father's blessing, as well as with a man she cannot love. She articulates to her tyrant guardian more clearly than most Restoration heroines her rationale for freedom of choice, a rationale that equates forced marriage with its supposed obverse:

> But (Sir) unless by Love made soft, and light,
> The yoke of Marriage all the world would fright:
> And, if my Love in Wedlock-bands be forc'd,
> Alas! I am not marry'd, but divorc'd. [II, 21]

So when her father presents her with Sir Arthur Addel, a man of considerable estate, Julia becomes a trickster, exacting from her foppish suitor an absolute blank promise to serve her, then insisting he cease courting her. Instead, since it is important "To try well, what must cost so dear" (III, 53)—that is, the estateless Single—she sets about to test Single's constancy and tame him of his jealousy, employing the unwitting Sir Arthur in her plots.

The plot-pot comes to a boil when Peregreen learns his father comes with an Indy-Merchant to marry him to a vast fortune. So Peregreen plans to elope with Betty. In a scene of great comic confusion, the most salient actions are that Sir Arthur is mistaken for Peregreen by Sir Salomon's servants and beaten; Betty is rescued by Peregreen and taken to Sir Salomon's supposedly for safety; and Peregreen comes into possession of Betty's basket, which contains the writings rendering her Sir Salomon's estate. At the critical instant, Peregreen realizes that Sir Salomon is Mr. Evans and that his ward is the merchant's daughter and therefore his intended. When Betty escapes to him, Peregreen presents her to her father, as Sir Salomon slinks off. Peregreen offers Sir Arthur his sister in marriage as payment for services rendered, a more appropriate, Country wife rather than the Town wife Julia, who would be too much for him. Then Peregreen insists to Wary that Single and Julia are already virtually married by precontract. When Wary complains that Single has no estate, Peregreen produces the writings. Betty now owns Sir Salomon's estate and therefore Single's legitimate patrimony, but Betty's property will soon be Peregreen's, so he generously renders to Single his due. Not to be outdone in generosity, the Cit Wary follows the Town wit's example: "I dare not resist the will of Heaven, which shews it self in the wonderfull turne of Affairs, which this day has produc'd. Daughter, enjoy your Love; and my blessing go along with it" (V, 99).

Here the sense of an ending receives the providential ratification much more common in heroic and tragicomic romance. But the real dynamic is the playwright's desire to reward the Town wits with the City wives and fortunes that should naturally accrue to them as hip members of the superior ruling class, that is, those who have learned the ways of the Town. Perhaps the most important symbolic figure at the end is the young

Peregreen Woodland dispensing rewards, manifesting both wisdom and generosity. He has displaced the play's title character, who because of a mean-spiritedness that makes him unworthy of his status (he has, after all, ordered the beating and apparent murder of Peregreen, who is both his guest and the son of his old gentry friend), is excluded from the closing comic embrace.[2]

Tunbridge Wells; or, A Days Courtship (1678), perhaps by the same Tom Rawlins who wrote *Tom Essence* of the previous year, returns us to the crossroads of the spa. Tom Fairlove, a sexual trickster on the make, meets his fellow Town wit Owmuch, "A Gamester, that Lives by his Wits and borrowing of Money" (dramatis personae). Owmuch is a younger brother for whom "Nature" designed fools as his "inheritance": "My happy Stars dispos'd me th'other day amongst a Collony of Elder Brothers, whence I chose a Brace to whom Fortune had been more bountiful than Nature" (I, 2). He sets up a couple of London whores at the wells, Brag and Crack, posing as a rich widow and her maid and attracting cullies to ply them with courtship gifts. But Owmuch's larger scam is to trick Sir Lofty Vainman, a foppish baronet, into marriage with Brag, then shake him down for a settlement. He justifies his trickery as universal practice if not universal right: "To thrive is but our Neighbours right t'invade, / And cheating's the chief knack of every Trade" (I, 11). And when Wilding, a rakish husband, tries to abet Fairlove's counterplot to get Sir Lofty for his own sister, Mrs. Courtwit, Owmuch justifies trickery even against friends of the same class, as Wilding affects patronizing disdain:

> *Owmuch:* Were you ten thousand friends, you shou'd excuse me; I'de not release my share in this Knights marriage, t'ingross th'amity of all mankind.
>
> *Wilding:* Thy base ignoble ways of livelihood beget a general scandal on the name, and garb of Gentleman, they'l grow contemptible, being used by thee.
>
> *Owmuch:* Thou art too young, and scrupulous a sinner; examine but the Town, and thou wilt find the gayer part, to have as little Land as thou, or I, and yet they keep guilt Coaches, their race and hunting Nags, Lacquies, and Pages; and what is more expensive then all these, Misses, whose cloaths may vie with Eastern Queens, and Pallaces with Cardinals for cost; and can'st believe these miracles performed by simple rules of honesty, and honour? Thou art not such a Novice.
>
> *Wilding:* I know there are sev'ral ways of livelihood, most indirect; but this damn'd down right cheating I affect not.
>
> *Owmuch:* Kind Nature gave to ev'ry Man his Portion, some in Wit, to others Lands or Moneys, and did contrive us for each others use. And

> I account it as unreasonable to waste Wits precious tallent on a fool
> without advantage, as to let Lands *gratis*—My brain's the nobler free-
> hold. [V.iv, 44]

Appearing to have defeated his fellow Town wits, Owmuch proceeds to
the marriage of Sir Lofty and Brag.

Soon after his cocksure manifesto and apparent triumph, however,
this trickster par excellence is outwitted—and what is worse, mostly by
women. He is first crossbitten when Crack decides to free-lance, impersonate the widow Brag in order to marry the "Quondam Mercer" Farendine (dramatis personae), who now affects to be a gentleman, and split
with the loot. But the supreme crossbiter is Courtwit, who determines
to help her brother win the desirable but *dangereuse* Alinda, rich sister to
Sir Lofty, who resists Fairlove's protestations as coming from one long
hardened in sin (to borrow a phrase from Etherege's Harriet). Courtwit
disguises herself as the parson who marries both Farendine and Crack and
Sir Lofty and Brag. She then advises her brother to exact a promise of
marriage from Alinda in return for the release of Sir Lofty from his apparently disgraceful marriage and consequent settlement. Fairlove does so
aside, then exacts a promise from Sir Lofty for Alinda's hand if he can
annul the marriage to Brag. When the parson's identity is exposed,
Owmuch and his whores are tricked. The play concludes with Owmuch
cursing amidst the hymeneal dance celebrating the wedding of not only
Fairlove to Alinda—the right couple to inherit—but also Courtwit and Sir
Lofty. Like Orrery's Francisco, the younger brother Fairlove provides for
his sisters, even marrying an absent one to the Country fool, Squire Timothy Fop, who was forced to accept Sir Lofty's awarding Fairlove with his
sister Alinda instead of him as promised.

The point of such endings in these plays is not growing disrespect for
the institution of marriage (Rothstein and Kavenik, 172) but a trans-
parency in Stuart ideology: the important thing is for Town wits and their
families to be settled in the political economy. In the hierarchy of symbolism, usually the most attractive, gay couple marries for more than mercenary considerations. Usually love and marriage for them go together. But
as we have seen in several plays, not every marriage combines a gay couple.

What is interesting about the ending of this play is not the apparently
mercenary marriages of Fairlove's sisters but Courtwit's courtship with
Wilding, which may or may not terminate when she calls for an end to
"our modish courtship" (V.iv, 41[misnumbered]), for she seems to invite
him to further (adulterous) courtship in the concluding dance. If so, her
figure, which celebrates her superior "Wits" that have "proved the best,"
anticipates that of the subversive women tricksters I shall treat below

(ch. 8). What else is interesting is Fairlove's last line of triumph over the trickster tricked: "No Wit can prosper without honesty" (42). In Restoration social comedy with just implicit threats against the dominant culture, tricksters tend to be not just sympathetic but benevolent, covered whenever possible by the veneer of official discourse. Against explicit threats, tricksters can become more aggressive, as we shall see.[3]

An anonymous playwright contributed *Mr. Turbulent; or, The Melanchollicks* (1681-82), or as I have it in a later redaction, *The Factious Citizen; or, The Melancholy Visioner,* a play that pits two tricksters against each other. Furnish is the Owmuch of the play, described in the dramatis personae thus: "Nephew to Mr. Turbulent, a swaggering, debauched Person, who has nothing, lives by his Wits, yet furnishes others with Money and Goods." He utters something in the spirit of Owmuch's trickster manifesto: "Fools are a Prey to Knaves, small Knaves to great, / Cullies to Gamesters; the whole World's a Cheat" (III, 46). Furnish seems the master trickster throughout the play, getting even with butts, whose money he has taken and spent and who now demand payment, by turning them on one another. But when he comes to cross-purposes with Lucy Well-bred, Turbulent's rich ward, he meets his match.

Lucy is in love with Fairlove. Yet she is not free to choose him because her uncle Turbulent controls her £5000 portion, and her receiving it is contingent upon her marrying with his blessing. But Turbulent hates Fairlove because he is a Town wit, while Turbulent and his cohorts are virulent, antigovernment Whigs. Fairlove protests he has money enough for both, but to Lucy it is a matter of principle: she wants enough money to live like the gentlewoman she is on her father's side. Her uncle designs her for Finical Cringe, "A Balderdash Poet, and an Apish Citizen" (dramatis personae). So Lucy, as does Caryll's Julia, administers to Cringe the absolute negative, siphons him off onto her cousin Priscilla, Turbulent's cracked Quaker daughter and heiress. Furnish, however, has plans to marry Priscilla to one of his factors in a scam to get her and Turbulent's money, including Lucy's portion.

Lucy must counterplot. She tells Turbulent that Furnish's factor, Hangby, disguised as Sir Peregrine Pricket, is a government informer. But Furnish shows up disguised as one of the summoned soldiers, still keeping control of the situation. Lucy springs her masterplot: the will that placed her in Turbulent's wardship says he remains her guardian until dead or until declared non compos mentis. She tricks Turbulent, to escape supposedly imminent prosecution for sedition, into feigning a madness so great that Dr. Quibus, who has a theory about melancholy and madness that challenges both Burton and Swift, has him committed to Bedlam.

Before committal, Lucy asks Turbulent aside if he will now give her her portion and his blessing on her marriage to Fairlove. When he refuses, Lucy proceeds with the marriages, including that of Cringe to Pris. Furnish has been arrested for debts, and Lucy, in the spirit of comic generosity, talks one of his dupes into springing for him.

In a sense, we end this study of Restoration social comedy that deals with implicit threats to Stuart hegemony where we began, with a nubile trickster duping a tyrant guardian, marrying one of the beautiful people, a Town wit, and thereby inheriting the earth. That is, they inherit the estate that is the material base of power that undergirds English patriarchal aristocracy. The trickery of these couples then (whether primarily that of a nubile trickster or her more experienced sister or a younger brother) and the freedom of choice in marriage it represents present no radical threat to aristocratic ideology. At the same time Stuart ideology as constituted in these plays is less idealistic than that constituted in Restoration "serious" drama. Hardly any of the denouements are rationalized in terms of a metaphysical dynamic: little or no Divine Providence, just some fortune and a lot of luck. A lot of love, too, bringing together in mutual admiration and respect a gay couple that is portrayed as deserving its inheritance.

But the dynamic that drives the endings of these plays is the kind of necessity Raymond Williams glimpsed: the necessity for the couples with the right stuff—both nobility and energy—to be the proper vehicles for the transmission of power and property through patrilinearity. This necessity drives the playwrights as well, as they reinscribe an ideology in changing times, when the ruling class is no longer (was it ever?) just landed Country gentry but includes liaisons with City daughters because of the need for infusions of City wealth—a wealth, as Christopher Hill notes, that drives up the size of dowries and leads, along with the practice of *strict settlement,* to a widening of the gap between large and small landowners and a concentration of power in a new oligarchy (203-4). But the economic realities that are embodied in this comedy signal not yet a shift to a bourgeois ideology. In *Marxism and Literature,* Raymond Williams writes about the enormous elasticity of tradition—its power to absorb the new. In that sense, the writers of these comedies are conservative, adapting the tradition to the shifting realities.

That tradition remains aristocratic: Durfey's Virtuous Wife remains married to the man who stole her from her lover. Lacy's Lord Arminger restricts the fortune hunters seeking marriage with his heiress wards to members of the upper (however alloyed/allied with New Money) class. Town wits still cast their mistresses or, at best, arrange marriages for them with dupes. Lords still retain their *droit du seigneur* and deposit their bastards elsewhere than on their estates. Virgins are still in, whores out (even sympathetic whores, like Behn's wronged Angellica and Rawlins's resourceful Crack). Estates are redeemed from those who stole them and returned to their rightful owners.

I do not see these plays as gradually evolving toward bourgeois ideology. Like the Thomas Kuhn of *The Structure of Scientific Revolutions,* I believe tradition holds until a critical mass of opposition overturns it. Some of the elements of that critical mass, no doubt, are present in these plays: younger brothers, for example, and uppity women. But I believe in a dramatic shift that occurs across the fulcrum of the Glorious Revolution. Till then, Restoration drama in general and comedy in particular remain essentially conservative. Several of the plays I have analyzed in this chapter are from the 1680s.[4] But no Restoration comedies are more conservative than the plays John Harrington Smith found so cynical and that we might, at first glance, find subversive—the Cit-cuckolding plays to which I now turn.

5

Town Tricksters Tup
Their Rivals' Women

An old black ram/Is tupping your white ewe.

Iago, in *Othello*, I.i.89-90

Therefore let no man be urgent to take the way homeward until after he has lain in bed with the wife of a Trojan to avenge Helen's longing to escape and her lamentations.

Nestor, in Homer's *Iliad*, 2.354-56

Women are raped by Serbian soldiers in an organized and systematic way, as a planned crime to destroy a whole Muslim population, to destroy a society's cultural, traditional and religious integrity.

Slavenka Drakulic, "The Rape of Bosnia-Herzegovina"

He tops upon her still, and she Receives it.

Contentious Surly, watching his wife be courted
before his face, in Leanerd's *Rambling Justice* I, 8

Depictions of war by conquerors and conquered alike—from the mythical past of the Trojan War to today's all-too-real postcolonial conflicts—have attempted to demonstrate dominance over their rivals by not just fancied but real tupping of their women, a verb I choose not only because of its Renaissance and Restoration reverberations, especially germane to my topic, but because of its connotations of animal behavior, of the brutal sexual dominance implied by *topping,* or climbing on top. Drakulic's poignant description of systematic rape in Bosnia-Herzogovina gets to the heart of the psychology: an attempt to destroy the cultural integrity of the enemy by contaminating the vessels of his patriarchal genealogy, by impregnating those vessels with his enemy's seed, the final cruel joke of hatred and revenge. Iago's taunting of Brabantio adds the dimension of fear of racial contamination, fear of the potency of the Other. Contentious Surly's agony is made especially tortuous by his fear of class domination:

he is a typical Restoration Cit, who is portrayed as gracelessly impotent in the face of his wife's seduction, ultimately not by the rambling Country (booby) justice but by the Town wit.

This aspect of Restoration comedy has been politely glossed over in histories of Restoration drama. Most notably, John Harrington Smith set the stage for the last half-century of criticism by delineating a subcategory of Restoration comedy, "Cynical Comedy," a category he wanted to contrast to those comedies that featured his chosen—and admired—trope of the gay couple. Smith points out that cuckolding is central to these comedies about "The Gallant in the Ascendant" (ch. 4, title). He means gallants that are not paired with equal, equally witty women to form the gay couple, but his phrase glancingly though unintentionally alludes to the class warfare embedded in Restoration comedy—and generally ignored in its criticism. This warfare is imaged especially in the trope of not just cuckolding in general but Cit-cuckolding in particular, wherein representatives of the dominant class tup with impunity the women of the emergent middle class.

I do not use the metaphor of warfare loosely. I am thinking of Michel Foucault's inverting the notion that war is just politics extended into the notion that politics is extended war (*Power/Knowledge*, 90-91). In words that seem to me applicable to the period after the restoration of the Stuarts and their continuing struggle for power Foucault writes: "[I]f it is true that political power puts an end to war, that it installs, or tries to install, the reign of peace in civil society, this by no means implies that it suspends the effects of war or neutralises the disequilibrium revealed in the final battle. The role of political power, on this hypothesis, is perpetually to re-inscribe this relation through a form of unspoken warfare; to re-inscribe it in social institutions, in economic inequalities, in language, in the bodies themselves of each and everyone of us" (90).

Restoration drama is one of the social institutions that continues the class warfare of mid-century England. Conflict in Restoration drama, as elsewhere in Restoration society, can be seen—at least in part—as an extension of the Civil War between the old feudal class and the emergent bourgeoisie, or better (since Hill among others has shown that configuration to be a rather quaint historical fiction [*Century*, passim]), between contending oligarchies: the Court and the Town and their allies against the City of London and, occasionally, its allies among the Country gentry.[1]

I should now like to argue that the conflict of those Restoration comedies featuring Cit-cuckolding is related to the same class warfare, aggressively reinscribes aristocratic ideology, and does so, in Foucault's terms, not only through *language* but through the *body-language* of stage performance, and indeed, through *bodies* themselves, where the perfect, potent bodies of Town wits dominate over the imperfect, impotent bodies of Cits and where the bodies of women become the contested ground for class dominance and, ultimately, symbols of the contested estate of England itself. However much wit these women are given, however much sexual energy of their own they display, they are merely counters in wars between men.

This displaced warfare breaks out with an unprecedented aggressiveness in the rampant Cit-cuckolding of Restoration comedy of the late 1670s and early 1680s, the time of the Popish Plot and the Exclusion Crisis. Smith identifies several earlier comedies that feature cuckolding, but only Thomas Betterton's *The Amorous Widow* (1670?) and Joseph Arrowsmith's *The Reformation* (1672-73)[2] provide genuine precedents for the class antagonism of the later plays. In the former, alongside a rather typical plot where a tyrannical guardian, the superannuated Lady Laycock, wants to dispossess her ward of her portion and is foiled by trickery into accepting a gay-couple marriage complete with portion, lies a Cit-cuckolding plot. The Town wit Lovemore courts the all-too-willing Mrs. Brittle, a woman of at least gentry class forced by her parents to "redeem" their "Estate" by marrying a Cit without so much as a by-your-leave (III.i, 37). After an assignation, Lovemore and Mrs. Brittle reenter (who knows exactly what liberty they have taken?), and he courts her with language prejudicial against her dull Cit-husband and celebratory of Cavalier potency and libertinism: "You will have time enough to lie by that dull, stupid Clod, your Husband, e'er the Morning: Methinks I grudge him the least Look of you, since he knows not how to value so rich a Jewel. Let him live, and pore o'er his Bags, his Dross, and worldly Gains, whilst we know better how to waste our youthful Hours in softest Kisses, and everlasting Joys" (V.i, 75).

If after their outrageous loveplay on stage in front of Mr. Brittle the rebellious couple does not actually consummate,[3] nevertheless the clear message of dominance in both language and body has been communicated *to the audience.* The middle-class component of that audience might have taken solace in the fact that Mr. Brittle is a petty bourgeois and not a rich merchant, but it also probably unwittingly internalized the lesson and its attendant discipline (in Foucault's sense)—or such would seem to be the intention (conscious or not) of such plays.

Arrowsmith's *Reformation* focuses on this same kind of aggressive Cit-cuckolding. The *reformation* in the title of Arrowsmith's play is a society for the reformation of sexual mores especially. It is ostensibly a libertine society that liberates, that encourages sexual promiscuity. At the center of this libertinism is a class bias. Instructing the two witty, nubile, aristocratic women the Town wits of the play would include in their society, Pedro explains to one of them that the liberty they take is "nothing Madam but what becomes all People that are Vertuous [read, *aristocratic and libertine*]; 'tis only such as drive a trade, and gain by seeming nice that should be otherwise" (III.ii, 33). Indeed, the play includes a hypocrite merchant, Lysander, who feigns sadness at leaving his wife for business but keeps a mistress for solace. Yet he is one-upped by his wife, who had given all her "Virgin Treasure" to her libertine lover Pisauro before she married this merchant strictly for "money" (I.ii, 5-6).

The society for reformation roundly attacks the traffic in women in this patriarchal Italian setting, and the word *trade* is a key link between that concern and the class conflict that is implicit throughout the play. When Leandro, a would-be wit and reformer, protests that he rather likes "the honest way of marrying" (he means the exchange system between men[4]), Pisauro responds with libertine doctrine: "Heaven forbid, but that somebody should like that dull trade: for if there were no wives, there would be no husbands to rob to maintain us younger Brothers" (II.i, 16). Pisauro and Juliana are a team of con artists who have fastened on a rich merchant so Juliana can keep Pisauro in such a manner that he as younger brother would not be able to maintain. Lysander is Juliana's "Loving Cuckold" (I.ii, 7), and it is no accident that he is a merchant. A Town wit's cuckolding someone from among his own class is relatively rare in Restoration comedy—and extremely dangerous, usually leading to swordplay (see below, ch. 7). But Cits are not only fair game, they are the class enemies of the Town wits. Thus they are portrayed as impotent and cowardly.

In this play, Lysander tries to play Othello when he attends a reformation party at his own house and catches his wife parading shamelessly—including participating in a kissing dance—with her adulterous lover: "[P]rithee chuck tell me, which of these is thy Gallant? or do they take't by turns" (IV.ii, 61). He tries to bravely counter by parading his own mistress and pretending to Juliana that they form a fashionable ménage à quatre: "Nay we'l be man and wife still in any place but bed, and that want you have provided for your self, ne're trouble your self. If you do more than e're I could *Pisauro,* and she prove fruitful, I promise here to be a Godfather. If I have the same success here, I expect the like kindness from you *Juliana*" (61). What Lysander has done, however, is to reveal his own impotence. He concludes the act with this cynical, sardonic tag: "The world may laugh, and names of scorn invent,/But to be Cuckold[']s nothing if content" (61). He has difficulty remaining content, passively accepting his cuckoldry, but instead of doing the aristocratic class-constructed *manly* thing and challenging Pisauro to a duel, he takes his anger out on his wife, threatening her with divorce and complaining about Pisauro's braving it not so much with her as with his purse (V.i, 63). His behavior is stereotypically bourgeois. Town wits do not sue for divorce or plan alimony or arrange to keep up appearances. They kill (in tragedies) or at least try (in comedies and tragicomic romances).

Despite its ostentatious libertinism, the play concludes with the two Town wits socialized into marriage with the nubile women who have exercised their free choice and finally obtained their tyrannical guardian's blessing and the promise of a settlement. But amidst the typical festive comic ending, Pisauro and Juliana again parade shamelessly together, and they have this extraordinary exchange with Lysander, whose threat of separation they meet with aristocratic insouciance:

> *Lysander:* Well met Madam, I hope you're pleas'd.
> *Juliana:* Since you are so cruel as to part, I must allow you truly noble.
> *Lysander:* I doubt Pisauro some of these fine feathers must molt.
> *Pisauro:* You're deceived Sir, with these I intend to purchase a rich wife, and pay some of my old scores to *Juliana*. [V.ii, 78]

Juliana's proclaiming him "truly noble" is (*pace* Rothstein and Kavenik, 171) patronizingly ironic: the only thing "noble" about him is that he is allowing her, begrudgingly, a separation. His lack of any aristocratic magnanimity is revealed in his taunting jeer to Pisauro, but the latter's rejoinder underscores his Cavalier triumph. Now Pisauro will merely switch roles with Juliana and become her kind keeper. Thus younger brothers will make their fortunes still at the expense of the rich, especially rich Cits.

Comedies that focus on this kind of Cit-cuckolding do not become prominent, however, until the Restoration compromise was seriously crumbling in the light of the distinct probability that an aging Charles II would die without a male heir and leave the throne to his Catholic brother James, duke of York. At roughly the same time that Dryden could begin *MacFlecknoe* with the shockingly appropriate lines, "All humane things are subject to decay, / And, when Fate summons, Monarchs must obey" before proceeding to the diminuendo, "This *Fleckno* found," writers of Restoration comedy began to return to the motif of Cit-cuckolding, a return that reached a crescendo during the Exclusion Crisis.

Tom Essence; or, The Modish Wife (apparently by one Tom Rawlins, 1676) features as the subtitle character Mrs. Monylove, a trickster so outrageous and delightful as to disguise herself as her own twin brother, who then disguises himself as her, all in order to trick her tightfisted Cit husband into marrying his richly endowed daughter to Mrs. Monylove's Town lover that they might live off the proceeds of the scam. The scam fails and the con artists end up with nothing, but in the meantime Mrs. Monylove has cuckolded her husband in his own house virtually by his own invitation. The fact that her husband's name in the play is Old Monylove indicates that his cuckolding is justified on two grounds, age and class. As the first act ends with this tag, "When old Fools Wed, they must with Horns dispence: / Horns are the just rewards for impotence" (I.[ii], 15), Monylove's age is stressed, but his impotence is also part of his larger class caricature, which includes Puritanical parsimoniousness, for he puts his own wife, disguised as her brother, to bed in the same room with her gallant because he wants to save expenses: she exclaims perversely, "Now this Old Fool will force me to Cuckold him, meerly out of Covetousness, that he will not foul a pair of Sheets extraordinary" (III.ii, 35). When he threatens divorce at the end, she brazens it out that she will get enough alimony to keep a gallant.

The class bias of the play is underscored in the farcical scenes concerning the title character, a perfume salesman who is jealous of his wife primarily because she might ruin the reputation he needs for trading credit. When he manifests pretensions toward higher class by insisting that knights' daughters and maids of honor have flirted with him, she puts him in his place. When she manifests similar pretensions by insisting she is a "Gentle-woman," he responds in kind, "Gentle-woman with a Pox— a Cittizens Daughter and a Gentle-woman—" (6). The crude, petty, bourgeois behavior of the Essences, farcical as it is, serves to pull the higher bourgeois Monylove toward their pole of class antagonism. If Mrs. Monylove does not win it all at the end, her class does. The witty couple Loveall and Luce are reunited, she a mature woman trickster who redeems his sexual energy from its wonted *variety*. And the young gentleman Courtly wins the eminently desirable and rich daughter of Old Monylove and his former wife, finally gaining his blessing and his apology that his threat to marry her to someone else was, in her best interests, designed to obtain for her "a greater Estate" (V.iii, 65). But Courtly bests him after all, for he grafts onto his higher class Monylove's middle-class fortune. Monylove remains at the end a cuckolded Cit maintaining his wife and her lover through alimony.

The high plot of Thomas Porter's *The French Conjurer* (1677), a play set in Spain but of course really about England, relates similarly to the low. In the low, Claudio plots with the clever bawd Sabina to seduce Leonora, the wife of Pedro, "a Gold-wire-drawer" (dramatis personae). In the high, Dorido plots to win Clorinia, the daughter of Avaritio, "A rich old covetous *Spaniard*" (ibid.). Whatever Avaritio's ostensible class, the butts of both plots represent miserliness, a trait associated especially in the English seventeenth century with middle-class culture. Avaritio would consign his daughter to a nunnery just to save her portion, and when the rebellious young couple, married in his face during the great conjuring trick of the last act, begs his blessing, he denies it with a curse—until he learns that Dorido's rich uncle has died, leaving him heir. Then Avaritio can afford to bless them. Pedro wants to keep his wife from visiting a nunnery, for fear that she will be too generous and spend too much of his money on their salvation. Sabina succeeds in tricking him to let Leonora go (she is dressed only in her petticoat!), and Claudio wastes no time in seducing her, but it is a seduction that concludes, however playfully, in threatened force—a threat she turns into a hilarious excuse: "Stay, Sir, if I must go, let us resolve to be as little wicked as we can. . . . But you shall promise me first you will not use me too roughly, for my poor Husband's sake" (IV.i, 29-30).

However wittily they engage, the class aggression is manifest, especially in the conjuring scene, where Leonora descends through a trapdoor in one of the circles to join Claudio, and returns exultant that the devil has embraced her not once but twice, at which she is "very well satisfi'd" (V.i, 45). The significance of the whole conjuring scene is that Town wits can have the women of their class enemies at will and with impunity. Indeed, Claudio comments about Leonora's flirting with him as she enters the scene, "Was there ever such a wittie charming Rogue! She courts me before her Husband's face" (41). An earlier comment by Sabina to Claudio clarifies the lesson of Cavalier dominance over bourgeois cowardice and impotence in late seventeenth-century England:

> Well, Senior, and now you put me in minde of *England,* I cannot chuse but pity your case, that such a noble young rich Don as you should be put to that toil, that charge, and that trouble, for the obtaining such a paltry creature as a Citizens Wife. An Intrigue with a Citizens Wife in *England,* is as common a Frolick as a Carnival here, and has full as little danger in't. There's no locking up their Wives, nor engaging whole Families to punish their frailties. If a Gallant be caught in the fact by a Wives Brother, nay, or a Husband himself, he may as easie come off for Adultery there, as a man may for Murther here. The Gallant gets but out of the way for sanctuary, and the Wife gets her Parents to make up the Breach, at worst, but to pay a new Portion, and all is well. The kinde Cit uses his Wife that wrongs him, as he does the man that robs him; he had rather have his stolen goods quietly agen, than to hang the thief and loose them. [I.i, 2]

The winter-spring theater season immediately before the Popish Plot (fall 1678) produces three Cit-cuckolding comedies, Behn's *Sir Patient Fancy* (probably January), Dryden's *The Kind Keeper; or, Mr. Limberham*

(March), and John Leanerd's *The Rambling Justice; or, The Jealous Husbands* (February). Behn's and Dryden's plays are vigorously anti-Cit and antiDissenter, but Behn's is much more subversive and thus shall be treated below (ch. 8). Dryden's celebrates the energy of the young Cavalier libertine Woodall, who threatens to tup Cit wives and mistresses at the boardinghouse run by the Puritan Mrs. Saintly—a boardinghouse that is really a bawdy house, not only because Woodall's father, Aldo, uses it as a resort for his whores to come to him as *patron* for a form of underworld justice, but also because the supposedly respectable women who live there are sexually promiscuous.

What justifies Woodall's rampant sexuality is an extension of the warfare between Royalist and Roundhead, by early 1678 percolating quite near the surface again and about to boil over. Mrs. Saintly rises every morning and goes ostensibly to exercise at a Dissenters' meeting house, "where they pray for the Government, and practice against the Authority of it" (I.i.10-12). Her attempt to seduce Woodall exposes her Puritan hypocrisy and demonstrates Cavalier superior, irresistible attractiveness. Pawning her off on his servant puts her in her place. Woodall doubles this symbolic class conquest by seducing the wife of the witwoud Brainsick, a pretender to taste in and even composition of operas and a delightful creation, whose rhetoric rivals one of Jonson's. Brainsick reveals his lack of class not only in the tasteless distillations of his brainpan but also in his crude bullying of his wife and of the primary object of class aggression in the play, the Mr. Limberham of the subtitle, who at some level, as critics have speculated for centuries, may have represented Shaftesbury but who primarily represents a Cit.

Limberham, who identifies himself as "a Member of the City" in the epilogue, is portrayed as old, "feeble" (I.i.348), and impotent. At one point he is mocked for being so little in command of his sexual powers as to have prematurely ejaculated (II.i.78ff). Thus he is justly supplanted by a representative of the more vigorous class. Woodall's father, Aldo, who does not yet recognize his son, coaxes Limberham's offended mistress, Tricksy, to a reconciliation: "What if he has some impediment one way? everybody is not a *Hercules*. You shall have my Son *Woodall* [a term he uses generally, not specifically], to supply his wants" (II.i.143-46). By implication, Woodall *is,* by virtue of his class, a veritable Hercules, at least sexually. Mrs. Pleasance, the witty woman of the play who eventually tames him, mockingly characterizes his potency to the wife and mistress he would satisfy seriatim: "'Tis a likely proper Fellow, and looks as he cou'd people a new Isle of *Pines*" (III.i.44-45)—a reference to a fictional castaway's populating his island with thousands of inhabitants (45n).

When fairly caught in his affair with Tricksy at the end, Woodall offers Limberham the opportunity for "satisfaction" (V.i.589). Of course, being a Cit, Limberham is ipso facto a coward. He submissively marries Tricksy and grants her "four hundred a year . . . for separate maintenance" (V.i.596-97). Meanwhile, Woodall, now recognized as young Aldo, socializes his sexual energy into a marriage with the witty Mrs. Pleasance, recently discovered to be a gentlewoman of considerable fortune. The class dominance of the ending is driven home in the Epilogue, where Limberham complains of (Royalist) playwrights,

> these Poets take no pity
> Of one that is a Member of the City.
> We Cheat you lawfully, and in our Trades,
> You Cheat us basely with your Common Jades. [7-10]

That is, Citizens often have aristocratic cast mistresses pawned off on them; moreover, Town wits "Put in for Shares to mend our breed, in Wit" (14) and the resulting bastards become highwaymen and whores.

The Rambling Justice is the most defiantly aggressive of these plays of 1678. Sir Generall Amorous, "A Gentleman of a free Nature, a Generall Lover" (dramatis personae), similarly appropriates religious language in libertine fashion to describe his adulterous affair with the wife of the old Cit Sir Arthur Twilight. Twice he refers to his affair as a "blessing" from "Heaven" (I.ii, 10; III.i, 25), and he rhapsodizes in a postcoital Rochestrian eroticism that is blasphemous: "How many minutes have we had of precious sweet delight! Oh let me dwell upon these hands a while, and breath my soul into each trilling Pore: thy melting lips have made me all a charm, and when I cast my arms about thy neck, I thought I grasp'd a God; the darkness of the Covert could not shade thy piercing beauty from me, for through those thick and darksome Clouds of Night, I could behold the glances of thy Eyes, which shot fresh joys into my panting heart. . . . by Heaven, all, all I say is earnest" (III.i, 25). The fact that he has just copulated with the wrong woman bothers him not overmuch, and when she, Petulant Easy, celebrates her rebellion against her oppressive husband, Contentious Surly, Sir Generall responds again in Rochestrian libertinism: "when love and freedom meet, a Husband is a kind of dull Animal, created to bear the name of Father, whilest we happy men enjoy with freedom what he fondly thinks himself monopolizeth" (ibid.). When Surly, crazed with jealousy, chases after his wife to chastise her, Sir Generall accosts him, accuses him of staining his honor with the imputation of adultery, and challenges him to fight. The dissenting Cit is forced into the submissive posture of cowardice.

Like Woodall, Sir Generall is a libertine interloping in a boardinghouse, whose host is Sir Arthur. Though Sir Arthur is jealously concerned for his wife's chastity, he allows Sir Generall to board because he is reputed to have money and land. At one point Sir Generall borrows money and a ring (to court Sir Arthur's wife) on the promise of a deed of conveyance of those lands (II.i, 17). This touch is a direct hit at the bourgeois practice of appropriating, legally or illegally, aristocratic lands as part of their emerging power. But Sir Generall delivers no lands.[5] Instead, he appropriates the Cit's wife, mollifying her (slight) reservations thus: "I should not urge had you content at home, but being rob'd of such a weighty blessing, and made a starvling to the joys of Wedlock, I come with real and hearty zeals, to give you those pleasures his Age and Impotence deny'd" (IV.i, 42). And he defies her husband: "Now nothing sure can cross me, this night I shall enjoy *Eudoria* and revell in the pleasures of her Love, what will Sir *Arthur* say when he shall miss his Wife? he can but vex or perhaps hang himself, let him do either, all's one to me so I but enjoy his Wife" (III.ii, 31). Indeed, when Sir Arthur is a witness to his own cuckolding, choking on overhearing the names cuckold for himself, whore for his wife, and even pimp for himself, he falls into a fit of coughing and interrupts. Sir Generall and his wife brazen it out to his face, Generall threatening to kill him. Sir Arthur is reduced to begging for his life, and when his wife joins him in begging, Sir Generall lets him live: "Consider Sir, 'tis but a Veniall sin, and not so great as it is Common; for but few Women inviolably observe the Faith they owe their Husbands" (V.i, 67).

But Sir Arthur can find no solace in Sir Generall's palliating rhetoric. Throughout the play he has been fascinated with the character of a cuckold, as long as such a character is not his own, and he has even abetted the cuckolding of Contentious Surly. When he discovers he has delivered his own wife into the hands of the cuckolder, he runs screaming hysterically off the stage, "I shall run mad, mad, stark mad; my Wife, my Wife, my Wife, I am a Cuckold, I am, I am, I am indeed, a damn'd procuring Cuckold" (III.iii, 35). And he gets this small consolation from his wacky servant Bramble:

> *Sir Art:* . . . a pox of Matrimony if this be the fruits on't, was ever Gentleman made a Cuckold before?
> *Bramble:* Yes Sir, especially Citizens; 'tis an Hereditary possession belonging to the Court of Aldermen, and scarce one scapes it, if their Wives are either Young or Handsome. . . . 'Tis something severe indeed, but the best is, you are not the first Citizen that has had his Wife run away with a Courtier. [V.i, 53-54]

The implication is, of course, that Sir Arthur cannot escape being toasted for the rest of his life as "the most Superannuated Cuckold in *Europe*," to which he can only reply submissively, "What, blush for a trifle? a Cuckold is a Christian" (V.i, 62). Moreover, in a mock fifth-act conversion (contrast with Woodall, but compare with Lee's Nemours) Sir Generall ends up marrying Sir Arthur's witty daughter Emilia, while his other daughter Flora cynically marries the booby rambling justice of the title, and all Sir Arthur can do is to hope both husbands will be cuckolds like him and Contentious Surly. He will even help Emilia be a whore to avenge herself on Sir Generall's inevitable inconstancy. But such posturing only reveals the impotence of the Cits. The entire play is thrown as a challenge in their teeth. Flora in the Prologue compares to Dissenters critics who "in the Pit as they in Pulpits rage,/preach up Rebellion to undoe the Stage." This is Royalist anti-Whig rhetoric, and the figure of the triumphant, insouciant, irresistible Cavalier Sir Generall Amorous represents as aggressive an assertion of class hegemony as we get until the Exclusion Crisis.

Meanwhile, between the spring of 1678 and the fall of 1681 only one major Cit-cuckolding play continues the tradition in the calm before the storm, Thomas Otway's *The Souldiers Fortune* (spring 1680).[6] Otway's play celebrates the ultimate triumph of two down-and-out Town wits. They are demobilized soldiers who are angry at the way society seems to reward nouveaux riches and parvenus instead of the younger sons of the aristocracy who have served their country loyally only to be pawned off with worthless debentures. They reserve their bitterest scorn for yesterday's rebels, one of whom they spot across the stage. Beaugard describes him as one (like Shaftesbury, the portrait implies) who brought his "King [that is, Charles I] . . . to the Block," joined the "never to be forgotten Rump Parliament," obtained a pardon at the Restoration, and now plots sedition against his too-generous "Master [that is, Charles II]" (II.385-406). Accompanying this superannuated rebel is a supposed lawyer who longs to be made "Recorder of some factious Town . . . To teach Tallowchandlers and Chees-mongers how far they may rebel against their King by vertue of *Magna Charta*" (II.422-25). The reason the Rump Parliament must never be forgotten is that the Civil War ever threatens to break out anew, especially with the Miltonic if not Lockean politics being opposed to Stuart monarchial theory.

So the primary object of Beaugard's class revenge is Sir Davy Dunce, not only because he bought his beloved Clarinda in a forced marriage while Beaugard was away in the army; not only because he is "a paralitick, coughing, decrepid Dotrell" (I.527-28)—those would be reasons enough in comedy; but because "he is one of those Fools forsooth, that are led by the Nose by Knaves to rail against the King and the Government, and is mightly fond of being thought of a party," reports Lady Dunce, who therefore has "had hopes this twelve month to have heard of his being in the Gate-House for Treason" (I.462-66). Now she hopes to cuckold him with her erstwhile lover. From the moment he sees Beaugard's portrait Sir Davy is threatened by Cavalier potency: "Odd a very handsome fellow, a dangerous Rogue I'll warrant him, such fellows as these now should be fetter'd like unruly Colts, that they might not leap into other mens pastures; here's a Nose now, I cou'd find in my heart to cut it off" (II.66-70). The preoccupation with his nose works off the folk trope that the size of the upper reflects the size of the nether nose. Yet for all his bravado, upon encountering him in the flesh Sir Davy fears Beaugard will slit his own "nose"—a trope that is tantamount to castration.

The play works off this motif of violence. Just as Beaugard begins his blasphemously erotic addresses to Clarinda—"Let's vow eternal, and raise our thoughts to expectation of immortal pleasures" (III.533-34)— Sir Davy discovers them together and, though his wife convinces him she abhors Beaugard's approaches, like a Cit coward, instead of challenging him, plots to have him murdered by cutthroats. The cutthroats are Beaugard's plants, however, and he and his lady engage in one of the funniest cuckolding tricks in all these plays: Beaugard feigns death, Sir Davy is scared to death, and Sir Jolly Jumble, the great pander of the play, convinces Sir Davy to leave the body in his lady's bed, where perhaps by "stroaking" she might revive him (IV.641)!

Sir Davy first beseeches his wife to cooperate—thereby supplanting himself with his own cuckolder—then goes to pray for repentance. He is repeatedly so frightened he is scared into praying in Latin. This is a trick worthy of Dryden, portraying the Whigs as really the crypto-Catholics, not the Tories. But even when he is scared into being "the civillest Cuckold" (V.489) by unctuously letting his wife go with Sir Jolly to his house to hide the dead body and to stay till the heat dies down, he remains vile and hypocritical underneath, for he immediately informs the constable. Beaugard meets Sir Davy's discovery of him alive and quick in Clarinda's arms with Cavalier defiance, threatening death to any who approaches (V.658), then blackmailing Sir Davy into treating Lady Dunce as if she were "my Mistress"—which of course she is and presumably shall remain as part of the "Covenants" between them (V.696, 732). "Covenants" is a nice word to be shoved down the throat of this self-confessed "common-Wealths-man" (V.428-29). The clear message of the play is that the only "Covenants" entered into by Cits, Whigs, and Dissenters will be those dictated by the dominant Town wits. This time it is Sir Davey, played by the irrepressible Nokes, the other great comic actor of the Duke's Company, who runs frenetically around the stage proclaiming his cuckoldom and signaling class impotence and defeat.[7]

On the eve of England's last great dynastic struggle, the Revolution called "Glorious" by the winners, as the Exclusion Crisis came to a climax at Oxford, English comic playwrights turned Cit-cuckolding into a particularly virulent example of the erotics of power (this poignant phrase is Braverman's, "Rake's Progress"). Ravenscroft's *The London Cuckolds* was produced by November 1681, Behn's *The Roundheads; or, The Good Old Cause* by December, Durfey's *The Royalist* in January 1682, and Crowne's *City Politiques*, scheduled for production in June, was delayed by censorship until January 1683.[8] All four of these plays portray Cits as silly, cowardly, impotent, Whig, and meddling in politics; Town wits as handsome, witty, libertine, potent, Tory, and worthy to dominate; and women as generally witty, attractive, sexually active, and naturally attracted to the dominant males. The Town wits tup their rivals' women, often in their face, and force them to accept it. And this is all performed before an audience, as is now a commonplace of the criticism of the drama, packed with Cits, as if to rub class dominance in their faces.

The London Cuckolds is the least overtly political of these plays. But there is no mistaking the class warfare.[9] Three Cits—Wiseacre, Doodle, and Dashwell—are cuckolded with impunity by three Town wits—Townly, Ramble, and Loveday. They are abetted by two witty, rebellious wives—Eugenia and Arabella—and by one ignorant Country wife, Peggy. Arabella is prescient about Peggy's fate, for her husband will not succeed in keeping her ignorant: "[T]his is not an age for the multiplication of fools, in the female sex" (I.i, 451), and indeed, Ramble ends up instructing her in "the duty of a wife" (V.ii, passim)—that is, satisfying a real (read, *Cavalier*) man sexually and cuckolding her Cit husband. When *her* Cit husband leaves her for his business at the Exchange with no more than a kiss (a typical portrayal of Cits as negligent of their women in favor of trade), Arabella reveals her unsatisfied sexual appetite to have a class bias: "I have a month's mind to greater dainties, to feast in his absence upon lustier fare than a dull City husband" (I.i, 451), who is "without a sting" (III.i, 480). She prefers to cuckold him with Townly, but if chance throw Ramble in her lap, she'll take him. Arabella takes great delight in belittling her husband by making him jump over a stool, for example, and even greater delight in outwitting his injunction that she answer every question put to her by a man with "No": she manipulates the questioning in such a way as finally to get Townly into bed with her.

Eugenia proves equally witty—and equally voracious—as she takes Townly by mistake for Ramble, then tricks Dashwell into not only sitting in the garden, disguised as her and waiting for Loveday, while she and Loveday frolic in his bedroom, but even into taking a humiliating beating from Loveday when he is finished. That Dashwell deserves such treatment is manifest in this exchange between Ramble and Townly:

> *Townly:* What is her husband?
> *Ramble:* A blockheaded City attorney; a trudging, drudging, cormudging, petitioning citizen, that with a little law and much knavery has got a great estate.
> *Townly:* A petitioner! Cuckold the rogue for that very reason. [I.i., 454-55]

Here both class and topical politics are evident: a petitioner is one who supported the Exclusion Bill. So when Dashwell is dressed as a woman in the garden and called a "Cotquean" (V.v, 543)—a man who does women's domestic chores—and when Loveday administers him a flailing, he has himself been symbolically tupped by the dominant males. And it is no accident that twice in the play Ravenscroft refers to the king, once as Arabella playfully makes her husband jump over the stool—first "for the king" and then "for the queen" (IV.iii, 517)—and once, more explicitly, as Peggy, like Wycherley's Country wife, naively protests to her husband that the "gentleman" (Ramble) who just courted her and kissed her hand in public "might be the king, they say he is a fine man" (II.iii, 474). This seemingly throwaway line, which alludes to Charles II's own sexual prowess, clearly associates the Town wits of the play with the Court party and gives a royal sanction, as it were, to their tupping their rivals' women. After all, Charles obviously flaunted his sexuality as a sign of potency. Ravenscroft's epilogue might serve for all these Cit cuckolding plays, but especially those of the Exclusion Crisis: Ramble says,

> . . . every cuckold is a cit.
> But what provoked the poet to this fury,
> Perhaps he's piqued at by the ignoramus jury,
> And therefore thus arraigns the noble City.
> No, there are many honest, loyal witty,
> And be it spoke to their eternal glories,
> There's not one cuckold amongst all the Tories.

We can cuckold you with impunity, but you cannot cuckold us, for we are the superior class—and therefore deserve to rule.

Two recent articles on *The Roundheads*—one by Robert Markley and the other by Elizabeth Bennett Kubek—have thoroughly analyzed the sexual politics of that play.[10] Let me just say here that Behn's Cavaliers (tellingly referred to throughout as *Heroicks*), who have lost their estates to the likes of Ravenscroft's Dashwell, consider cuckolding Cromwell's generals—whose sexual as well as political ineptitude proves their lack of worth to dominate. They call such cuckolding "an Act of honest Loyalty, so to revenge our Cause" (IV.i.19), especially if Loveless can "Cuckold the Ghost of old *Oliver*" by sleeping with Lady Lambert, Cromwell's former mistress (I.173-74). General Monck's taking of the City of London is appropriately described by Cits as a rape, for he uprooted her gates and "lay her Legs open to the wide World, for every Knave to view her Nakedness" (V.439-40). In other words, disloyal Cits deserve to be cuckolded, and the City of London herself, for her infidelity, deserves to be raped into submission by the real men of England, the Royalists. Here the body of woman is clearly a metonymy for the contested land, and rape is clearly both a literal and a metaphoric weapon in wars between men. The witty women themselves, as Kubek demonstrates, despite the fact that this play is written by a woman, are put back in their place—supine before real men.

Like Behn, Durfey sets *The Royalist* during the Interregnum and intends it (especially the first act, which ends in the title character's being stripped of his estate), as he says in the preface, as a "*Memento* of *past* or as a *Caveat* of *future* Mischiefs and Diabolical Practices" (sig A2r, italics reversed). The danger posed by Roundhead republicans in the past—as by exclusionist Whigs in the present crisis—seems perhaps best epitomized in this stanza from a witty song sung by the loyal Lieutenant Broom. Note how the political and the sexual are compounded:

> The Name of *Lord* shall be Abhorr'd,
>   For every Man's a Brother;
> What Reason then in Church or State
>   One Man should Rule another?
> When we have Pill'd and Plunder'd all,
>   And Levell'd each Degree,
> Wee'l make their plump young Daughters fall,
>   *And Hey then up go We.* [IV.ii, 50, italics reversed]

Not only will distinction be destroyed but our women tupped and our genealogical eggs scrambled. The theme of leveling gets played out especially in the low-plot, low-class scenes, where Slouch and Copyhold, two of the Cavalier Sir Charles Kinglove's tenants, come to London to exercise their heady sense of elevation, only to be jostled about by pimps and pretentious footmen: Copyhold, "If these doings last, woe be to all merry Meetings ifaith; why one knows not now who's the Landlord, nor who's the Tenant; which is the King, and which the Cobler" (III.ii, 26). They go on to argue that there's no refuge in the law, for the strongest control it:

might now makes right, for "the Head and Fountain of the Law"—that is, Charles I—"lyes a bleeding" (III.ii, 27). Ironically, of course, there is no real difference between class rape that goes low-high and class rape that goes high-low: both are acts of dominance, cloaked in whatever language of legitimacy, even religious.

Durfey focuses the high plot of the play on sexual warfare, on Cit-cuckolding, ostensibly as revenge but really as naked power. The libertine Royalist Heartall—the two terms are virtually synonymous, for the surplus sexual energy of the Cavaliers is the sign of their potency and right to reign—first seduces the niece of the chairman of the Committee of Sequestration, Sir Oliver Oldcut, then pawns her off on the corrupt Justice Sir Paul Eitherside. On their wedding night she makes Eitherside promise abstinence under pretense of keeping their marriage a secret from her uncle for the nonce, but at the same time she gives him the key to her chamber. Unable to restrain himself, the old lecher discovers his bride in bed asleep with her lover—on stage. Seizing Heartall's breeches, he plans to get her portion by law and turn her out of doors, but when he demands her portion from Sir Oliver, the latter reveals that she has no money. Meanwhile, Eitherside has publicly humiliated himself as a cuckold.

Because Sir Oliver sequesters his estate, Sir Charles Kinglove, the Royalist of the title, decides to take revenge by cuckolding him with his wife Camilla, who like all the women in these plays is spontaneously attracted to the manly Cavalier. Camilla repeatedly portrays her husband as impotent and knows she "was design'd for nobler Fortune" (II.i, 11). She insists to Sir Charles, "though I am fetter'd to this tainted Limb, this Canker of the festring Common-wealth, yet I have Loyal blood within my veins" (III.iii, 35). They dialogue delightfully thus, breaking into a form of duet:

> *Sir Charles:* Thou must [have loyal blood], I know it. Thou soft lovely
> Creature. Those that have Wit like thee, must needs be Loyal.
>
> This Marry'd Lump, this, Husband, is thy shame:
> *Camilla:* My shame indeed, and Husband but in Name.
> And tho in Name I must his Wife appear.
> *Sir Charles:* And tho in Name thou must his Wife appear,
> Thou art the Mistress of a Cavalier.

As in *The Roundheads* the latent loyalty within witty women is ostensibly a sign of the *naturalness* of Royalist supremacy. Since Marx's *German Ideology* we have known how to critique dominant systems that portray their foundations as natural and universal. But the real foundation here has to do more with what iconoclasts from Machiavelli to Nietzsche have called *virtù*, the sheer male power of dominance. The loyalty of the submissive woman here is like the loyalty of the submissive land before power that succeeds in portraying itself as legitimate and natural.

Sir Charles and Camilla contrive to trick Sir Oliver out of two of his teeth, which are delivered to Sir Charles, and into patiently bearing fillips on his nose—both acts of symbolic castration. Most outrageously, they make him witness their embraces while he sits in a supposedly enchanted pear tree and comments thus on their "Carnal Copulation": "Now, who's that? 'dsheart the Colonel, and Kissing her, and she Clasping him . . . what still cling'd? still lockt together? why Colonel, Goat, Stallion, how eagerly the strong-backt Dog gripes her?" (V.i, 56). The animal references underscore the aggression of such tupping.

Typically, this play too ends with the Cits announcing their cuckoldry to the world—that is, to the audience. Addressing and taunting that audience in a way that implicates them in his rebellion, Captain Jonas, described in the dramatis personae as "A Seditious Rascal that disturbs the People with News and Lyes, to Promote his own Interest," as he is led off to prison for consorting with a whore, says with heavy irony, "Therefore good people, what ever you think of me, I believe you to be good people; very good people; as good Subjects; as true to th'King and Kingly Prerogative; as unwilling to Rebell and Mutiny; and as heartily Conscientious in your dealings as my self. And so farewell t'ye" (59). In the prologue Durfey has insulted the Whigs in his audience by saying only they would refuse an adulterous intrigue—implicitly because they lack Tory potency; at the end he forces them to watch their party humiliated sexually through the trope of synecdoche, cuckolded Cits standing for the whole of that party and identified with regicide rebels.

On the other side of the political symbolism, aside from the central character, there are two important symbols for loyalty. At the opening of the play in the center of the stage is a royal oak fenced around that Sir Charles Kinglove apostrophizes as a symbol of legitimate Stuart hegemony, for it harbored Charles II after the battle of Worcester and allowed him to escape the regicide Roundheads. The other symbol is in a way related: Philipa, a rich heiress in love with Sir Charles but abandoned by him because her father became a traitor, is a character, like Wycherley's Fidelia, out of romance. She follows Sir Charles dressed as a man and surreptitiously defends the absent Philipa as being not incompatible with Sir Charles's loyalty: "A Roundhead's Daughter might have got a Cavalier, that might have liv'd to take his Grandfather by the Beard" (I.i, 6). When Charles II in exile needs £20,000 posthaste, Philipa does not hesitate a minute to send it, and Sir Charles's union with her at the end represents the triumph of loyalty and the reunion of "Great *England*'s Monarchy" (V.i, 63) with the body of its loyal land.[11]

In Crowne's *City Politiques* class warfare rises closer to the surface than in any of these plays (so close to the surface that its production was delayed from spring 1682 to winter 1683). Though the locale is displaced to Naples, there is no doubt that we are in London, where City rebels defy the legitimate government, arm themselves, and speak sedition. Critics have attempted to identify several of the characters as representatives of specific individuals during the Exclusion Crisis, and there are some important resemblances, as between Doctor Sanchy and Titus Oates, the infamous perpetrator of the Popish Plot, and the Catholic bricklayer and the "Protestant Joiner," Stephen College, one of the perjurers in the plot who was executed for treason. Several characters have traits of Shaftesbury; the podesta has traits of Slingsby Bethel, one of the defiant Whig sheriffs of London during the crisis; the viceroy in some sense could be seen to represent the duke of York; and both Cavaliers at points represent Buckingham and/or Rochester.

But it is important to see that these characters represent types as well, that Bartoline, for example, does not represent necessarily any particular Whig lawyer but the class of corrupt lawyers who would sell their opinions to the highest bidder, who are really nominalists, antinomians—and to recognize such a portrayal as a salvo of political propaganda from Royalists who claim that theirs is the party of de jure power. When the governor tells the podesta that the viceroy will not knight him until he prove himself, the podesta threatens (behind his back, of course),

> Since he is so huffy and stormy I'll be a storm. . . . A whirlwind that shall rumble and roar over his head, tear open doors by day and by night, toss his friends out of their coaches and beds into jails; nor shall all the preachings and pulpit-charms of their priests
> > Dispossess me or fright me in the least;
> > A Whig's a devil that can cast out a priest. [I.ii.133-41]

Despite all of their own sanctimonious rhetoric, these Whigs are portrayed as religious hypocrites, defiant of the divine sanction that supposedly underwrites de jure rule and poised to wreak havoc on their country. Dr. Sanchy says of praying, "[I]t is but a thing of form to please the people" (II.i.289), and the bricklayer obtusely opines, "I care not a farthing for reason, law, nor Scripture if they side with the Tories. I prefer Whig nonsense before Tory reason" (IV.i.79-81). Indeed, the Whig claim to government is portrayed as de facto power; concerning the question whether their cause is right, the bricklayer and the podesta have this telling exchange:

> *Bricklayer:* We have a hundred thousand men, and they are always in the right. Set me in the head of such a general council, and I'll be pope, the only infallible judge.

Podesta: Ay, and have what forms of worship you will. When a cannon's the preacher [pun intended], who dare shut up the conventicle? And nothing opens and divides a text like gunpowder. [IV.i.396-401]

This battle over the right/power to govern is figured especially in the play as a battle over estates, over land, because, although England was in transition from a land-based to a trade-based political economy, land remained the ultimate status symbol for both the threatened aristocracy and the emergent bourgeoisie. When Florio, the Cavalier disguised as a reformed Puritan in order to have access to the podesta's wife, hypocritically pretends to be concerned for the misguided Tories and prays, "Heaven turn these wicked men; I love their souls," the bricklayer responds with the rhetoric of power instead of religion, "Heaven turn 'em out of the kingdom, for I love their lands" (IV.i.402-3). The podesta allows the reformed Florio, who is apparently dying of syphilis, to live in his house and be nursed by his wife, Rosaura, out of greed for his "estate," which he hopes Florio will bequeath to her (II.i.434) and which the equally greedy Bartoline hopes Florio will bequeath to his child bride, Lucinda. The Cavalier Artall remonstrates with his erstwhile witty companion Florio, accusing him, as now one of the Whigs, of trying to "babble and scribble us out of our estates" (I.i.127); he employs the metaphor of swallowing estates whole (I.i.137), a metaphor elaborated on by Craffy, the podesta's son, whose rebellion against his father culminates in giving evidence against him and his faction: "They are moderate drinkers o' wine, but will carouse water abundantly; for they'll drink your rivers, fish and all, and put your land into it for a toast, if you'll let 'em. And yet sometimes they have very narrow swallows; they cannot down with a little church ceremony [as in taking communion in the Anglican church, according to the Test Act], but they'll swallow church lands, hedges, and ditches" (V.iii.206-11).

The battle over landed estates itself gets figured as a battle over women, over the wives of these seditious Cits. Artall disguises himself as Florio in order to seduce the wife of the lawyer who corrupts the whole process of the transfer of property and who would cheat his fellow Whig out of Florio's estate. The closing words of Act IV are the podesta's frantic ravings about losing his "estate" because of his rebellious knavery (IV.iii.168-69), and Act V immediately opens with Artall's rhapsody over his affair with Lucinda: "I am strangely taken with this sweet young creature; 'tis so pleasant to drink at such a fresh spring, which never brute defiled or muddied" (V.i.1-3). On the surface, this is a hit at Bartoline's impotence, an impotence that he acknowledges throughout the play and that he forces the podesta to acknowledge (see esp. II.i.384-87, where he calls wearing breeches at their age an imposture, for they "prechend cho what yey ha' not"). But it also identifies women with the springs that run through the land. It is no accident that Bartoline, when he catches Artall and Lucinda in each other's arms, threatens to take away Artall's estate.

When Artall protests he has too good a title, Bartoline boasts that he and his fellow Whig lawyers have infinite tricks to poke holes in titles and that the only title Artall will end up with is to "the jail," which will become his family seat (V.i.53-69). Artall responds by taking Lucinda under his wing and threatening Bartoline with the power that has always been symbolic of feudal hegemony, the power of swords. He threatens to let into the country French swords (what the Whigs always feared—and justly), and the threat is a clever ruse to draw Whig wrath onto Florio, for whom Bartoline still takes him. But it is also a revelation of the force that always justifies supposed de jure power, despite his Royalist rhetoric: "I'll let in the enemy, and cut the throats of such rogues as you, who abuse your trade, and like so many padders make all people deliver their purse that ride in the road of justice. Better be ruled by the swords of gallant men than the mercenary tongues of such rascals as you are" (V.i.101-5).

Florio, a libertine whose scam is as outrageous as Horner's, delights in the prospect of being called the "_____" of the podesta's wife (I.i.10). The text is left blank for the actor or reader to fill in, but if the word were as mild as *seducer,* surely Crowne would have filled it in himself. Surely he invited us to supply a more aggressive word. Crowne also makes the analogy between Rosaura's body and an estate explicit:

> *Florio:* I do not know
> But my fair love, like an o'er fertile field,
> May breed rank weeds if she be idly tilled [that is, by Cits or their sons];
> Lest love for fools should in her bosom live,
> She shall have all the tillage I can give. [I.i.337-41]

When he finally seduces Rosaura, he proclaims triumphantly, "Then we may securely hoist sail for the haven of love. All the mud that barred it up we have conveyed away, and I will come ashore on these white cliffs, and plant my heart there forever" (V.ii.199-202). The "white cliffs" are not only her breasts and/or her mons veneris but they are also the very White Cliffs of Dover. For the power struggle comically portrayed in these plays is ultimately over the control of Albion herself.

One of the subtler jokes in this play is the way in which these Cavaliers' pretended rhetoric of reformation echoes (as in Lee's *Princess of Cleve*) Rochester's deathbed conversion. It is as if Crowne the Royalist wrenches Rochester's dead body back from the Whig moralizers who had temporarily triumphed over it. Rochester's libertinism, a function of aristocratic class superiority at the moment when its hegemony was being most seriously threatened, is hurled back in the teeth of the emergent bourgeoisie and its middle-class morality as a sign of the Stuarts' right to rule with impunity not because of law or morality but because of sheer amoral power. Caught in flagrante delicto (like Horner and Sir Generall Amorous, Florio tups his rival's woman right behind the back wall of the stage, where they are observed in the act by Craffy), Florio and Rosaura brazen it out at the end, turning Whig principles against the podesta:

> *Florio:* Our [Whig] principles are: he is not to be regarded who has a right to govern, but he who can best serve the ends of government. I can better serve the ends of your lady than you can, so I lay claim to your lady.
> *Rosaura:* And you have my consent.
> *Florio:* So, I have the voice of the subject too; then you are my wife and I'll keep you. [V.iii.179-85]

Of course, no real theory of government is here being affirmed. Florio gets and keeps Rosaura by the power of sheer class supremacy.

In the end the Whigs defeat themselves, appropriately, by their own hypocrisy, lack of loyalty among themselves, and their own false witnesses gone amok. But they are also defeated by Craffy's Oedipal rebellion against his father, a rebellion figured throughout the play as his incestuous desire for his father's wife. His story can be read as the anarchy that inevitably follows from Whig disrespect for the law. But it can also be read as an allegory of Monmouth's own Oedipal rebellion against his father. Of course, no father's wife was literally involved in that rebellion. But on the symbolic level, once again the body of woman can be seen as a figure for the land itself. If the king's bride is his loyal country (as figured throughout the period; see for example Dryden's poetry), then the confusion Craffy makes throughout this play between his father's wife and his father's estate enhances the possibility of an allegorical reading. Perhaps that possibility, more than anything else in the play, resulted in its being banned temporarily.

The rhetoric at the end of Crowne's play is not that of the typical providential justice underwriting legitimate rule. It is the rhetoric of class. The governor warns the rebels, whose power has now been quashed, "And so, gentlemen, henceforward be wise, leave off the new trade you have taken up of managing state affairs, and betake yourselves to the callings you were bred to and understand. Be honest; meddle not with other men's matters, especially with government; 'tis none of your right" (V.iii.390-95).[12] Rights are thus functions of class, and the class superiority of England's aristocracy has been vigorously reasserted in these plays about Cit-cuckolding.[13]

Cit-cuckolding is finally a trope not just for class dominance, however. It is obviously a trope for gender dominance as well. The seduced women in these plays are figures for the contested land. They along with the estates are symbols for the power of the dominant class. But the women are also figures for real women, who unfortunately throughout human history have been tokens in power relations between men. When those relations break out into real, open warfare, women really get raped. Even in the displaced warfare of these plays, there is no real liberation for women. They may escape oppressive relationships with Cits, but they still remain objects of exchange between men as men vie for control. Tupping your rivals' women, especially in their very faces, is a sign of class dominance, but it is always the men who are on top—of both the rivals and the women.

6

Satiric Butts Get Disciplined

In the social comedies I have just analyzed, I have treated in passing several satirical character types: the tyrannical guardian, the Cit (cuckolded or not), the superannuated lover, the parvenu, the Country bumpkin, the Country wife, the clever whore. The Town wit and the witty woman are defined against these foils so that they appear to be the right couple to inherit. Thereby the Town itself, not so much a place as a site of power relations with City, Country, and Suburbs, is portrayed as the nexus of the Nation. Cits are portrayed as parsimonious, cowardly, impotent fools; the Puritanical version, as sanctimonious, hypocritically lecherous, and politically subversive. Bumpkins are portrayed as unsophisticated, tasteless, uncouth fools. Parvenus too are portrayed as tasteless, lacking the breeding (that ubiquitous aristocratic keyword meaning both birth and training) proper to their social aspirations, even as they affect fashion, wit, manners, learning, even poetic inspiration. There is a reason for these stereotypes: If the Town has the monopoly on breeding, wit, grace, taste, talent, why then it is the natural home of the natural leaders of the nation. And it can afford to obfuscate its dependencies on both City and Country as part of its self-mystification.

If there were world enough and space, I would love to share with readers all the delightful satiric butts I have met in my travels through the comic archives. Playwrights and actors infused into an astonishing number of them great comic energy. But I have space for a look at only a few to try to unpack that energy and comment on its ideological significance. It makes sense (to me at least) to focus especially on more Jonsonian plays, that is, ones more packed with satiric butts. In choosing the few, I make evaluative judgments that may be idiosyncratic, but besides the canonical plays I shall treat by Wycherley and Shadwell, I hope to interest scholars and students alike in at least a few noncanonical plays that I have come to consider comic masterpieces and that I would love to direct or act in myself. In this section, I shall treat punitive characters from social comedy.

Later in the book, I shall return to energetic characters that are not satiric butts but the locus of daemonic if not democratic forces.

The trickster-tricked motif among the sympathetic characters in Wycherley's *Love in a Wood; or, St James's Park* (1671) is so minor I earlier relegated it to a footnote. But it is a major motif among the punitive characters. Sir Simon Addleplot, as the dramatis personae describes him, is "a Coxcomb, always in pursuit of Women of great Fortunes"—and always failing, for despite his title he has nothing of the wit or grace of the Town wits,[1] is an inept parvenu who bought his title from "a Court Landress" (V, 98). Indeed, Ranger, one of the real, Town wits, characterizes Sir Simon thus: "That Spark who has his fruitless designs upon the bedridden rich Widow, down to the sucking Heiresses in her pissing cloute" (I, 21). Disguising himself as the usurer Gripe's clerk Jonas, Sir Simon hopes thereby to gain access to Gripe's daughter Martha, his heiress apparent worth £30,000, for Sir Simon has squandered what little estate he has and is about to run out the remaining annuity. He conspires with Dapperwit, another parvenu, a pretender to wit, to elope with Martha, but Dapperwit plans to crossbite him and get Martha for himself, with Martha's complete cooperation. Mrs. Joyner, the great marriage broker and bawd of the play, warns Sir Simon about conspiring with people smarter than he, but he complains, "That's the hardest thing in the world for me to do, faith and troth" (I, 16). Mrs. Joyner, along with the audience, interprets the comment as unintended self-satire.

This marplot figure has another bow to his quiver and hopes his disguise gives him access to Gripe's sister, Lady Flippant, "an affected Widow, in distress for a Husband, though still declaiming against marriage" (dramatis personae). When he is forced to bring her into company at a French ordinary, Lady Flippant reveals aside that she, like Dapperwit, is engaged in crossbiting Sir Simon: "Does he bring us into company, and *Dapperwit* one? though I had marryed the Fool, I thought to have reserv'd the Wit as well as other Ladies" (I, 24)—that is, reserved Dapperwit as her kept gallant. One of Sir Simon's more delicious ineptitudes is not recognizing Lady Flippant in the park while he satirizes her to her masked face for running out on him from the ordinary: "[S]he is as arrant a Jilt, as ever pull'd pillow from under husbands head (faith and troth) moreover she is bow-legg'd, hopper-hipp'd, and betwixt Pomatum and Spanish Red, has a Complexion like a Holland Cheese, and no more Teeth left, than such as give a Haust-goust to her breath; but she is rich (faith and troth.)" (II, 34). What is so delicious is not only the ineptitude, the sour metaphors, but the fact that he reveals his complete lack of decorum by uttering this kind of character sketch as a courtship address to another woman he has met by chance in the park. For her part, the widow vows revenge through marriage.

Turnabout is fair play, and Sir Simon, disguised as Jonas, is forced to overhear a similar satirical character sketch of himself from the wit, Ranger. Moreover, in this scene in Act III, even as he delivers by his own hand Martha's letter to Dapperwit, Sir Simon must endure Dapperwit's pretending not to know him and kicking him—always funny business on the stage, as pretenders even with titles must endure being put in their place, that is, their real class status below the ruling class.

Sir Simon addles his own plot, for it is too contrived and he too stupid. As Jonas he conveys to Martha letters between her and Dapperwit, supposedly facilitating Dapperwit's courtship of her for Sir Simon. But when they meet, Dapperwit and Martha embrace each other and kiss repeatedly, she supposedly pretending not to recognize Sir Simon under Jonas and thanking Dapperwit for being a go-between with Sir Simon. Sir Simon protests: "I wou'd have kept the Maiden-head of your lips, for your sweet Knight, Mrs. *Martha,* that's all; I dare swear, you never kiss'd any man before, but your Father" (V, 92). Jonas leaves to put on Sir Simon, and in a hilarious scene, Martha pretends to discern Jonas under Sir Simon and refuses to marry her father's man. Sir Simon repeatedly protests his credentials, the wedding preparations. Martha and Dapperwit determine it is best not to waste the latter, so they invite Sir Simon/Jonas to witness their marriage.

Sir Simon's response is interesting: "What, ruin'd by my own Plot, like an old Cavalier[?]" (V, 99). As Weales points out in his note (124 n. 6), by no means did all the Cavaliers fare as well as Robert Howard's Colonel Careless or even Durfey's Sir Charles Kinglove or Cowley's Colonel Jolly in getting back their estates by hook or crook. So many an old Cavalier was forced to "plot on still" as Sir Simon plans to do by trying to get Martha's father Gripe to prevent the marriage. But Wycherley also seems to suggest something deeper, more sinister: By what plot of their own were old Cavaliers ruined? By some scheme to get money in a world never quite fixed after the Restoration, where loyal Cavaliers had to compete for estates against vicious Cits and their lawyers? It seems no gratuitous detail that when Lady Flippant pursues the reluctant Jonas around Gripe's desk, he protests the need to proceed with "a Lords Mortgage" with dispatch (IV, 74). Wycherley has set out to punish the members of the upstart new order not just for fun but for vengeance in the name of the ruling class.

Often the pet peeves of Restoration comic playwrights are witwouds, wannabes who pursue fame and patronage that are out of their reach because they are out of their (class) league. The real wits complain of this play's Dapperwit: "[W]hy shou'd you force your chaw'd jests, your damn'd ends of your mouldy Lampoones, and last years Sonnets upon us?" (I, 18). He manifests his lack of class and breeding by proceeding to malign Ranger the moment he is out of the room and by plotting against his supposed friend Sir Simon, and Vincent upbraids him for both transgressions of Cavalier code. He too condemns himself out of his own mouth. Insufferably loquacious, he attempts to court women with his volubility. Lydia leads him on into a disquisition about wits, which concludes,

> Your Judg-Wit or Critick, . . . can think, speak, write, as well as all the rest, but scorns (himself a Judg) to be judg'd by posterity; he rails at all the other Classes of Wits, and his wit lies in damming all but himself: he is your true Wit.
>
> *Lydia:* Then, I suspect you are of his Form.
>
> *Dapperwit:* I cannot deny it, Madam. [II, 38-39]

Dapperwit's solipsism begins to suffer comic revenge. Having taken Ranger to see his jewel of a mistress, Lucy, he is denied entrance, ostensibly because she believes he brought his friend to go snacks but really because she has bigger game arriving soon, Alderman Gripe himself. So Dapperwit, having protested he would sooner stop writing poetry than desert his darling Lucy, lurches toward Martha and exults in his good fortune and great wit as he invites his fellow wits to his wedding party: "I have marry'd an Heiress worth thirty thousand pound, let me perish" (V, 108). But the crossbiter is crossbitten when Gripe, furious at losing his daughter and especially his money, determines to marry Dapperwit's cast wench Lucy "and get Heirs to exclude my Daughter, and frustrate *Dapperwit*" (V, 110).

It is Dapperwit who calls a spade a spade anent Lady Flippant. Flirting with him to convince him that Sir Simon is no threat to her affection, Lady Flippant asks Dapperwit if he is jealous. He responds, "If I had met you in *Wheatstones*-Park with a drunken Foot-Soldier, I should not have been jealous of you" (I, 25). As he points out, referring to the fact that Whetstone's Park was a notorious red-light district, he has just called her a "Whore in plain english." But Lady Flippant's desperate need for a husband with an estate (since she has no jointure of her own and is virtually out of money) and her rampant sexual appetite cause her to be willing to accept Sir Simon as husband with Dapperwit as gigolo; or to ask if the Town wits at the ordinary have "Fortunes" (I, 26); or to flirt in the park with Ranger and the disguised Sir Simon; or to pursue in a very funny scene even the impecunious clerk Jonas. Aside to the audience she complains about hard times for people of quality (with hearty sexual appetites): "'Tis much for the honour of the Gentlemen of this Age, that we Persons of Quality are forc'd to descend to the importuning of a Clerk, a Butler, Coach-man, or Footman; while the Rogues are as dull of apprehension too, as an unfledg'd Country Squire, amongst his Mothers Maids" (IV, 74). Testing her honesty (in case he must rely on his fall-back plan), Jonas pursues her into the other room and returns horrified, as he narrates his adventure to Mrs. Joyner: "She threw down my Ink glass, and ran away into the next room; I follow'd her, and in revenge, threw her down upon the bed; but in short, all that I cou'd do to her, wou'd not make her squeek" (75). Frustrated, Lady Flippant finds Jonas "not fit for my brothers service" (75)!

When Lady Flippant goes back to St. James's Park on the make, however, she comes up empty, as she relates in a comically poignant speech: "Unfortunate Lady, that I am! I have left the Herd on purpose to be chas'd, and have wandred this hour here; but the Park affords not so much as a Satyr for me, (and that's strange) no Burgundy man, or drunken Scourer will reel my way; the Rag-women, and Synder-women [cinder-women], have better luck than I" (V, 96). Defeated, she slinks into the final scene and informs Mrs. Joyner that she must now settle for Sir Simon indeed (making no more mention of vengeance). But we know from Mrs. Joyner's aside as she agrees with both to join them ("[L]ike the Lawyers, while my Clients endeavour to cheat one another; I in justice cheat 'em both" [109]) that they are about to discover their ultimate crossbite: that neither has any money. The rag and cinder women may indeed fare better than she, picking up what turns up.

The point of Wycherley's satire on Lady Flippant is manifold. First, as Gripe's sister, she is a Puritan and therefore a sexual hypocrite, who constantly pretends she is uninterested in either sex or marriage when her appetite for both is voracious. Second, she is, if we read Sir Simon's satirical character sketch of her as verisimilar, a superannuated lover and ought therefore to yield to the younger generation instead of running around at night with Lydia and Christina, meddling in their affairs and trying to manage her own. Finally, as her "Persons of Quality" speech indicates, she is, like Lady Fidget and her friends after her, a weapon in the class war: not that all women, even women of quality, are at heart rakes, but that wives of aldermen who aspire to quality are. City *ladies* are, by definition.

If Wycherley is cruel to Lady Flippant, he is ruthless to her brother. Mrs. Joyner, knowing he overhears, gives him a supposedly flattering character that would earn him no credit among the Cavaliers: "He is a prying Common-Wealths-man, an implacable Majestrate, a sturdy pillar of his cause—"; she continues to flatter him directly: "You cannot backslide from your Principles; / You cannot be terrify'd by the laws; / Nor brib'd to Alegiance by Office or Preferment" (I, 12-13). The last line speaks volumes. It infuriated the Court party that preferment in the City earned no allegiance for the king.

Beyond this suggestion of sedition lies the common, Jonsonian satire of the Puritans for hypocrisy, a hypocrisy Wycherley delightfully bandies in the continuing dialogue between Gripe and Mrs. Joyner, played with gusto one must surmise by the great comic actors Lacy and Corey:

> *Gripe:* You are a Nursing mother to the Saints [that is, you are a bawd];
>   Through you they gather together [that is, they copulate];
>   Through you they fructify and encrease; and through you
>   The Child cries from out of the Hand-Basket [that is, the bastard
>   seeks lodging at the foundling hospital, funded by the Saints].
> *Joyner:* Through you Virgins are married or provided
>   For as well [that is, they are declared virgins and he draws up the por
>   tions and joyntures accordingly]; through you the Reprobates Wife
>   Is made a Saint [that is, as magistrate, he lets her off for a bribe of
>   some kind]; and through you the Widow is not Disconsolate, nor
>   misses her Husband [because he takes care of her sexual needs]. [14]

Gripe's pursuit of Crossbite's daughter and Dapperwit's mistress Lucy is one of the funniest parts of the play. He has agreed to take care of all her and her mother's necessities in order to keep her as his mistress. From the moment he and Joyner enter the Crossbites' humble abode, Joyner works him for money to raise their standard of living (and to pocket for her own convenience). In his state of high sexual stimulation, he gives Joyner money just to get rid of her. She leaves muttering, "I never knew any man so mortify'd a Miser, that he would deny his Letchery any thing" (III, 63). But he takes liberality as a sign the Town "white Peruques" spoil the women, "and that's the reason when the Squires come under my cluchess; I made 'em pay for their folly and mine, and 'tis but Conscience" (64)—that is, as magistrate he gets even with the upper class for raising the stakes in the traffic in mistresses by making them pay for both their own and the City's sexual transgressions, by charging fines large enough so he can afford the traffic, even if he doesn't want to spend out of his £30,000 estate. As he courts the falsely modest Lucy, and as his expectations rise, Joyner bilks him out of more and more money, till she obtains his grandfather's seal ring (which he must have bought, she says, for he has no natural coat of arms). Joyner finally leaves, and Lucy, going along with the pretense that he is a dancing teacher, puckishly asks him, "I don't see your Fidle, Sir, where is your little Kitt?" Lacy's Gripe must have been spectacularly funny: "I'le shew it thee presently Sweetest" (65). Lucy cries out, Crossbite and witnesses break down the door, and the skinflint Gripe is shaken down for a substantial blackmail.

The £500 Gripe must grant Lucy for a portion gripes him, and Joyner works him back up to a pitch by assuring him she will make Lucy give him his money's worth. But Gripe has not finished suffering his poetic justice. While he seeks Lucy again, Martha escapes to marry Dapperwit, and the only way Gripe can get even is to publicly disgrace himself by marrying a cast wench. His only consolation is that he gets the £500 portion back. "[B]esides," he assuages his shame, "'tis agreed on all hands, 'tis cheaper keeping a Wife than a Wench" (V, 110).

Corman writes, "Ranger and Lydia have occasional moments of brilliance, but it is Gripe and Dapperwit, Sir Simon Addleplot and Lady Flippant who are the most effective characters in *Love in a Wood*. These are the characters," he adds, citing Katherine Rogers, "who serve as focuses for 'the moral awareness which was to distinguish Wycherley among his contemporaries,' a moral awareness that left him, and not Shadwell, as the heir to Jonson's comic mantle" (30). *Comme je suis d'accord,* but the "moral awareness" is not some universal humanistic ground from which to satirize; it is the specific ground of the Restoration Town playwright, satirizing these four butts as deviant from the class norm of the hegemonic group he represents. These exuberant creations are tricksters who must be tricked not, like Lydia and Ranger, so they can be taught lessons that socialize them as part of that superior hegemonic group but so they can be punished and separated from it.[2]

If Wycherley bested Shadwell at Jonsonian comedy, it was not for the latter's lack of trying. In his first two plays all the creative energy goes into humors characters (witness the title of the second, *The Humorists* [1670]), into which he even tends to make his romantic leads (witness the main title of the first, *The Sullen Lovers; or, The Impertinents* [1668]). But it is the impertinents in both plays whom we remember: the fops Sir Positive At-all and Brisk and the witwouds Ninny and Drybob. In *Epsom Wells* (1672) Shadwell gives us one of the great Country bumpkins of the Restoration in Clodpate. But he achieves his apogee of Jonsonian comedy in *The Virtuoso* (1676), where he creates several marvelous punitive characters to whom he administers punitive discipline indeed.

Sir Formal Trifle, played by Nokes, and Sir Samuel Hearty, played by Leigh, are the fop and the witwoud par excellence. They serve the typical function of foils to the brilliance of the Town wits, who manifest in their elegant discourse and their bearing that they are superior to these foolish nouveaux knights. Sir Samuel's most delightful idiosyncrasy is his use of disguises to further his amatory designs. To gain access to one of the virtuoso's nubile nieces (from whose presence he has been banished as a wit!) Sir Samuel first disguises himself as Longvil's servant, whose impertinence is punished with repeated kicking. In exasperation, Longvil threatens to run him through the guts with his sword. When Bruce restrains him because killing him would "be something uncivil," Sir Samuel protests in comic outrage, "Uncivil! What a pox do you talk? Uncivil! Why 'twill be murder, man. Uncivil, quoth a—Well, I must be gone with a cup of content to the tune of a damn'd beating, or so—This is a fine, nimble piece of business that a man cannot make love to his own mistress" (II.i.188-93). Clarinda maliciously persecutes Sir Samuel, exposing him to her uncle Sir Nicholas, with the result that Longvil orders him dowsed under a pump and tossed in a blanket.

Having been kicked, beaten, pumped, and tossed in a blanket for his troubles throughout the play, he dons the disguise of a woman, only to be treated as a bawd and dropped down a trapdoor through which has disappeared only a moment before Sir Formal in punishment for his tedious oratory. Let us listen to Sir Formal in order to understand why they would want to get shut of him. Clarinda has challenged him to discourse "upon seeing a mouse enclosed in a trap" (he is to be the mouse imminently):

> I kiss your hand, madam. Now I am inspir'd with eloquence. Hem. Hem. Being one day, most noble auditors, musing in my study upon the too fleeting condition of poor humankind, I observed, not far from the scene of my meditation, an excellent machine call'd a mousetrap (which my man had plac'd there) which had included in it a solitary mouse, which pensive prisoner, in vain bewailing its own misfortunes and the precipitation of its too unadvised attempt, still struggling for liberty against the too stubborn opposition of solid wood and more obdurate wire; at last, the pretty malefactor having tir'd alas, its too feeble limbs till they became languid in fruitless endeavors for its excarceration, the pretty felon—since it could not break prison, and, its offence being beyond the benefit of the clergy, could hope for no bail—at last sat still, pensively lamenting the severity of its fate and the narrowness of its, alas, too withering durance. After I had contemplated awhile upon the no little curiosity of the engine and the subtlety of its inventor, I began to reflect upon the enticement which so fatally betray'd the uncautious animal to its sudden ruin; and found it to be the too, alas, specious bait of Cheshire cheese, which seems to be a great delicate to the palate of this animal, who, in seeking to preserve its life, O misfortune, took the certain means to death, and searching for its livelihood had sadly encountered its own destruction. Even so—[III.iv.96-124]

Clarinda springs the trap. The joke in this kind of specious eloquence is *on* the satiric butt but *in favor of* the playwright him- or herself. That is, the audience knows the character a fool but loves him for the sake of the artist who could so brilliantly portray him. And when so fine an actor as Leigh lends his talent and his body to the role, the figure of Sir Formal is infused with a quantum of comic energy.

The audience would have delighted especially in watching Leigh/Sir Formal come on sexually to Nokes/Sir Samuel. Leigh was great at playing bisexual or homosexual characters (see ch. 8 below for an analysis of Leigh as the abbé in Southerne's *Sir Anthony Love*), and Nokes came to be known as "Nurse" Nokes for his cross-dressing roles (like the nurse in Otway's Romeo and Juliet play, *Caius Marius*). Fearing discovery and being sent to Bridewell to be whipped, Sir Samuel allows Sir Formal a kiss, which provokes this hilarious exchange:

> *Sir Formal:* The sweets of Hybla dwell upon thy lips. Not all the fragrant bosom of the spring affords such ravishing perfumes.
> *Sir Samuel:* O Lord, sir, you are pleas'd to compliment. [Aside.] Ah lying rogue, my breath smells of tobacco.
> *Sir Formal:* Our time may be but short; pardon the unbecoming roughness which my passion prompts me to. Come, my dear Cloris.
> *Sir Samuel:* Lord, what a pretty name is that. I was ne'er call'd Cloris before. [IV.i.38-47]

Sir Formal cannot control himself, resorts to "a rape," and Sir Samuel expresses his shock then throws Sir Formal down: "'Sdeath! The rogue begins to pry into the difference of sexes and will discover mine. I must try my strength with him.—Out lustful Tarquin! You libidinous goat, have at you" (65-70).

Both these parvenus suffer punitive poetical justice in the end. Sir Formal, fooled by Clarinda into thinking he marries her, marries only her maid Betty and receives this final rebuke from the witty Clarinda: "Sir Formal, she's as good a gentlewoman as you a gentleman" (V.vi.72-73). Sir Samuel is arrested and reincarcerated as a bawd. Though he escapes, throws the concluding masquerade party to further his designs on Miranda, and arranges to have himself delivered into the concluding presence in a chest, he receives his final rebuke from Bruce, who is now Miranda's guardian: "I will cut your throat if you attempt to make love to her any more" (111-12). The violence of this last threat constitutes the play's last assertion of class difference: parvenu males are warned not to overstep their bounds and court aristocratic women, the preserve of the Town wits.

Shadwell treats Snarl punitively from his opening scene. He is described succinctly in the dramatis personae as "an old, pettish fellow, a great admirer of the last age and a declaimer against the vices of this, and privately very vicious himself"—a perfect role for Cave Underhill, with his wonted dour look. At his entrance on the stage he attacks his grandnieces as representative of a degenerate age: "[T]he last age was an age of innocence. You young sluts you, now a company of jillflirts, flaunting, vain cockatrices, take more pains to lose reputation than those did to preserve it. I am afraid the next age will have very few that are lawfully begotten in't, by the mass" (I.ii.101-6). He has articulated one of the central concerns of aristocracy, the perpetuation of its power through lineage. Yet he is mistaken in his judgment of these young women—choosing in a world of promiscuity to remain chaste, they socialize the promiscuity of their chosen Town wits—and he is a hypocrite about his own generation. As a result, the women punitively correct him, first verbally: Clarinda banters, "Pish. You are an old, insignificant fellow, nuncle, such as you should be destroyed like drones that have lost their stings and afford no honey"; he retorts, "What pleasure can a man have in this coxcombly, scandalous age? In sadness, I am almost asham'd to live in't, by the mass"; she: "Then die in it as soon as you can if you do not like it" (I.ii.134-46). It is Snarl who is impertinent, passing judgments, casting a pall on the youngsters. They steal his cane and pipe, flinging the one away and breaking the other. And while he bends over to pick up the pieces, one of the women knocks off his hat and periwig, the other knocks him down. This is generational rebellion against a superannuated malcontent.

It is almost as if Shadwell's characters are asking for it. Indeed, Snarl literally is. Even though "this snarling fellow's sometimes in the right" as he satirizes the virtuosos (II.ii.261), he loses his moral authority with the audience when, as he castigates the age for its sexual degeneracy, he fondles his kept mistress Figgup, grows passionate, and begs her to cane him with birch, a masochism she gets no sadistic pleasure from:

> *Figgup:* I wonder that should please you so much that pleases me so little.
> *Snarl:* I was so us'd to't at Westminster School I could never leave it off since. . . . But dost hear, thou art too gentle. Do not spare thy pains. I love castigation mightily. [III.ii.65-71]

The worst poetic justice that could be administered to Snarl would be to lose that authority publicly, and that is what he gets. At their next assignation, Snarl and Figgup are surprised and take refuge in a woodhole, but are dragged out in front of two other couples there for the same purpose, who pretend to be scandalized at his hypocrisy. His nephew Sir Nicholas gloats, "Is this the fruit of your virtue and declaiming against the vice of the age?" (IV.ii.179-80). Snarl tries to brazen it out, protesting Figgup's innocence and even drawing on his nephew. But Lady Gimcrack's bravo Hazard discovers the birch rods and Snarl deliquesces.

Twice Snarl is humiliated by the public flaunting of his scandal, the first time as he ascends his soapbox to condemn Sir Formal (Clarinda must have told Sir Formal in their conversation aside for him to have received the news). He vows revenge against his nephew and his hangers-on and assembles the dispossessed weavers who are in turn dispersed by Bruce and Longvil. The second time occurs as he makes an appearance barefaced at Sir Samuel's masquerade, ready to play the malcontent. Clarinda and Miranda taunt him, then Sir Samuel and Hazard until he exclaims aside, "O my shame comes upon me!" (V.iv.148). He and Figgup leave, Snarl blustering hypocritically, "In sadness, it is a shame such bawdy doings should be suffered in a civil nation" (166-67). He returns, dragging in Figgup and triumphing, "Where is this coxcomb, nephew, this virtuoso? I was with a whore in German Street, was I?—And your ladyship reproach'd me too. She is your aunt, in sadness" (V.vi.53-55). In sadness, indeed. Snarl inflicts upon himself, out of spite, his own final punishment—to be married to a common wench, whom everyone knows to be a whore. He consoles himself in the mad fiction that she is at least his own whore and not another man's.

Ironically, Shadwell, who can attack libertine Town morality as well as any satirist of his time, pillories a representative of priggishness that opposes the *tempora* and *mores* of the new Town generation. Although Bruce and Longvil are no better than they should be in their relations with Lady Gimcrack, they are converted by play's end to be trustees first of the desirable young women's fortunes and ultimately of their bodies, upon which they will cultivate a new generation of Town wits. Significantly, those challengers to their superiority are all punished rather severely, even physically. The cultural function of this motif appears to be *punishment* on stage, *discipline* in the audience, which is intended to internalize the lesson.

Perhaps the most brutal punishment is reserved for Sir Nicholas, the virtuoso himself. Shadwell defers his entrance until the middle of the second act, and the suspense is worth it. Learning to swim by lying on a table and imitating the actions of a frog in water tied on a string secured between his teeth, Sir Nicholas must have presented an absolutely hilarious spectacle to the audience. Moreover, he manifests the insensitivity to experimental animals at which animal-rights activists cringe. Then he rhapsodizes on his ability to fly, plans to fly to the "world in the moon" (II.ii.35). Bruce and Longvil, those Lucretian philosophers, ask the practical question: When does Sir Nicholas plan to try his skill swimming in water? Sir Nicholas: "I content myself with the speculative part of swimming; I care not for the practic. I seldom bring anything to use; 'tis not my way. Knowledge is my ultimate end" (84-86). Sir Nicholas's descriptions of his experiments with air, transfusion, a prototelephone system that sounds like a seventeenth-century version of the Net—all these are very, very funny, especially with Snarl playing a Jonsonian Macilente-style commentator, whose nastiness boils over. So far Shadwell's technique is to display Sir Nicholas's foolishness.

In the fourth act, however, Shadwell begins punishing. While Snarl and Figgup hide in the woodhole because they are interrupted by Lady Gimcrack and Hazard, her kept bravo, Sir Nicholas and his kept whore Flirt arrive. Lady Gimcrack goes on the attack. Sir Nicholas counterattacks that he knew from Flirt that she and Hazard would be there. Then they both begin to realize that Flirt is Hazard's whore, and each complains of being double-done:

> *Sir Nicholas:* O this villain has made me doubly a cuckold. . . .
> *Lady Gimerick:* This strumpet has doubly betray'd me. [IV.ii.109-15]

Hazard and Flirt provide the Gimcracks with the rhetoric to cover their retreat, a rhetoric Sir Nicholas believes while his wife only pretends to.

Sir Nicholas is saved from the rebellion of the weavers, but while he is distracted, those nieces over whom he keeps so tight a rein (reign) slip out of his grasp. He arrives at Sir Samuel's masquerade, finds his wife, but she takes him for Hazard and laughs, "It makes me break my spleen almost to think, what an Ass we made of Sir Nicholas today" (V.iv.186-87). Enraged, he chases her off stage. When he returns and begins to threaten a patriarch's justice, she throws his love letters to his whores in his face. He publicly proclaims Flirt mistress of his house and casts his proper lady from him—only to have Lady Gimcrack proclaim that she has enough of a separate maintenance to live on without him (and with Hazard). Sir Nicholas now deliquesces and offers truce, but news arrives that the creditors from whom he borrowed money for his experiments have "seiz'd on all your estate in the country" (V.vi.29).

Sir Nicholas appeals to his wife, who contemns him now more than ever: "No, sir, I thank you. My settlement is without incumbrance, and I'll preserve it without you, which you are the greatest [incumbrance] a woman can have" (36-38). Turning to Snarl whose inheritance he holds in reserve, he discovers Snarl has married Figgup and plans to get heirs to disinherit him. Finally he turns to his nieces, whom he has kept out of circulation in order to preserve their fortunes for himself, only to be told they have chosen Bruce and Longvil as guardians. "Am I deserted by all? Well, now 'tis time to study for use," he proclaims, and the audience is teased for a moment into believing he has learned the lesson of his poetical justice, but he continues, "I will presently find out the philosopher's stone. I had like to have gotten it last year but that I wanted May dew, being a dry season" (130-33). As Michael Alssid points out, Sir Nicholas remains the mad projector (71). And yet any credibility he still might have within the scientific community will be destroyed when Lady Gimcrack sends his letters to the college. Even Flirt deserts him when he no longer has the money to keep her. Like the weavers his inventions (metaphorically if not literally) dispossess, he is estateless.

Why is so much special punishment meted out to Sir Nicholas, whose projects seem so innocuous? Why strip him entirely of his estate? Conservatives throughout the latter part of the seventeenth century attacked the Royal Society and its experiments. The aristocracy in its ideology lined up with the Ancients in the controversy with the Moderns. Witness the Lucretian pose struck by Bruce and Longvil. It is as if gentlemen do not engage in crass or crude experiments that challenge received opinion. Under the guise of respect for Tradition, Restoration comedy, just as it masks the Town's reliance on both Country and City, masks the aristocracy's alliance with the new science and trade. Whether Sir Nicholas accurately represents the Royal Society or not, he functions as a trope for the repeated emphasis in the play on useful (applied) as opposed to speculative (pure) science. From Bruce's nostalgia for a simple bricklayer to Lord Munodi's desire for a science that could produce a green revolution in *Gulliver's Travels* to Senator William Proxmire's "Golden Fleece Awards" the modern world has applied a supposedly common-sense standard to science that is really the bourgeois demand that science serve enterprise. Making the Town wits the locus for the standard by which we judge the virtuoso's madness is designed to give the illusion that aristocratic ideology can appropriate and dominate the powerful new force of science. It is always in the ruling class's best interest to portray scientists as mad. Then it can appropriate their discoveries even as it belittles or co-opts their little moralities about how those discoveries might be used. It is part of the discipline government subtly instills.

Does Lady Gimcrack not escape punishment? It could be argued that keeping Hazard is no great reward but actually a form of punishment, for we know he has no loyalty to her but will just use her money to pursue the gambling his name implies and the whore who will no longer stay with the penniless Sir Nicholas. Yet Shadwell invests her with something of the free spirit of English women he later lionizes. At one point in the play she receives a letter from Hazard beseeching her to meet him at their place of assignation "as well for a great deal of love as for a little business." Alone on the stage, she addresses the audience as confidante: "Well, I will go though it cost me money. I know that's his little business. I know not why we ladies should not keep as well as men sometimes. But I shall neglect my important affair with these two fine, sweet persons [Bruce and Longvil]; but that's uncertain, this is sure" (III.i.237-44).

Lady Gimcrack sounds exactly like Dorimant. And that's the point. She has appropriated to herself the prerogatives of the male libertine and has assaulted his double standard. There is nothing noble or magnanimous about her motivation here and throughout the play. She is not the kind of successful heroine trickster I shall examine below (ch. 8). Rather meanly she plots for herself at the expense of her nieces. But she does get away with it, thanks to some clever retirement planning. Shadwell employs her mainly as an instrument of punishment on Sir Nicholas. But he also invests her with a free-spirited energy that enables her figure, unlike those of the other butts, to transcend, warts and all, the punitive poetical justice of the ending. Unlike Sir Nicholas, Lady Gimcrack still has an estate.

Why Rawlins's *Tunbridge Wells; or, A Days Courtship* has not received more attention I do not understand. Perhaps it was simply eclipsed by the brilliance of the other plays produced during 1678, the annus mirabilis of Restoration comedy.[3] A great deal of the play's power resides in its Jonsonian humors characters, especially in their language. The one modern critic who has recognized the excellence of this play, John Harrington Smith, writes that it "can boast some of the most distinguished dialogue in the minor comedy of the period" (82). I have already analyzed Owmuch's trickster manifesto above and will not drag him back on the stage, but others deserve curtain calls in this section.

Crack's scam with Farendine is exploded by Courtwit's disguising herself as Parson Quibble, and Farendine, having undergone a conversion of sorts, will return Crack's and Brag's gleanings—much to the chagrin of Owmuch, who had planned to go snacks—to their original owners. I for one wish Crack had gotten away at least with the loot, her waggishness is so attractive, so witty. She advises Brag to persevere in the rich widow scam: "No Chimistry is like a Womans Wit" (II.i, 12). Concerning Parson Quibble, she complains, however, "His Tyth Geese and Pigs come in so slowly they'l scarce discharge a Treat of *pettit Pasté* and brandy." Then, in a delightful parody of Jacobean diction, she warns of the approach of two of their marks, "Obscure, I hear some footing" (12). To the witwoud poet Witless, relentless in his pursuit of the "widow" Brag, Crack offers this tongue-in-cheek advice: "You mispend your fury; my Lady's not of the Tribe of *Hellicon,* and were you heir apparent to *Parnassus,* she'd not accept it for a joynture" (IV.ii, 33). She thus chases away the one pretender from whom she and Brag can draw no booty. Planning to crossbite

Brag by marrying Farendine and absconding with said booty, Crack philosophizes that the mercer will be no worse for the bargain: "[N]or will my Mercer lose by the exchange, since I'm the fresher merchandize o'th'two; and for our Portions, hers is in Fee-tail, and mine in Capite, a nobler Tenure" (V.iii, 40). Indeed, she is superior by her wit, heads over tails. She prays to the god of thieves and tricksters that she might succeed: "*Mercury* thou Favourer of Wiles, assist my love!" (41 [misnumbered]).

When Owmuch angrily reveals to Farendine that he has married Crack instead of Brag but Crack counters with the offer of the booty, Farendine expresses a wonderful folk rationale for accepting her (and the booty) over Brag: "Thou art indeed much younger, and mayst crown me oft'ner with the City night cap, if thou call'st that a fortune" (V.iv, 45). Well, stripped of the booty at the end, Crack's "City night cap" and her *caput* may be all she has left to survive! She is a casualty in the power conflict between the Town tricksters, Owmuch and Fairlove, and if the play's final lesson is that Fairlove's victory means a triumph of the idealized official discourse that legitimates it—"No Wit can prosper without honesty" (50)—then there is no place for Crack in the comic closure. No trick has gained her an estate.

There is no place for Mrs. Paywel either. She is an alderman's wife trolling for a gigolo at the wells, and Mrs. Parret is her bawd. When Owmuch asks if there be any infertile women at the wells who need sexual assistance—"Waters are but waters Mrs. *Parret,* there goes more to the composition of an Heir, than minerals" (I, 5)—Parret describes an alderman's wife who "is kindly willing to spare the decrepit years of her Husband, and to mannage his Cash to his ease, and her own satisfaction" (5). Meanwhile, Mrs. Paywel complains to the wells' Dr. Outside that she longs for a boy, a male heir, but that the alderman comes "short" of it (Parret's pun, III.i, 22). Her subsequent comment reveals that she too would be a trickster for an estate: "Many a Woman wou'd have supplied his defects elsewhere rather than suffer such an estate to go out of her line" (22). Out of *her* line! This uppity City wife threatens patri- with matrilinearity—an implied consequence of sexual promiscuity in all these comedies and an inherent problem in the too-complex system for reproductive control. As Lévi-Strauss puts it in "The Structural Study of Myth," it is easy to see when one comes from one; it is difficult when one comes from two.

Mrs. Paywel is uppity in terms of status as well. When she encounters the Town couple Wilding and Courtwit, she prides herself on her equality with Town and Court women, to the point of offering to show the lace on her smock in public. Wilding comments, "'Twould much oblige the Company"; Courtwit adds, "And no wayes disoblige the Court" (23).

Mrs. Paywel snorts her retort, "They rail at me already for wearing such rich points on my petty-coats, and swear they don't become a Tradesmans Wife, but did they see what's under my petty-coats. . . . I'le come one day with all my trappings, and dazle their weak eyes; and let'em know a Banckers Wife can vie jewels with the proudest of 'em" (23). Of course, as the play presents her, she would rock back on her heels and expose what's under those petticoats to virtually anyone, thereby revealing her inherent lack of worth to attain higher status.

Even though Mrs. Paywel plots for an assignation with Owmuch and goes so far as to shake her legs with him right in front of her stupidly "indulgent" husband (dramatis personae), she fails of her desires. At the crucial moment, Owmuch is so physically repulsed by her as to hesitate long enough that Alderman Paywel returns unexpectedly. In a funny scene Owmuch hides in the closet while Mrs. Paywel and Parret administer the wells' waters to the alderman's eyes that are supposedly so bloodshot he could not have seen a man in his wife's room. Alderman Paywel keeping his eyes shut for the waters to work, Mrs. Paywel smuggles out Owmuch, giving him a jewel in prepayment of future services back in London.

This subplot contains the same ideological content as the Cit-cuckolding plays: Cits are impotent, Cavaliers potent, City wives *naturally* attracted to the perfect bodies of their class superiors, with the actual or potential consequence that City children are often the by-blows of Town wits. The frustration of Mrs. Paywel's desires, however, is not just part and parcel of the official morality of the play's conclusion. Unlike Lady Gimcrack, she is punished for her appetites and aspirations. The uppity woman of this play is put in her *proper* place.

Of the three butts who pursue Brag, Witless the witwoud poet and Farendine the qoundam mercer are the more interesting because of their dialogue. Witless enters with a rhetorical flourish aimed at the "Widow" Brag: "Where's this magnetick of beauty; here's an Ode shall make her fairer than Nature designed her, it contains 999 Stanza's, writ all *a la vole;* my Muse ne're drew bit for't" (II.i, 13). He goes on to brag about a play he has written that caused the actors, when reading it, to burst their buttons. Then, in a delightful moment of reflexivity, he asks if they have seen *Tunbridge Wells,* the very play they're all in! Like *Epsom Wells, Tunbridge Wells* takes the audience on a fictional trip to a crossroads that reveals interimplication. But the interimplication is not merely some epistemological trip wherein we discover our complicity in the failure of language; it is a sociopolitical trip where we discover the dialogics of power relations.

Rawlins endows Witless with wonderfully horrible verses (a difficult thing to do). He courts Brag with these:

> When most Stupendious Thunder from the Earth
> With silent noise concealed this Ladys Birth,
> The Bull in Paralax did bray so lowd
> That Fate by him had like to have been cowd. [14]

But as with Jonson's Sir Politic Would-be, the problem with Witless is more than his aesthetic abrasiveness. His pretensions lead him to violate the political responsibility of the poet. Witless claims poets can "depose Kings, subvert States, creat and annihilate unborn Worlds" (III.ii, 27). He means in plays, but the implications are dangerous when parvenus talk sedition: "I went not treacherously about to incense the People, and foment Rebellion, but contrived my Stratagem with such artifice [as the parson would], they [the kings in his play] destroyed each other playing a Prize at Cudgels" (27). Witless violates decorum as part of a larger transgression of a metaphoric sumptuary law the play enforces: Don't dress up, you're out of your league, and, like the parson, you are dangerous to well-established hierarchical relations precisely because the dress you wear is public, political discourse.

When Crack mockingly opines that Witless might as well profane the Restoration rhymed heroic play as well as comedies, he answers smugly, "Poor Chamber Utinsil; thy heart is no more proof against Love in rhime than thy sleazy Smock against him thou likest" (II.i, 13). The comment is very funny. But serious plays that deal with kings and states are about more than just "Love in rhime," they are about relations between kings and subjects; comic plays too, at least those I am calling social, enforce boundaries and reinforce hierarchy. Witless does not understand. But the Shadow, the playwright Rawlins, do. Thus Witless is expelled from the stage long before the denouement, not just because he has no money but because, like one of Pope's dunces, he has defiled the aristocratic *nature* of poetry.

The description of Farendine in the dramatis personae teaches us from the start how to read him: "A Quondam Mercer disgusted with his Profession, and from a sedentary Fool being turned a Riotous Coxcomb pretends to all the worst Qualities of a Gentleman." Being a pretender to higher status he misses the mark. He sounds like a Town wit, but out of key, as he rails against the City he believes he has transcended: "Know I defie that inclosure of horned Beasts, where hypocrisie stalks like Religion, and fraud wears the Cloak of Sobriety; I dwell within the Precincts of Gentility; keep a Warehouse within the sent of his Majesties Kitchin, wear my sword, maintain my Miss, converse with the *Huza*'s, storm Punks, beat Watches, and reel to bed by three in the morning" (II, 12-13). He has become not a gentleman but a hector. But Rawlins uses him to satirize the gentlemen who abuse their gentility: "That generous humor [Brag's fake swooning at the very name of Citizen] does improve my hopes; I want but little of a Gentleman, except a Priviledge not to pay my debts; for I can swear as lowd, talk as profainly: Drink as deep, and Court a Miss as lewdly: Therefore I'le order straight my Journy-man to shut up Shop, turn all my Wares to cash, defraud my Creditors with a composition, and make me large returns of th' overplus, that I may put my self into a Garb, Purchase a Knight-hood, and atchiev'e [*sic*] the Widow" (15). For every parvenu, is there a lacuna in commerce?

Farendine's main function, however, is to satirize pretenders who violate that metaphoric sumptuary law and try to dress up to another status. When Fairlove dissolves Sir Lofty Vainman's marriage to Brag (because his sister Courtwit has impersonated Parson Quibble and thus no marriage transpired), Farendine begs Fairlove to free him from his marriage to Crack as well, offering Fairlove money and the appropriated booty too; furthermore, he promises, "I'le never more pretend to th' qualifications of a Gentleman" (V.iv, 48). In other words, he has been cured of his mad ascension.

Although Parson Quibble is funny as a punning Welshman and Squire Timothy Fop is funny as "A Coxcomb that pretends to know all persons and business" (dramatis personae), their types of hypocrite and pretender are not portrayed with the signal eloquence and energy of Sir Lofty Vainman. Sir Lofty has a grandiloquence that ranks with Sir Epicure Mammon and must have been a great part for Nokes or especially Leigh. Rawlins's description of him informs us he is "A Baronet of great means and little sense, a great affecter of figures and hard words" (dramatis personae). He is a Restoration W.C. Fields. Witness his response to making Fairlove's acquaintance: "Odoriferous Mr. *Fairlove*! I reverence thy Name sublimely, and to ellucidate the redundancy of my devotions, I'le enter it upon the knuckles of my Pedestals" (I, 6). What this last phrase means is itself elucidated by the stage direction "*writes upon his knees*" (6). He makes Courtwit's acquaintance thus: "You shall make an impropriation of me, and be the sole Incumbant of my amours. Pardon me, Madam, tho I illustrate my ellocution with those clerical metaphors, know I am a Baronet of 2000 *per Annum*" (7). On the other hand, the flexible Sir Lofty responds to Brag's matching his rhetoric stroke for stroke in repartee, and particularly to her pretending to share with him intimate secrets, with this wonderful Fieldsian rapture: "Madam, my auricular aurifices dilate themselves to entertain your secret!" (II, 17).

Not only is Sir Lofty's love in vain, but he is full of the vanity of self-love. Having manifested his cowardice by quaking away when Owmuch brings swords ostensibly sent by Fairlove with a challenge (such cowardice is itself a sign of self-love as opposed to gentlemanly honor and courage), Sir Lofty approaches Fairlove warily later in the play and submissively protests, "I am transcendantly perplexed by the participation of some sinister misapprehensions between us. . . . By the quiddity of my Knighthood, I was as innocent of any intentional injury, or injurious intention, But *con licenza*, that figure must not laps quotation" (IV.i, 31-32). So carried away by his own eloquence, he interrupts his apology to write his own words in his commonplace book!

The wealthy fool is a power football kicked back and forth between Fairlove and Owmuch. Both need his estate: Owmuch to supply his wants through the bonds and bribes he will get by settling the quasi-divorce between Sir Lofty and Brag; Fairlove to supply his sister with financial security. Owmuch appears to win the match. Completely tricked by Owmuch and Brag, Sir Lofty steals off to marry her with this rhapsodic verbal ejaculation: "Come Widow, this Night I'le celebrate the Bacchanalia's of Hymen; and inebriate my Knight-hood in the profundities of *Venus*" (IV.iv, 37). But when Sir Lofty discovers Brag is a whore, or in her words "an obliging Lady," Sir Lofty exclaims, "An obliging Lady, Zooks an obliging Lady, what a Lacquer she has found for a Whore? I'd give half my demeasnes for an emancipation" (V.iv, 47). Brag demands a settlement of a thousand a year for life, and Owmuch adds to the demand an immediate two thousand, one for him and one for her, apparently. Fairlove counteroffers to free Sir Lofty from Brag if he grant him his sister's hand and also a thousand for the person who gets him off (meaning Courtwit, for whom Fairlove will now have provided a portion).

So Fairlove tricks himself and his sister into estates. Since by doing so he causes Sir Lofty to deprive Squire Fop of the sister he promised, Fairlove even provides Fop with a substitute wife, another sister as yet unprovided for. His rationale is as follows: "Y'had almost 'scaped my memory; But since I have robbed you of one Wife, the best justice is to help you to another; a Medly of poor Wits and Rich Fooles make the best mixture in Nature; and I've a Sister in *London* at your Service" (41-42 [misnumbered]). This is the doctrine of brothers sans estates. But we might ask the further question why both Fop and Sir Lofty are absorbed in the hymeneal embrace and, therefore, symbolically into the society of Town wits. Perhaps this play reveals more than others that the ruling class is not homogeneous.

When we first meet Fop, his talk of trade sets Owmuch's teeth on edge: typical gentry snobbery. Yet Fop's marriage to Fairlove's sister acknowledges the increasing alliance of the gentry with the merchant class in order to keep its head above the shifting economic currents of England.

When we first meet Sir Lofty, he brags about his lineage all the way back to the time of King James I: again, typical gentry snobbery, this time on the part of the playwright, against nouveaux riches who since Jacobean times rose into an expanded peerage through the sale of honors. Yet perhaps the comic energy of these characters, especially Sir Lofty, is an aesthetic sign of the economic energy of an emergent class without the absorption of which English aristocracy would collapse. However much the surface tropes still nominate these parvenus as "Fooles," however much the concluding dialogue between Courtwit and Wilding teases us into the thought that at least she if not her sister will manage these fools and perhaps scramble their eggs, the *mixt way* of comedy may in this instance, at least, transparently constitute the ideology of a heterogeneous ruling class.

Of course one of the most common satiric butts in Restoration comedy is the *fanatical* Puritan. The anonymous *Mr. Turbulent; or, The Melanchollicks* (1682) has the greatest collection in a single play. Indeed, though it has other butts like the projector Grin Sneak, the witwoud Finical Cringe, the quack Dr. Quibus, and the matchmaker Lady Medler, all these are minor in comparison to the fanatics. It is a play I might have classified as dealing with explicit threats against Stuart hegemony, though Furnish's Cit-cuckolding activity is marginal. *Mr. Turbulent,* whose second title was *The Factious Citizen; or, The Melancholy Visioner,* is definitely an Exclusion Crisis play, however.

The main fanatics are Timothy Turbulent, "One that hates all sorts of Government and Governours, and is always railing against the Times" (dramatis personae); Rabsheka Sly, "A Creature of Mr. Turbulent's, and one of his private Cabal, a private Sinner, and Railer against the Times" (ibid.); and Abednego Suck-Thumb, who has no special description but is the most wonderful of these, a brother Saint who sucks his thumb in silence until he sees amazing visions. The French Dr. Quibus's anatomy of melancholy puts both Turbulent and Abednego in the third degree, with Turbulent heading toward the fourth (actually, Quibus thinks Abednego is already there, though he is his convenient type for the third degree). The third degree, characterized by black bile, is religious, where the melancholy visioner of the subtitle "sees Visions of de Angels, and de strange Beasts, and de Monsters; dis causeth de Prophesie, de Fanatick, de Sects, and de Schisms, and de Hereticks, de Divisions, de dark mists in de fancy, and in de imagination, and de strange Chimeras, and all de strange delusions in de varld" (II, 21). The fourth degree, characterized by choler, "causes all de quarrels in de world, and makes de fiting, de Riots, de Routs, de peevishness, de angriness, de beating one another, de disputing, de Railings, de Revilings, de Treasons, and de Treasonable Speeches, de Turbulences, de Rebellions, and opposition of de Governours, and de Government, of de Kings and his Laws, and of all unquietness in de world" (21). (This is Swift's madness in *A Tale of a Tub*.)

The nearly mad Turbulent spends the entire play ranting and railing against the government and everyone else that bothers him. Dr. Quibus tries to treat him through diet, beginning with a general flushing with enemas and emetics. The trickster Furnish plays off Turbulent's appetite to get his fanatic daughter for Furnish's fellow trickster Hangby, but at the crucial moment Turbulent's rebellious niece Lucy bursts in to warn him that soldiers have come to arrest him for talking sedition. Turbulent retires in haste to don his armor, which is made of brown paper, and hides in a press. The soldiers dump out his black box of favorite radical books: prophecies and visions; writings of the Levellers, Muggletonians, Quakers, Ranters, Anabaptists, and the Family of Love—all fanatical sects. Furnish, disguised as one of the soldiers, tells Turbulent's man Pollux to burn the books! They find Turbulent hiding in a press, wrapped in the brown paper armor, standing like a statue.

Even the Town wits Fairlove and Friendly are brought in to make fun of Turbulent. At one point they say he/it is a statue of Oliver, but Pollux says, "Indeed Sir you are mistaken, he never lov'd *Oliver* in his life, nor any Governor, nor Government—you do him a great deal of wrong: He was then the same Mr. *Turbulent* that he is now" (IV, 53). Furnish expresses surprise that this railer against idolatry would himself have set up graven images, so he pulls a pistol and pretends to shoot it. The statue drops its truncheon, and they all feign surprise but pretend to believe it is still a statue. Closing Turbulent back up in the press, Lucy speculates archly that he was so frightened he probably soiled his armor behind— crude, cruel, but effective Whig-bashing by displacing the current crisis backwards. The implication is that once a Roundhead, always, and that the followers of Oliver have always really been anarchist—and hypocrites and cowards to boot. But there is a subtler message in this fourth-stage madness: be quiet, leave government to your betters, to those bred for it. Or we will burn your books.

This lesson becomes clearer when we analyze what Furnish does to the Slys. Ostensibly upset and intent on revenge because both dun him for debts, Furnish sets them to spying on one another at a local tavern. Moreover, because Mrs. Sly means sexual debts as well, he tries to silence her with a threat to her husband. She had better keep his mouth shut lest he be tried on the statute of *scandalum magnatum* for railing against the government. She defends a man's right to speak in his own shop and house. He counters by wondering why they bother with such things:

What does it have to do with oil and olives, mustard and salt? But there is nothing innocent about such questioning. It is a form of surveillance and intimidation. So when he sets them to spying—she because Furnish says Sly is a womanizer, he because Furnish says his wife retaliates in kind—they end up disciplining one another: fighting at Turbluent's till the constable and watch are called and they are hauled away to jail. At the end, though they have been released from jail, they are silenced by the merrymaking of the triumphantly married Town couple, literally driven off the stage by the—to them—horridly abrasive, profane sound of the hymeneal fiddles.

Like *City Politiques, Mr. Turbulent* stages a full-scale seditious meeting of a caricatured Whiggish cabal, featuring Turbulent's and Sly's tirade against the government. Their tirade is conducted in full fanatical cant. They lament the times when they could speak freely, as in what Sly calls "the good times of the Rump, when any one might rail against Kingly Government, and the idols of Monarcy [*sic*], without check or controul. . . . But I will speak, and I must speak, and I cannot but speak against Monarchy, which is the very tail of the Beast, that arises up with seven heads out of the Bottomless Pit" (II, 24 [misnumbered]). They continue in contrapuntal rhapsody:

> *Turbulent:* 'Tis the Idol of the World and ought to be pull'd down, and laid in the Dust—It must be overturn'd—overturn'd—overturn'd—
> *Sly:* For it permits the wicked and abominable men to do what is good in their own eyes—and suppresses the fiery zeal, and the zealous fury of those who stand up for Reformation.
> *Turbulent:* And suffers the gathering together of Minstrels, and the noise of the Flutes, and the tinkling Cymbals in the Streets.
> *Sly:* And the Morris-dancers, and the Rope-Dancers, the Puppet-Plays—the Bull-bating, the Bear-bating, the Horse-Races, and the Cards, and the Dice, oh abominable!
> *Turbulent:* And the Players of Interludes, and the Men and the Women singers.
> *Sly:* But Babylon must fall—must tumble, must be pulled down—
> *Turbulent:* And it shall fall, and it shall tumble, and it shall be pulled down. [24]

The scene concludes with a cryptic vision by Abednego, prophesying, of course, though they are too stupid to see it, their own ruin.

Aside from this brief vision, the playwright keeps Abednego, played by Tony Leigh, in reserve, sucking his thumb, for the dramatic effect of his uncontrollable, spontaneous outburst—surely one of Leigh's finest speeches. When the trickster Lucy informs Abednego that Turbulent has lost his reason, Abednego launches on a diatribe against reason as

> the Filth and Scum of the Carnal Brain: It is the Sut and Fume of Hell: it ought to be banish'd and not made use of: it is the Froth of a corrupted mind: it is the Carnal Weapon of the wicked, learned men—And I say again, we ought to live above Reason, beyond Reason, and to Act against Reason, and contrary to Reason, and to pull down Reason, and to over-throw, overthrow, overthrow—the Idol Reason. . . . 'Tis that which causes the Rulers of the Earth to impose Laws on us: 'tis that which causes the outward Worship, and the congregating in Stone Churches: 'tis that which causes the Orders and the Ceremonies, the Institutions, and the Schools, and the Universities, and the Study, and the Books and subtle Questions and Answers among the men of the World—'Tis the very Root of all Evil, and it must be confounded; and if Brother *Turbu-lent* has lost his Reason, he is become perfect. [IV, 58-59]

Method in madness is always the playwright's design. Here of course, the playwright lays bare the (supposedly) inherent radical anarchy of Puri-tanism, its irrationality, its anti-intellectualism, antinomianism, anti-insti-tutionalism. Thus the political center portrayed itself as rational in the face of a challenge it succeeded in portraying as lacking any standard of judg-ment outside its solipsistic, idiosyncratic, unverifiable individual inspira-tion. Of course in the face of such a threat, the only hope of society would be sober skepticism, rational empirical procedure, the conservation of tra-ditional institutions and rituals. At least that would seem to be the ideol-ogy intended to be projected through the play.

The final scene is Bedlam. The political opposition is mad.[4] Turbulent gets into a shouting match with the Slys, and Pollux comments, "So—so—the Brethers and the Sisters are falling to pieces" (V, 72). The play closes in Tory wish-fulfillment: the Town wit and his witty lady trium-phant; the Quaker daughter redeemed from her parents and converted from abstemiousness to the Cavalier pleasure of dancing; and the mad fa-natics literally sealed off in the interior scene, silenced in mid-rant. It is a scene of triumph in the culture wars that were the extension of the Civil War. And the punishment inflicted on the enemy onstage was obviously designed to instill discipline in the audience—ostensibly through fear and intimidation, perhaps even shame and guilt, but more realistically through the co-optation of the center toward the politics of common sense and controlled, rational discourse. The metaphoric Moor-fields of the play do not have to be the site of confrontation between Town wit and satiric butt that Friendly creates at the beginning. Instead they can be the site of mutual respect between reasonable men and women to which Fairlove is attracted, where "Men and their Wives ordinarily walk here together very lovingly" (I, 4). But the "irenic" quality Rothstein and Kavenik properly sense in Fairlove's comment (252) signals not so much peace between contending classes as the appeal, as in Dryden's major poems, for a coalition of the center against the extreme left.[5]

"[W]hen one wishes to individualize the healthy, normal and law-abiding adult, it is always by asking him how much of the child he has in him, what secret madness lies within him, what fundamental crime he has dreamt of committing" (Foucault, *Discipline and Punish* 193). Foucault is writing about "the means of correct training" (Pt. 3, ch. 2) as part of the discipline of education in post-Enlightenment Western Europe. Nevertheless, we can perhaps argue that the punitive aspects of Restoration comedy perform the same kind of cultural work. They attempt to normalize behavior by portraying deviance as childish or mad. So in the slapstick action of farce fops and witwouds and parvenus and bumpkins and projectors and uppity women are literally or metaphorically spanked, beaten, pumped, tossed in blankets, tumbled, and run off the stage if not out of town. Even the more knavish tricksters are taught their lesson not to contest with their betters. And the fanatics fare worst of all, at least in *Mr. Turbulent,* for they are perpetually incarcerated in Bedlam where they will suffer the gaze of the normal. The members of the audience watch in relative silence, internalizing the lessons in a less punitive form of discipline.

Night after night, the institution of the theater produces knowledge that reinforces the relations of power between and within classes. At its best, Restoration social comedy negotiates some freedoms within those confines, relative freedom of marriage choice, for example. But it remains fundamentally conservative. The right couples inherit the estates, singing to the others, "I hear you knockin' but you can't come in"; the others, chastened, exit singing, "Oh, yes, I'm the great pretender"; and the audience sings in relief, "It ain't me, babe." The laughter that lingers in the emptied hall after social comedy is more Hobbist than we care to admit: half self-congratulation, half participation in the punishment.

Part Two
SUBVERSIVE COMEDY

Like social comedy, subversive comedy also ends in comic celebration, but there is a centrifugal energy in tension with the centripetal. In Ravenscroft's *Careless Lovers,* while one couple with the right stuff is united and granted the estate, the other, unredeemed sexual tricksters, doggedly retains their promiscuous prerogatives, thereby threatening to scramble the genealogy that the entire system of property exchange through marriage was designed to protect. But *The Careless Lovers* is something of an anomaly in Restoration comedy. Subversive comedy tends to focus on other manifestations of centrifugal energy. Sometimes this energy strains the seams that hope or pretend to stitch together a superficially homogeneous ruling class out of the heterogeneous elements of a tenuous oligarchic coalition (ch. 7). Sometimes it strains gender ideology and creates a space for rebellious upper-class women, if only in the margins of official society (ch. 8). Sometimes it threatens the ordering force of aristocratic ideology with democratic elements whose energy is so boisterous as to be positively uncontainable (ch. 9 & 10).

7
Town Tricksters
Tup Each Other's Women

As in the rivalry between Rains and Bevil, on the one hand, and Woodly, on the other, some—though a very few—Restoration comedies focus on intraclass sexual rivalry. The implosion that threatens in this potentially deadly rivalry symbolically hints at the uneasy truce between factions within the ruling class. For Town wits to try to cuckold one of their own brings the dynamics of sexual competition not only to the Town but, by implication, into the Court itself, where Charles II's promiscuity can be seen, as Dryden for one portrays it in the opening of *Absalom and Achitophel*, to be subversive of the very fabric of political society. If you portray Charles as King David, your audience knows that the demise of Absalom represents the visitation upon David of the consequences of his sexual transgressions. As I have argued (*Word as Bond,* 129-209), Dryden's poem can be read as David's tragedy. In the world of Restoration comedy, tragedy is, of course, avoided. Rivals are pulled back from the brink—or they simply wink at the transgression and pretend to accept the rival's word that nothing ever happened (as in *Epsom Wells*). But the breach is never fully healed and the threat for further subversion remains.

Chronologically the first of these plays, the anonymous *The Mistaken Husband* (1674), resembles Restoration social comedy, for the ending features a converted younger brother rake, the union of the right couple poised to inherit an estate, a punished and disciplined tyrannical guardian, and even a long-lost son restored to his estate and generously dispensing largesse to bring the play to a happy conclusion. What spins out centrifugally on a tangent at the end is the fact that the play rewards a trickster's calculated if not callous supplanting of a friend in his marriage bed.

Manley, a typical down-and-out younger brother figure used to living beyond his means, has eloped with the daughter of a rich merchant Learcut, who, nouveau riche that he is from his humble origins as a cheese monger, has married up and taken on airs. So Learcut considers Manley

unworthy of his daughter, refuses to yield her £8000 portion, and ties him
up in lawsuits till he is in virtual debtors' exile abroad. There Manley
meets the scapegrace Hazard, to whom he tells his entire story. A
proto–Martin Guerre, Hazard steals enough information and identifying
tokens—including scars—to impersonate Manley and to complete the un-
consummated marriage on a stolen night nine years later.

When Hazard's Town friend and comrade in impecuniousness, Underwit, balks at Hazard's scam, Hazard crows younger brother/trickster
doctrine with a flair:

> I will not
> Stain my Family: a Younger Brother of the house of
> *Mercury,* and baulk at any thing that's not impossible! [I, 3]

Underwit protests that Hazard "swore" to Manley he would help reinstate him with his wife (5). Hazard responds outrageously,

> I'le forget that; for men whose Lands and Wealth
> Lie in this Circle   [*Pointing to his Head.*]
> Must not stick at trifles.
> . . . If I
> Miscarry, hang me up for a *Pryapus* to scare
> High flying Wits.

Even as a scarecrow to other Town tricksters his enormous phallus would
signal his threat not to the City or the Country but to the Town itself.

Pretending that a rich uncle has left him a wealthy merchant, Hazard
earns the approval of Learcut, who wants to know only if in their night of
stolen love the bedded couple have begotten a grandson to be his heir.
Hazard plans to work fast to secure himself, his "wife," and Learcut's plate
and jewels. He loads the latter on a ship he won gambling, which appropriately lies at "Cuckolds Haven" (III, 28). That reference underscores
the fact that Hazard has indeed cuckolded a member of his own class, a
transgression that in the tragedy of the period has deadly consequences
(Otway's *The Orphan,* Southerne's *The Fatal Marriage* [to extend my
period a few years to mention an immensely popular play with a quite similar plot]). And what about Mrs. Manley? She is not entirely convinced
Hazard is really her husband. But her state of mind matters not to this son
of Mercury: Hazard plans to share her with Underwit when they reach
America. Meanwhile, pretending to have been robbed by his servant, he
cons £1000 out of Learcut (shades of Owmuch and Furnish) and smuggles him on board, planning to plunder his household down to a
jointstool. Hazard's plot is sadistic: Learcut is incarcerated in scary cir-

cumstances, and Hazard returns to Mrs. Manley dripping wet, informing her that Learcut, trying to save money on passage and insisting on sculling himself out to the ship, unfortunately hit a buoy and was dragged under by his bag of guineas. Hazard narrates the feigned disaster with relish and concludes maliciously, "Yet he had the comfort, which no other Usurer ever had, to have his Gold go with him" (33).

Inevitably, Manley returns, demanding his own. Hazard, upbraiding himself for having left Manley wherewithal to return, exclaims, "Had I only taken order for his Diet [that is, poisoned him!] he might have stay'd there yet, and not like an unmannerly Cuckold have interrupted me in my banquet on his Spouse. Wit repair this Errour, or thou shalt for ever do pennance in durty sheets, and wast thy Treasury in writing speeches for the City Pageants" (IV.iii, 38). Hazard determines to brazen it out. Again when Underwit protests at his devilish scheme, Hazard invokes his deity:

> Commit not Sacriledge to Mercury;
> Nor rob him of his honour, he's the God of Coyners boy, and
> Sublimates his wit.
> He flies into my fancy when I'm mov'd there. [39]

This Jonsonian trickster confronts Manley, affirms *his* identity as Manley, claims Mrs. Manley as *his* property even as she swoons in recognition of her error. At this moment of deadly rivalry, Manley reaches for his sword, only to be arrested by Underwit and the watch, who take him off to prison. And when Mrs. Manley complains bitterly to Hazard, he offers her libertine doctrine: "How many Women whose names stand white in the Records of Fame, have acted willingly what you were wrought by fraud to suffer; only they keep it from the publique knowledge, and therefore they are innocent. How many Fair ones, were this your story acted in a Play, would come to see it sitting by their Husbands, and secretly accuse themselves of more. So full of spots and brakes is humane life, but only we see all things by false lights, which hide defects, and gloss 'ore what's amiss" (IV.v, 46). All Mrs. Manley has to do is become Wycherley's Lady Fidget, Restoration comedy's greatest hypocrite. Instead, she informs Hazard that though she has come to love him and forgives him, she can live and sin with him no more. Hazard acts as if he is moved, but in the next moment he is callous when her maid reports her attempted suicide, and he continues to plot with Underwit their escape with Learcut's entire fortune, having inherited his (supposedly) posthumous estate through Mrs. Manley.

Surprisingly, however, Hazard visits Manley in prison, assures him Learcut is really alive and Mrs. Manley is still a virgin, and offers to reinstate Manley, maintaining that such was his plan all along. Hazard is no sentimentalist, though. If Manley refuse his offer, he will really drown Learcut and suborn witnesses to send Manley to Tyburn for being a highwayman. In other words, Hazard forces Manley to accept his word that Manley has not been cuckolded. Manley capitulates, but the bone sticks in his throat: he'll believe her "unstain'd"; if not, "I am not the first Gentleman hath borne / A Horn in's Crest" (V, 62). A bit like the Prince of Cléves (either de LaFayette's or Lee's), when Hazard offers to swear, Manley stops him, "for an Oath / Will not make me believe a tittle more" (62).

The apparent denouement brings both men to Learcut's (who, having been sufficiently chastened, has been released by Underwit). Hazard presents Manley to his wife, insisting his entire scam was performed to convince Learcut of Manley's value. Hazard asks only permission to visit occasionally as a friend, and Mrs. Manley willingly agrees to frequent visits. The arrangement is critically unstable, and Manley repeatedly murmurs aside about being a cuckold. The implication is that his cuckoldom will be reconfirmed in every one of those visits. We too cannot believe that this son of Mercury will become a gracious loser. It would be like the Prince and Princess of Clèves inviting the duc de Nemours to Sunday dinner every week.

So the playwright rewrites the denouement. Underwit turns out to be Learcut's long-lost son. He seeks from his sister aside the truth about her chastity, and she apparently tells him, for he now brokers a different resolution. Underwit offers Manley his wife's portion. Manley agrees, happy to be rid of the "Skittish Jade, and have money to boot" (V, 69). But Underwit really needs not his cooperation, for more than seven years has elapsed and by law Mrs. Manley is free. Learcut offers Hazard his daughter's hand. Sounding like Dorimant, he forswears all his "wild follies and debaucheries" (70). But his mercurial puckishness is not all gone, for, with regard to their already having consummated their future marriage, he wittily proclaims, "'[T]is true I have had her before hand but that's but being my own Cuckold" (69). Thus the audience dodges a silver bullet aimed at the heart of its belief in the ideology of the ruling class: that they (we) take care of their (our) own. Yet would not they—the Town husbands themselves, this time, not the Cits—leave the theater muttering aside, like Manley, "I'm a cuckold, I just know it, whatever the playwright says. Hasn't he informed me what sins my wife conceals as she sits beside me?"

Wycherley's *The Country-Wife* (1675) is certainly the best known, probably the greatest of Restoration subversive comedies. Juxtaposed to the centripetal movement of Harcourt and Alithea toward marriage, complete with the £5000 portion she was in danger of losing, is the centrifugal movement of Horner, his ladies, and the Country who is rapidly becoming a Town wife. Horner is the unconverted rake, whose great sexual energy remains uncontained and, combined with his great trickster wit, therefore threatens to disrupt the orderly transmission of power and property.

On the surface the play features interclass cuckoldry. Though Wycherley is somewhat vague about his class, Sir Jaspar Fidget is described as "this grave Man of business" (I.i, 262), preoccupied with the "business" of the Court (passim); moreover, he neglects what the Cavaliers consider his proper business with his wife (she says hilariously in the closing tag of Act II, "Who for his business, from his Wife will run;/Takes the best care, to have her bus'ness done" [290]). Clearly, Sir Jaspar lacks Cavalier taste, manners, and the ability to value his wife. He looks very much like a City knight who has enough money to have gained interest at Court, probably over trade matters.

The Country squire Pinchwife, who is about to be cuckolded himself, warns Sparkish, apparently a parvenu member of the lesser gentry with only a "crackt title" (I.i, 268), to go ahead and "be a Cuckold, like a credulous Cit" (II.i, 280) by allowing Harcourt to court his fiancé before his face. And Pinchwife himself is twice compared to an alderman (IV.i, 331; V.ii, 342), once proclaiming he must endure cuckolding with "a City-patience" (III.ii, 310). So there is a running analogy between these Country and City fools who obviously deserve to be cuckolded. If the gallant is in the ascendant in this play, to use John Harrington Smith's phrase, it is because he represents not just class superiority (we learn that Horner's estate and lineage are far superior to Sparkish's [V.ii, 347]) but the superiority of that subset of class represented by the Town wits, a privileged minority that distinguishes itself from not only Cits but Country boobies because it is the jet set identified with the Town and the Court as the loci of real power in the kingdom.

Perhaps if Wycherley were hauled before some tribunal to answer charges that he attacked the class he was patronized to defend, he might answer that he meant no more than other Cit-cuckolding comedies. But what is subversive about *The Country-Wife* is the ambiguity of the class status of the *women of quality*. Ubiquitous is this phrase in the mouths of Sir Jaspar's wife, sister, and cousin. And while Wycherley might puckishly maintain he meant City ladies, their language ramifies largely. The ladies complain that they are neglected by "Men of parts, great acquaintance, and quality" (II, 283), who spend their attention on lower-class women. In response Lady Fidget utters an immortal line: "'[T]is an errant shame Women of quality shou'd be so slighted; methinks, birth, birth, shou'd go for something; I have known Men admired, courted, and followed for their titles only." Maybe as the wife of a City knight she is taking on airs and wants to be pursued because she is a "Lady." But one can understand why the upper-class women apparently took umbrage at Wycherley's play (see the dedication to and the discussion of the play within *The Plain Dealer*). He appears to travesty them as well. Mrs. Squeamish adds, "Ay, one wou'd think Men of honour shou'd not love no more, than marry out of their own rank." The conversation returns to the topic of men of quality breeding beneath themselves, then surprisingly reveals that women of quality are forced to the same expedient.

In the great banquet scene, the ladies apostrophize the brimmer of wine as that which makes husbands blind, gallants bold, and, Squeamish adds, "for want of a Gallant, the Butler lovely in our eyes" (V, 350). Restoration society—if not all patriarchal societies—was prepared to accept the system of *droit du seigneur* for draining off surplus sexual energy. But not a *droit de madame*. The system of honor and reputation was intended to control women's sexual activity to protect against adulteration. Intraclass adultery would be bad enough for women, but interclass would be absolute anathema. In his mad protection of his sister, Crowne's Lord Bellguard of *Sir Courtly Nice* refuses to allow a good-looking servant in the house, protesting, according to Leonora, "he will not be brother in law to er'e [*sic*] a butler or footman in England" (I.220-21).

Such cross-class transgression is not the threat Horner among the ladies represents, however. And the ladies of the Restoration, having internalized the sexual discipline of their patriarchy, may have been the front line of protesters. But the men of quality would have been the ones to fear this don juan in their seraglio.[1] Wycherley's women obviously prefer upper-class gallants, if they can get them. When Wycherley thus satirizes women of quality, the satire is a communication *between men,* for the threat is between men—of the same class.[2] In one of the most extremely aggressive acts of sexuality in all of Restoration comedy—the famous/infamous china scene—Wycherley stages not class dominance, not even gender dominance primarily. Just behind the partition closing off the inner stage (and I would use French doors with sheer curtains so the audience could see a shadowy Horner tupping a willing, frolicking Lady Fidget, then she topping him), a Town blade copulates with a woman of quality. That calls for Abelard's punishment, turning Horner into the eunuch he impersonates.[3] The audience's position is that of Dr. Quack, Horner's confidant and, in effect, pimp, the voyeur who watches from behind the screen not so much Horner's cuckolding activity but the cuckolds' delivering of their women to him. The men in that audience would have to suffer ambivalence: they could say, "It ain't me," because the cuck-olds are contemptible Cits and bumpkins; but because of the fluidity of the ladies' category, they must also say, "Hey, that could be my wife!"

That the play is not just a winking joke between men but much more threatening can also be seen by the response Horner's omnivorousness—and the rampant, aggressive male promiscuity it represents—provokes. Several times in the play, even the booby Pinchwife contemplates reaching or actually reaches for his sword: to threaten his wife and his sister but to kill Horner for at least breach of promise with his sister if not adultery with his wife. Perhaps the audience perceives the saber rattling as mere blustering. But when Horner's best friend, Harcourt, who has sought advice from Horner about how to win that sister, Alithea, from the fop-pish Sparkish, now having won her accosts that friend for tarnishing her reputation, Horner's choice to protect his Country tart instead of honor-ing his friendship and class solidarity with Harcourt causes serious trepida-tion in the system.[4] Harcourt defends the only woman of real (moral) quality in the play against Horner's (passive) aspersions on her honor when he denies not he received her into his chamber. By his own (witty) admission, Horner is "on the criminal's side [Margery's] gainst the inno-cent [Alithea]" (V, 355). The two Town wits then have this unwitty ex-change aside, that is, between (the real) men:

> *Harcourt:* I must now be concern'd for this Ladies [Alithea's] Honour.
> *Horner:* And I must be concern'd for a Ladies [Margery's] Honour too.
> *Harcourt:* This Lady has her Honour, and I will protect it [implying his lady has not her honor: nb. the strength of the auxiliary "will"].
> *Horner:* My Lady has not her Honour, but has given it me to keep, and I will preserve it [a strong answering "will"].
> *Harcourt:* I understand you not [How can he when he thinks Horner's a eunuch?].
> *Horner:* I wou'd not have you. [356]

So Horner, to his peril, chooses his scam over his friendship, despite all those early protestations that homosocial camaraderie is superior to heterosexual activity. He has fractured homosocial bonding, and only Quack's and Lucy's lies avoid the inevitable deadly rivalry between Horner and Harcourt. But when the play concludes with no poetical justice that makes Horner really impotent, leaving him instead potent and still on the make, the audience laughs at its own expense: the women of quality ner-vously because they have been misognyistically slandered; the men of quality nervously because at some level they recognize that class solidarity is just a pleasing necessary fiction. If Richard Braverman is right about the symbolic link between Horner's autonomy and the king's ("Rake's

Progress," 152-54), then Charles II's own promiscuity itself gives the lie to that solidarity and sanctions its rupture. If the king can do it, then a for-tiori so can Horner, Rochester, Buckingham, and any other don juan, even one's best (aristocratic) friend.[5]

At the climax of Otway's *The Atheist; or, The Second Part of the Souldiers Fortune* (1683), the title character, in a flush of repentance when he re-ceives what he believes is a mortal wound, confesses to a feigned cleric that he has committed adultery "With my Bosom Friend's Wife, and one that deserv'd much better of me" (V.821-22). The line has relevance not so much to Daredevil's situation; it merely provides the occasion for comic business between him, played by Cave Underhill, and the cleric, played by Tony Leigh, as the latter, really the unscrupulous old Cavalier Beau-gard Sr., attempts to ferret out the name of the woman for his own promiscuous purposes. But Daredevil's seemingly throwaway line has spe-cial relevance to the action being conducted around him, as the vengeful jealous lover Lucrece manipulates Beaugard Jr. into an assignation with his best friend Courtine's wife, Sylvia, even as Courtine, believing Beaugard to be frolicking with his own mistress, Porcia, guards the door to the inner closet of Daredevil's bedchamber behind which the couple commits. When Beaugard and Sylvia emerge, Courtine is furious, and Beaugard can only meekly petition, "Nay, let us not quarrel *Ned:* I'll give thee a friendly account of this matter to morrow between our selves, in the mean time be satisfi'd, I have not wrong'd thee" (933-36). If Daredevil, in the symbolic center of this scene, be not the real atheist (manifesting his fear of an af-terlife of divine retribution), he is surrounded by metaphorical atheists to the patriarchal system and its underwriting religious code.[6]

Superficially, *The Atheist* resembles another *mature woman trickster mans her land* play. Porcia, "Daughter of a very rich Merchant" and "the onely Heiress of an immense Fortune," has been twice tyrannized over by male guardians: first by the "Raskals" who virtually "sold" her to the high-est bidder (II.137-42); now that she is a widow by a fanatically misogynis-tic brother-in-law, who unfortunately controls the great part of her fortune. Her deceased husband, in the ultimate abuse of wardship, has be-queathed her, as if she were a completely objectified piece of his property, to his rival from whom he had won her. The brother-in-law, Theodoret, and the intended fiancé, Gratian, are nearly as cruel to her as the duchess of Malfi's brothers. They imprison her, and Theodoret repeatedly screams misogynistic rant in her face, justifying himself thus: "[I]f possible, I would not have a good Breed spoil'd" (V.247-48). So Porcia, who has met Beaugard on a ramble in disguise and who has found a kindred spirit that despises marriage as much as she, nevertheless determines to marry

Beaugard, to give herself and her remaining jointure to him, in order to escape patriarchal tyranny: "I dread my Brother's Fury, / Ev'n worse than Matrimony. Here, Sir, I yield my self / Up yours for ever" (IV.584-86). She justifies herself with the rhetoric of mid-century rebels: "With hopes of Liberty I am indeed [transported]: it is an English Woman's natural Right. Do not our Fathers, Brothers and Kinsmen often, upon pretence of it, bid fair for Rebellion against their Soveraign; And why ought not we, by their Example, to rebel as plausibly against them?" (V.430-34).

Porcia's appeal to the rhetoric of revolution of the mid-century is, of course, problematic. Her word "pretence" undercuts the political rebellion of the Civil War; it nevertheless does not fully undercut her articulation of a right of women "to rebel as plausibly against" patriarchal tyrants. As usual in Restoration social comedy, Porcia's rebellion cuts not across class lines. Moreover, the Beaugard of the sequel of *The Souldiers Fortune* has inherited his uncle's estate. So through their trickster machinations and despite their reservations about marriage, the right couple comes together at the end of the play to possess a large combined estate and to beget heirs for it. The marriage seals the transfer of Porcia's jointure under the protection of her man. No structural damage has been done to the system itself.

This centripetal motion of the ending cannot obliterate the centrifugal motion of the other plot, however. The discovery of her apparent adultery has precipitated Sylvia's abrupt departure in disgrace and Courtine's bitter proclamation as she leaves of a separation not so much in fact as in spirit: "Your humble Servant, my Dearest! I am only glad of this fair opportunity, to be rid of you, my Dearest: henceforth, my Dearest, I shall drink my drink, my Dearest, I shall whore my Dearest; and so long as I can pimp so handsomly for you, my Dearest, I hope if ever we return into the Countrey, you'll wink at a small Fault now and then with the Dairy-Wench, or Chamber-Maid, my Dearest" (V.942-49). In other words, because the unscrupulous Lucrece, out of pure malice, dons breeches and seduces Sylvia into rebelling against the double standard and behaving just like her husband, who has come to Town to escape the tedium of their marriage by whoring, Sylvia must suffer the consequences within a system that has not been radically altered. She is deprived of any moral ground whence to condemn her husband's adulteries; his *droit du seigneur* has been reaffirmed with a vengeance.

Not since Dryden's *Marriage A-La-Mode* had there been a Restoration comedy that dealt so relentlessly with what critics so often and so idly speculate about: What *really* will be the fate of Dorimant's marriage to Harriet? As I have argued in *Word as Bond* (76-79), the unhappy married couple of that tragicomedy's comic plot rediscover not only their attraction to each other but the pragmatic basis for the patriarchal code of the word, for leagues and covenants that control promiscuity and establish property rights in a woman's reproductive capacity. Otway's Courtine and Sylvia make no such rediscovery. Neither is heard from again as the play closes. Moreover, the play ruthlessly dissects their apparent right-couple marriage, complete with estate, at the end of the original *Souldiers Fortune* by looking into its future.

Even the misogamist Beaugard has too rosy a picture of marriage. Witness this exchange with Courtine, who has just escaped the prison of the dismal Country house for the freedom of the Town:

> *Beaugard:* Married! That is, thou call'st a Woman thou likest by the name of Wife: Wife and t'other thing begin with a Letter. Thou liest with her when thy Appetite calls thee, keepest the Children thou begettest of her Body; allowest her Meat, Drink, and Garments, fit for her Quality, and thy Fortune; and when she grows heavy upon thy Hands, what a Pox, 'tis but a Separate-maintenance, kiss and part, and there is an end of the Bus'ness.
>
> *Courtine:* Alas, Beaugard, thou art utterly mistaken; Heav'n knows it is quite on the contrary: For I am forced to call a Woman I do not like, by the name of Wife; and lie with her, for the most part, with no Appetite at all; must keep the Children that, for ought I know, any Body else may beget of her Body; and for Food and Rayment, by her good will she would have them both Fresh three times a day: Then for Kiss and part, I may kiss and kiss my Heart out, but the Devil a bit shall I ever get rid of her. . . . By the vertue of Matrimony, and long Cohabitation, we are grown so really One Flesh, that I have no more Inclination to hers, than to eat a piece of my own. [I.214-36]

Moreover, Sylvia infringes on his *droit du seigneur* among Country maids, so he has come to the Town and hopes he "will not see Country, Wife, nor Children agen these seven years" (285-86). The economic necessity built into the sense of the ending of social comedy is thus jeopardized: Courtine affects insecurity with regard to the paternity the system is designed to protect. It is part of the comic wisdom of Dryden's play that men are really no more secure than Courtine here but must, as the witty Doralice insists, rely on trust. But the mutual trust of the erstwhile gay couple Courtine and Sylvia has gone the way, it would seem, of all flesh.

Courtine seeks the escapism of Beaugard's unbridled libertinism. They wax rhapsodic like new versions of Rains and Bevil, Bruce and Longvil:

> *Beaugard:* Is not this Living now? Who that knew the Sweets of Liberty, the uncontroll'd Delights the Free-man tastes of, Lord of his own

Hours, King of his own Pleasures, just as Nature meant him first;
Courted each Minute by all his Appetites,
Which he indulges, like a bounteous Master,
That's still supply'd with various full Enjoyments;
And no intruding Cares make one Thought bitter. . . .
Courtine: Nay, not one Rub, to interrupt the Course
Of a long, rolling, gay, and wanton Life.
Methinks the Image of it is like a Laune
In a rich flow'ry Vale, its Measure long,
Beauteous its Prospect, and at the End
A shady peaceful Glade; where, when the pleasant Race is over,
We glide away, and are at rest for ever. [III.1-16]

Of course, since Beaugard has inherited an estate that is "well Tenanted" and yields £2000 per annum based on "old Rents" (I.245-46), he can afford this life of hedonistic luxury. Courtine too, supported by the estate for which he sold his liberty to marry Sylvia, can also afford to leave his responsibilities in the Country and take a sabbatical in the Town. Beaugard's insouciance is an affectation, for the very City, Court, and Country pursuits he pretends to escape by his Town bachelor existence are those that sustain it:

Who, that knew this [libertine life and philosophy], would let himself be a Slave/To the vile Customs that the World's debaucht in? Who'd interrupt his needful Hours of Rest, to rise and yawn in a Shop upon *Cornhill?* Or, what's as bad, make a sneaking Figure in a Great Man's Chamber, at his Rising in a Morning? Who would play the Rogue, Cheat, Lie, Flatter, Bribe, or Pimp, to raise an Estate for a Blockhead of his own begetting, as he thinks, that shall waste it as scandalously as his Father got it? Or who, *Courtine,* would marry, to beget such a Blockhead? [III.17-26]

His own uncle and Sylvia's and Porcia's fathers were the ones who engaged in such pursuits so that Beaugard and Courtine and their Town ilk can afford the Town posture of scorning them. Yet the repeated suggestion that the aristocratic patriarch cannot be sure of the parentage of his heir is subversive. Instead of the Town cocksureness of the Cavalier who insists his City cuckold ought to be grateful for the nobility he has contributed to the Cit's blockhead race, Beaugard insists no race is pure or noble. His misogamist stance therefore threatens not only the continuity of his own patrilineage but the ideology that underwrites it.

Beaugard's patrilineage is problematized already, for his father, jealous that his eldest brother bequeathed his estate to his nephew instead of his younger brother, goes so far as to join forces with Theodoret in an armed assault on his own son. Ironically, "Father," as the text calls Beaugard Sr., has from the opening of the play branded his son "a Rebel" because he refuses to marry—and thus carry on the lineage (I.74). Indeed, Father has considered Son a rebel since his son flirted with Father's whore as a youngster (Beaugard maintains he did nothing more than call a whore a whore). And Son describes a relationship that corresponds with Beaugard's and Courtine's antipastoral descriptions of ill-begotten children and their treatment:

> [T]he next thing you did [after getting married yourself], was, you begot me; the Consequence of which was as follows: As soon as I was born, you sent me to Nurse, where I suckt two years at the dirty Dugs of a foul-feeding Witch, that liv'd in a thatch't Sty upon the neighb'ring Common; as soon as I was big enough, that you might be rid of me, you sent me to a Place call'd a School, to be slash't and box't by a thick-fisted Blockhead, that could not read himself; where I learnt no Letters, nor got no Meat, but such as the old *Succubus* his Wife bought at a stinking Price, so over-run with Vermin, that it su'd to crawl home after her. [I.7-18]

Blockheads beget blockheads who are taught by blockheads. So much for the breeding of a gentleman. Beaugard survives being thrown out by Father only because of the generosity of Uncle, whose £200 allows him to buy a commission and go to war.

Of course, Beaugard is himself no blockhead but a Town wit, and he is no absolute rebel or atheist against patriarchy: no matter what his father does to him, he loans him money (which he knows Father will lose gambling) and refuses to contradict him downright or talk about him behind his back: "Prithee [Courtine] no more on't [maligning Father for his gambling], tis an irreverent Theme; and next to Atheism, I hate making merry with the Frailties of my Father" (II.11-13).[7] But the fabric of patriarchalism has been made threadbare—not only by Beaugard's actions with Sylvia, Courtine's desertion of his right-stuff marriage, Beaugard and Courtine's disparaging of estate building and managing, and Father's denial of his son—but by the Atheist's uttering what cannot be said: when Courtine argues against atheism by insisting that religion and its accompanying fear of hell are what "makes People live in Honesty, Peace, and Union one towards another," Daredevil responds, "Fear of Hell! No, Sir, 'tis fear of Hanging. Who would not steal, or do murder, every time his Fingers itch't at it, were it not for fear of the Gallows? Do not you, with all your Religion, swear almost as often as you speak? break and prophane the Sabbath? lie with your Neighbours Wives? and covet their Estates, if they be better than your own? Yet those things are forbid by Religion, as well as Stealing and Cutting of Throats are" (II.388-99).

So when Father would cut his son's throat and steal his estate— "Now, if my Rebel be run through the Midriff in this business, I am the next Heir at Law, and the two thousand Pounds a year is my own, *declaro* . . . I am none of thy Father" (IV.79-81, 626)—he merely acts like all power-seeking, hypocritical rebels against the system who mask their transgressions behind its ideological veils. Indeed, the rebels are not rebels at all but exploiters. Father's denial repudiates a system so corrupt as to hang at the end of the play by the thin thread of his son's persistent loyalty. But that loyalty is not vindicated by divine providence, by some transcendent system of retributive and distributive justice. Beaugard, acting as reconciling patriarch at the end, definitively attributes the dynamic of the denouement to "Chance" (V.1040). By sheer force of personality, Beaugard assumes control, consigning his father to a nursing-home existence with the placebos of wine and tobacco but no estate-destroying gambling; forcing Theodoret, whose private army has been disarmed and confined, to accept the situation willy-nilly; and apparently consigning Courtine to silence. Yet does the audience still hear echoes of this exchange?

> *Courtine:* Nay, when Cuckolds or Brothers fight for the Reputation of a back-sliding Wife or Sister, it is a very pretty Undertaking, doubtless. As for example; I am a Cuckold now.
>
> *Beaugard:* All in good time, *Ned;* do not be too hasty. [The dramatic foreshadowing is palpable!]
>
> *Courtine:* And being much troubled in Spirit, meeting with the Spark that has done me the Honour, with a great deal of respect I make my Address,—as thus,—*Most Noble Sir, you have done me the Favour to lie with my Wife.*
>
> *Beaugard:* Very well.
>
> *Courtine: All I beg of you, is, that you would do your best endeavour to run me through the Guts to morrow morning, and it will be the greatest Satisfaction in the World.*
>
> *Beaugard:* Which the good-natur'd Whoremaster does very decently; so down falls the Cuckold at *Barn-elms,* and rises again next day at *Holborn* in a Ballad. [II.259-74]

If these echoes linger—and how could they not?—then even if we were to imagine the typical duel between Beaugard and Courtine, there would be no triumph of justice, no vindication of the wronged Cavalier that we would expect from his ideology. If Beaugard has the power to make his tupping his best friend's wife good, so be it. Nor would the audience not hear, through the mention of Barn-elms, echoes of the famous duel fought there between the duke of Buckingham and the earl of Shrewsbury (see Ghosh's note). In other words, Otway's play has revealed the lack of any real class solidarity between Town wits as part of a larger picture of the naked rapacity behind the facade of Stuart ideology.

It is as if Wycherley in *The Plain Dealer* (1676) explores the Courtine figure from another angle—that of the cuckolded Cavalier who takes his vengeance. As others, most notably Peter Holland (ch. 6), have noted, the play frustrates almost all our expectations. Let me focus on a set he does not discuss, the expectations of other buddy-cuckolding plays. The cuckolder is usually more attractive than the cuckoldee, from Bevil and Woodly in *Epsom Wells* to Hazard and Manley in *The Mistaken Husband* to Beaugard and Courtine in *The Atheist*. And there is usually a cover-up, a word passed between men that nothing really happened, a word accepted in order to avoid deadly rivalry between members of the hegemonic aristocratic subclass, the Town Wits. But the original cuckolder in *The Plain Dealer*, Vernish, is less attractive than his cuckoldee, Manly, who unwittingly cuckolds him in turn, not knowing his ex-betrothed is his best friend's wife. And although the cuckolding action has taken place in the dark—only a nice guy like Percy Adams could make a case that it has not taken place—rather than being covered up all is brought to light as Manly exposes the new cuckoldee to witnesses.

In other words, *The Plain Dealer* is, in this one aspect at least, more aggressive than the buddy-cuckolding plays I have discussed so far. Because critics have been looking for its meaning in a clear moral message or have simply been throwing up their hands to conclude that it has no meaning but no-meaning itself, they have, at least until recently, not seen the sense of its ending. Now, thanks to important essays by Helen Burke and Richard Braverman, we have begun to read the play for its ideological significance. According to Burke's essay, the most thorough, the two plots of the play are related through the law and Lacan's Law of the Father, both placed in the service of the perpetuation of patriarchal control of women and property and both threatened by uppity women ("Family Property"). To put my spin on Burke's reading, the play is a comedy because the ending is a restoration, indeed a re-restoration of Stuart ideology as its Restoration compromise was beginning to crack in the mid-1670s when, Braverman argues, "the political wind shifted with the parliamentary reaction to the Declaration of Indulgence" ("Rake's Progress," 150). But this restoration is effected in the play not with the subtle masking of social comedy but with the aggression of the Cit-cuckolding plays. And it has revealed too much to be able to paper over the cracks in Stuart ideology.

Unlike the typical pair of Town wits that commonly begins a comedy at the center of things—of Town, of the women, of signification itself—Manly and Freeman are eccentric in that they are naval officers sans ship and Cavaliers sans fortunes. Freeman is a younger brother without prospects, and Manly appears to have sold his estate to escape the degenerate world of the Town and to venture his remaining capital for a fortune in the East Indies. The radical sign of the degeneracy of the Town, which throughout the play is a synecdoche for the World because it is the center of the subculture that dominates not only England but the increasing world of its imperial conquests, that radical sign is *distrust*. One cannot trust appearances, for everyone is a self-interested hypocrite, and the ethical core of aristocratic mores has been violated by an inconstant lover and an inconstant friend. Burke is right to point to the setting of Act III, the courts at Westminster Hall, as crucial to the meaning of the play, for they, the symbolic site of the preservation of words and bonds, are instead the symbolic site of corrupted words and bonds. More important, on the material rather than the symbolic level, they are the site of the transition from the old aristocratic to the emergent bourgeois order (or, to put it more accurately, from a Court-dominated to a Parliament-dominated oligarchy). The latter, with its attendant lawyers, is encroaching on the estates of the former. A defender of the old order would of course portray this transition as disorder. And what better, more traditional way to signify disorder than two uppity women.

The ending of the play is a wish-fulfillment, as previous critics have argued, but they have missed the wish: the reestablishment of the establishment, figured not just in the witty dominance of Manly over the fools and fops of the play but especially in the rape of the uppity women. The Widow Blackacre, who would dare to control her dead husband's estate by keeping it from her son and from other men wanting to marry her and put her back into *covert baron*, is finally tricked by Freeman at the very moment she is tied to a chair for what the audience assumes to be a rape until Major Oldfox assaults her with words instead. Another audience expectation, following the social comedy pattern of the union of a witty male trickster with an equally witty widow, is frustrated at the end of the play: Freeman does not marry the rich widow but instead through blackmail exacts an annuity plus the payment of his debts.

Why the frustration of this particular expectation? To make the ending that of satire? I think not. After all, the trickster has succeeded, and we are invited to celebrate his success. The meaning has to do with the play's misogyny: whatever its psychological implications, if the revolutionary socioeconomic realities of the late seventeenth century are figured as the disorder of uppity women, it makes more ideological sense for Freeman finally not to marry the widow but deprive her of what she secretly wants, the "Consideration" in recompense for what she gives up out of her estate, the "duty" of the kept gallant (V, 509)—a duty Freeman cleverly frees himself from by changing the metaphoric terms of settlement to those of divorce. The widow reveals at the very end that she is a typical woman, who really just wants a real man, at least for sexual service. And the worst punishment she can suffer is to be deprived of one and, more appropriate for superannuation, to be left prey to the Oldfoxes of the world. After all, the Widow Blackacre was played by an aging Katherine Corey, who a few years earlier had created Duffett's fetid, grotesque amorous old woman in the play of that name.[8]

If the one plot of the play ends with the encroachment upon the uppity woman's estate for the freeing of a real man from dependence, the other plot ends with the dispossessed dispossessing the dispossessors and regaining a modicum of his estate. He exacts his revenge on the inconstant lover and friend who dispossessed him (of his jewels as well as supposed place in their hearts) by two acts of sheer male aggression to reestablish dominance: a form of rape and a duel.[9] He tups his rival's wife in a bed trick with his real phallus, a phallus so real that Olivia is absolutely "sure" the one with her in her bedroom was not a woman (V, 490), and he defeats his rival with his symbolic phallus, his sword. His right to dominate at the end—the right to dominate of the real, loyal Cavaliers, so loyal they would sink their ship containing their own wealth rather than have His Majesty's Ship captured by the enemy Dutch—is symbolized by his being rewarded with Fidelia's estate: the faithful Fidelia, who has followed Manly everywhere and has finally shown even her timid courage by attempting to divert Vernish to fence with her during the duel. Manly's view of a world of radical distrust is altered at the end, his faith in it restored by a new friend, who is enough of a plain dealer to tell him his motivation for reconciling with the world is tempered by the mercenary concern of Fidelia's estate, and by a new, un-uppity lover, a sign of word-as-bond. His reconciliation to the "World" of the Town (V, 515), then, is not intended to be psychologically realistic; it is symbolic of the restoration of Stuart ideology, that the aristocratic men of "intrinsick worth" (I, 394) deserve to rule and deserve unquestioning loyalty. And Fidelia is a figure for that loyalty, for the lands of England, for the land of England itself, reunited once again with her lawful lord who has been in exile.

But if the ending of the play is comic in its action of the restoration of aristocratic order, it is nevertheless subversive. Not just epistemologically, as others, most notably Holland and Markley have argued, but ideologically as well, as Markley began to analyze (*Two-Edg'd Weapons*, 178-94) and as Burke has clearly demonstrated ("Family Property"). It is subversive in their sense because it has revealed that its ideology is based not on the traditional discursive codes that made it appear natural, for those codes are threadbare. I would add that the aggressive actions taken to restore the ancien régime allow us to peep through the worn ideological garment to see the naked truth: its base is not a Christian ethic with its attendant metaphysic, which critics including myself have mistakenly sought in vain, nor any real aristocratic order, which is belied throughout by repeated satiric disclosures of genealogical impurity, but is, as it always has been, sheer power. The misanthrope Manly triumphs not because of virtue but because of *virtù*—because he becomes a trickster whose wronged phallus asserts itself in the dark and reestablishes dominance. What makes this restoration more subversive than those of Cit-cuckolding comedies is that Manly has asserted himself against members of his own class who have broken their troth and thereby their class solidarity. The lingering question of the play is how long can the Court party and its hired guns, among them the playwrights, hold the Restoration compromise together.[10]

The most aggressive of all these buddy-cuckolding plays must be Otway's *Friendship in Fashion* (1678). The atmosphere of the play is extraordinarily predatory, with "malice" and "revenge" repeated key words of motivation. Goodvile, neither Cit nor Country bumpkin but a full-fledged Town wit, attempts to pawn off a cast mistress, his own cousin Victoria, on his best friend and fellow Town Wit, Truman; furthermore, he plans to seduce the fair Camilla, then pawn her off on another friend and fellow Town wit, Valentine. So Truman and Valentine plot to revenge themselves on this breach of class solidarity by Truman's cuckolding Goodvile with his beautiful, young, witty wife. Meanwhile, Lady Squeamish, described by Truman as a "decay'd woman with all the exquisite silliness and vanity of her Sex, yet none of the charms" (III.173-75), attempts revenge on Valentine for deserting her for the younger Camilla. And Malagene, the scandal mongering parasite whose name means "ill-bred," seems a very figure for the virulent malice of the play.

Friendship in Fashion features a couple of parvenu fools, Caper and Saunter, and a nouveau Country knight, Sir Noble Clumsy. But we cannot dismiss Malagene as just another parvenu, for he is Mrs. Goodvile's cousin; nor Lady Squeamish as the widow of a City knight, for her origin is never disclosed and she may well be the aging but still promiscuous daughter of a peer.[11] My point is that, as with *The Country-Wife*, the playwright has left the status of some of the satiric butts ambiguous enough for the audience to find no refuge in placing them in the class or status of the normal *punitive* characters of Restoration comedy. Moreover, there is no doubt of the stature of Goodvile, a fact emphasized by his being played by Betterton. Informed by Malagene that Truman and his wife had an assignation in the garden, Goodvile exclaims, "By this light I am a Cuckold, an Arrant Rank stinking Cuckold" (IV.520-21). This is not Nokes or Leigh running around the stage farcically screaming he is a cuckold. This is the Sir Lawrence Olivier of his time, not usually associated with satiric butt roles. Nor is his rhetoric farcical but (as with Sir Salomon) borders on the heroic rhetoric of the contemporary tragic protagonist Betterton so often played: "Now if I am not a Cuckold let any honest Wittall judg, ha, ha, ha. How it pleases me! Blood! Fire! and Daggers!" (V.45-46).

Goodvile's status is evidenced not only by his rhetoric. Truman and Mrs. Goodvile acknowledge he is no fool but "has Wit" (V.401-2) and is thus a worthy adversary. Moreover, he has power: the power to threaten Malagene with murder if he does not serve him; the power to assert his honor with his sword, which he twice draws against Truman; and the power of the lord of his manor, a power that produces "that shining Pelf that must support me in my pleasures," as Mrs. Goodvile taunts the disguised Goodvile come to trap her and Truman (V.549-50). Indeed, the play threatens to destroy the very basis of social continuity and class dominance as these class predators nearly effect implosion.

Mrs. Goodvile says that Goodvile's wit is exactly what will "be his ruin" (V.403). He is a comic overreacher, believing he can get away with dumping cast mistresses on friends and thus violating that code so special to Western aristocratic societies at least since Cicero wrote *De Amicitia*. Thus the title of the play indicates the inversion of tradition resulting in a dog-eat-dog world even in the ruling cohort. Believing he is seducing Camilla, Goodvile is tricked by his fellow wits into copulating with Lady Squeamish, giving Mrs. Goodvile the opportunity to wonderfully revile him: "[H]ave you a stomach so hot that it can digest Carrion that has been buzz'd about and blown upon by all the Flies in the Town? Or was it the fantasticalness of your Appetite, to try how so course a Dish would relish, after being cloyed with better feeding?" (IV.332-36). But Goodvile's first response to discovering his mistake is to displace his anger onto Victoria and Valentine, whom Lady Squeamish and he mistakenly believe to be the other couple in the garden. His outrage leads him to grab "Victoria" (who is really his wife) and call out "Valentine" (who is really Truman). Truman defends himself by insisting Goodvile had invited him to court Victoria. But he has also heard Goodvile accuse "Victoria" of perfidious falseness to him, her lover, and, announcing that he is "ready with my Sword to make good" (IV.240), hurls Goodvile's own perfidiousness in his teeth: "One would have thought Sir, that you who keep a generall Decoy here for Fools and Coxcombs, might have found one to have recompenced a Cast Mistress withall, and not have indeavour'd the betraying the Honour of a Gentleman and your Friend" (259-63). When Truman is subsequently "rough" with Lady Squeamish (280), rubbing salt into Goodvile's psychic wounds, Goodvile dares him to justify his own honor, and the two draw swords and fight until Valentine separates them before blood is spilled.

More threatening than even spilled blood in an intraclass duel, however, is the scandal that Goodvile allows to escape his own Town house and gardens. He defiantly proclaims in his wife's face and in front of witnesses that Victoria has been his mistress, thus publicly acknowledging not only adultery but incest. And his wife publicly upbraids him about his adultery with Lady Squeamish. The implosive fourth act repeatedly rings with the threat that Malagene will "publish" the scandal. Goodvile assures the distraught Victoria he can control the destructive forces he has unleashed by a cover-up. But his rhetoric upon his clandestine return from his feigned voyage out to the Country estate in order to trap Truman and his wife upon his return to Town reveals that he is on a course not only self- but society-destructive. He exclaims to the whores he has brought with him: "[S]ome hot-brain'd, Horn-mad Cuckold now would be for cutting of Throats; but I am resolved to turn a Civil, Sober, discreet Person, and hate blood-shed: No: I'l manage the matter so temperately that I'l catch her in his very Arms, then civilly Discard her, Bagg and Baggage, whilst you my dainty Doxies take possession of her Priviledges, and enter the Territories with Colours flying" (V.507-14). This ploy is not some Lysander-like posturing from Arrowsmith's *The Reformation,* for in just another minute or so Goodvile will respond to Truman's "basely done" by giving him the lie direct and pulling his sword again (V.643-48).

Goodvile means to dismantle the structures Restoration social comedy underwrites, the estate and the family. One whore will take her coach and six to the Exchange and a play, where she will entertain some amorous fop, Goodvile thus exchanging his wife for a "*Bona Roba*" as he calls her (522). His other whore will supplant his wife as "Housekeeper" and "manage all th'affairs of my Estate and Family, Ride up and down in my own Coach attended by my own Footmen; Nose my Wife where ere you meet, and if I had any, breed my Children" (525-28). This last duty would scramble the eggs in a way different from Careless in *The Careless Lovers.* If the traffic in marriage was designed to provide a proper vessel for aristocratic seed—and at best a proper helpmeet who indeed managed the aristocratic estate—then Goodvile's plan would replace the wife and children that are the proper end of comedy (and of society) with whores and bastards. We are sent back to Goodvile's earlier protestation to Victoria, "Leave thee! By Heav'n I'de sooner renounce my Family, and own my self the Bastard of a Rascal" (II.132-33). He is, in effect, the rascal who has renounced his family to breed bastards.

The system Goodvile threatens is that obscured by Restoration comedy but visible occasionally through the arras. Mrs. Goodvile's mocking reference to the pelf that supports her Town pleasures opens with a continuation of a mock pastoral she began earlier. Pretending she is unaware of Goodvile's presence in masquerade, she says tauntingly to Truman, "Ah were but Mr. *Goodvile* here now, what a happy Day might this be! But he is Melancholy and Forlorn in the Country, summoning in his Tenants and their Rents" (V.546-49). Earlier she feigns rhapsodic appreciation of his triumphal return to his Country estate:

> Oh what joy will fill each neighbouring Village! to hear our Landlords Honour's coming down. The Bells shall jangle out of Tune all Day; and at night the Curate of the Hamlet comes in the name of the whole Parish to bid his Patron welcome into the Country, and invite himself the next Lords Day to Dinner. . . . Then the next Morning our Tenants dainty Daughter is sent with a Present of Pippins of the largest Size, cull'd by the good old Drudg her Mother, which she delivers with a Curt'sie, and blushes in expectation of what his Worship will bestow upon her. . . . Then come the Country Squires, and their Dogs, the cleanlier sort of Creatures of the Two: Straight w'are invited to the noble Hunt, and not a Deer in all the Forest's safe. [V.69-88]

Mrs. Goodvile's mockery aside, Otway reminds us of the complicated Country power relations that enable Town lifestyle: the fawning sycophantic behavior so as to curry favor and not incur the wrath of the master of the manor. The ruthless exacting of those rents lies behind this remarkable exchange between Town wits and friends: Goodvile, his lust for Camilla growing warm, encounters Truman and Valentine at his soirée and flushes,

> *Goodvile:* Well, Gentlemen! Now you have left the Ladies, I hope there may be room near your hearts for a Bottle or two.
> *Truman:* Dear *Goodvile* thou art too pow'rful to be deny'd any thing. 'Tis a fine cool Evening, and a swift Glass or two now were seasonable and refreshing, to wash away the Toil and Fatigue of the Day.
> *Valentine:* After a man has been disturb'd with the publick Impertinences and Follies he meets withall abroad, he ought to recompence himself with a Friend and a Bottle in private at Night.
> *Goodvile:* Spoken like men that deserve the life you enjoy[.] [III.665-75]

Aristocratic ideology from Sarpedon's famous speech to Glaucus in *The Iliad* maintained that such men indeed *deserved the life they enjoy*, while the men who really toiled and became fatigued every day were simply obliterated from aristocratic literature except as the occasionally mentioned foot soldiers who won the Great Men's victories. Even Otway's casual references refer mainly to the mid-level managers, the curates and squires. Only the poor woman and her daughter, who understand perfectly how women get ahead down on the farm, are represented from the lowest class—only the sex slaves, not the field hands.

The play pulls back from the brink. Mrs. Goodvile, a trickster even more daring and resourceful than Truman, who has been praised repeatedly for her management of her husband, manipulates him in the final act to believe that her actions were all just a trial of Goodvile, an attempt to win him back through jealousy. She has said she could bring him to his knees, and she does—a gesture, he protests, "To let the World see how much a Fool I can be." "[A]rt thou Innocent?" he finally begs to know (V.722-23). When she protests that she is and exits "*in a rage*" (731 s.d.), I for one cannot believe her. However much our knowledge of what happened in the garden may be obscured, at least we have heard too many protestations of love between Truman and Mrs. Goodvile to believe they will remain chaste and unadulterate. The breach in the system gets patched over by Goodvile's assertive command, "*Truman,* if thou hast enjoyed her, I beg thee keep it close, and if it be possible let us yet be friends" (735-36).

Friendship in Fashion concludes with this apparent reconciliation, at least between male friends. Moreover, Valentine and Camilla enter into a clandestine marriage, celebrated at the end. And Victoria's tarnished honor and reputation get redeemed by marriage to the foolish but lovable Sir Noble. All the anger and revenge and malice get displaced onto the typical *punitive* characters, Saunter and Caper: the latter's perpetually dancing leg tied up behind, the former's perpetually singing mouth gagged. Goodvile's banishment speech at the end is directed not toward the adulterous sinners in the garden but the fools of one class low: "See here these Rogues how like themselves they look. Now, you paultry Vermin, you Rats that run squeaking from House to House, up and down the Town; that no man can eat his Bread in quiet for you. Take warning of what you feel, and come not near these Doors again on perill of hanging. Here [he addresses the footmen], discharge them of their punishment, and see'em forth the Gates" (748-54). None of the other transgressors really get punished—except for Lady Squeamish, who is oblivious, and Goodvile himself, who must consign his ignominy to oblivion. He may parade his quasi-heroic stature one more time, warning the audience in a gesture of male bonding, "Especially you gay Young marry'd Blades, / Beware and keep your Wives from Balls and Masquerades" (769-70). But he and the audience both know that any children he finally gets from his marriage will probably be Truman's. The comic ending cannot mask the "Devil" Goodvile suspects "in this Business" (734).[12]

Goodvile's "Devil" is not metaphysical, however; it is the return of reality repressed by aristocratic ideology: the predatory rapacity that class solidarity—and Restoration social comedy—cannot totally efface. Nor can the endings of these five plays, which, amidst traditional comic marriages, feature sore thumbs that insist on sticking out. The mood of the endings seems to me progressively darker in the plays as I have arranged them. I am not surprised there are so few such buddy-cuckolding plays. Corman writes, "Comedies revealing deep disillusionment or cynicism almost inevitably fail in this period" (14). He specifically mentions several "plays admired by twentieth-century critics," including Otway's *Friendship in Fashion*. It is remarkable that Wycherley's *The Country-Wife* and *The Plain Dealer* became permanent plays in the repertoire, for surely they reveal cynicism (in the former) and disillusionment (in the latter). Both plays, as is commonly known, were extremely controversial, and it is not insignificant that Wycherley wrote no more for the stage. Plays that reveal rotting seams in the supposedly seamless ideological garment of the ruling class must have been painful, disruptive, and subversive indeed.

8
Naughty Heroine Tricksters
Get Away with It

As we have seen in Part 1, woman's wit in Restoration comedy most often works to land men or man land, that is, to enable a freedom of choice that nevertheless socializes centrifugal male energy in service of the preservation of the estate and its transmission through genealogy. Despite the desire of feminist criticism for a more radical interpretation, woman's wit is thus a trope that is essentially conservative of aristocratic ideology even as it may modify its traditions slightly in favor of more female freedom.[1] But Otway's Mrs. Goodvile is a different kind of woman trickster in Restoration comedy. She employs all of her woman's wit and wiles to revenge herself upon her husband and cuckold him with his best friend. No amount of ambiguity about whether they have actually *committed* in the garden and no amount of male conspiracy to cover up can blunt the edge of her threat. She is not a Lady Flippant or even a Lady Gimcrack or a Lady Fidget, characters we may be able to dismiss as satiric, punitive. Mrs. Goodvile is the heroine of the play, its main female protagonist, played by the immensely attractive leading lady, Elizabeth Barry. And she gets away with adultery, an adultery that the audience is supposed to applaud, an adultery that threatens her own class's fundamental power structure.

Yet, as I pointed out in my *DLB* article on Otway, he undercuts Mrs. Goodvile's heroism—at least for a twentieth-century audience—by his portrayal of her as having internalized the age's misogynistic treatment of her wiles as specifically feminine.[2] A few other comic playwrights of the Restoration give us fully subversive heroine tricksters in truly subversive plays. The radical nature of their subversion is limited by the imaginative prospects (or discursive formations) open to the playwrights. Their radicalism consists more in a Bakhtinian than a Foucauldian sense, more in the carnivalesque undercutting of official discourse than in any shift in epistemes or social structures and paradigms. Thus I shall examine subversive heroine tricksters who operate mostly from the margins, who are essentially parasites on the hegemonic political economy, but who nevertheless obtain space of their own on those margins in which to maintain a combination of agency and (subversive) integrity. Discovering and analyzing the truly subversive plays with truly subversive women tricksters seems important for our ability to generalize about woman's wit as it was portrayed in Restoration comedy at a time when women's liberation was emerging in Western Europe, especially in France and England.[3] If the subversion we discover is more carnivalesque than paradigmatic, we should nevertheless celebrate its liberating élan.

One category of subversive heroine tricksters includes women who are part of a team of con artists who prey on normal society. The greatest of these marginal couples belong to Behn's later plays.[4] Like Arrowsmith's Juliana, Behn's Lucia, Lady Fancy, in *Sir Patient Fancy* (1678), is also married to a foolish (old) Cit. She too has a gallant, Wittmore. Unlike Behn's own Julia, Lady Fulbank, from *The Luckey Chance; or, An Alderman's Bargain* (1686),[5] Lucia does everything she can to cuckold her husband with her lover. Indeed, like Juliana and Pisauro, they were lovers before the marriage, and Lucia may not be Wittmore's alone either. Her maid, Maundy, comments as she waits to usher a lover up to Lucia, "Now am I return'd to my old trade again, fetch and carry my Ladies Lovers" (III.ii.76-77). Indeed, the plural is not impertinent, for the lover she is about to carry is not Wittmore but Lodwick by mistake.

Interestingly, as opposed to Lady Fulbank, though the heroine is tricked sexually and is initially disturbed, she dwells not in melancholy but comically shrugs it off. When Wittmore thinks he has been cuckolded by his friend with his mistress, he is furious. But Lodwick lies to him and says he and Lucia were interrupted, and Lucia later thanks him aside for being a "Man of Honour" (IV.ii.213) and preserving her reputation with her gallant. Once again, deadly rivalry between Town wits, one of whom has in a sense cuckolded the other, has been averted.

Wittmore is no match for Lucia's wit. As things get too complicated for him to manage, he throws his hands up in exasperation: "Look ye, I'me a Damn'd dull fellow at invention" (IV.i.234). Another of the young bucks, Leander, concludes that they had best leave matters to the women, for "women are best at intrigues of this kind" (IV.i.241-42). Lodwick's mother and sister, Lady Knowell and Lucretia, both do assist in the tricking. But the prime trickster is Lucia, whose ready invention escapes every near-disaster. She manipulates her hypochondriacal Puritan husband by feigning piety, making up lies on the spur of the moment, cuckolding him under his very nose, and robbing him blind. When Sir Patient surprises Lucia and Wittmore in her closet, she ingeniously and hilariously tricks him and arranges Wittmore's escape, saying that she would not mind if he were caught except that she has not yet secured the £8000 she intends to steal: "[B]ut now to be found out wou'd call my Wit in question, for 'tis the fortunate alone are wise" (IV.iii.162-63). She prays for help from no Christian providence but "all ye Powers that favour distrest Lovers" (IV.iii.199)—not the "distrest Lovers" of romance but those of the subversive counterculture.

When she is finally discovered, she brazenly exclaims to her outraged husband, "Rail on, whilst I dispose my self to laugh at thee" (V.672). She can afford now to triumph, because she has secured the £8000: "*Wittmore,* I have now brought that design to a happy conclusion for which I married this formal Ass" (V.267-68).[6] Sir Patient can divorce her (or, the implication seems to be, get an annulment, since their marriage settlement was contingent on her being "Honest" [V.703]), bearing the ignominy of being a cuckold, but he cannot prove she has his money. Wittmore articulates their scam: "[W]e have long been Lovers, but want of Fortune made us contrive how to marry her to your good Worship" (V.709-10).

Behn's team of con artists, then, like Arrowsmith's, are upper-class parasites who, because he is, as Behn writes in the dramatis personae, "a wild young Fellow of a small Fortune" and, as he describes himself, "a younger Brother," and because she has no other status than his "Mistress" (V.711-12), cannot support themselves independently and therefore prey upon their cultural inferiors. Admittedly, they are themselves preoccupied with possession, a concern truly transgressive tricksters should contemn, for the sexual economy they rebel against is one of possession for means of genealogical identification. Moreover, like Arrowsmith's transgressive couple, they remain marginalized, excluded from the dominant patriarchal political economy. By means of their scam or its repetition, they may amass some wealth, may consequently garner some independence. But they cannot engender a legitimate heir, cannot create a place and a space of their own which is enduring, transmittable. Yet even if they cannot legitimately replicate themselves, they at least have some breathing room on the margins where they can maintain a kind of integrity, a being true to themselves. Behn, in other words, gives us an alternative comic response to the Law of Strict Settlement—and one in which the prime agent of trickery is a resourceful woman. Her promiscuity, which is subversive to the system of sexual control for the expanding and inheriting of estates, instead of being condemned turns dispossession into a parasitic survival the audience is invited to applaud.

If Lucia never articulates such a counterdiscursive position vis-à-vis patriarchal England's hegemonic code, La Nuche, the parasitic prostitute from *The Second Part of the Rover* (1681), herself not a trickstress of the order of Lucia, does so. In a sense, she is Behn's most subversive character. As Robert Markley has shown, the nostalgic *golden age* of unencumbered sexuality such as Behn describes in her poem of that name is the fantasy world that La Nuche and Willmore create for themselves.[7] From that perspective La Nuche attacks Beaumond, who thinks he is upbraiding his fiancée, Ariadne, for an assignation but is actually revealing to La Nuche, whom he is supposed to love, his concern for his rights as a husband. Her attack assaults the bulwark of feudal patriarchal aristocracy's control of reproduction: "[T]hou shame to noble Love! thou scandal to all brave debauchery, thou fop of fortune; thou slavish Heir to Estate and Wife, born rich and damn'd to Matrimony" (IV.67-69). Key aristocratic value terms, "noble" and "brave," are appropriated to a libertine ethic, and the religious myth employed to enforce Western man's genealogical control is inverted, so that monogamy becomes damnation. It is not the free lovers who are slaves to passion but the aristocrats who are slaves to a system of property exchange. La Nuche finally frees herself from another form of economic slavery, dependence on the underworld system of control of surplus sexual energy, a system portrayed as the reverse mirror image of the upper-world's system of marriage for economic exchange: both are insufferably mercenary and materialistic for Behn's libertine couple.

Absent from this ending is the Hellena reality principle: La Nuche may well be stuck with bastards when Willmore almost inevitably violates their verbal "bargain" that "no poverty shall part us" (V.506-7). Furthermore, the two of them, like Wittmore and Lucia, have been preoccupied throughout the play with possession of each other: Willmore has been so jealous of rivals as to engage repeatedly in swordplay, and La Nuche cannot bear to think of him with another woman—certainly strange behavior for libertines and whores. Finally, the problem with the courtly love language they employ is that it replicates the official sexual discourse of constancy: "Nay, faith Captain, she that will not take thy word . . . deserves not the blessing" (V.510-11). La Nuche does not achieve the Princess of Clèves's wisdom that the only way to avoid inconstancy is to abstain from the game.

The ending of *The Second Part of the Rover* points in two directions. To be successful transgressive tricksters, Willmore and La Nuche will have to invent a scam like that of Wittmore and Lucia. They may have eschewed the two parallel economies of upper- and underworld sexual politics. But they will either have to remain parasites on the upper-world, or they will have to turn aristocratic romantic fantasy into bourgeois individualism. The latter mode will await the novels of Defoe and his successors to be fully realized.[8]

Despite Hume's failure to delineate the widow as a significant character type in late seventeenth-century comedy (131-32), she is certainly familiar to readers of Etherege, Wycherley, Vanbrugh, and Congreve. We have already noted several witty widows who man their land—and some uppity ones who get put in their place. But there are some subversive widows who successfully rebel against the patriarchal paradigms of either reintegration into society through marriage or exile within it (the Widow Blackacre still cannot actually inhabit the Inns of Court but only their environs).

The duke of Newcastle, probably with help from Shadwell, wrote a delightfully subversive play entitled *The Triumphant Widow; or, The Medley of Humours* (1674). But the title character Lady Haughty's triumph is quite different from Newcastle's other comic widow Lady Pleasant's Beatrice-like marriage with her Benedick, Boldman, in *The Humorous Lovers*. Besieged by suitors, Lady Haughty vows never to marry and, though she facilitates several marriages throughout the play, remains true to her word with regard to herself. Curiously, her ethic runs counter to the folk ethic in this raucous farce. Footpad, one of the most delightful rogues in Restoration comedy (and whom I shall treat in the next chapter), at one point is disguised as a peddlar selling, among other things, strange, new ballads. When Gervas the orange man uncovers one of Footpad's ballads about a lusty widow, they engage in the following exchange along with a bystander:

> *Gervas:* A lusty Widow is no strange thing.
> *Footpad:* Yes a lusty Widow, that lives and dies chastly.
> *Gervas:* Is't possible a lusty Widow live and die chaste?
> *2 Man:* Lord, Lord, what lying things these Ballets are, and to be in print too!
> *Footpad:* All the Parish Hands are to the Certificate to confirm it.
> *2 Man:* Puh, 'twas plain malice in 'em, to asperse a lusty Widow so.
> *Gervas:* The Parish should have had a lusty young Vicar, and he'd have converted her i'faith. [I, 6-7]

Yet when Lady Haughty's maid Nan asks, "Did your Ladiship find such great affliction in Matrimony, that you are such a violent enemy to it?" the widow responds, "So much, as I am resolved never to be so constrained again, I'le continue as free as Nature made me; why should we submit to that foolish Animal Man?" (II, 32). And at the end of the play (like Lady Mary Wortly Montagu in "The Lover: A Ballad" a generation or two later), she describes an impossible ideal man and concludes,

> Till such a man I find I'le sit alone,
> And triumph in the liberty I owne:

I ne're will wear a matrimonial Chain,
But safe and quiet in this Throne remain,
And absolute Monarch o'er my self will raign. [V, 98]

Like the widows Barbara Todd describes as increasingly resisting marriage over the next century, Lady Haughty defiantly resists reintegration into hegemonic sexual economy. Luckily she has the independent estate to do so. And yet. Perhaps there is something more than folk humor in the play that suggests Lady Haughty's behavior is to be seen as negative, unnatural. After all, Newcastle has named her *Haughty*. And in a very curious, apparently Freudian slip, someone—Newcastle, scribe, prompter, compositor—has misattributed a concluding speech that obviously belongs to Justice Spoilwit, whom Lady Haughty has refused but for whom she has found no suitable spouse, to Lady Haughty herself. When Colonel Bounce responds to her ideal portrait, "God take me, I'de not be such a man for such a Widow," the play prints the following rejoinder:

> *Lady:* Nor I neither, I desire to be a Politician and a States-man, for nothing but that I may have power to do wrong, there is such pleasure in it. [V, 98]

The point would seem to be that Justice Spoilwit will sublimate his frustrated sexual desires. But the misattributed lines suggest that the lady's haughtiness reflects an uppitiness that projects her into a men-only domain. It may be a haughtiness the play subtly, even unconsciously resists. But Newcastle also signally terms her "triumphant." The play remains at least subversive in its ambivalence.

The most successful transgressive widow I know in all Restoration comedy is Shadwell's Lady Cheatly, the eponymous heroine of *A True Widow* (1678).[9] Perhaps his title indicates male condemnation of her: she is a *true* widow, what all widows are at heart, a trickster, out to not just equal but supplant men. Unlike the other subversive heroine tricksters I have discussed, Lady Cheatly is not a sexual transgressor but an economic one. Thus, more so than the others she anticipates Moll Flanders. She sets up as a banker in order to amass a fortune for herself and convince men of her own worth and that of her daughters, whom she hopes to marry off in the marriage market (or keeping market—she doesn't care about morality but about the best deal). Needing to be sure of her mark before she marries him—that is, that he has a large estate—she remonstrates with one of her suitors, "Sir, Though I have a great esteem for your Person, yet we Widows that have some Fortune, are to consider something besides Passion" (II, 308). Her witty daughters, Theodosia and Isabella, may eschew her pragmatism and marry for love (as they eventually do), but not Lady Cheatly. When her unwitty daughter, Gartrude, despite the best efforts of her fellow trickster, the "very wise and discreet, half Bawd, half Match-maker" (dramatis personae), "Lady" Busy, to pair her with a rich keeper, allows herself to become soiled by both the wealthy gallant, Stanmore, and a boorish fop, Selfish, Lady Busy rather nakedly forces Gartrude to recognize the reality principle of this play and marry the fool, Young Maggot: "[Y]ou must marry him, if he will, and be glad on't too: *Stanmore* has forsaken you; *Selfish* can't keep you; your Mother will turn you out of doors, and you will starve" (IV, 346).

Lady Cheatly justifies her trickery on the grounds that men—her brother and others—despoiled her of her late husband's estate: turnabout is fair play. She beats men at their own game of control. By means of disappearing ink, she defrauds her depositors. But her steward, as if infected by the leveling effect of her rebellion, tries to assert his lower-class male dominance and blackmail her into marriage with him. She tricks him into trusting her, even though he knows better, and just when she is on the brink of exposure, she succeeds in getting even her dupes to lie for her and escapes on their bogus bourgeois credit as opposed to the steward's judicial oaths. Although she had set her sights closer to the Court end of the Town, she settles for the wealthy Cit, Maggot, in marriage because, as she tells another of her disappointed dupes, "he is governable" and can help protect her from creditors (V, 360). Indeed, when she confesses to Maggot that her estate "belongs of right to other People," he deserts his middle-class morality and embraces her trickster's ethic: "Right? 'Tis no matter for Right: I'll show 'em Law" (V, 361). Hiding behind and subverting the emergent bourgeoisie's precious code of law, this true widow will indeed govern not only her husband but her part of the world. She has tricked all the other tricksters—or like Lady Busy, uses them to her advantage—and emerges a truly triumphant, transgressive trickster—independent and in control.

Two of the most successful subversive heroine tricksters are free-lance con artists. Despite the fact that the play is a tragicomedy, because such a thoroughly subversive comic heroine is so rare on the Restoration stage I cannot forbear treating James Howard's Mirida from *All Mistaken; or, The Mad Couple* (1665), who freelances as a woman rake teasing her suitors with no intention of ever getting married: "My humour is to love no man but to/Have as many Love me as they please / Come Cut or Long tail," she announces with wicked double entendre (II, 19). She too is a male creation, but she seems to me radically subversive of aristocratic ideology. *All Mistaken* is a split-plot tragicomic romance. Unlike the normal pattern, where both plots end in a reaffirmation of feudal patriarchal order—the one on idealistic, the other on pragmatic grounds (as I have outlined in "Ideology")—the pattern of this play never rectifies the ironic tension between high and low.

The high plot features a duke and his lover Amphelia, both of whom pretend to be inconstant out of a jealousy infused by the villainous Ortellus, and another noble couple, Zoranzo and Amarissa, whose relationship is also threatened by jealousy. The low plot features Philidor and Mirida, both pure libertines, whose postures continually parody and mock those of the romantic lovers: Zoranzo is imprisoned; Philidor imprisons his several betrotheds, bastards, and their nurses in a garret. Philidor and Mirida pretend he is dead and read a bogus will to outrage his entourage and then lock them in a vault; Amarissa vows to die with Zoranzo in prison and lie with him in his grave. At one point Philidor and Mirida are captured by their antagonists and bound together back-to-back so they cannot even delight in one another's body; both Amarissa and the duke suspect Amphelia and Zoranzo of copulating while chained together in prison. When the duke discovers that the woman he has feigned love to is really his sister, a fact that releases him from his bonds to and from her brother's vengeance, he would have no word but *sister* spoken, especially by infants and nurses, a detail that wrenches us back to the pursuit of Philidor throughout the play by infants and nurses. The entire upper plot is a labyrinthine wandering through misperceptions and misrepresentations until pledged words are restored; Philidor's entire enterprise is to be freed from his promises and their attendant responsibilities, while Mirida's is to be free of obnoxiously persistent suitors, especially one fat and one lean, whom she tortures mercilessly. The high plot restores word-as-bond; the low plot explodes it, especially in the mock-proviso scene, in which they both pledge to be bound by no ties: theirs will be a totally open relationship.[10]

The heroic plot embodies what Bakhtin labels *official discourse*, while the comic is pure *carnivalesque*. John Harrington Smith's dismissal of Howard's play as nothing more than a grotesque parody of Dryden's *Secret Love; or, The Maiden Queen* (1667)[11] and the short shrift it has received from Restoration drama critics in general probably indicate a distaste for the play's rampant, scatological slapstick. To cite only the most egregious example, Mirida's fat lover, Pinguister, is trying to win her love by acceding to her outrageous and sadistic command that he lose weight, especially by incessant jogging and purging. He is constantly running off stage to relieve himself, and at one point a rustic clown pursues and beats him for defecating in his mouth while he was sleeping (III, 34). At another point Mirida pretends to comfort the exhausted Pinguister by putting his head in her lap, but she proceeds to roll away from him as he rolls after like a hogshead. Assuming a bully-breeches role, she goes so far as to fence with him and disarm him (V, 53-56). However slapstick, the action is still interpretable: Mirida threatens patriarchal control.

Howard's carnivalesque represents the chaotic energy of life (and the excesses of the grotesque body) triumphing over restrictive forms. When the duke tries to fold his mad kinsman, Philidor, into the hymeneal closure of tragicomedy, it is Mirida who first protests, "Hold Sir, I forbid that banes [*sic*]" (V, 67). The duke tries yet once more to enforce his official discourse by the sheer power of his hegemonic position, but Philidor and Mirida resist:

> *Duke:* This day, Hymen shall light his
> Torch for all.
> *Philidor:* With your Pardon Sir, not for me
> And my Female.
> *Mirida:* No faith, I'le blow it out if he dos. [V, 68]

When he first meets her, Philidor exclaims of Mirida, "[S]ure 'tis I / In Petty coates" (II, 19). And there is probably a sense in which she is the projection of a male fantasy, a woman as libertine as man in his wildest dreams. There is surely nothing realistic about her. Indeed, when the reality principle of bastards enters Philidor's discourse with her, she rejects the topic out of hand. And we never learn if she has consummated her relationship with Philidor. Especially as his scheme to have his betrotheds and nurses release him from promises succeeds, by the end of the play both Philidor and Mirida represent pure desire, a pleasure principle that asserts itself in the teeth of the *real,* the ultimate reality principle:

> *Mirida:* Heaven send thee and I many a fair year,
> To be mad together in.
> *Philidor:* I as you say, give us but time enough,
> And when we grow Tame, let the
> Bell Tole for us[.] [III, 36]

Like Boccaccio's sexual tricksters, articulated in the midst of the Black Plague, Howard's tricksters, female as well as male, outrageously assert that the only proper response to death is not to utter patriarchal words and not to marry and produce heirs to carry on both family and estate but to chatter irrepressibly, profanely, blasphemously—"faith," "Heaven" send us time indeed—and to do the *olde daunce* on the very grave itself.

Southerne's *Sir Anthony Love; or, The Rambling Lady* (1690) features the greatest of these free-lancers if not the greatest subversive heroine trickster in all of Restoration comedy, the rambling lady of the subtitle who masquerades in drag as Sir Anthony.[12] In it woman's wit seems to achieve not only a significant level of liberation but also a very high level of *jouissance,* of sheer delight in the nature of carnivalesque play.[13] Moreover, the playfulness extends to the destabilization of notions of class as well as gender.

First, using their wits the typical women victims of tyrannical guardianship are liberated. Floriante and Charlott, daughters of Count Canaille, plot to escape his control of their bodies and persons through "Disobedience" (II.i.337-38), despite the count's unsuspecting confidence that Floriante at least

> too well knows
> What's owing to a Father and her self,
> To my Authority and her own Birth,
> Now to dispute what I design for her[.] [II.i.367-70]

Charlott, the typical "mad" half of the team (II.i.358), is, like Behn's Hellena, consigned to a convent, and she is witty enough to know exactly why: she says rebelliously to Count Verole, who, designed for Floriante, has just recommended that Charlott be placed in such a "retreat from a bad World," "[I]f my Sisters Fortune, in your Opinion, had not wanted mending more than my Manners . . . I might have continued in this bad World" (II.i.388-93). Floriante rebelliously continues the argument with Count Verole, seeing perspicaciously that he seeks Charlott's displaced portion not for her but him "self," for he will "command" any money after marriage, promising to be liberal but in reality after having "enclos'd" her like open land proceeding to possess her fortune and enslave her person and abuse them both (II.i.399-405).

Not naive about marriage or the male libertinism celebrated throughout the play, Floriante finally concludes of her impending union with the rake Valentine, "Well, since Marriage at best is a Venture, I had as good make it myself, as let another make it for me, at my Cost" (V.vii.27-28). It is true that, as Weber has cleverly shown (*Rake-Hero,* 171), Floriante and Sir Anthony's being dressed in each other's clothes in the final scene reminds the audience that Sir Anthony has eschewed marriage with her gallant, Valentine, and, not fearing Floriante "in a Wife" (IV.ii.82), intends to remain Valentine's mistress. But the suggestion may not be as disturbing as both Weber and Pearson (117) take it; it may be a delightfully subversive image of a successful *ménage à trois.* If so, Southerne has granted Floriante freedom of choice not for the usual reason of uniting the right couple for the social continuity of estate building and preservation but for subversive pleasure.

It is also true that Charlott is not married to a man she loves at the end but has married the fop Count Verole. And Volante is not married to the putative man she loves (Sir Anthony) but the ponderous Ilford. Yet there is nothing of the cynical atmosphere at the end of, say, *Friendship in Fashion* or *The Atheist*. Charlott, who has enough joie de vivre to eschew romantic dying to escape a nunnery (II.i.345-47), does not care *who* provides her with an escape alive: she protests that she is "Not so much in love with the Count, as I am out of love with a Nunnery: Any man had been as welcome" (V.vi.43-44).[14] She insists on her own agency: "I thought fit to provide for my self" (V.vi.25). Moreover, Volante, whom Sir Anthony describes as "too Witty, to be very Wise" (II.i.260), has wised up enough by the end of the play to be cured of her attraction to Sir Anthony by the plain dealing of Ilford, who has refused to take advantage of her in the planned bed trick. When he restores her "liberty" from the counterfeit marriage with Sir Anthony (V.ii.73), she (offstage) freely yields herself up to him in marriage. It would seem that the "Glory" of the "Wit" of all three women (II.i.407) has liberated them from oppression. But none is radically subversive, not even Floriante, whose husband's future escapades with Sir Anthony/Lucia would not threaten the continuity of estates.

The glorious wit of Sir Anthony, however, is thoroughly, radically subversive. She is the supreme agent of trickery. She frees herself from white slavery by escaping from and duping the keeper who bought her first of £500, then of a purse (by threatening with a phallic pistol), and finally of marriage, divorce, and a settlement of £500 a year. She tricks the other tricksters of the play, especially the pilgrim (who never retrieves from him/her his casket of jewels) and the abbé. When the wits are at a loss, s/he exclaims, "What's to be done? Any thing's to be done" (II.i.114). Out of comic perversity she tortures Ilford by pretending to court his beloved and finally makes him acknowledge that she is "the Ascendant" (IV.iv.172). When the abbé giggles, "Have I caught you my little *Mercury!*" (V.iv.43), the audience recognizes the appropriateness of the appellation in that Mercury is not only swift but the god of thieves and tricksters.

At the end of the play Sir Anthony is not socialized into any structure of official society but remains free to carry on the "Trade" of free love (I.i.526), that is, of subversive female sexual promiscuity. The marriage into which she has tricked her keeper, Sir Gentle Golding, provides the necessary cover of respectability as well as status (Valentine comments that Sir Gentle has made her "a Lady" [V.vii.131], that is, the wife of a knight, albeit a City one), and the divorce provides the necessary money in terms of separate maintenance for her to carry on the life of trickster, female rake, free-lance con artist. She has obtained that special freedom she declares earlier belongs to English women: "Cuckoldom is the Liberty, and a seperate Maintenance, the property of the Free-born Women of *England*" (II.i.158-59).

Sir Anthony seems to enjoy her trickery for the sheer fun of it. Her servant says she is "as busie as a projector" (III.iii.11), and we are inevitably reminded of those master trickster-projectors, Jonson's Subtle, Face, and Dol Common. She exposes the pilgrim "for the dear Jest" of it (III.i.7; cf. V.iv.33), referring to her plot as "our Farce" (III.iii.2), as if she were a comic playwright herself, designing endless "Frollicks" (IV.iii.99; V.iii.5). Valentine becomes a spectator to the "ridiculous" skit she stages with Sir Gentle (IV.ii.94 ff), and she intends him to be her substitute in a supposed tryst with a woman. The "pleasure" she talks about sharing with him (V.iii.7) would be not only vicarious sexual pleasure but the ecstasy of the trick itself.

But Sir Anthony's triumph represents more than the dominance of woman's wit announced at the end by Sir Gentle: "When we have Mistresses above our Sense,/We must redeem our Persons with our Pence" (V.vii.146-47). She destabilizes not only gender relations but class relations. From the beginning she mocks the foundation of aristocracy, genealogy: when Valentine tries to refute her notion that courage is just culturally learned with the traditional datum that birth counts for something—"there's something in Family sure"—Sir Anthony puckishly responds, in a rejoinder worthy of Swift, "Wooden Legs, in a great many, *Valentine*." Ilford tries to hold up the aristocratic end of the argument by insisting "Courage often runs in a blood—" only to be interrupted by Sir Anthony: "They say so of the Pox, indeed. The Sins of the Fathers may run in the blood sometimes, and visit the third and fourth Generation: But their virtues dye with the men" (I.i.103-08).

This motif continues throughout the play through the exposure of Sir Gentle Golding as anything but gentle in the aristocratic sense, both because he appears to have bought his title and to have no aristocratic "Family" (II.i.546) and because he is incapable of "trust" (V.vii.59) and generous behavior. The motif continues especially through the repeated spoofing of Count Verole's rank. Even the abbé joins in: "Virtue created first Nobility, / But in our honourable Ignorance / Nobility makes Virtue" (II.i.34-36). Count Verole's cowardice throughout reveals him as not having the merit that goes along with his rank. Sir Anthony dissects him in this exchange:

> *Verole:* I am of [God's] creation.
> *Sir Anthony:* Of the King's you may be,
>   But he who makes a Count, ne're made a Man,
>   Remember that, and fall that mighty Crest.

Verole: It seems you know me then.
Sir Anthony: By that coy, cock't-up Nose, that hinders you
    From seeing any Man, that does not stand
    Upon the Shoulders of his Ancestors,
    For long Descents of farr-fam'd Heraldry:
    I take you for a Thing, they call a Count;
    For had you not been a Count, you had been nothing[.] [II.i.416-26]

Sir Anthony, on the other hand, according to Valentine "deserves" an estate if he doesn't have it, more so than most of those that do (I.i.330). As opposed to the count, Sir Anthony knows him/herself (II.i.436). She seems to represent the emerging master trope of self-reliance and its attendant notion of bourgeois upward social mobility. Indeed, Valentine sums up this motif:

> Thus all things are provided for by Fate:
> The witty Man enjoys the Fool's Estate.
> So Rich and Poor, let 'em compute their Gains,
> One has his lot in Lands, and one in Brains. [IV.ii.199-202]

Valentine's "Poor" here include not just dispossessed peasants but dispossessed younger brothers, whose plight has been referred to throughout the play (see e.g. II.i.170-71; III.i.63ff.).

In this play, however, as opposed to the younger brothers of plays like Orrery's *Guzman* or the anonymous *Mistaken Husband*, it is the witty poor (probably lower gentry) woman who uses her brains to enjoy the fool's estate. Apparently having come from humble origins and having been sold into white slavery for money, Sir Anthony at the end is not only a lady, but, being Golding's legal wife, could produce "another Man's Child upon her Body" which could "inherit" his "Acres" (V.vii.137-38). Although Valentine seems to promise that she would not do that, would not (unlike the bitter Lysander in *The Reformation* [IV.ii, 61]) ask her cuckold to stand as "Godfather" to such a child (V.vii.137), the point is that she has the power to scramble the genealogical eggs.

Moreover, the scrambling of gender throughout the play best imaged in the constant changing of clothes extends to the lubricious abbé. With the help of the pilgrim, who wants revenge for being bested by a superior trickster, he arranges a supposed assignation between Sir Anthony and a woman, an assignation Sir Anthony cannot, out of her love of fun, turn down. But the woman proves to be the abbé, whose friendliness toward the pretty young man had a basis not clearly manifest, and Sir Anthony becomes the object of a homosexual seduction—which could turn into a homosexual rape, with the aid of the pilgrim (now disguised as a palmer). Sir

Anthony is forced to reveal her real gender—and to deeply disappoint the abbé, who now must treat with her to "muzzle the Scandal" (V.iv.139).

Not only do the repeated cross-dressing and gender switching serve to destabilize notions of gender, then, but so also does the homosexuality. Supplementation is no longer just between men (as it usually is in the libertine world of Restoration comedy), but a cross-dressing woman and a homosexual priest are both supplanters of other genders and, in the case of Sir Anthony at least (but remember the abbé's notions of nobility), classes. Even worse, the abbé gives a blessing of five thousand crowns to all three of his nieces, to be supplemented by "a Thousand extraordinary for her who brings me the first Boy" (V.vii.92-93). "Brings me" can, of course, simply mean *give birth to,* and the abbé's generosity could be read as a reward for and (hypocritical) support of the fulfillment of the primogenitive system. But given his clandestine homosexuality, at least Valentine, Sir Anthony, and the audience must interpret "brings me" in a more sinister sense: the abbé is a pederast who will subvert primogeniture by furthering gender instability.

This final scrambling of (patri)lineal order is treated by the play not as darkly but rather comically sinister, and the ending is traditionally celebratory. It is as if the audience were invited to observe along with Valentine, "How this fooling has run away with the time!" (III.iv.179). Valentine has said earlier to Sir Gentle, "[W]e make a shift"—that is, they improvise to provide Sir Gentle with the sexual partner he desires. Sir Anthony's rejoinder sums up the play's purpose and its power: "Make a shift! We make a Carnival; all the year a Carnival" (II.i.572-73). The play's carnivalesque centrifugally disrupts the centripetal force of official discourse—the control of gender, class, genealogy—ultimately by threatening aristocratic codes of identity that exist for purposes of power transmission and suggesting their replacement by radical and not just bourgeois individualism, an anarchic individualism without patriarchy, without rigidified boundaries of gender and class.

There is a nice progression through the greatest of these subversive plays. In *Sir Patient Fancy* the tricksters are parasites who invade the City from the Town yet can be said still to live on the margins of aristocratic society, subverting its controlling code of patrilineal genealogy. In *A True Widow* the trickster moves from the margins of (counterfeit) aristocracy into respectable bourgeois society, subverting its controlling codes of law and finance. In *Sir Anthony Love* the trickster seems free at the end to move in and out of both aristocratic and bourgeois society at will, anarchically subverting all boundaries. If anyone could have built a room of one's own at the end of the seventeenth century, it would have been Sir Anthony.

9

Male Folk Tricksters
Erupt from Below

I have already examined the punitive treatment of satirical butts who provide superb vehicles for the great comic actors of the Restoration and who infuse it with enormous comic energy. Restoration comedy of the 1660s contains sympathetic, low-class tricksters who infuse this comedy with a remarkable, boisterous folk energy that explodes on the stage and threatens to take over entire plays, as indeed, in some signal instances, it does, making them fully subversive comedies. These folk tricksters and their energy persist, although less pervasively, until 1690.[1] They leaven an essentially aristocratic form and subvert it through what Jackson Cope calls *the dramaturgy of the daemonic* or what I prefer to call *the dramaturgy of the democratic*. These characters have something of a chthonic quality that links them to the earth, the mud, and thus to the daemonic, to the life force on this planet that through the green fuse drives the flower regardless of any official discourse or institution or estate. But they also have a political dimension: sometimes they are placed in service of aristocratic hegemonic discourse; more often they are subversive of that discourse and create a space for the voices of the dispossessed to be heard, an energy of the Third Estate that will not be denied.

In treating the right coupling plot of Cowley's *Cutter of Coleman Street*, like most critics, despite the fact that he is the title character, I merely glanced at Cutter and barely mentioned his cohort Worm. Yet these pretenders from the Suburbs, who appropriate military rank, provide a good deal of stage business. They enter the stage full of bogus news and gossip that represent what Bakhtin analyzes as the grotesque, excessive "Language of the Marketlace" (*Rabelais,* ch. 2). Bakhtin writes, "The culture of the common folk idiom was to a great extent a culture of the loud word spoken in the open, in the street and marketplace" (182). And it served to articulate a dual image of the world—upper and lower, life and death, evoking both praise and abuse—that militates against official discourse: "In the development of class society such a conception of the world can only be expressed in unofficial culture. There is no place for it in the culture of the ruling classes; here praise and abuse are clearly divided and static, for official culture is founded on the principle of an immovable and unchanging hierarchy in which the higher and the lower never merge" (166). Despite Bakhtin's exaltation of the marketplace and of the novel as places where the lower disrupts (and despite his disparagement of drama as almost always official, "monologic" discourse—for example, in *Problems of Dostoevsky's Poetics,* 17), Restoration comedy strikes me again and again as the site of such disruption. Here the loud voice and brawls of the bogus "Colonel" Cutter are juxtaposed to the witty deliberations of the real Colonel Jolly, that gentleman trickster seeking to regain his estate.

Commissioned by Jolly to pursue his ward-niece (and thus alleviate him of the necessity of doling out to her her entire portion at once), Cutter and Worm fall out with one another, shout disparagements of each other's character, and come to actual blows. And they appropriate and parody the language of the upper sphere: Worm shouts as he attacks, "Have at you, Cutter, an' thou hadst as many lives as are in Plutarch, I'd make an end of e'm all" (II.iv.14-15). Jolly's daughter Aurelia also enlists Cutter and Worm in her own plotting, employing them as spies against Truman Jr. and Lucia, and they reveal to Jolly the nature of Lucia's counterplot, though they think the poison she administers to Jolly to force a deathbed permission for her to marry young Truman is real. After they reveal the plot to Jolly, they engage in a hilarious, Rabelaisian scene of deathbed drinking.

Lucia responds to the courting rogues by complaining that men of such ill repute attach themselves to the true cause of Royalism, and she longs for Heaven to restore the king, who as the country's physician will cure such ulcers. Moreover, like Shakespeare's Prince Hal, once he seems assured of winning the Widow Barebottle—thus regaining his own estate—Jolly can afford to repudiate his low-class accomplices and boon companions. He disowns Worm, who plans his own trick to gain Lucia only to be one-upped by the (class) superior trickster Colonel Jolly. So as the play moves toward the restoration of Jolly's estate—and the promise of the king's restoration—at least one of the body politic's ulcers would seem to have been cured by excision.

Worm has planned all along, however, that if his plot to impersonate Lucia's father fail "'twill be at least a merry 'bout for an hour, and a mask to the Wedding" (IV.vi.122-23). In the final scene when Jolly emerges triumphant with his new wife to confront Worm with his fraud, Worm escapes punishment by cleverly maintaining that he and his accomplice were merely enacting such a masque. Moreover, the title character of the play has not only escaped drudgery as Jolly's factor in his schemes, he has imitated the master with his own trickery, donning the mask of a convert and securing the widow's daughter Tabitha by parodying her Puritan cant outrageously and hilariously. Cutter begs Tabitha no longer to call him Cutter, for the Devil is a cutter, but Abednego, for he shall suffer martyrdom (*la petite mort*) but will rise from the dead. We saw in the Introduction that his resurrection in character takes the form of reverting to Cavalier with sword, hat, and feather, a transformation matched by Tabitha's repudiation of her mother and her mother's religion as she prepares to become a (Cavalier) mother herself.

Thus Cutter's triumph is not merely that of the *daemonic*. It is thoroughly politicized. When Tabitha and her mother marvel at the miracle of Cutter's conversion, protesting miracles cannot exist in this age of "Cavalerism," Cutter responds that miracles shall not cease "till the Monarchy be establish'd" (III.xii.38-39). The women hear *Fifth Monarchy*, but the audience hears the other, *restored monarchy*. At the same time, Colonel Jolly's and Lucia's attempts to excise these ulcers fail, and they are included in the hymeneal embrace of the ending, as Cutter enters equally triumphant with Jolly and bringing the fiddlers for the marriage dance. The upper-class tricksters win estates, but so do the lower-class tricksters win, if not estates exactly, rewards of brides and a status-stability that redeems them from Suburb subsistence: Cutter becomes Jolly's stepson and even Worm is provided with a wife in Lucia's maid Jane. Thus while Cutter and Worm serve a political function—let us remember their song about old Noll's being hanged from a tree at the restoration of the king—they also serve a more Bakhtinian, subversive function of disrupting the discourse to force the inclusion of folk elements. Such inclusion incipiently subverts Stuart ideology by democratizing the register.

It is a commonplace of criticism of Sir Robert Howard's *The Committee* that Teg (Teague), the Irish servant, was a big hit in a role created by the great early comic actor, John Lacy, who also probably played Cutter.[2] He was a hit especially because of his slapstick treatment of Obadiah, the solicitor to the Committee of Sequestration who facilitates the confiscation of Royalist estates and whose name implies his Puritan connections. At one point Teg gets Obadiah so drunk he actually joins in Royalist songs like this one:

> Not a thought shall come in
> But what brings our King,
> Let Committees be damn'd with their gain:
> We'l send by this stealth
> To our Hearts our Kings Health,
> And there in despite he shall Reign. [III, 114]

Colonel Careless praises Teg for having "vanquish'd the [Good Old] cause in this overthrow of this / Counterfeit Rascal its true Epitome" (115). Later Colonel Blunt charges Teg with another distraction of Obadiah as he rescues Careless: "[M]ake him once more drunk, and it / Shall be call'd the second edition of *Obadiah*" (127)! To keep Obadiah from interfering with the denouement wherein the Cavaliers resecure their estates, Teg threatens to stab him to death, finally releasing him with the demand that he "shall love the King" (V, 134). Amidst the closing hymeneal dancing, Teg aggressively forces Obadiah to dance with him: "*Obadiah* shall be my woman too, / And shall dance for the King."

Such aggressive forcing of his opponent into a submissive, female posture marks Teg's role as a conservative reinforcement of the reaffirmation of Royalist dominance that the rest of the dramatic action embodies. And in giving this role to an Irishman, Howard invites Irish Catholic loyalty to his restored (crypto-Catholic) king and allows a modicum of in-your-face vengeance to the Irish, who had been mercilessly crushed in the early 1650s by Cromwell in retaliation for their rebellion in the 1640s. Careless takes up this servant of a dead friend, for obviously there is no place for an Irishman in troubled England, yet he cannot endure "to see any miserable / That can weep for my Prince, and Friend" (I, 77). Teg cannot keep a straight face in front of the posturing erstwhile scullion, Mrs. Day, and when she remonstrates with him for being an Irish traitor, he insists, no, he's an Irish "Rebel" (III, 100)—a loaded epithet even on the restored stage.

But Howard has also given voice to the most dispossessed of all the peoples of the contemporary British Isles. As Hill summarizes, the Act for the Settlement of Ireland (1652) "provided for the expropriation of the owners of some two-thirds of the land, and for the transplantation of the bulk of the Irish population to Connaught" (115). Though this particular "transplantation" was never carried out in full, it nevertheless resulted in massive dispossession among the "uninfluential landowners," and the word "transplantation" itself reminds us that this period also marks the transportation of Irish slaves to the plantations of the West Indies as England began to acquire more of them under Cromwell.[3] Lacy as Teg invested the character with all the energy of the greatest comic actor of his time in England, thus giving his voice a resonance that transcends his immediate political role and reverberates in the echo-chamber of the hollow lives of not-so-great Britain's landless.

Perhaps acted around the same time as these first new and important Restoration comedies was Thomas Thompson's *The Life of Mother Shipton* (1662?). If the title character of this play, the witch Mother Shipton of

English folklore, is not portrayed as a successful trickster (see ch. 10, for treatment of her), Thompson provides some male alternatives that carry through her subversion. A bunch of beggars occupy Shipton's abandoned peasant hut as a "pretty pallace for us Princes of the ragged Regiment" (II.i, 10, misnumbered). Especially in the light of the heroic play's protagonist's asserting *I alone am King of me!* they sing an amazing song celebrating their superiority:

> A Beggars a Prince, we gather from hence
> We are not confined as some Princes be,
> Though we are not so rich,
> Wee've as princely an Itch,
> And my mind, my mind is a Kingdome to me.
>
> We loose no grate purses,
> Nor have not the Curses,
> Of Orphans: of Widdows, or poor Caveliers,
> And before that I shall, from a Dignity fall,
> 'Till be eight times, nine times ten hundred years.
>
> We scorn all their jears,
> And live not in fears,
> Of being imprisoned by black rod or Tower,
> And as for the stocks, of it self it unlocks
> Within the space of a mery short hour[.] [10]

The reference to the poor Cavaliers is especially poignant in this *contemptus mundi* warning against ambition. But because the beggars become the dupes of the abbot and of Radamon, perhaps we cannot take them too seriously. Furthermore, their vision of superiority is actually as empty as the traditional pastoral vision.

From Thomas Middleton's *A Chaste Maid of Cheapside,* however, Thompson purloins another plot for his play, featuring the trickster Shiftwel (Allwit in Middleton's play, a name that is an anagram for Wittol but which also suggests his subversive wit). Shiftwel is a freeholder on Sir Oliver Whorehound's estate. Sir Oliver exercises his *droit du seigneur* on Shiftwel's wife, keeps them both, as it were, as she pumps out bastard after bastard. Shiftwel is a willing pander, with many mistresses to ease his pain, he tells his friend Moneylack. But Shiftwel has mortgaged his little estate to fund his pleasures (imitating the vices of his betters), a mortgage that is now forfeit to Scrape the Usurer. Buying time with quick wit, Shiftwel, disguised as the gentleman Frankheart, courts the widow Lady Lovefree, whose estate he figures will redeem his. Her man Roger characterizes her as spoiled, idle, and no fit huswif, and Shiftwel responds in a parody of the rhetoric of Town wits, "Thou art too earnest my old fac'd *Saturn,* I like her near the worse, huswifery is the superficies of a gentle Female, and the parenthesis of a Lady which may be all left out" (17). This is the rhetoric of the social climber, for whom the ultimate status symbol is the wife (or, as in this case, mistress) who, like her betters, does not have to participate in the work that sustains his life-style. His glib tongue wins the widow, who maintains she is but a woman who cannot resist its magic. Calling their love pure and constant, they fall to, and Shiftwel becomes Lady Lovefree's kept man.

Meanwhile, Sir Oliver discusses with his servant David how Shiftwel has fallen prey to Scrape. David moralizes that thus men who aspire "above their pitch" receive their just reward (V.v, 43, misnumbered). But Thompson does not bring Shiftwel crashing down in the poetic justice that concludes the rest of the play. Covering his bets, Shiftwel plots against Sir Oliver in order to obtain a settlement for life for himself and his wife. His friend Moneylack poses as a sergeant and arrests Sir Oliver for trespass and battery (both against Shiftwel's wife). Lady Lovefree, who is in reality Lady Whorehound, Sir Oliver's wife, taking her revenge on him for his promiscuity, watches in shock when Shiftwel himself comes to enforce the warrant, realizing she has been tricked, that he is not Frankheart. She steps forth and reveals herself, asks forgiveness for having paid Sir Oliver in kind, as does Sir Oliver for his transgressions with Mrs. Shiftwel. But instead of being dismissed as a failed trickster, Shiftwel succeeds through his bogus complaint in tricking Sir Oliver to agree to paying him £100 per annum during his life, plus a jointure to Shiftwel's wife of the same annuity and a marriage portion for Moneylack's bride-to-be, Shiftwel's sister. This last provision proves prudent, for when a real sergeant arrives to arrest Shiftwel on Scrape's suit, Moneylack posts bond for the debt owed by his now brother-in-law. The plot ends in the "*high Festival*" of comedy (V.v, 51). Thus unlike Dickens's Madame Defarge this victim of *droit du seigneur* triumphs over his (not so oppressive) oppressor. With his new income, the *villain* will continue to aspire above his "pitch."

John Wilson's *The Cheats* (1663) would seem to be a social comedy that rewards a Town wit trickster with a fit, witty wife and an estate. Afterwitt's estate has been mortgaged first by his father and now by him to Alderman Whitebroth, a City trickster engaged in multiple fraud. In poetic justice he has fallen in love with the alderman's daughter, Beatrice, whose "Red Petticoat must piece up all" (I.ii, 7). Abetted by his irreverent libertine friend, Jolly, the free-lance trickster par excellence, Afterwitt plots to obtain Beatrice, her father's heir, complete with his estate. Beatrice loves Afterwitt well enough but plays *dangereuse* with him, demanding Platonic love while he protests the needs of the body. She also demands that he court her father, for she has no intention of running away romantically. As her maid Cis tells Jolly, "She loves him well, but her fathers Estate better" (IV.v, 58). Afterwitt and Jolly blackmail the Suburb trickster Mopus, a feigned astrologer, whom they catch tousling the constable's wife, Mrs. Double-Diligence. Mopus feigns a prophecy that Beatrice will marry Afterwitt, and she does, without even securing her father's estate. Meanwhile, Jolly conspires with a cheating lawyer, Runter, and a hypocritical Puritan divine, Scruple, and with two Suburb hectors, Bilboe and Titere Tu, to con Whitebroth with multiple tricks, including a drug that makes him think he is dying and thus needing a will; blackmail for his affair with the same constable's wife; and a false deed of conveyance of the estate to Afterwitt and Beatrice. Afraid most of the sex scandal, Whitebroth capitulates and blesses the rebellious gay couple.

What is remarkable about the ending, however, underscores what is remarkable about the play. Whitebroth's comic embrace of the young couple redeems him from being a mere punitive satirical butt: "Come Son and Daughter, the business is done, and I forgive you both—And if that settlement be not large enough, I'll make you a new one upon demand—You shall have your own Estate back, in present, and as you love your Wife, the rest after our deaths:—And so, you have my blessing" (73, misnumbered). There is really no poetic justice on the cheats at any level. Mopus, who was bored, gets some action. Scruple gets a benefice on Afterwitt's estate. The servants Tim and Cis have the pleasure of seeing the right couple succeed. Runter cares not what side he serves as long as he gets his fee. Mrs. Double-Diligence is happy with her husband, who remains ignorant of her multiple adulteries, and will probably continue at least the affair with Bilboe, as will Mrs. Mopus with Titere Tu. Bilboe gets an amazing £500, which he will undoubtedly share with his fellow hector. On the other hand, whatever the forgiveness embodied in the comic embrace, Whitebroth *has* been severely satirized for his fraud, the Puritan sisters and Scruple for their hypocrisy, Mopus for his bogus science, Runter for his mercenariness, the hectors for their cowardice. And Tyro, the Country booby whose pretensions to Beatrice have been destroyed by Afterwitt in a typical manifestation of Town superiority, is run out of Town and not even included in the closing embrace.

Yet the cultural work the play performs seems finally not to underscore the superiority of the Town wits so much as to celebrate the sheer energy of trickster wit, an energy that dissolves class boundaries in the carnivalesque. The play opens not with the wits plotting the securing of women and estates but with the Suburban tricksters, Bilboe and Titere Tu, who like Cutter and Worm have appropriated uniforms and ranks and like Shiftwel have appropriated the rhetoric of their betters, including their ubiquitous Latin tags. They are successful parasites, feeding off those same betters as highwaymen, thieves, and con artists. When they entertain their married mistresses at a midwife's residence (another underworld parasite), they parody the behavior of libertine Town wits, indulging in Billingsgate dialogue. Mrs. Double-Diligence wants to know if Titere Tu is married. Bilboe responds wittily, "Every mans Boots serve his turn." Titere Tu parries, "And better so, than going bare-foot" (II.iv, 24). The couples want to make merry, and they do with this exuberance:

> *Bilboe:* Hang pinching, we'll never pine our selves, though our Heirs smart for't.
> *Mrs. D-D:* Here Major—Here's an old *Elizabeth,* has not seen light these seven years.
> *Bilboe:* And ev'n let her go—She has been Pris'ner long enough of all conscience:—Come Captain, let's be merry.
> *Titere Tu:* By this hand 'tis true:—[*Speaking to Mrs. Mopus.*]
> I love thee above all flesh alive:—Fear nothing—All's well, and as right as my Leg.
> *Bilboe:* And that's crooked to my knowledge.
> *Mrs. Mopus:* Nay good Sir; —You do but jest? [26]

The line about not being parsimonious, even if it means their heirs suffer, is hilarious, given that their heirs will be cuckoos in others' nests. And we know what leg Mrs. Mopus worries about! Titere Tu starts singing a song about cuckolds, but the women demand a new song (again note the parody of the typical upper-class courtship scene), so Bilboe obliges with a song about cuckolds which insists that they are men after all, that is, human beings: if not, "most of our Fathers were Beasts" (27). So much for any myth of genealogical purity.

Equally carnivalesque is the dialogue between Whitebroth and Double-Diligence, who tells a farcical story of the previous night's watch, which resulted in his and his watch's being doused by chamber pots: "[W]e were most lewdly bepist, and some Pates broken" (II.v, 29). White-broth sees it as "The King's Majesties Authority affronted, in the representative person, of my Neighbour *Double-Diligence,* the Constable." True enough, but the exchange represents typical subversion of official authority in constable scenes since the time of Shakespeare and Jonson. Double-Diligence needed a warrant to arrest the perpetrators but during the alderman's sickness could only get one signed by his wife, which no one will honor. Shades of *Bartholomew Fair.* Sounding like Justice Overdo, the alderman protests that since man and wife are "one person in Law," she is as good a Justice of the Peace as he (30).

Scruple has the verbal energy of a descendant of Jonson's Zeal-of-the-land Busy while Mopus resembles Jonson's Face. Their hilarious exchange about the original language in Eden—Mopus championing Hebrew, Scruple Welsh!—sets the play awash in competing Rabelaisian cants, the kind we have heard before in the chapter on punitive elements of social comedy. They develop a begrudging admiration for each other as pseudo-scientists. Meanwhile, Bilboe and Titere Tu quarrel like Jonson's Subtle and Face, but it is not so much their words as their bodies that dominate the stage, as they indulge in mock combat—for each is too cowardly to actually fight. At one point Titere Tu has one leg "*over*" (the apron?) but then takes sword in both hands, "*winks*" (obviously at the audience), and runs at Bilboe (IV.i, 45). Bilboe flees but comes back when Titere does not pursue. Bilboe reminds him of who made him what he is. When Titere takes credit, Bilboe swears he must kill him. They fight again, till Bilboe praises his fighting, calls a halt, they banter some more, then embrace.

This kind of slapstick action takes place in scene after scene. There is a Monty Python quality to it. Hired by Tyro to avenge his humiliation at the hands of Afterwitt in front of Beatrice, Bilboe pretends to have been run through. Titere Tu reassures Tyro that Bilboe will nevertheless fight on for him: "Ne'r doubt him Squire—I'd as liefe have him upon his stumps, as twentie others upon no leggs" (IV.iv, 55). The great length of the play is an endorsement of this comic exuberance. Moreover, it slips out of any attempt to read it as social comedy, not only because this exuberance dominates but also because we cannot take Afterwitt finally as the representative of a superior class served by all this trickery. For Whitebroth narrates a history that threatens any such reading as he explains the relationship between him and the Afterwitts (one that complicates the class politics of the play):

> To see how this World goes round:—My Great-Grandfather was a wealthy Citizen, and left my Grandfather, a Gentleman forsooth! But what between my Father, and him, they so order'd the business, that they left me, nev'r a Groat.—This Fellows Grandfather, was a Law-driver, and swallow'd my Father up; His Father set the Estate a moving, and this, will set it quite away:—His first Ancestor, cheated mine, and I hope I shall be able, to requite his love, upon his posterity:—Thus you see, the wheel comes round, to the same point again—This City, is like the Sea; few Estates, but ran of't at first, and will run into't at last. [III.ii, 35]

Afterwitt is not an aristocrat but the descendant of a lawyer who cheated himself into an estate. Nor is Whitebroth a gentleman either but the descendant of a wealthy City merchant. So behind the myth of aristocracy lurks oligarchic rivalry, and whoever has the power has the escutcheon of the moment. Moreover, despite Stuart ideology of the City, it is now, as the financial center of the country, the effective source of estates, into which and out of which they flow through various mergers and settlements facilitated by lawyers. Afterwitt's restoration is a subversive parody of the restoration of the Royalists and the king.

Mopus's Swiftian wisdom would seem to be right: "There are but two sorts of people in the World, *Aut qui captant, aut qui captantur;—Aut Corvi qui lacerant, aut Cadavera, quae lacerantur* [either those who capture or those who are captured; either crows who lacerate or cadavers which are lacerated]; which, the great *Albumazar,* has most significantlie render'd, by Cheators, and Cheatees—If it were not for fools Sir, how should Knaves live?" (IV.ii, 52). In apparently idle chatter with a boy about his Latin, Scruple may give us a metaphoric understanding of the play. Scruple asks the boy the meaning first of *byssus* then of *abyssus.* The boy answers, "*Byssus,* A bottomless Pit; *Abyssus,* A more bottomless Pit"; Scruple: "A—Child, Thou art in the right; There is a Great—great—great Bottomless bottom;—Indeed there is" (III.iii, 36), but is there? If his words have transcendental significance, Hell is that bottomless bottom, but the play suggests that there is no bottom, no ground, only words, only cant, only cheating. Who is on top is a function of wit, but who has the wit is no longer a function of birth, of class. Jolly, the rootless, probably younger brother of a Town wit, may have the greatest wit in the play, but he gets nothing for his troubles but the sheer love of play—surely no material manifestation of class superiority. And he must share the honors with the surviving Suburban parasites especially. Just as the play begins with him, Bilboe has the last, Rabelaisian word: "[S]ince we have had so good fortune to day, we'll henceforth boyle our Beef in Sack, and make the Beggars drunk with the Porridge" (77, misnumbered). The daemonic energy spills over democratically.[4]

One would expect the author of *The English Rogue,* Richard Head, if he turned his hand to drama, to write a play about tricksters. *Hic et Ubique; or, The Humors of Dublin*[5] seems as autobiographical as the early chapters of *The English Rogue,* for it features failed English petty bourgeois— "Quondam Citizens of London" (dramatis personae)—displaced to Dublin and thrown upon their wits, such as they are, for survival.[6] And they are accompanied by two parodic libertines, Hic-et-ubique and Phantastick, who, if they are younger brothers, emanate from fallen gentry indeed. Yet there is a Cavalier trickster, Peregrine, whose name indicates his stature and who wins the witty woman in the end.

This play is not social comedy with satiric butts, however. Yes, Peregrine merits the love and hand of Cassandra, daughter of Alderman

Thrive-well the vintner, in what would seem to be the typical reintegration of an estateless aristocrat through marriage with City money. Though he was angling for someone else, Thrive-well accepts their marriage in festive mode: "Marriages are made in Heaven, and questionlesse it was there decreed your Union; therefore my blessing on you both" (V.vi, 63). Peregrine displays aristocratic sensitivity when he falls in love with Cassandra at first sight, and she, though properly *dangereuse*, knows how to value "worth," especially when it is conjoined "with constancy" (IV.i, 44).

But Peregrine himself is not typical. No banished Cavalier or resourceful younger brother, he is the son of Old Peregrine, the East India merchant, "born to land" that his father must have purchased, but, like a nouveau riche, bred to no "Trade" and now affecting the ultimate Cavalier insouciance: he says of his estate that he

> enjoy'd it so long, till I was weary on't, and then was never at rest, till out of that dirty lump, I had extracted a pure and portable *Elixir.* In short, to free my self from that trouble & vexation that are the inseperable companions of Lands and Tenements, I sold 'em. (*Caveat Emptor*) The monies I have long since spent, yet want not; the Earth's large, and has enough, (and to spare) to supply the wants of all her industrious children. He that has wit, (I think [ ]) needs no plow; the apprehension of which perswades me, not to be confin'd to any place. My great Grandfather *Adam,* (Emperor of the whole world) left me something every where, and I find it truly paid me where e're I come. [I.iii, 9]

This is as pure a trickster manifesto as we get after Jonson's Mosca, and Peregrine's name surely alludes to the character of the same name in that same play, *Volpone.* Peregrine's posture is defiant of Williamsesque socialization. He is not restored to an estate in England but has only married the woman whom he loves and with whom he will thrive well not in the Town but in Dublin, probably at her father's expense. If at Thrive-well's death we are to assume Peregrine will inherit his estate, we need to remember that it consists merely of a tavern; moreover, we cannot envision Peregrine as an innkeeper but would expect him to sell the enterprise and let the buyer beware as he continues a carefree pursuit of Adam's legacy. Like Shadwell's Bevil and Rains, Peregrine longs to be free from the "trouble & vexation" of managing "Lands and Tenements," but unlike them he appears to remain free in the ultimate pastoral fantasy of carelessness. Yet given his origins, he seems to represent not Cavalier but bourgeois wish-fulfillment: to out-aristocrat the Cavaliers themselves.

Thrive-well himself seems a figure for the survivalist. Denied the preferment in Ireland promised him if he came over from England (like the soldiers from the New Model Army who were promised land) and having spent all his money, he could not lower himself to become a drawer, so his wife was forced to turn some apparent tricks to get him enough credit to set up a house for lodgers. They fed off itinerant gallants and earned enough to purchase the current tavern. Thrive-well philosophizes that the English gentry ought to send their sons to Dublin rather than on the Grand Tour, for here they would learn survival skills, learn to "live" rather than merely to affect "wit and manners" (I.v, 14).

Out of sows' ears, Thrive-well attempts to create other tricksters in his image. He leaves his pupil Contriver on the stage to utter this manifesto (reminiscent of the English Rogue's):

> Umh—how happy are all my projects, gramercy good brains. I am now clearly of the belief, my Mothers imagination was strongly fixt on *Oliver* or *Mazarin,* when she conceiv'd me, or that she long'd to eat five or six leaves of *Machiavel's* politick Discourses. When I was but a Boy I could have cheated all the Boyes in a whole School of their bread and butter, and have eaten it all afterwards: As for Calves and such like humane Creatures, them I couzened at my pleasure, by sucking their Dams. Now since I write my self Man, go thy way, when e're thou dyest, there's none will survive to bring thy ingenious plots to perfection. [IV.ii, 45]

This is disruptive discourse from below: the malicious image of the mother's imagination wandering during copulation to two of the century's most successful energy figures; the delicious image of the duping of unsophisticated lads by seducing their mothers. These are images from what Bakhtin calls "The Material Bodily Lower Stratum" (*Rabelais,* ch. 6). Tricksterism as survival is a manifestation of that corporate, immortal body of "humane Creatures" who, as Faulkner says, *endure.*

Not all the tricksters in Head's play triumph. Contriver's projects, including that for Thrive-well's daughter, fail after all, and he is reclaimed by his wife, newly arrived from London. But despite his parody of Restoration tragical poetic justice—"How just is Heaven! I see there's no shelter from Divine vengeance, no refuge from the All-seeing eye" (V.vi, 63)—he is enclosed in the concluding comic embrace, chastened and forgiven. Trust-all, despite the Restoration official discursive position that a gentleman's word is his bond, seems never to learn that you really can not trust anyone and must, like Contriver's mother, swallow a few leaves of Machiavelli's *Discourses* in order to survive. Bank-rupt thrives better because he masters the canting discourse of a mountebank. When Phantastick visits him for a cure for the clap, Bank-rupt breaks out into rhapsodic, Jonsonian mock moralizing to Recipe, his medical sidekick: "I knew him in another Condition; but commonly the Effects of Prodigality concludes [*sic*] in misery: those that sayl in Ships of Pleasure, near mind-ing the Sea-marks of Discretion, are oft suckt in, and swallowed up by the Quick-sands of Delight, or are violently dasht against the Rocks of Luxury" (V.i, 54).

Like Mrs. Hadland in *The Counterfeit Bridegroom,* Mrs. Hopewel survives by utilizing her feminine beauty and wiles. A woman alone in a strange country, she vows to seek aid from every deity in heaven to help her "play bad cards at the best advantage." She will pretend to be a widow, yet not wrong her husband, for she will get rich men to court her, ply her with gifts, yet retain her integrity. She has her own trickster manifesto: "Nature took pains in forming me beautiful, and age has not so much impair'd it, but that there's enough still to attract both love and pity from any brest that is amorous. Why may not I then follow the presidents of thousands of our sex, that in the ebb of their prosperities, have angled with their wits (baited with their beauties) in the swift streams of affection, whence they have drawn up large and rich fishes, without breaking the honourable line of their reputation" (I.iv, 11). She succeeds in duping Collonel Kil-tory of his estate, though Head backs off from full, Jonsonian tricksterism in this instance and has the Hopewels render it back in exchange for a loan that will enable Hopewel to set up honestly.

Hic-et-ubique and Phantastick are the Bevis and Butthead of Restoration comedy. Their constant comic asides are insufferably sophomoric, and despite their efforts to court Mrs. Hopewel, they are relegated to their landlady, Sue Pouch. Forced to sell his remaining cloaks, Hic-et-ubique breaks out into hilarious heroic couplets:

> Three Cloaks and all ingag'd, O cruel Fate
> That wu'd not leave me one, to Palliate
> My weather-beaten Body, and inclose
> My naked sides from my deriding Foes.
> My Angry Hostess, (heedless of the weather,
> Grown fat with foggy Ale, and bound together
> With the warm thongs of Fortune) has forgot
> What cold and hunger is, and she will not
> Shake hands with Pay, holds it is unjust
> To listen to the Arguments of Trust[.] [IV.iii, 47-48]

This is the landlady at whom he has railed earlier in Rabelaisian images of the bodily excessive: "[T]hou Tun of Heydleberg, thy bunghole's so big that I am afraid to come near it, lest falling therein, I hazard a drowning. Had *Gargantua* liv'd, thou mightst have taught him, without much endangering of him, to have kneaded dough in thy trough" (III.ii, 37). But now he is forced to compound with Sue Pouch and marry her for his debts, a consummation she has devoutly wished all along: "Why this is it I aym'd at: Youth joyn'd with Age is like a Warming-pan to a bed in Winter" (IV.iv, 51).

Despite his silliness and crudeness, then, Hic-et-ubique is also folded into the hymeneal embrace at the end of the comedy. In a sense, he and Phantastick are figures for the excessiveness of the play: uncontrollable, uncontainable, they and it constantly spill over into gratuitous exuberance. They really have no essential connection with any plot, and their volubility is a kind of filler that supplies no lack. For example, Phantastick laments his worsening clap, posturing rhetorically like a reformed sinner:

> Why shu'd I raile at Fortune, calling her Whore, unconstant Queane, and the like; when my own foolish self, is the sole Author of my present misery. Had I not been infatuated, I might easily have prognosticated my future condition, by the courses I then took. I cannot stay at home, the distemper of my body maketh me every where restlesse. Neither durst I stir abroad, for fear of Arrests. Oh insupportable condition! from bad premises, I cu'd now draw a worse conclusion: Farewel fond Femal [*sic*] pleasures, and welcome that Pilot that will steer me to the land of forgetfulness, where my weather-beaten Vessel may be safely moor'd up, from the tempestious, and swelling billows of all misfortunes[.] [V.iv, 59-60]

To him Hic, delightfully picking up the ship metaphor:

> [T]hou canst not steer aright; surely thou'st lost thy Rutter: You must be firing so often, that I thought you'd blow out your Brich-pin. Surely thy touch-hole is very foul, for thou recoylest wickedly; let me see thee walk,—Bad, bad—I fear th'art past mending by a Sereing, so that the utmost of thy expectation is e're long to be all at flitters. Well, I am sorry that so good an Hackney should so quickly be beaten of his speed, and dry founder'd. You see how drinking and whoring makes you draw your leges after you; come, thou must be stew'd, else thou'lt ne're be wholesom meat for the worms. [60]

Even Phantastick is included at the end: Hic-et-ubique takes him into his service as his tapster, though he is not sure his legs will carry him up and down.

What we have at the end, then, is a community of tricksters in a tavern, some floating to the top of success, some sinking below, as we, the audience, celebrate their verbal and bodily excesses—and the playwright's own indulgence in amorphousness. Displaced from London's Town to the boondocks of Irish backwardness, the characters and the play remind us of the rest of the world, the "humane Creatures" excluded from the canon of official discourse—from Stuart ideology to Literature as one of the Fine Arts.[7]

The subtitle character of the fine comedy by John Lacy, *The Old Troop; or, Monsieur Raggou* (1664)—a play in which everyone is a sneak or a thief—steals the show. Set in the Civil War, *The Old Troop* features a troop of Royalist soldiers spending more time scavenging the countryside than fighting. Their only visible opponents are a troop of Roundheads at the significantly named Thieves-den Garrison who do the same, covering their skulduggery with sanctimonious rhetoric. The most outrageous act of requisitioning from the local Country folk occurs when, led by Flea-flint, the troop demands of a household food, water, wine, women, hens, turkeys, swine, cows, calves, sheep, and so on. When the woman of the house maintains she has nothing to give, Ferret-farm orders her, "Send to the Market Town, and buy Provision, and be hang'd, or I'll set fire o' your house, you damn'd dery damn'd whore" (III, 20). But they have no money to buy provision. Long before *Modest Proposal,* the lieutenant scares them by threatening to eat their children, asks his men if they know how to prepare them, especially the cook, Monsieur Raggou: "Begar me tink so; for vat was me bred in de King of *Mogul*'s Kitchen for, tere ve kill twenty shild of a day? Take you one shild by both his two heels, and put his head between your two leg, den take your great a knife and slice off all de buttack, so fashion; begar, dat make a de best Scotts Collop in de varle" (21). The lieutenant wants a man-child, the implication being that the troop devours not only livelihoods but heirs as well. Raggou counterproposes, "Do you hear? get me one she-shild, a littel whore shild, and save me all de Lamb-stone and Sweet-bread, and all de Pig-petty-toe of de shild: do you hear, you Roundhead Whore?" (21). Yet the lieutenant and the cornet begin to worry:

> *Lieutenant:* This foolery will be nois'd about the Country, and then the Odium will never be taken off.
> *Cornet:* Why, what can they make on't? all understanding people will know it to be mirth.
> *Lieutenant:* I know they will; but the envious Priests will make fine talk on't, and make a great advantage on't too: Though they know it to be nothing but mirth, they'll preach their Parishioners into a real belief of it, on purpose to make us odious. [21]

This is Bakhtinian carnivalesque versus official discourse.

The women from the neighborhood all worry about these barbaric Cavaliers. One finally advises the others to bring out their animals to save their children. Meanwhile, a nurse brings two children! The rogues are hard-pressed not to be crossbitten. They ask if she's not scandalized to sacrifice her children, but she insists they're not hers but belong to a London woman in arrears in her child-care payments! The children are twins, and Raggou pretends they're forbidden to eat twins, asks instead for pregnant women to eat: "Lieutenant, it be de best meat in de varle; begar a woman with shild is better meat den one hen with egg at *Shrove-tide*" (23). When the women bring provisions, the troop demands drink too, and they offer them anything rather than their children. Raggou leaves them with this consolation: "Take some comfort; for if we should eat your shildren, you sall no be a loser by dat; for look you good woman, how many shildren we eat in a Parish, so many shild we are bound to get before we leave it; dat is very fair" (23).

The scene is a wonderful example of how both Raymond Williams and Mikhail Bakhtin are right. Behind the comedy is the harsh reality of a countryside ravaged by war and requisitioned into poverty by competing armies, whatever their ideologies. But the reality is filtered through the kind of materialist folk humor that makes it endurable even through its outrageousness. As with our students when we try to teach them Swift's masterpiece, the moralist in us is shocked at not just the idea of infantile cannibalism but Raggou's graphic descriptions of *ragazzo* buttock soup and *ragazza* sweetbreads and pig's knuckles. At the same time, we are "understanding" enough to recognize it all as "mirth," gallows humor worthy of wartime memories.

We assume Lacy wrote the part of Monsieur Raggou for himself (Leo Hughes, 27) and infused it with his great comic energy. Unlike James Howard's contemporary English Mounsieur in the play of that title and countless similar French satiric butts in Restoration comedy, Raggou, despite being vilified by his lieutenant as "a nasty slovenly rogue" who "stinks above ground" and "has not had a shirt on's back time out of mind" (I, 7), beats his English antagonists time and again with his "*French* wit" (V, 38) until the very end when his marriage to Dol Troop represents not so much a satirical denouement as a delightful, appropriate union between the two greatest tricksters of the play. Perhaps Lacy, like Sir Robert Howard, chose to treat favorably another of the detested allies of the Royalists as a piece of in-your-face bravado vis-à-vis the Roundhead sympathizers of his audience.[8]

Be that as it may, Raggou's antics are hilarious folk rhetoric and *lazzi*. When Dol Troop tries to lay her bastard, still in utero, at Raggou's feet, he protests he swore to marry her in French, which will not hold up in English law! He protests further when she threatens, "Begar, Madam *Dol,* you be de great Whore de *Babylon;* begar, me vil make appear noting can get you wid shild but the May-pole in de *Strand;* and den me can make appear, by good witteness, dat me have no May-pole abouta me. So adieu, Madam *Babylon:* Pox take you, me fader your dam son of a Whore shild!" (II.i, 9). The rhetoric works here because of its appropriation of the images of the whore of Babylon and the maypole from both Christian and pagan superstition, on the one hand, and Puritan cant on the other. The imagery culminates when Dol confesses, in effect, that the entire troop has fathered her child, to which troop she is as "faithful . . . as ever Wife was to a Husband": Raggou exclaims, "O, ho, are you so? me tink now, Madam *Dol,* you are de Whore de *Babylon;* for one whole Troop may make a Maypole" (II, 13-14).

Monsieur Raggou's major farcical actions include duping his landlady of a huge cheese, which he tries to hide in his enormous coat sleeves; cross-biting Flea-flint by counterdisguising himself and plundering the neighborhood in his stead; getting the best lodgings in town; and when the troop tries to scapegoat him for their plundering by planting evidence on him for the constable, escaping through a series of hilarious disguises. The first of these is to trade coats with another Frenchman and appropriate his puppet show, with which he dupes his pursuers. One of his puppets he portrays as the Whore of Babylon, who makes "great love" to that phallic "May-pole" again (IV, 29). He then pretends to be a Dutchman and sells the show to Flea-flint, who is also on the lam. Raggou's most outrageous disguise is as a matching post, which a painter paints and a joiner, attacking the painter for breach of contract, takes for the work of a competitor. Finally, Raggou disguises himself as an old woman who thinks she tricks the troop's captain out of the reward for Raggou by turning in her/himself!

The captain's countertricking him so that his only escape becomes marriage with Dol Troop may seem to be a class triumph, a sign that the aristocrat retains class superiority. And the play's concluding promise of the king's poetic justice on the plunderers and hypocrites from both camps would seem to underwrite such a conclusion. Particularly the Roundheads' crimes will be redressed, for though the loot captured with them is forfeit to the king, he generously "had rather have his Subjects hearts than Money" (V, 37). Captain Honor closes the play with this tag:

> I wish that the great Timber, the Pieces of State, that lie betwixt the King and Subjects,
>> I wish that they would take a hint from hence,
>> To keep the Peoples hearts close to their Prince. [39]

In other words, he appeals to the lords of the manors, of the estates with their timber, those Justices of the Peace, who, as Christopher Hill argues throughout *The Century of Revolution,* were indeed the backbone of the country, to act as the timber of the nation and uphold the king by keeping the people loyal.

In order to interpret the sense of this ending, however, we need to examine a subplot. Tom Tell-troth, despite his name, is another rogue, who works through Dol Troop the camp follower to get his beloved

Biddy through a trick marriage. Tell-troth is a turncoat, having served first the Roundheads, now the Royalists. His reason for switching is to follow his beloved, offering his services as a spy now to Captain Honor. He maintains that all loyalty is mixed with self-interest and warns the king accordingly, "[S]o that, good King, wheresoe'er you see me, trust to your self" (IV, 27). Moreover, when Tell-troth reports to Captain Honor that he has tricked the governor of Thieves-den Garrison to capture the Roundhead captains and appropriate the booty to himself, thus making him more easy for the taking by the Royalists through false promises of preferment with Parliament, Captain Honor, true to his name, at first disdains double-dealing. But when Tell-troth suggests the captain have the lieutenant swear the oath so that the captain can have the booty without forswearing, the latter, despite his touted honor, agrees. No honor among thieves with a twist, then. This is a world where all are thieves, where the witty tricksters prevail. Even the king's motivations can be seen as the pragmatism of power relations. His restitution to a Country gentleman of the wealth the Roundheads had swindled through religion *buys* him loyalty—a loyalty indeed mixed with self-interest. In such a world not only hypocritical Puritans can rise "from Coblers to Commanders" (IV, 27). There being no inherent (moral) difference between classes, what is to keep an arch-trickster, an arch-disguiser like Monsieur Raggou from rising to the top? We shall see that motif played out fully in Behn's *The False Count*.

First, however, we need to examine at least one intervening, remarkable lower-class trickster.[9] As one might expect from the duke of Newcastle, who collaborated on a more humors style comedy with both Dryden and his nemesis Shadwell, *The Triumphant Widow* (1674), whose titular heroine we examined briefly in the last chapter, contains multiple, memorable folk tricksters. These tricksters erupt repeatedly into the action of the high plot, insisting on the presence of the lower orders. The first subset comprises Footpad and his comrogues, who plan to prey on the suitors to Lady Haughty. One of the rogues praises Footpad for his "Breeding," and Footpad responds, "I am beholden to my Parents for that, truly they did breed me very well, rest their Souls, they were both slain at *Tyburn*, I heard 'em there at *Good people take warning*, but I had more Grace than to take it" (I, 2). The rogues universalize roguery, singing,

> Since ev'ry Profession's become a lewd Cheat,
> And the little, like fish, are devour'd by the great;
> Since all Mankind use to rob one another;
> Since the Son robs the Father, the Brother the Brother;

Since all sorts of men such Villains will be,
When all the World plays the Rogue, why should not we? [3][10]

Disguised as a gypsy, Footpad addresses the goddess Fortune: "Have at thee Fortune, they say thou art a Whore I will have a bout with, though thou art grown so common, thou favorest every Blockhead" (II, 28). The arch-trickster of the lower order, he repeatedly dominates Fortune, first lightening the pockets of Lady Haughty's ridiculous suitors under the guise of fortune-telling and later, disguised as a cripple, lightening one of them of a bag of £100 while the latter engages in a farcical duel and scurrying off, only to return with comrogues to lighten the participants further of clothes, hats, swords. Despite his Raggou-like disguises, however, Footpad is caught by the constable at last and sentenced to hang at Tyburn as his breeding seemed to foreshadow.

Within Lady Haughty's household, there are two more subsets of folk-subversive characters: John the master cook and the denizens of the kitchen, and James the butler and the chambermaids. John is in love with the chambermaid Mall, James with the chambermaid Margaret. The former courts with greasy metaphors, making Mall sit in his lap and endure his kisses. And his courtship songs sound like recipes! This is the best of the stanzas:

> Thou should'st skim Love upon the top,
> Or with a Sop
> To soak it, or else to dip it,
> Many a Sippet
> Would keep't within Love's circle, then
> Stir it agen;
> And if it rise, 'twill down, you know,
> If that you blow. [II.i, 25]

James the butler courts with insult and answerable bawdry. As he and Margery argue, he insults her body, and she responds, "[T]hou unconscionable Item of searing Candle, Bumbast, and Canvas"; he, "There's stiffening too, good Mrs. Wasp, with a sting in your tail"; she, "Not so much as you should have put in, you cheating Rogue, you cozened me in that too" (III, 40). The kitchen bursts open again for a scene of parody of the upper plot and class. The cooks entertain with a delightful mock epic about cooking, spoken "*in a very tragical tone*" (III.i, 46 s.d.). Here is the best part of it:

> A Chine of Beef slasht mangled to the bones,
> Shoulders of Venson in their own blood wallowing,
> Our Ordnance Marrow-bones dismounted quite,

> The wriggled Brawn so massacred with wounds,
> Tripes hanging out most hideous to see,
> With excrement of Mustard dropping down.
> There Oysters now gaping for their last breath,
> Lobsters and Crevices all bloody red. . . .
> None made retreats but Crabs, that I could see,
> The Forlorn hope of Porrige all was spilt,
> And the Reserve of Fruit and Cheese thrown done,
> Some few were rallied, for the fight 'ith' Hall;
> But being charg'd, they could not stand at all.
> So the dead bodies, scatter'd bones, and crusts,
> Were in the Alms Tub buried first, and then
> Rak'd up by rav'nous Crows and Kites call'd Beggers,
> Wherewith their hungry maws and scrips they fil'd. [47]

The musician responds, "I see moving passion is a great matter, though in Kitchin Poetry" (48). In another eruption, James and Margery trade hilarious insults—for example, Margery's "You Raggamuffin, you Drawlatch, you Scurff, you Nit, . . . you Jail bird, you Mungrel, you Widgeon" (IV, 64). They mock each other's (non)origins, each other's parents:

> *Margery:* Indeed you are of an ancient Family, that which belongs to
>   your no House, is an old Coat powder'd with Vermine. . . .
> *James:* You are of a Royal stock indeed, have I not seen your Mother
>   with a Petticoat of more patches than one can number, indented at
>   the bottom, and so short, I saw up to her old cruel Garters, with her
>   Stockins of three colours, three stories high, with Incle about her
>   Hat, knitting at the Gate for an Alms? [IV, 64]

Yet there is no radical difference between the folly of upstairs and the folly of downstairs, where Lady Haughty's suitors fall all over themselves in silliness.

Emerging from all the folk interruptions, dances, squabbles, energetic outbursts, both servant couples ask Lady Haughty's permission to marry. She queries James and Margery about possible fornication, a word they take to be "too fine a word for us poor folks to understand" (V, 79). Lady Haughty grants their requests, noting that it is a day for both marrying and hanging. She has sent a reprieve for Footpad, but it may arrive too late, as Newcastle stretches out his scene in parody of criminal biographies and Newgate confessions. The mob gathered at the foot of the scaffold interrogates Footpad, and he facetiously responds, "You examine me as if you would hang me, after I am hang'd" (V, 91). One man says, "Prethee Mr. Thief, let this be a warning to you for ever doing the like again";

Footpad, again facetiously, "I promise you it shall" (92). The women think he is too pretty to be hanged. He offers to trade places with their husbands: "I had rather be Epilogue than Prologue to this Tragi-Comedy; I see you have no mind to go to Heaven yet for all your pretended zeal, you would still live in this vale of misery and transitory peregrinations; but if any be ambitious to be exalted, I'le render him my place" (92). The folk comment on the fine speeches they have heard from the scaffold. So Footpad obliges: "Well, good people, if I may be bold to call you so, this Pulpit was not of my chusing, I shall shortly preach mortality to you without speaking; therefore pray take example by me, and then I know what will become of ye, shortly I will set a Death's head before ye, to put you in mind of your ends, *Memento mori*" (93). One of them remarks that he is a scholar who "does Latine it." "I will be, I say, your *memento mori,* hoping you will all follow me: I have been too covetous, and at last taken for't, and am very sorry for't; I have been a great sinner, and condemn'd for it, which grieves me not a little, that I made not my escape, and so I heartily repent it, and so I die with this true Confession" The people are so moved they begin to pray mercy for him. But then comes the reprieve and the Monty Python response:

> *1 Man:* Pish, what must he not be hang'd now?
> *2 Man:* What did we come all this way for this?
> *1 Woman:* Take all this pains to see nothing! [94]

In the final scene Footpad enters, Lady Haughty hopes he will leave off thieving, and he gestures, "If it be possible to break an ill habit, I will, Madam, I give your Ladiship a thousand thanks; for as the case stood, you could not have done me a greater courtesie" (97).

The point of all these eruptions into the more typical high plot would seem to be that not only is there no great divide between upstairs and downstairs, the folk energy and wisdom of the lower-class characters are in marked contrast to the suitors' posturing. Well before the bourgeois satires of Southerne and Gay, then, upper-class decadence was being contrasted with lower-class exuberance, hypocrisy with a refreshing forthrightness if not exactly honesty. Lady Haughty's fit match is obviously Footpad. But not even Archer will marry Cherry in 1707. The democratic window of Restoration comedy invited no precipitate defenestration.

In the fall of 1681, Behn had produced, amidst her Tory comedies, a comedy she announces in her prologue as Whig, *The False Count; or, A New Way to Play an Old Game.* Since the prologue itself is stridently anti-Whig and since the play features Cit-cuckolding, what could she possibly have meant? The answer would appear to lie in her treatment of Antonio, the merchant whose class status is treated favorably. But the real subversiveness of the play lies in its destabilization of status hierarchy even as it seems to redefine and restabilize it.

Don Carlos is the young, aristocratic governor of Cadiz, who has just inherited his father's "Estate and Honour [as governor]" (I.i.21) but has failed to secure Julia, to whom he is precontracted by mutual vows but whose father has given her away in marriage to the merchant Francisco. The main plot of the play aims at the adulterous union of this gay couple in the teeth of her jealous old husband. Though he now claims to be a "Gentleman" who leads a life of leisure (IV.ii.101), Francisco was not born a wealthy merchant. Antonio describes his origins as "an *English* Cordwainer, that is to say, a Shoo-maker, Which he improv'd in time to a Merchant; and the Devil and his Knavery helping him to a considerable Estate, he set up for *Gentleman*" and retired to Spain (I.i.55-58). He manifests the character traits usually attributed to satirized Cits: penuriousness (too stingy to live in England, would live in slavery rather than spend the money to ransom himself), impotence (can not satisfy his wife), cowardice (would shoot Carlos in the back but refuses to face him, would sacrifice his wife's virtue to save his own skin), ignorance (can be tricked into thinking a villa in the Spanish countryside is Turkish), sycophancy (fawns before lords and sultans), hypocrisy (denies his Christianity to save his skin as well).

Carlos's clever servant Guzman plots an elaborate trick to gain Carlos access to Julia: when Francisco goes aboard his galley, Carlos's company pretend to be Turks, kidnap Francisco's party and bring them to Antonio's villa, where Carlos plays the Great Turk, who chooses Julia for his harem. Francisco, played by Nokes, is forced into utter abjection with the fear of being strangled if he does not relinquish his wife, nay persuade her to become the Turk's mistress—that is, to "Pimp" for her (V.56). Nokes must have been hilarious in the role, especially in this scene where, goaded by Guzman, who is disguised as a bassa and was played by his great comic partner Underhill, Francisco begs Julia to abandon her strict virtue and capitulate:

> *Guzman:* Nay, doe't and doe't handsomly too, not with a snivelling countenance, as if you were compell'd to't;—but with the face of authority, and the awful command of a Husband—or—thou dyest—
> *Francisco:* My dear *Julia,* you are a Fool, my Love . . . to refuse the Love of so Great a *Turk;* why, what a Pox makes you so coy? . . .[*Angrily.* [A]m not I your Lord and Master, hah? . . . [A] Pox of her Vertue,— these women are always vertuous in the wrong place.   [*Aside.*
> —I say, you shall be kind to the sweet *Sultan.*
> *Julia:* And rob my Husband of his right!

Francisco: Shaw, exchange is no robbery.
Julia: And forsake my Vertue, and make nown Dear a Cuckold.
Francisco: Shaw, most of the Heroes of the world were so;—go prethee
Hony go—do me the favour to Cuckold me a little, if not for Love,
for Charity. [58-91]

This main plot concludes in one of Behn's fantasy divorces, as Carlos, upon the authority of their precontract, seizes his "own" and Francisco, cured of his jealousy, willingly relinquishes her (319). Thus a middle-class male who has married above his class is put back in his place by the superior aristocrat.

The second plot of the play complicates its ideology, however. Antonio the merchant is also the friend of Carlos, and their relationship resembles that between the typical Town wits of Restoration comedy. Antonio's father arranges a marriage for him with Isabella, Francisco's daughter by a former wife. But Isabella has taken on airs and considers Antonio beneath her. Into her mouth Behn puts the anti-Cit sentiments that pervade hers and others' comedies. Antonio reports she calls him "base Mechanick" (I.i.98), and she herself exclaims, "Merchant, a pretty Character, a Woman of my Beauty, and 5. Thousand pound, marry a Merchant—a little, pety, dirty-heel'd Merchant[?]" (I.ii252-54). To Antonio's face she protests, "Sawcy Impertinent, you show your City breeding, you understand what's due to Ladys, you understand your Pen and Ink how to count your dirty money, trudge to and fro chaffering of base commodities, and cuzening those you deal with, till you sweat and stink again like an o'er heated Cook" (312-16). She insists upon a radical "difference between a Citizen and a true bred Cavalier" (328-29) and leaves Antonio abruptly with a "farewel, Cit" (334).

Isabella's is the rhetoric of Stuart ideology, which insists upon the same radical difference. Yet the play subverts that ideology by portraying Isabella as a fool and Antonio as inherently noble and rewarding her with one from the lowest class, him with one from the highest. Antonio is given the better part of the concluding tag of the play to read out its moral—a different class message than that of the main plot: "You base born Beauties, whose ill manner'd Pride, / Th'industrious noble Citizens deride, / May you all meet with *Isabella's* doom" (V.383-85). Indeed, Isabella is a fool. But for Cavalier Behn to call her "base born" in contrast with "noble Citizens" is quite remarkable, especially when the epithet of usual opprobrium, "industrious," is added to the seemingly inappropriate "noble." She seems to be making a distinction between petite and haute bourgeoisie. Isabella is the daughter, after all, of a "Leather-seller" (I.ii.262), and Antonio reproves her "ill manner'd Pride" by pointing out, "[I]f there be any inequality in our births, the advantage is on my side" (310-11). Her own father has characterized Antonio as "one of the richest Merchants of his standing in all *Cadez*" (250-51); moreover, Behn puts in his mouth a reproof of her ambition to marry up that sounds uncharacteristically nonfoolish: "Come, come, Mistress, I got by the City, and I love and honour the City; I confess 'tis the Fashion nowadayes, if a Citizen get but a little money, one goes to bulding houses, and brick Walls, another must buy an Office for his Son; a third hoysts up his Daughter's Topsail, and flaunts it away, much above her Breeding; and these things make so many break, and Cause the decay of Trading: but I'm for the honest *Dutch* way of breeding their Children, according to their Fathers Calling" (285-90). Behn seems to want it both ways: to satirize Cits for social climbing and thus to confine them to the City, and yet to praise merchants of the haute bourgeoisie—perhaps to help build a political alliance that disengages that part of the middle-class from its inferior brethren and engages them with the Court party as part of the naturally noble ruling class. Yet how did the haute bourgeoisie become haute? How did Antonio's father get that villa in the Country? Did he not build houses and walls? And is his son not moving up? Behn's play both reveals the already existing alliance between aristocracy and haute bourgeoisie, achieved through economic and sexual intercourse, and at the same time denies the efficacy and desirability of such status flexibility.

The play undercuts even this emergent ideology. If Nokes has a wonderful role as satiric butt, he is upstaged by his greatest comic partner, Tony Leigh, for Leigh was given the most dynamic role in the play, that of the chimney sweep Guiliom. Guiliom is employed by Guzman to impersonate a viscount in order to chastise Isabella for her parvenue pretensions. Carlos has reservations about Guiliom's ability: "This Fellow's of a quick Wit and good Apprehension, though possibly he cannot act the Don so well" (I.i.110-11). Even Guiliom seems reticent, relying on "good instructions," a phrase he employs twice when interviewed for the job (II.105, 113). Though he repeatedly slips into the homely metaphors of his trade, Guiliom gives himself and Carlos the lie, however, for he rises heroically to the occasion, as he singles out Isabella for his affection:

> Oh! I am doubly wounded, first with her harmonious Eyes,
>   Who've fir'd my Heart to that degree,
>   No Chimney ever burnt like me.
> Fair Lady,—suffer the Broom of my Affection to sweep
> all other Lovers from your heart. [III.ii, 148-52]

When she protests she is to be married that very day, he explodes into delectable rant: "To day; name me the Man—Man, did I say, the Monster, that dares lay claim to her, I dain to love,—none answer me,—I'll make him smoak by *Vulcan*—and all the rest of the Goddesses. . . . I cannot brook a Rival in my Love, the rustling Pole of my Affection is too strong to be resisted. . . . I say no more, but that I do Love,—and I will Love, and that if you are but half so willing as I, I will dub you, Viscountess *de Chimeny Sweperio*" (154-73). The false count fakes anger with his rival Antonio (who goes along with the joke), reconciles, and offers him a soot-blackened hand to kiss. Corrected in one of his verbal faux pas for swearing "By *Mars*, the God of Love!" Guiliom stubbornly insists, "I say, I'll have it *Mars*, there's more Thunder in the sound" (IV.i.6-10). He is, of course, in on the joke of the Turkish kidnapping, and when Francisco fears being made a eunuch, quips delightfully, "Shaw, that's nothing, 'tis good for the Voice—how sweetly we shall sing, ta, la, ta la la, ta la, *&c*" (62-63). His antics on the stage, especially his mock fencing, must have split the audience's sides. He is a figure for boundless comic energy erupting, like his vulcanic goddess, from below.

Guiliom's primary function is to humble Isabella, whose ambition soars beyond his lordship to be a very sultana: "oh that I were a She Great *Turk*" (IV.i.149). Certain she will be chosen by the great Turk, she assures Guiliom, "Because you were my Lover once, when I am Queen I'll Pardon you" (191-92). Spurned, she fawns repentant, but Guiliom returns cold retorts to her plaints and finally rejects her with gusto:

Isabella: Oh, Heavens! and shall I be no Viscountess?
Guiliom: Not, for me, Fair Lady, by *Jupiter*,—no, no,—Queen's much
  better,—Death, affront a man of Honour, a Vicount that wou'd have
  took you to his Bed,—after half the Town had blown upon you,—
  without examining either Portion or Honesty, and wou'd have took
  you for better for worse—Death, I'll untile houses, and demolish
  Chimneys, But I'll be revenged. [304-10]

Amazingly, Isabella is now so desperate to rise and not fall back to the level of Antonio that she brooks Guiliom's hilarious but gratuitous sexual innuendos. She weeps, he melts. As they make plans for the wedding, they conclude the scene and their courtship in a parody of romantic dialogue (note the verse):

Guiliom: And, is it pure and tender Love for my Person,
  And not for my glorious Titles?
Isabella: Name not your Titles, 'tis your self I love
  Your amiable, sweet and charming self,
  And, I cou'd almost wish you were not great,
  To let you see my Love.

Guiliom: I am confirm'd—
　'Tis no respect of Honour makes her weep;
　Her Love's the same shou'd I crie—Chimnie Sweep. [318-26]

Antonio sweetens his class revenge against Isabella by not only insuring that both settlement—of £10,000—and marriage be consummated but by arranging for her to rencounter Guiliom in his *propria persona*. Mocking her prior protestations that she loves him without titles and laughing in the teeth of her father's threat to cut her off without portion, Guiliom taunts her—"No matter, her love's worth a million; and, that's so great, that I'm sure she'll [be] content to carry my Soot-basket after me"—and, the stage direction informs us, "*Goes and kisses her, and blacks her face*" (357-58, 360s.d.). This gesture is the final put-down of the uppity City daughter, a blackening that levels her downward toward her origins. Earlier Guiliom has mockingly wondered, "[W]hat clod of Earth [that is, what "Citizen"] cou'd bring forth such a Beauty?" (III.ii.144) and Francisco has answered, lamenting her prior engagement but unwittingly speaking more truth than poetry, "Alas, my Lord, I am that clod of Earth, and to Earth if you call it so, she must return again, for she's to be married to a Citizen this Morning" (145-47). The blackening kiss repeats this *earth to earth* parody of Christianity's *ashes to ashes, dust to dust.*

Yet out of these ashes with their ideological import rises the figure of Guiliom himself, representing an energy that finally really does transcend class. When Carlos comments to him, "Thou want'st not confidence," Guiliom retorts with folk wisdom, "No, nor Impudence neither; how should a man live in this wicked world without that Talent?" (II.115-17). His implicit satire on the lords he impersonates reminds us that nobility is a mask for knaves—even "the best States-man in Christendom" is "loose in the hilts" (III.ii.229-30). More important, the race goes to the swift, the mercurial, the tricksters who can change shape at will. When Carlos remonstrates with Francisco that "as cases stand"—that is, since his daughter is now damaged goods—he is not likely to find a better match for her than Guiliom (V.365), Guiliom boasts of his own ability—whatever hers—to rise: "And, for the Vicount, Sir; gay Cloths, Money and Confidence will set me up for one, in any ground in Christiandom" (366-67). No wonder there were sumptuary laws! Carlos allows as Guiliom just might "pass" (369), and Francisco himself concludes, "I was but a Leather-seller my self, and am grown up to a Gentleman; and, who knows but he, being a Chimney-sweeper, may, in time, grow up to a Lord" (371-73).

In sum, in the denouement Behn has unraveled any monologic ideology, revealing that the daemonic energy of the earth makes a mockery of any official discourse, any status stability. Rising from the ashes like a comic phoenix, the chimney sweeper soars toward an inevitable peerage, false count become a true—at least as true as any other, even the "noble Lord" Carlos he welcomes at the end into his society of happiness (377). Fittingly, he has the last line of the play, capping Antonio's tag about all proud but baseborn beauties meeting "with *Isabella's* doom": "—And, all such Husbands as the Count *Guiliom.*" (385-86). The line means may all such women meet with the additional doom of having husbands like himself—partly as punishment, but the line means more than that. It is a boast, a piece of self-congratulation: any woman would be glad to have a husband with such energy. And that means sexual energy as well. Has he not just pleased Isabella in bed? Has he not the ability, then, to please even real sultanas, real queens? He is as potent as the potentate Carlos, as the supposedly radically different Cavalier. And so is Antonio. And they are all chimney sweepers with ashened faces, children of the earth. In this play, Behn is a closet Leveller.[11]

In Nahum Tate's *A Duke and No Duke* (1684) it is as if Guiliom gets his chance to be not only a lord but a duke. Trappolin, also played by Tony Leigh, is a Rabelaisian character, a pimp who services several ministers of state. Banished ostensibly because of his vicious enormities (but really because of his love for Flametta, who is also beloved by the powerful lord Barberino), Trappolin encounters Mago, whose name is self-explanatory and who transforms him into the spitting image of Lavinio, the legitimate duke of Tuscany and a de Medici. Trappolin returns to the court in Florence and lambastes Lavinio's lords for mistreating himself as Trappolin. Demanding a definition of the duty of a statesman, Trappolin, whom I shall call in this role No Duke, juxtaposes his own, Rabelaisian sense against that of official discourse. Barberino's answer is a late feudal aristocratic standard:

> To study first his Royal Masters profit,
> And next to that his pleasure; to pursue
> No sinister design of private gain;
> Nor pillage from the Crown to raise his Heirs,
> His base-born Brood in Pomp above the Race
> Of old descended Worth; to know Desert,
> And turn the Princes favour on his Friends;
> And keep an open Ear to just Complaints. [I, 13-14]

No Duke counters with a satirical topsy-turvy: "Why there 'tis. I have travel'd, and can tell you what a Statesman should be. I will have him ten times prouder than his Master; I, and ten times richer too. To know none of his old Friends, when he is once in Office; to inform himself who has

Merit, that he may know whom to do nothing for; to make Sollicitors wait seven years to no purpose, and to bounce thr'o [*sic*] a whole Regiment of 'em, like a Souldier through the Gantlet" (14).

The duke has put Brunetto, a captive at his court, in prison for aspiring above his station to the duke's sister, the Princess Prudentia. No Duke visits Brunetto and assumes no airs, invites Brunetto to just call him Lavin or Medices. They engage in farcical stage business, as Brunetto refuses to sit at No Duke's right hand, while No Duke insists he not sit on the left. No Duke invites Brunetto to talk with him as if they were in a tavern. No Duke releases Brunetto and encourages him to wed his sister posthaste. Prudentia reveals to him that Brunetto is really a prince, and No Duke says he no more thought of Brunetto as a prince than himself! His crude earthiness breaks out in a passion for Prudentia, which produces a "Carnal Reason" for lamenting their love (II, 18), but he reluctantly grants his consent to her as well for the marriage. He is like Sancho Panza as governor of his island, inhabiting a body that is full of crass desires and folk common sense.

It turns out that this is judgment day for causes the duke decides from the Chair of State. Several people have come to appeal for justice. What we get, of course, is saturnalian misrule complete with parodic solomonic wisdom. An old woman, widow to a man who died in the duke's service, has had her daughter debauched and ruined by one with his own wife and son. No Duke's judgment is that she gets to debauch the son and therefore ruin his fortune in turn. Of course the joke is that patriarchy does not work that way, for the son cannot really be ruined by such a deed. Another widow complains that a coachman drove over her only child. No Duke decides he has to give up being a coachman till he impregnate her with a substitute! She complains that the remedy is even worse than the offense, but he silences her. So far this folk patriarch has shut up both women. Next is a Puritan, complaining that a tiler fell off the roof of the mansion he was having built, landed right on him, and bruised him despite the dozens of articles of puritanical garb he was wearing. No Duke affects indignation at such an outrage, says the Puritan must ascend the roof and fall on the tiler. By then he has had enough and needs to feed his body.

Meanwhile, the real duke, who has been fetching his bride abroad, returns with her and finds things upside down, as if "[s]ome strange fantastick humour has possest / In general the Citizens of *Florence*" (II, 22). Several switches occur as each duke assumes the stage and power, none funnier than No Duke bellying up to the new duchess, Isabella, kissing her smack on the lips, and, when she expresses surprise at his humor, saying he has been drinking, grabbing her by the hand, and leading her off to consummate and drink together!

Apparently too drunk for sex, No Duke is discovered when the scene is drawn to have fallen asleep surrounded by flasks of wine. To the chagrin of ambassadors from Savoy (whence hails Brunetto, whose real name is Horatio, brother to the current duke of that province), No Duke acts like the peasant—and pimp—he is. Finally confronted by the duke, No Duke throws Mago's powder in his face and transforms him into himself, Trappolin. Mago finally enters to undo the confusion, returning the duke and No Duke to their proper selves, assuring the duke that No Duke has not cuckolded him, and informing Horatio that his brother is dead and he is now duke of Savoy. The duke generously now allows the marriage of Horatio and Prudentia, but he insists on Trappolin's banishment. Horatio rewards Trappolin for his own generosity toward him and takes him to Savoy. Lo and behold, Mago turns out to be an unjustly banished count and reveals that Trappolin is his son—a real count-apparent after all.

What is the reason for all this identity confusion, especially in a play with poignant similarities to the current political situation, where a brother, recently in exile, awaits the death of his sovereign brother? Order and legitimacy seem reestablished at the end. Lavinio is back on the throne accompanied by his chaste duchess, and he reads out of the action a typical lesson of official late feudal discourse: "God's! [*sic*] what abject Things,/When in your Hands, prove Scourges of a State" (V, 41). Trappolin, then, "abject" creature that he is, can be rationalized as a scourge of god. He himself reads a different lesson but one still compatible with official discourse, *sic transit gloria mundi:* "You see by me what a Prince may come to" (ibid.). Identity confusion provides a kind of mirror for magistrates.

Jo Haines's epilogue causes us to reinterpret these lessons, however: while bashing Cits for foolishly believing their wives chaste when there are so many studly Cavaliers around, Haines admits,

> There's no Man here had Married I'me afraid,
> Had he not first suppos'd his Wife a Maid,
> Thus, 'tis Opinion must our Peace secure,
> For no Experiement can do't I'me sure.
> In Paths of Love no Foot-steps e're were Trac'd,
> All we can do is to suppose her Chast;
> For Women are of that deep subtile kind,
> The more we dive to Know, the less we find.

Cuckolding (even pre-Cana cuckolding) lovers leave no footsteps. All the pitiful subjects of patriarchy can do, in reality, is suppose their women chaste. The secret is out. All the eggs are scrambled, and there is no such thing as legitimacy. Like Guiliom, Trappolin opines as he views his new self, "The Dress is just like him, and for ought I know, it is Dress that makes a Duke. . . . Trust me for Duking of it: I long to be at it. I know not why every man should not be Duke in his turn" (I, 10). Trappolin's becoming a count at the end is a sop to the fears of the aristocracy, to Stuart ideology. Every count is a false count, every duke a no duke, for the patrilineal aqueduct that leads to the palaces of the great has leaks and breaches. Barberino's key phrases—"base-born Brood" and "the Race / Of old descended Worth"—are merely verbal fences against the Rabelaisian reality Trappolin represents.[12]

10
Female Folk Tricksters Climb on Top

In this category of subversive comedies featuring folk tricksters, women again seem to merit their own separate treatment. I shall once more examine sympathetic folk tricksters exerting their energy in comedies they do not dominate, then examine plays they simply take over.

James Howard, creator of the irrepressible Mirida, bequeaths to us in *The English Mounsieur* the vivacious Wiltshire Country lass, Elsba. While Lady Wealthy is taming Welbred, his libertine comrade Comely, uncharacteristically for a Town wit, determines to leave London to go down to his estate in the Country in order to breathe the country air, to hunt and hawk, eat and sleep soundly, and never dream of women: "Now i'le away, a country life / Shall be my Mistriss and my Wife" (IV.i, 39). But as he is leaving, he runs into the Wiltshire couple William and Elsbeth. They have come up to Town "about this Maiden's Vather's Will," says William (40), and are staying where William's father "uses to lie at . . . When [he] comes about Law Suits" (41). Howard thus parodies the aristocratic pattern: at best Elsbeth's father was a freeholder. But Howard invests her with not so much material wealth as irresistible *élan vital,* for he wants to test the envelope of hierarchy. This moment in the play, deferred so late, radiates the brightest energy as it interpolates the conversion of the hippolytan squire to love of the Country lass. Comely finds himself strangely moved that Elsba's to marry Will. Some beast has tried to bite her leg, so Comely gets to see it as her skirts are raised, wishes he were as fortunate as Will to be handling it. He insists, as an aristocrat, that he would, of course, handle the leg more gently. Left alone, Comely muses, "[W]hat sudden fate hath chang'd my mind! . . . sure I'me in love" (42).

The comic necessity apparently at work is frustrated, however, by class consciousness. But not in the manner we might expect. Comely begins his courtship of Elsba with the (class) confidence that she cannot love her clown as much as this Town wit. But she is indifferent to his courtship, protesting she loves only Will. She is worried that he is lost in London and says if he died, she would never sing again milking her father's cows. Comely gets nowhere with her and asks to contest with William when he returns over which one talks the best love. Elsba agrees but is sure Will will win. Will returns, awed with the sight of the procession of the bull and bears on bear-baiting day. Comely exhibits class superiority: "'[T]is a very hard case this Clown must be my Rival" (56). But against Comely's essentially Platonic rendering, Elsba prefers William's homely one:

> I do love thee, I find by the Comfashiousness of my heart, I could suck thy Eyes out of thy head, I could eat thy lips though I were not an hungard, I could lick thee all over as our Cow does her Calf. O *Elsba,* my heart do Thunderclap my breast when I think o'thee, a wou's methinks sometimes though I never am anger'd with thee, I could tear the cloaths off thy back, Smock and all, my heart does leap and caper when I do see this leg and thy Coats tuck't up as thou com'st home from Milking Vathers Kine. [V.i, 56-57]

Later Comely tries to court Elsba not with Platonisms but with the material, gorgeous trappings of his class and estate. She resists with wonderful country humor: "O wo'us! [apparently for *wou's,* Wiltshire for *wounds*] *William* would not know me in all this bravery, but Sir if you would give me all these things and Roast-meat twice aday into the bargain, I could not have the Conscience to take my heart from *William,* he and I are going just now, if you'l be my Father and give me, i'le thank you? [*sic*]" (V.ii, 61). Defeated, Comely concludes despite himself, "I can't but love her too for being constant to her Clown" (61).

Thus Howard circumscribes metaphorical *droit du seigneur.* Comely can not have Elsba not because of his own class disdain of marriage with a peasant but because she will not have him. And not so much because of Country virtue as because of Country taste. She prefers Will's roast beef to Comely's caviar. Their lovemaking will be grotesque, carnivalesque as they tear off their clothes and lick each other all over like cows, sucking each other's eyes out. And like the gods on Olympus before the lovemaking of Mars and Venus, the aristocrats can only stand and envy. At the end Comely displays his Country treasure before the ladies, who mock him with class contempt for falling in love with someone so beneath him—though they are forced to admit she is pretty, and they bet, in their envious snobbery, she can dance well. Dance she does, doing a Country jig that absorbs into it the English Mounsieur's Crafty wife, who chauvinistically disdains the French mode and joins Elsba in the English. But the treasure of Elsba's comic spirit cannot be possessed, can still only be admired, as Comely offers her an annuity and vows to travel in order to forget what he cannot have. Comely's concluding ennui, his comic *tristesse* is an unconscious, ludic acknowledgment of aristocracy's failure to contain what it oppresses.

Perhaps the most obvious class of female folk tricksters contains the clever women servants. The most famous such servant in Restoration comedy must be Lucy in Wycherley's subversive comedy, *The Country-Wife*. Not only does she empower the eponymous Margery to evade the sadistic patriarchal control of her jealous husband, Pinchwife, providing her with the ruse to impersonate her sister-in-law, Alithea, in order have her own husband deliver her to the chambers of the cuckolding Horner, but she empowers Alithea to escape her trothplight to a fool. She boasts of her plot and her agency, "So 'twill work I see– . . . Now cou'd I speak, if I durst, and 'solve the Riddle, who am the Author of it" (V, 346, 355). Although in the case of Alithea she intervenes to free her to follow her heart and to be united with Harcourt in a traditional union of mutually intelligent lovers, Lucy's rationale is folk subversive: she says aside of Sparkish, "Well to see what easie Husbands these Women of quality can meet with, a poor Chamber-maid can never have such Lady-like luck; besides he's thrown away upon her, she'l make no use of her fortune, her blessing" (III, 301). Directly to Alithea she makes the same point: "Lord, Madam, what shou'd you do with a fool to your Husband, you intend to be honest don't you? then that husbandly virtue, credulity, is thrown away upon you" (IV, 313).

And although she has worldly wisdom enough to know that expecting love to follow marriage is folly and to recommend instead mutually united hearts, she is no romantic, especially about the honor code: "[W]hat a Divel is this honour? 'tis sure a disease in the head, like the Megrim, or Falling-sickness, that alwayes hurries People away to do themselves mischief; Men loose their lives by it: Women what's dearer to'em, their love, the life of life" (IV, 313). So when the archtrickster Horner is almost at a loss in the face of exposure, Lucy comes forward (for a bribe—Horner pledges to "give" her an unspecified amount [V, 358]) to try to cover his adultery with Margery. Her protestations alone do not work, but when the Quack doctor arrives to affirm Horner's ruse of impotence, Lucy articulates the last protestation of Margery's innocence, which she has Margery affirm through the "lyes" Lucy and the other subversive ladies have taught her to tell to protect the illegitimate satisfaction of libertine desires (V, 360). Thus, Lucy escapes any poetic justice traditionally meted out to transgressors, especially women, and thrives on gratuities from gallants and ladies whose desires she serves. She remains a parasite on the political economy of the hegemonic system but exercises independent agency, serving not only her mistress but the Town Wits who reward her services.[1]

Earlier in the analysis of punitive elements in Restoration social comedy (ch. 6), because they are not satiric butts but successful tricksters, I deferred treatment of Wycherley's pair of outrageous bawds in *Love in a Wood*, Mrs. Joyner and Mrs. Crossbite. The dramatis personae describes the former as "a Match-maker, or precise City Bawd" and the latter as "an old cheating Jilt, and Bawd to her Daughter." City women are almost always satirized in these comedies as hypocritical, superannuated, lecherous, ambitious. But these two women are a notch down the social scale into the lower classes, and their escape from the poetic justice of class dominance at the end marks a celebration of their vitality.

From his mock dedication of *The Plain Dealer* to the notorious bawd Mother Bennet we can infer Wycherley's attitude toward such scandalous women: "[W]hatsoever your Amorous misfortunes have been, none can charge you with that heinous, and worst of Womens Crimes, Hypocrisie; nay, in spight of misfortunes or age, you are the same Woman still; though most of your Sex grow *Magdalens* at fifty" (383; italics reversed). Wycherley also informs us what he thinks of the profession:

> [Y]our house has been the house of the People, your sleep still disturb'd for the Publick, and when you arose 'twas that others might lye down, and you waked that others might rest; The good you have done is unspeakable; How many young unexperienc'd Heirs have you kept from rash foolish Marriages? and from being jilted for their lives by the worst sort of Jilts, Wives? How many unbewitched Widowers Children have you preserv'd from the Tyranny of Stepmothers? How many old Dotards from Cuckoldage, and keeping other mens Wenches and Children? How many Adulteries and unnatural sins have you prevented? [381]

Years before de Mandeville Wycherley has articulated a public defense of the stews based precisely upon the notion of siphoning off surplus sexual energy in order, ultimately, to preserve property, protecting "Heirs" from foolish marriages, husbands from "Cuckoldage," and the system from adulteration.

So bawds like Joyner and Crossbite are parasites, living off the superflux which shows neither the heavens nor society more just. Joyner lets fall into her lap all the money the male fools in the play will spend to serve their lust, and as they try to crossbite each other, she crossbites them with this satiric rationale of the more successful trickster: "[L]ike the Lawyers, while my Clients [Sir Simon Addleplot and Dapperwit] endeavour to cheat one another; I in justice cheat 'em both" (V, 109). Crossbite and her daughter Lucy are equally successful. They hesitate not a millisecond to dump Lucy's keeper Dapperwit, who has kept them from living recently merely "upon Green Cheese, Tripe, and Ox-cheek"

(III, 51), in favor of Alderman Gripe, who will relieve all their "necessities" (52) and satisfy all Lucy's incipient bourgeois longings "sooner; [*sic*] than by *Dapperwits* assistance" (53). Looking to make excuses for the break, Crossbite and Lucy persecute Dapperwit for his supposed "bargain" to share her with Ranger (57), and Lucy concludes triumphantly, "And now to let me out to hire like Hackney; I tell you my own dear mother shall bargain for me no more; there are as little as I can bargain for themselves nowadays, as well as properer women" (59). The joke has a leveling effect: proper women, in Wycherley's world, bargain as much as proper whores. The patrilineal system is really not protected at all.

Joyner bilks Gripe into a liberality beyond his class but not his lust. And Crossbite snares Gripe in flagrante delicto—well, in hot pursuit—in order to blackmail him. In his Puritan cant Gripe demands, "[T]hou young Spawn of the old Serpent; Wicked, as I thought thee Innocent [read, *virgin*]; wilt thou say I wou'd have ravish'd thee?"; Lucy: "I will swear you did ravish me" (III, 66). When Gripe finally capitulates to avoid hanging, Crossbite hilariously reinterprets what has happened thus: "Indeed, now I consider; a Portion will do my Daughter more good, than his death; that wou'd but publish her shame; money will cover it, *probatum est*, as they say—let me tell you, Sir, 'tis a charitable thing to give a young Maid a Portion" (67). Ironically—and risibly—Gripe gets this portion back when he marries Dapperwit's erstwhile mistress to revenge himself on Dapperwit's stealing of his own daughter by getting new heirs on his new wife. Thanks to the unpunished trickery of Joyner and Crossbite, Lucy gets into the £30,000 estate her son—by whatever father—will inherit. The parasites have feasted.[2]

A few Restoration comedies give remarkable voice to bawds and whores—not Behn's high-class courtesans but the Suburbians like Shadwell's Mrs. Jilt all the way down to camp followers like Lacy's Dol Troop. Dol has an incredible Rabelaisian speech that infuses her trickery with the subversive gaiety of the bodily excessive:

> I cannot say I am with child, but with children; for here has been all Nations, and all Languages to boot; if the several Tongues should work upwards now, and I speak all Languages? Why, I am not the first learned woman; but I believe the first that ever came by her learning that way. If I should have for every man that has been dealing here a child, and if the children should be born with every one a Back and Breast on, as they were got? Bless me, what hard labour should I have! But, for all this, I hope I do not go with above a Squadron of children. But to my business. I mean to lay this great belly to every man that has but touch'd my Apron-strings. I thank the Law, 'tis very favourable in this point; for

when I have plaid the whore, the Law gives me leave to play the rogue, and lay it to whom I will. [I, 6]

Dol's multiple birth of polyglot warriors would rival the birth of Gargantua. She gets away with her scam to charge every member of the troop with paternity and pocket the resulting bribes, and she outrageously responds to the captain's threat to slit her nose if she not identify the one true father, "Why truly, I cannot lay it to any one man; but Gad is my judge, 'tis the Troops child, Captain[,] . . . and as Gad's my comfort, I have been as true and faithful a Woman to the Troop, as ever Wife was to a Husband, Captain" (II, 13). Abetting Tom Tell-troth's scheme to win Biddy, Dol tricks the captain and the lieutenant, who think they are tricking her into marriage with a girl. Dol substitutes Tell-troth for herself. In the end, instead of receiving some form of poetic justice for her egg scrambling, Dol gets a reward of sorts in a marriage to Raggou that legitimates her child. If marrying this stinking cook seems no bargain, it seems so only because of our bourgeois sensibilities. Their marriage is a perfectly appropriate union of the two greatest energy figures in the play. The ensuing parodic jousting jig between two hobby horses in armor celebrates folk humor that has, momentarily, transformed the world of the English Civil War into carnival.

Buckingham's adaptation of *The Chances* (1667) folds into the Fletcherian tragicomedy the raucous Jonsonian characters of the second Constantia and her mother. Buckingham doubles not only the high-class Constantia, precontracted wife to the duke, with a low-class version, but also Fletcher's boisterous landlady with a loquacious bawd. Down on her luck, Mother has sold 2 Constantia to an old braggart soldier, Antonio. Discoursing to her kinswoman, Mother outlines how she taught her daughter all her tricks, woman's wisdom, and helped her practice just to keep her elbows in. With highfalutin rhetoric she obfuscates her dealings with Antonio, "one whom my ebb of fortune forc'd me to enter into a negotiation with, in reference to my Daughter's Person" (V.iii, 58). After a night of his fumbling impotence, 2 Constantia and Mother have robbed him and fled, but Mother flags on their escape route: "Hold *Cons*, hold, for goodness hold, I am in that desertion of Spirit for want of breath, that I am almost reduc'd to the necessity of not being able to defend my self against the inconvenience of a fall" (IV.i, 44). 2 Cons tells her to hurry so they can get to the port, the shore, and make good their escape from Antonio. Again Mother responds like a female W.C. Fields for whom language is a class distinguisher:

Out of sight o'the Shore? why, do ye think I'll depatriate?
2 Cons: Depatriate? what's that?

> *Mother:* Why, ye Fool you, leave my Country: what will you never learn
> to speak out of the vulgar road? [44]

After more of this delightful dialogue, 2 Cons finally says, "Would not this make one stark mad? Her stile is not more out of the way, then her manner of reasoning; she first sells me to an ugly old fellow, then she runs away with me and all his gold, and now like a strict practitioner of honor, resolves to be taken, rather then depatriate as she calls it" (45). They take refuge in an inn, where Don John, a Fletcherian blade Buckingham has turned into a full-scale Restoration rake (a don juan), comes seeking the other Constantia. 2 Cons sexually manipulates him into protecting them, protesting she has great need of him. A decade before *The Rover* Don John sounds like the sex-starved Willmore: "If thou hast half so much need of me, as I have of thee Lady, I'll be content to be hang'd though" (47). When she unveils to him, he exclaims, "I'm so amaz'd I am not able to speak. I'd best fall to presently, though it be in the Street, for fear of losing time" (47). She offers to follow the world over and do anything for him, so he will do nothing with anyone else. He concludes, "O Heavens, I'm in another World, this Wench sure was made a purpose for me, she is so just of my humour" (48). Buckingham has, in short, imitated James Howard with a lower-class Mirida who has entranced her Philidor.[3]

Here is their mock-proviso scene. 2 Cons wants to know if he will be kind to her—always. Don John: "Always? I can't say so; but I will as often as I can" (V.iv, 59). They exchange witty but pagan vows:

> *Don John:* I swear then by thy fair self, that look'st so like a Deity, and art
> the only thing I now can think of, that I'll adore thee to my dying
> day.
> *2 Cons:* And here I vow, the minute thou do'st leave me, I'll leave the
> World, that's kill my self. [59]

Before they can get off to bed, however, Antonio charges in after 1 Constantia, captures her, and demands his gold (she is obviously veiled). 2 Cons steps up to disabuse him, he seizes her, claims he bought her, spent the night abed with her; she dares him to tell what he did all night! Deflated, Antonio bargains with her to get back his gold from Mother; he will then leave her alone. Mother protests outrageously that she stole Antonio's gold only because he had not set up a pension for her so she could give him gifts and therefore had to steal the purse only to make a gift of it.

Amidst the hymeneal closure of tragicomedy, Don John and 2 Cons stand out in bas-relief: as the Duke calls for the consummation of joys, exhausted with sexual frustration, Don John exclaims plaintively,

> And when shall we consummate our Joys?
> *2 Cons:* Never;
> We'll find out ways shall make 'em last for ever.
> *Don John:* Now see the odds 'twixt marry'd Folks and Friends:
> Our Love begins just where their Passion ends. [V.iv, 62]

Although Don John has pledged, "I will never more touch any other Woman for her sake" (61), they do not marry in the end. Instead, their relationship is juxtaposed to the typical closure of social comedy: they shall never "consummate" their joys but enjoy them perpetually in a free love between a Town wit and a Suburban jilt. Buckingham heretically democratized the gay couple.

The most remarkable set of voices, however, are those Dryden gives his whores in his social comedy, *The Kind Keeper.* In a funny parody of the Family of Love, the lubricious old Aldo refers to himself repeatedly as "Father" of a "Family" of prostitutes: "I love the poor little Devils. I am indeed a Father to 'em, and so they call me: I give 'em my Counsel, and assist 'em with my Purse. I cannot see a pretty Sinner hurri'd to Prison by the Land-Pyrats, but Nature works, and I must Bail her: or want a Supper, but I have a couple of cram'd Chickens, a Cream Tart, and a Bottle of Wine to offer her" (I.i.235-40). Aldo is a benevolent version of Gay's Peachum. If the California editors' glossing of "Land-Pyrats" is correct and Aldo is calling bailiffs robbers, then he is establishing a counterdiscourse to the official; he is, in a sense, legitimating the underworld as the more genuine, the more caring. For the "Counsel" he offers is revealed to us in an extraordinary, saturnalian scene where Aldo plays an alternative patriarch who hears, as if he were king of the underworld, complaints from the members of his family. He also maintains an "Office" provided with (dwindling) supplies to relieve their suffering. He philosophizes: "[H]ow will this glorious Trade be carri'd on, with such a miserable Stock? . . . Well, somewhat in ornament for the Body, somewhat in counsel for the mind; one thing must help out another, in this bad World: Whoring must go on" (IV.i.9-14). "One thing must help out another" has more meanings than the California gloss. It has the proverbial meaning of mutual help, yes, but it also refers to the necessity of supplementing material with merely verbal support and to pimping and whoring as necessary aids (to aristocracy) in this bad world.

Dryden does not sentimentalize the scene, however. The participants hilariously appropriate the religious and prudential rhetoric of official discourse. Mrs. Overdon is the first plaintiff, and her business opens with this exchange of mock compliments:

> *Mrs. Overdon:* Ask blessing, *Pru:* he's the best Father you ever had.

Aldo: Bless thee, and make thee a substantial, thriving Whore. Have your
   Mother in your eye, *Pru;* 'tis good to follow good example: How old
   are you, *Pru*? hold up your head, Child.
Pru: Going o' my sixteen, Father *Aldo.*
Aldo: And you have been initiated but these two years: loss of time, loss
   of precious time. Mrs. *Overdon,* how much have you made of *Pru,*
   since she has been Man's meat? [15-22]

Mrs. Overdon's complaint is that she has not made as much off Pru's
maidenhead as she had hoped, no matter how many times she has sold it,
but she is not ready to marry her off to a Cit yet in hopes she still might
get an upper-class keeper and a "Coach for her" (25). Besides, she has
spent too much on her education to give up yet: "[P]ray let her try her fortune a little longer in the World first: by my troth, I shou'd be loth to be at
all this cost, in her *French,* and her Singing, to have her thrown away upon
a Husband" (43-46). Aldo remonstrates with Mrs. Overdon for her swearing and counsels Pru to say her prayers and go to church Sundays so she
"thrive the better all the week" (49). And Aldo charitably offers to keep
Pru himself while he finds her "an able young" keeper; his only price
is that she do his "little business"—which business, since he is an old
fumbler, as he tells Woodall his son in disguise, would be "little" indeed
(50-51). Amidst the humor, however, we cannot blink the implication
of "Man's meat": this is a "bad World," where upper- and middle-class
women are commodities exchanged between men in a marriage meat
market, and where lower-class women are fast-food hamburgers sold in or-
dinaries to momentarily assuage the munchies. Dryden humanizes these
latter, allowing them to strut and fret their hour upon the stage.[4]

Like Nan in Behn's *The Revenge,* Mrs. Pad has "perform'd the last
Christian Office" of her keeper, following him to Tyburn, and Aldo, calling her a "Widow," rigs her out with new clothes and offers to help her
gain "the very Judge who sate on him" as her new keeper (52-70). The
next plaintiff has more to complain about. Her keeper, the gamester
Caster, whom she ironically calls "that Son of a Whore" (74-75), will not
share his take even though she lures his marks, beats and starves her, and
has now left her with "a Bastard of the Rogues in my Belly" (87). Aldo will
provide midwife and wet nurse and swaddling clothes for the child, plus
help in bringing Caster before the law. When Mrs. Hackney bursts in complaining that Mrs. Termagant has stolen her keeping lord, the exchange is
hilarious in its parody of upper-class political, sexual, and status concerns:

Hackney: She has violated the Law of Nations; for yesterday she inveigled
   my own natural Cully from me, a marri'd Lord, and made him false to
   my Bed, Father.

> *Termagant:* Come, you are an illiterate Whore: He's my Lord now; and, though you call him Fool, 'tis well known he's a Critick, Gentlewoman. You never read a Play in all your life, and I gain'd him by my Wit, and so I'll keep him. [106-12]

What is being parodied is the agreement among aristocracies of all (patriarchal) nations that women who steal other women's husbands must be condemned, even stoned to death. And one whore attempts to climb the social ladder by stepping on another's fingers on the rung beneath.

Mrs. Hackney would seem to have the last laugh, leaving Mrs. Termagant with her wrung-out cully, who can borrow no more money till his father dies, and her clap to boot. Aldo's peacemaking rhetoric to Mrs. Termagant is hysterically funny: "Then there's a Father for your Child, my Lord's Son and Heir by Mr. *Caster*" (116-17). Can Aldo arrange things so that there is no sinister bar to this Caster's bastard's inheriting this married lord's estate? The very prospect celebrates the dispossessed's invasion of the propertied class's genealogy.

Acting like King Lear, Aldo further settles the dispute by dividing all of London into the spheres of influence of these two "Suburbians" (143): the City to Mrs. Hackney, the Town to Mrs. Termagant. Mrs. Pad concludes the business of this Family of Love: "Then all Friends, and Confederates: Now let's have Father *Aldo*'s delight, and so *Adjourn the House*" (124-25)—as if it were Parliament itself. And as Lord of Misrule, Aldo responds with monarchial gestures of ritual and liberality, "Well said, Daughter: lift up your Voices, and sing like Nightingales, you Tory Rory Jades. Courage, I say; as long as the merry Pence hold out, you shall none of you die in *Shoreditch*" (126-29). Inviting the hallelujahs that would adorn a messiah, Aldo promises the "merry Pence" of what Bakhtin calls *merry time* to help his whores avoid the fate of Jane Shore, dying in a ditch, by obtaining for them all at least the safety net of keeping if not actual places in the hierarchy. The whores make no reappearance, but their sister Tricksy, daughter of a cobbler and a sempstress (a former whore herself), tricks her kind keeper Mr. Limberham out of not only an annuity but finally marriage and a separate maintenance. Thus she obtains legitimation, a higher rung on the status ladder, and perhaps an inheritance for any son born to her by any caster of the dice. It is as if Dryden recognized, at some level, the need for welfare if not social justice in the world of these estateless women.[5]

Thompson's *The Life of Mother Shipton,* in addition to the other, male peasants and the *villain* Shiftwel, gives remarkable voice to the landless, destitute lot of the title character as a young peasant woman:

Miserable *Shipton* in what a poor condition has it pleased the powers to place thee! sure all the Eyes of Happiness did look a Squint at my nativity, and all the Destinies combin'd to wrap me up in endless poverty. . . . How pleasant and thrice happy is the fortune of other Mortalls, how bravely do they live and injoy themselves and their estates! How like petty deities are they seated in their pallaces! and to such poor Cottage bred Creatures as my self extend their generous Hospitality! how nobly do they pass over their lives and with odours and perfumes enter their earthly graves whose fame is still surviving by their Princely Pedigree? why was not this my lot poor miserable *Shipton*! . . . What pleasant life have I? forlorn desolation? What estate or subsistance? The Alms of the Parish? What Grave but a Ditch? And for my pedigree can only boast of poverty? I was wretched by my Parents indigency, and by their death in my Minority, thrice, thrice more Miserable! Am I not flesh and blood? Has not Nature bestowed on me the like perfections, each Mortal now can boast off [*sic*]? Why am I so low then when others are so high? Why do I court the ground when others in their glorious pinacles grasp the sky? Well henceforth wil I scorn their Alms and gifts of Charity.

Directly or indirectly I will find a way,
To make me rich in Pride and Money too, but stay. [I.i,1-2]

She pauses to think that she is "too presumptuous" and offends "these powers we are bound in the strictest obligations to obey: No be content in time thou wilt see Heaven will give thee more felicity" (2). But the poignancy of her complaint and the heavy irony of her false praise of the "generous Hospitality" of the landlords undercut her piety. The devil Radamon comes at this critical instant and promises her wealth and fame, and she bites, marrying him on the morrow for the "Fortunes and Estates" he offers her (I.vi, 11).

The Mother Shipton plot becomes a virtual morality play. Transformed to a gorgeous lady at first, she soon dwindles to a poor old hag who must at her devil-husband's bidding perform witchcraft as prophecy. Her most interesting prophecy is to the abbot of Beverley, who fears the church's loss of more abbeys. In what might be interpreted as a leveling (if not Leveller) note, Mother Shipton prophesies the downfall of the rich through pride, but she also prophesies further suffering for the poor:

> The poor shall grieve to see that day
> And who did feast must fast and pray.
> Fate so decrees their overthrow,
> Riches bring Pride and Pride brings woe. [III.vi, 31]

The poor apparently will suffer because that which sustains the economy, the estate, will crumble. Mother Shipton's final conversion and salvation would seem to underwrite the aristocratic system: "Is it a sin to covet riches when one suffers the contempt of the wor'd [*sic*] by reason of poverty? yes coveting ambitiously is execrable" (V.iii, 45). Nevertheless, especially given Shiftwel's subversive success, the moralistic ending of the play cannot silence Mother Shipton's subversion of class either.[6]

The first Restoration comedy to become fully folk-subversive due to the presence of one of these lower-class women tricksters is Porter's *A Witty Combat; or, The Female Victor* (1663?). The heroine of the subtitle is Madame (Mary) Moders. And she was a real person in more ways than one. Born in Kent and married to a shoemaker, Mary Carleton, as she came to be known in a series of stories about her, ran away from her first husband, then married another in Dover. She apparently ran away from him, too, suddenly appearing on the Thames as a rich German princess who attempted to con one Carleton into marriage but got caught in a crossbite when he turned out to have no more money than she. According to Ernest Bernbaum, we do not know whether Porter's play was really performed in 1663. But we do know it was performed in the spring of 1664, with Moders appearing as herself![7]

 The play opens with some servants marveling at her cunning, but when a gentleman seeks her, calling her a pretty thing, one of the watermen characterizes his recent fare as also astonishingly beautiful: "Pretty thing quoth a, she was worth ten pretty things; she was a thing to thank God for" (I.i, sig B2v). On the make for a rich mark, Mary must constantly be wary of others' trying to cheat her, beginning with her landlord and his wife. She inhabits a comic world of distrust and must survive within it. Toying first with a fiction that she had run hither to some "brave *Englishman*," she decides to mystify herself with an even more romantic narrative:

> But that's too lame, I'd rather have it thus;
> A Noble Person that to view the World
> With an experienc'd eye, throwes off her State,
> And like to the late active *Swedish* Queen,
> Retires into a Hut without her Retinue.
> This meetes my fancy and comes neerest to
> Their Wit (if they have any) here's a Field
> For us to play in[.] [III.ii, sig D1v; N.B. the blank verse]

The news of Queen Kristina of Sweden's abdication of the throne in 1654 had stunned Europe. Mary's comparison of herself as German princess to Kristina is indeed a witty gambit on her chosen field of play.

 Mary is engaged in a battle of wits, for her landlord and lady intend at first to bilk her. Sending out letters she knows they will intercept, Mary says of the maid who spies on her for her hosts, "My Education has not been so slender,/Nor my Wit left naked of Rudiments,/To be a Price for thee and thy designes" (III.ii, sig D1r). Then the landlady's brother, John Carleton, a second son and a law student, decides to masquerade as a lord. He wants to be sure she has an estate, and his sister responds defensively, "What do you doubt me there too *Iohn?* yes she has an Estate and a glorious Estate *Iohn,* but what it is I do not know *Iohn,* yet I can shrewdly guess *Iohn*" (III.iii, D3v). John asks good questions: "Is it in her own hands[?] . . . "Where lies it[?]" Having convinced him, Mrs. King advises him, "Then put your self *Iohn* into an Equipage beyond yourself *Iohn,* appear as I would have you like a Lord, *Iohn* with your Coach and Foot-boyes." The fact that a landlady is his sister indicates that the Carletons are not very high up the gentry ladder or have already had to compound downwards, marrying their daughter disadvantageously. Old Mrs. Carleton maintains that she can know Madame's essence at a glance, but she seems to have fooled herself with her own fiction that John is a lord and that she must be sure he not marry beneath himself, beneath the Carletons. The mask is slipping and all class looks like pretense.

Sounding like a Cornelian heroine, Mary triumphs:

Glory depends on Conquest, I have brought
(After so many Tryals of my Wit,)
My amorous Lord, and his averse Allyes
Upon their knees to supplicate my love[.] [V, sig E2v]

Post hymen, Old Carleton visits to see if Madame will settle her estate upon John, which he needs to settle his accounts (with the landlord, Mr. King, among others). Mrs. King is confident their scam has worked: "Her Estate will make amends for all, and though he is a false Lord now, her Estate will make him currant; money will buy Honour at any time Chuck" (V, sig F1v). But Old Carleton discovers the truth, and of course, rather than acknowledging having been bested by superior trickery, assumes the high moral ground and excoriates Mary as *ingannatrice:* "A very Pusscat, a subtle Carrion, and a cursed cheat. . . . An Estate, where lies it? at the Brick-hills, foolish boy; she is not worth a groat, but what thou hast out of thy prodigal affection given her, her Jewels are but counterfeit, and she a base imposture. . . . Boy she's a Strumpet, a vagrant, a wandring Baggage that has two Husbands beside thy self; a paltry Shoomaker is one of them" (sig F2r).

Alone Mary anticipates trouble: "I do expect a storme, and suddenly, by my bad dreames; which tell me I must wade through mud and Water;

signifying troubles dangerous ones: yet I shall pass them all, cleer as a sheet that has been whiten'd by the whitsters hand." She laughs in their faces when they come for her with a constable, and she comes off at her trial for bigamy with not only confidence but "impudence" (sig F2v), that trump suit of tricksters. When she emerges having been "quit" for lack of evidence, a gentleman comments, of course upbraiding her for witchcraft, "[H]ere's the beast will none spit at her, how she stares and gloats like old *Grimalkin* or mother *Gurtons* Cat 'ith Colehole."

The real emotion behind all this moral posturing, Porter implies, is envy that this great trickster got away with it. Thus the subtitle, *The Female Victor.* She is not a victor in the sense that this particular scam succeeds but in the sense that she escapes (poetic) justice. With cheeky aplomb Mary addresses the audience in the closing tag (in lieu of an epilogue), rubbing their faces in her signification:

> I've past one Tryal; but it is my fear
> I shall receive a rigid sentence here;
> You think me a bold Cheat, put case 'twere so,
> Which of you are not? now you'd swear I know;
> But do not least that you deserve to be
> Censur'd worse then you yet can censure me.
> The Worlds a Cheat, and we that move in it
> In our degrees do exercise our Wit:
> And better 'tis to get a glorious Name
> However got; then live by common Fame.

Madame remains at large, waiting for her next gull, already like the later Moll Flanders larger than life by her reputation as a great folk trickster. Despite her class, she has achieved parodic *gloire* thanks to her woman's wit. Two thirds of a century before Gay's *The Beggar's Opera* she has revealed the subversive truth that *all the world's a cheat* and that even a peasant can play Kristina—nay, Anastasia—as well as the best of them.

Twenty years later another female folk trickster takes over a play, the title character of Ravenscroft's *Dame Dobson; or, The Cunning Woman* (1683). Like the earlier Mother Shipton, Dame Dobson is a fortune-teller. Her Igor-like assistant, Decoy, admires her so much he says, "Though you are no Sorceress, yet you have the wit to make the World think so, and that's the same thing as if you really were one" (I.i, 1). As usual, a woman with power must be a witch, especially if she threatens male prerogatives. Dobson threatens a major one in that she appears to be a marriage broker, more than anything else. There is a countess under her influence, whom a certain colonel wants to marry. But Lady Noble pays Dobson handsomely to obstruct that match, leaving the colonel free for her to marry—after her husband dies! Noble must know if she will survive him, and Dobson arranges an elaborate trick with a vase: if it break, hubby will die first and Noble will be free to marry the colonel.

Meanwhile, Hartwell is trying to land a widow, Lady Rich. He has tried absence to make the heart grow fonder, but it only makes Lady Rich jealous. So Hartwell pays Dobson handsomely to provide the widow with a trick vision of him at Tunbridge Wells staring at her picture. Lady Rich wishes him present. Dame Dobson advises that she send him a letter telling him so, which she will have delivered immediately by spirits. Lady Rich watches (through a mirror trick) Hartwell receive the letter and return one immediately, which falls at her feet. She rushes out to antici- pate his return from Tunbridge. He returns later to narrate that at their meeting the lady agreed to sign a contract before witnesses.

Dame Dobson is an agent in another important match. The colonel's aristocratic cousin, Mrs. Clerimant, impregnated by a courtier, comes to learn if he will marry her. Dobson informs her the man will marry a lady of great quality. Despondent, Mrs. Clerimant asks for an abortion. Dobson refuses. Apparently, like Moll Flanders, Dobson has her limits, won't commit murder. Instead, Dobson will arrange a marriage with the cow- ardly Cit Gillet, who has paid Dobson for an enchanted sword with which to impress his mistress who is enamored of soldiers. The mistress has mar- ried one of them, and Gillet's swaggering earns him only forceful ejection from the wedding. Dobson fools him with a fortune that he will marry an- other, arranges for a vision, and develops an elaborate, totally byzantine courtship between Gillet and Mrs. Clerimant at a jeweler's (with herself to receive a jewel of great price). Mrs. Clerimant is not worried about Gillet's class, just wants her reputation saved, so Dobson prophesies that she will get "the Credit of making a good Match for a Court Lady that has more Beauty than Honesty, is a fit Wife for a Citizen that has more Money than Wit" (III.ix [misnumbered], 42).

The colonel believes Dame Dobson a fake and is determined to expose her so that the superstitious countess will marry him at last. But when he finally forces her brother Goslin, masquerading as the devil in one of her seances, to admit she is indeed the cunning woman of the sub- title, Dobson defiantly maintains the colonel should be happy she has found his cousin a better husband than she could expect, thereby saving her reputation and the colonel a nurse's fee. Dobson offers to return any money the colonel feels he has been duped out of, but he wants nothing more than a prediction that he will find favor with the countess at last. The countess says Dobson is not trustworthy, offering her own palm for him to read, and he divines they shall be married presently. Lady Noble slinks off to avoid shame. So this part of the play resembles Restoration social comedy, the union of the right aristocratic couple, the marrying of an aristocratic woman with a man from the middle class to save her reputation.

These plot lines must be ferreted out from the chaos of the play, however. Dame Dobson's room is the hub for all sorts of other action. One bit seems also typical of Cit-cuckolding social comedy. Mrs. Featly, daughter of a Cit, is the wife of an aging, very rich alderman through an arranged marriage. Her husband can provide her with no sexual satisfaction, so she is in love with a gentleman whom she keeps with her own money. But the gentleman is inconstant to her, and she does not want to support his affair with someone else. Dame Dobson will consult a devil to see if her gallant is really false, but Mrs. Featly is scared to death. Dobson assures her that not all who come get to see a devil; the devil must love her. The stage directions read, "Beat[rice, another assistant] *appears upon the Table with her head dress'd antickly, and her naked Neck and Shoulders—Eyebrows blackt, great Pendants in her Ears as big as Pidgeons Eggs*" (V.i, 60). They make Featly actually touch the head, then ask if her lover is cheating, and Beatrice says no. Featly gives Dobson a whole purse and leaves, scared to death. Thus Dobson sides with the Town wit against the City-wife mistress and makes a fool of her by means of the folk trick of the talking head.

But there are other actions that are more folk-subversive. Susan the Country girl wants Dobson to read her mind and discover that she is in love with her lady's son, who has plied her with gifts to extract a declaration of love but wants one thing more before he will marry her. Dobson sagely warns her not to ruin herself, but Susan is preoccupied with the size of her budding breasts. Dobson advises her to stroke them and coax them verbally to grow, predicting as she leaves that the young landlord will indeed ruin her.

Jenkin, a Welshman (played by Tony Leigh in a small part for him), complaining that his wife has run away and dressed like a man with a sword, asks for a potion to win her back: "Look you, pray you! make her very strong Glisters of Love that may keep in her Bodies, and work up to her hearts, And that will do it, look you" (V.i, 54). His wife shows up, miraculously, at Dobson's room requesting the dame to make her a real man, change her sex, give her the missing piece, because "[o]f all Conditions, that of a Woman is most miserable!—I have a Hat and a Sword towards Manhood: Come—supply the deficiency of Nature—Suit my Body to my Soul. And make me a Man compleat in all points" (56). Dobson counsels her to return to her husband and appease him; she has a powder to make him love her more. But Mrs. Jenkin, like Sir Anthony Love, wants to have fun till the money runs out. Dobson warns her to watch out, for her honor, but also not to advance too far with the women.

In order to convince Lady Rich of her powers, Dame Dobson arranges for her old servant, Mrs. Francis, to enter shrieking with an enormous belly. Dobson effects a cure by passing the tympanum from her belly to Decoy as they sit in two chairs. Lady Rich is properly amazed; Francis pays handsomely and leaves pleased; Decoy waddles off with his new burden.

We learn early that Dame Dobson deals in corpses from the executioner and discover why only much later, when Dobson is trying to frighten the colonel into believing in her powers. She threatens him with a horrible vision. Thunder and lightning come from the chimney, then body parts fall down; he is a bit nonplussed at that. Then she makes the body come back together during more lightning and thunder and walk into the center of the stage. She is Dr. Frankenstein turned puppeteer.

These bits—images of a Country simpleton stroking her breasts to make them grow; an ignorant Welshman asking for enemas that will float love up to his wife's heart; a rebellious Welshwoman seeking the missing phallus that will grant her real power; grave-robbed, dismembered body parts tumbling down then miraculously coming together—are reminiscent of the elements that Bakhtin analyzes in Rabelais, elements of a material folk existence that persists in spite of systems and hierarchies and represents humanity's only real immortality. These comic bits signify that Dame Dobson represents woman as giver and taker of life, as womb/tomb, Bakhtin's carnival woman: "In this tradition woman is essentially related to the material bodily lower stratum; she is the incarnation of this stratum that degrades and regenerates simultaneously. She is ambivalent. She debases, brings down to earth, lends a bodily substance to things, and destroys; but, first of all, she is the principle that gives birth" (*Rabelais* 240).

At the climax of the play, like the Jonsonian trickster that she is, Dame Dobson has gathered her booty in trunks, ready either to retire or to relocate, but the constable and watch can haul her off to prosecution. What saves her from prosecution at the end is not only that she has pleased some of the aristocrats and that others are happy just to escape without public shame. It is a recognition of her power, her carnival energy, which gets appropriated by the aristocracy but surprisingly in terms of emergent bourgeois ideology: Hartwell pleads, "For the good Service Dame *Dobson* has done me, I am oblig'd to be her Intercessor: And my request is, you'll all Pardon her what is past, and not prejudice her *Reputation* by Discourses in Publick, since 'tis her *livelyhood*, and *ingenuity* ought not to be discourag'd" (V, 70; emphasis mine). Dame Dobson has protested to the colonel earlier that she is as good as her word, but we are at that historical moment of transformation of aristocratic word-as-bond into bourgeois credit—which term means, etymologically, he / she believes. Putting her trickster spin on the new system, Dame Dobson responds to Hartwell, "Nay, let 'em tell all; if the World upbraid me, it will laugh at them; In this Business it is more Credit to deceive than be deceived." Like Shadwell's Lady Cheatly, Dame Dobson represents the trickster gone (Bourgeois) legit. But wherever she goes, she will take her folk origins, bones and all, with her.

The greatest exemplar of Bakhtin's carnival woman on the Restoration stage is the title character of *The Amorous Old-woman; or, 'Tis Well If It Take* (1674), traditionally thought to be by Thomas Duffett. The title role was played by Katherine Corey, who also played several of these female folk tricksters—Lucy, Mrs. Joyner, and Dame Dobson—and who must have been the greatest comic actress of the King's Company and perhaps of the Restoration stage, lending to these roles the comic energy they demand.

The play is formally a tragicomedy, with aristocratic lovers and friends pursuing honor and marriage in the high plot, but its low plot is one of the funniest of Restoration farces. Strega, "an old Rich deformed Lady" as the dramatis personae identifies her, is worth twenty thousand crowns per annum and attracts men who want to marry her for her fortune. Her name in Italian means "witch," an appellation once again applied to an uppity woman, in this case one who would dare at her age—she has a great-great-granddaughter—to be in control of her own wealth and seek another husband, her eighth (even more than the Wife of Bath). Garbato, the young blade who acts as go-between for Riccamare, the aristocrat who wants her for her money, describes her thus: "[S]he / Has a breath more noisom than a Jakes, / Able to belch a Pestilence, but Gold is a / Rich Restorative, and she's as mellow as / An Angelot Cheese, that has been mortifi'd / Fifteen Months in Horse-dung" (I.ii, 4; set as verse, but obviously doesn't scan). Here are Rabelaisian images of excrement, plague, and rottenness, emphasizing her chthonic nature.

Garbato adds later that she is "made of loose parcels" (II.ii, 19). Indeed, when Riccamare approaches her in her chamber, she lies in bed and is gradually dismembered by her servant, the Cervantean Sancopanco. As her first husband loved her for her youth, now she wants her eighth to love her for her wisdom and experience, not, like the other six in between, just for her riches. She says if Riccamare can stand to observe her five imperfections and still love her, she will have him. She parcels herself out on her dressing table. The observing men comment that she seems, puppet-like, to move herself as if by wire or clockworks. First she takes off her eyebrows; then she pulls out an eye. Riccamare still likes her as he would "a Treasure on a Dunghill, / I endure the stench o'th' one, for the lucre / Of the other" (III.vi, 42). Out come the teeth. Off comes the hair.

But when she takes off the leg, it is too much: Riccamare insists at least on flesh: "Dost think I'le ingender with Bedstaves,/And beget a generation of Scourg-sticks?" (43). He leaves her to the devil, later comparing her to that other witch, Mother Shipton. Strega thinks she can at least take consolation in the fact he is an elder brother, but when she learns he is a younger, she despairs of another husband (because younger brothers are more desperate for riches and also more attractive). She laments that she has chased him away.

But Furfante the Rogue and Buggio the Liar now interest Cicco, the old, blind senator, in Strega. Furfante comes courting for Cicco. This time, Strega and Sanco-panco decide not to display her imperfections, for it is a disguising age. The world has turned upside down since her youth and modesty has been exchanged for modishness. Sanco-panco convinces her that she is breeding new teeth, growing young again. Blind Cicco courts her without being able to see those imperfections, of course, and they finally go off together in amorous dalliance. The servants congratulate themselves.

The next time we see them, they are married, and Cicco is so rich he can now afford a generous portion for his daughter, who marries whom she desires after all, the trickster Garbato, who turns out to have inherited a deceased uncle's "fair estate" as well. And Riccamare makes amends for his machinations in the play by naming Cicco's daughter as his own heir (more than the usual younger brother after all). In other words the play ends in the typical marriages of comedy—one of the characters calls it "a rare Comedy of Mirth" (V.vii, 70)—but with an exaggerated amassing of estates. Moreover, the focus at the end is not on the young but the old couple dancing: like the Wife of Bath, Strega is rejuvenated by another marriage. She is a Swiftian tulip, sprung from dung. In her "material bodily aspect" she represents what Bakhtin calls "the real being outside all hierarchical norms and values" (*Rabelais*, 403). That "real being," for Bakhtin, is the "very process of becoming, its meaning and direction" (212): "The victory of the future is ensured by the people's immortality" (256).[8] But Strega is not a romanticized representative of the people. She *is* the chthonic in all its deadly as well as lively aspects.

Restoration subversive comedy, then, features centrifugal forces that refuse to be contained in Stuart ideology, that sometimes represent a breakdown of that ideology (buddy-cuckolding plays) or perhaps a counterideology that begins to offer the dispossessed, from aristocratic women to the landless folk, a space in the margins or even the opportunity to move up the hierarchy as part of an emergent bourgeois ethos. At its most radical, however, it seems to challenge the very idea of hierarchy. Particularly in the figures of these folk tricksters, Restoration comedy celebrates a leveling, democratic energy. If Bakhtin has romanticized the folk, so have some of these dramatists. The plight of the dispossessed remained bleak and unremediated. But the plays have portrayed a boisterous, raucous comic humor that laughs in the teeth of both the reality principle and official discourse and rejoices in the resilience of the classless trickster, who can inform any morph with his or her wit—who, to purloin a line from Milton, can create a soul under the ribs of death. If such a figure is merely the trope of art, it infuses dramaturgy with the daemonic energy of the democratic as a trope of hope.

Part Three
COMICAL SATIRE

In the lead essay in a recent collection on postmodern approaches to satire edited by James Gill, my collaborator and friend Deborah Payne addresses the vexing problem of our seeming inability to distinguish comedies from satires in the drama of the period. Some, like Rose Zimbardo and Laura Brown, see virtually all the comedies as satires.[1] Payne sees virtually none as satires. The part of her argument I wish to focus on here is that "the very semiotic texture of theatre makes dramatic satire almost impossible to realize utterly on the stage. . . . Inevitably, dramatic satire drifts toward comedy, the genre more in keeping with the theatre's particular strengths" (4). In an essay in another new collection on satire edited by Brian Connery and Kirk Combe, Christian Gutleben argues similarly that the ludic impulse in art is socially centripetal, resulting in comedy rather than satire, which is centrifugal. However plausible such arguments, I should like respectfully to disagree. My position is closer to that of Dustin Griffin in his recent book—that the ludic is inherent in satire, especially the more menippean kind. This kind is at the center of Bakhtin's theory of the dialogic, and although Bakhtin focuses on the novel and identifies, in several of his works, most drama with official discourse, why cannot drama be satire, sometimes speaking with a collective corrective voice, sometimes with more menippean, dialogic voices?

Payne would object that drama lacks the prime requisite of satire, a controlling, normative narrative voice. But an author or a director can organize a play or a production in such a manner to communicate either collective condemnation or a jumble of absurdity. One has only to think of *Dr. Strangelove* or *Waiting for Godot* for an example of each. Payne gets this theory of controlling voice mainly from Alvin Kernan's *The Plot of Satire*. I would say she was in the right church, just the wrong pew. In Kernan's more interesting because less rigid book, *The Cankered Muse*, he is onto something more suggestive when he applies the concept of menippean satire to drama and concludes that there is a form of drama that dramatizes the satiric scene and relies on irony to communicate its satiric intent (intro. and passim). Kernan, like Payne, is perplexed by the problem of endings. He sees, however, that the lack of comic reconciliation at the end of some plays is key to their being considered "comicall satyres." I should like to pick up this lead where Kernan dropped it and where all subsequent criticism has simply let it lie.

Most of us would agree that we can recognize objects of satire in Restoration comedy: Cits, country bumpkins, fops, parvenus, termagants, superannuated amorousness, cowardice, parsimoniousness, affectation—to name a few major ones. The question whether a comic play with satiric elements remains a comedy or becomes a satire per se, however, depends entirely on the ending. Comedies end in closure, celebration, centripety, even if subversive elements spin off centrifugally. Satires end sometimes in the closure of poetic justice, a justice that is often draconian or apocalyptic. For Kernan, *Volpone* is such a comical satire (and I have come to agree with him despite my treatment of it as subversive comedy in *Word as Bond*, ch. 3). But more often satires end in nonclosure, as Griffin argues so well (ch. 4), communicating Milton's lesson, *And so the world shall run, to good malignant, to bad men benign,* or Rabelais's lesson, *boire.*

Let me give two examples from minor and therefore perhaps more transparent Restoration comedy to illustrate the function of endings. A la Ben Jonson's *Every Man out of His Humour,* John Wilson's neglected play, *The Projectors* (1664), employs the plot structure of the satiric review, exposing the folly of character after character, from money-grubbing dupes who seek the easy buck through bogus *projects* or inventions, to uppity women engaged in a cabal for women's rights. Our audience expectation is for Jocose, the Jonsonian satirist-manipulator, to conclude the play with laughter at his dupes. But as his name already perhaps should have warned us, he is not Jonson's envious Macilente but a lover of comic laughter: he gives them back their money and invites everyone to a festive comic embrace. Payne would seem to be right: the nature of drama forces the playwright to conclude in comedy. But in an anonymous play of the same year, *Knavery in All Trades; or, The Coffee-House,* what looks like a raucous, folk-subversive comedy celebrating the triumph of servants over masters (the play was performed over Christmas holidays by apprentices) all of a sudden suffers a draconian poetic justice on a few of the scapegraces. I contend that this ending changes the generic nature of the play from comedy to satire because it eschews any concluding embrace or celebration and substitutes the whip of the moralist. That the ending is tacked on—indeed, the font of the closing pages is totally different and there are no page numbers—does not negate the fact that it changes the genre of the play from comedy to satire. Of course, we have only the printed and probably censored version of the play. Could it have sustained performance in its printed form? Are there any performed plays that have satiric endings?

Yes, rarely, which fact in a way proves Payne's point, who admits that there could occasionally be a real dramatic satire like Jonson's *Volpone*— but only rarely. Yet this *rarely* certainly qualifies her "*Inevitably,* dramatic satire drifts toward comedy." But let me make the point about satiric endings in performed plays first with regard to tragical satires. In 1668 Sir Robert Howard's *The Duke of Lerma* explored the almost Nietzschean excess of the old Jacobean Machiavel and frustrated the audience's expectation of poetic justice upon him by allowing him to escape as a final mocking gesture at the audience's complicity in hypocrisy.[2] In the 1670s the grotesque *Sodom,* Thomas Shadwell's shrieking *The Libertine,* and Nat Lee's outrageous *The Princess of Cleve* explored and exploded the excesses of the Cavalier libertine ethos. The ending of *Sodom* is apocalyptic; of *The Libertine,* draconian; of *Princess,* a bitter, cynical mockery of the conversion of the rake. In the early 1680s Thomas Otway's *Venice Preserv'd* ends in the destruction of any remaining idealism in a world dominated by the corrupt and the grotesque and witnessed by the mad. These, I would argue, in contradistinction to O.J. Campbell, are, like Shakespeare's *Troilus and Cressida,* tragical satires, for they feature death and a dark atmosphere of wholesale corruption.[3]

I would reserve Campbell's category of *comicall satyre,* a phrase taken from Jonson, for plays of a lighter atmosphere, where perhaps the ludic has more free reign. Two other categories of satire seem important and useful: corrective and absurdist. As Griffin has argued, critics of the mid-twentieth century insisted that all satire has at least an implied standard (28-34). In a sense, the rest of Griffin's book is an argument that the presence of such a standard is a vexed issue. Those that have such a standard, I call corrective; those that do not, I call absurdist—that is, they call into question the very grounds for judgment. Restoration comical satires come in both kinds.

11

Tricksters Scourge
and Get Scourged

The most prolific writer of comical satire in the Restoration is the under-rated and insufficiently studied Thomas Durfey. Critics have recognized the moralist in Durfey's later comedies but have not known what to do with his earlier ones. In 1916 Robert Stanley Forsythe articulated a posi-tion still maintained, at least implicitly, by Hume and Rothstein-Kavenik: "D'Urfey seems . . . to have much difficulty in providing endings for his plays. Indeed, in several of the earlier plays there is no real conclusion, but a mere stopping of the action at the end of five acts" (1:6). But Forsythe's characterization of the endings sounds like the characterization of the ending of satire by Griffin in his chapter on closure and by Connery-Combe in their introduction: satires often just stop because neither the folly of the world nor the anger of the satirist has ended. Hume and Roth-stein-Kavenik explicitly deny Durfey any status as a satirist (Hume 309, 334-35; R-K, 207-8), yet they fail to interpret the endings of these plays.

What are we to make of these endings? In *The Fool Turn'd Critick* (1676) the ending frustrates our expectations of a marriage joining a gay couple and their estates. Instead, the only marriage is between the epony-mous fool and a servant with no portion, much to the chagrin of the fool's father, Old Winelove, who wanted his son to learn the ways of the Town wit and to marry well. The rake/hero, who thinks he tricks his friend/rival not only out of the witty woman but into a clandestine mar-riage with the friend's pregnant whore, gets tricked by the bride's father, Sir Formal Ancient, posing as a parson; moreover, he gets tricked even out of the pleasure of seeing his friend duped, for the parson who conducts his marriage is also fake. Sir Formal dismisses his daughter, who has bounced back and forth between the rivals like an inconstant tennis ball and is ironi-cally named Penelope, and will deal with her later for attempting to marry without his permission. The only gestures toward closure are empty: Sir Formal forces Old Winelove to laugh at his bad fortune and go off and get drunk together; the rivals male bond in a handshake of renewed friendship. But they must leave the stage with false insouciance. Durfey would appear to have roundly satirized the kind of rakes Robert Jordan would term "extravagant." No new generation emerges to populate estates with heirs of superior progenitors. Indeed, all the explicit attempts at estate building have been frustrated.

Squire Oldsapp; or, The Night-Adventurers (1678) has an equally hollow ending: All the males in the play pursue the squire's kept mistress, Tricklove. We expect that the apparently happily married wit Henry will be reconciled to his faithful wife, Christina, and that his rakehell friend Welford will be married to the witty Sophia. But they, along with the obviously satirized humors characters, end up exposed to the virtuous women at the end in their continued lustful pursuits, and all the men can do is to try to silence the women for the supposed purpose of protecting their honor. We in the audience are once again denied any comic reconciliation and can only remember the disguised women's final comments before they are silenced: Christina complains, "Oh Heaven! is this the Fate of Marriage?" and Sophia says wittily of Welford, "if he keeps this custom, I find I shall buy his Loaf at a dear rate" (V.iv, 63). Henry, who has responded to his wife's question about being a good husband with typical Town contempt for husbandry of his estate, will obviously continue to waste it in pursuit of other women. And Sophia's comment throws her potential union with Welford, which was supposed to match his "good Estate" with her "six thousand Pound" (V.ii, 57), into a cocked hat. The cynicism of the ending is encapsulated in Oldsapp's closing the play by inviting everyone to join in a celebration of Tricklove's unquestionable fidelity.

In *Trick for Trick; or, The Debauch'd Hypocrite* Durfey takes the extravagant rake to the limits of the comical. Exaggerating Fletcher's witty, combative lovers in the play's source, *Monsieur Thomas,* Durfey takes their tit-for-tat tricks to the level of violence. Cellida, having already railed at Thomas for publicly besmirching her reputation once, is forced to watch him do it again in her father Sir Peregreene's presence, so she vows revenge. She arranges to have him tied up by her servants and in the presence of his own father and hers confess that he lied. The presence of the fathers is especially significant, for they were negotiating for a union of children and estates. But Thomas's not so clever servant Launce manages to get free and liberate his master. They then proceed to assault Cellida and her cousin Sabina, intending to rape them, while the stage direction tells us Thomas "*goes to undress*" Cellida, while she screams to Heaven for help, while her father looks on horrified and cries in vain for mercy, and while his father, appropriately named Sir Wilding Frollick (shades of Old Winelove), wants his son to be as wild as he and urges him on. They are stopped only by the arrival in the nick by Sabina's brother, Valentine. Cellida's father tries to kill Thomas and, when restrained by the brother, threatens prosecution under the law. But Sir Wilding protests they are rich enough to resist the reach of the law. Sir Peregreene and the women storm out with this astonishing parting repartee:

> *Thomas:* Now, Madam, cou'd not you have sav'd all this, and been willing?
> *Cellida:* Impudent Man! cou'd no entreaty prevail with ye? Well, from this instant I'll shun thee as I wou'd the Plague; and if I do speak of thee, it shall be with Scorn, and Derision—to curse thy il Nature—and Ingratitude—to which purpose I this Moment banish all sparks of Love—and do here solemnly vow—Never to see thee more.
> *Sabina:* Nor I, unless it be to revenge this baseness. [*Exeunt*
> *Thomas:* A Pox on't, this comes of Interruption, if they had but stay'd a little longer, that I might have had earnest of her, all had been sure;—but one Weeks humble Address shall make all well again, shall it no, Sir?
> *Peregreene:* No Sir, Nor believe I'll put up this affront so tamely: [*Exit* You shall hear from me, assure your self.
> *Wilding:* Ah, let him go, *Tom*—the Old Fool frets—ha, ha. [V, 62]

The play ends with Valentine forgiving Thomas and his servant for their assault on his sister, apparently because of some unspecified "Interest" he has in the "rest" of Tom's "Frollicks" (62). Whatever that means, the failure of Valentine to severely chastise Thomas constitutes a male bonding that is inherently misogynistic. Sir Wilding invites the young men for a collation of what can only be viewed as the most cynical celebration of such male bonding. Thomas concludes the play with a mock conversion, saying to his male buddies,

> Come, you shall go 'faith—for I am resolv'd to give my farewel to Intrigues, with a free and merry heart; and 'tis fit that you that are my Friends, shou'd be now my Witnesses, as you shall be when I go through the t'other Gate, Marriage. And tho' this kind of life is least troublesome; t'other is certainly most safe: especially, if a Man can change his Temper, else 'tis a Plague to him. For Marriage to a Debauchee, is a second Purgatory; It gives him onely a Prospect of Joy, or Torment, without knowing which he shall arrive to. But I hope I know my self better, than to venture without great Consideration to such Uncertainties.

After this cynical rationale for marrying a clean, proper virgin, Thomas slips lubriciously into the sing-song of the closing tag:

> Loose Love like a thin Garment serves us ill,
> And though wee'r pleas'd with it, we shiver still;
> But I'm confirm'd, let th'Age be what it will,
> What ever Nature in a Miss design'd,
> Wives only are the Blessing of Mankind. [63]

Marriage with whom? Cellida? After what has happened, no one in the audience could possibly take this ending straight. The actor would have to perform the speech as the final, most extravagant, most outrageous instance of Thomas's cocksureness. The only analogue for this ending is the outrageously cynical ending of Lee's *Princess of Cleve*, where Nemours, in a parody of fifth-act conversions, pretends to be the reformed rake who will now marry the tamed Marguerite. Durfey parodies Fletcher's concluding gay couple union. No gay couple united here, no estates joined. Just Thomas making an obscene gesture at the audience.[1]

These early comedies of Durfey seem to me to be conservative, corrective satire, designed to expose libertinism's dangerous threat to civil society and the peaceful transmission of power and property through marriage. But the greatest antilibertine comical satire of the period is Shadwell's *The Woman-Captain* (1679). Mally Bevil, the eponymous heroine of the play, is a satirical scourge, first against the Cit who bought her and his Puritan values. Mally complains to her old, miserly husband Gripe, "[M]y Mother betray'd me in my Youth to the slavery of thy Age" (II.344-45). So she exerts her "Christian Liberty" and "the right of an English Woman" (361-68) and liberates herself by tricking her way out of her confinement, then pretending to be her twin brother, a captain in the army, who comes to take revenge on Gripe for his barbarous, indeed enslaving treatment of Mally. At one point in her confinement he threatens to cane her. Like Ravenscroft's Hillaria, she wrests the cane from him and threatens him instead with "Correction" (II.374). An avatar of Pinchwife, he then counterthreatens, "[I]n, in, or this knife shall be embrued in thy Blood" (385-86).

    Correction becomes the key motif in this plot. Mally's plan is to coerce Gripe into returning her portion of £3000 or granting her an annuity of £400. Her coercion takes the entire play, however, for being a caricature of the abstemious Cit, Gripe is exceeding slow to learn discipline. As the woman captain, Mally's first act is to return naked violence with naked violence: she threatens to run Gripe through for his mistreatment of "his" sister. Restrained by her coconspirator, her real brother's sergeant, she yields to his argument that the regiment needs troops. Enlisting him in the army bound for Flanders (the one Otway and his soldiers were disbanded from), the captain turns Gripe and his servant Richard over to the sergeant for discipline in the manual of arms. Mally claims "the right of an English Woman" not only to free herself but "to Hector her own Husband" (III.469-70). And hector him she does, repeatedly caning him when he fails at military exercise. She has him tied neck and heels, then threatens him with what he interprets "worst of all"—to confiscate his "Writings" (V.361-63), which contain those "Mortgages" he, like a typical Cit real estate pimp, has been gathering from the extravagant aristocracy (IV.201): "How fast his Worships Land will melt into my Coffers" (II.30-31).

Their final interaction is extraordinary. Since bullying him has not worked, Mally reverts to her feminine self and manipulates him by wheedling. For his part, Gripe can not wait to get his hands on her to kill her, and he punctuates their dialogue with asides on the manner of the murder: from strangling, to running her through with a sword, to inserting a knitting needle under her arm, to smothering her and pretending she died of apoplexy, to administering an opiate that cannot be detected. Such raw violence, rare in Restoration comedy, deserves poetic justice. The final justice Shadwell administers is for Mally to soften up Gripe not with male but female weapons, batting her eyes, toying with him, cuddling, kissing, promising—if he but sign a deed releasing her with wealth, she will return the deed to him, as well as the writings the captain has sequestered. Mally succeeds not so much as a woman bully, then, as an *ingannatrice* who manipulates the words and bonds of official, patriarchal discourse.

The ending of the play is not the celebratory ending of social or subversive comedy, however. Mally has gained her freedom and at least a separate maintenance by using men's own gullibility against them. But she is quite different from Lady Fancy or Mrs. Cheatly or Sir Anthony Love. She pairs up with no male, indeed has eschewed escape in the "lewd Company" of the libertine rakes of the play (II.495-96). She has therefore retained her chastity, and there is no suggestion she will lose it later. Instead, she is a successful uppity woman who represents not only women's freedom from male oppression but also patriotic values. She is an agent of satire not only on niggardly, jealous Cit husbands and land pimps but on the extravagant Town wits of the decadent aristocracy.

For Mally as woman captain chastises Sir Charles Swash as well as Gripe. This Town swashbuckler has degenerated into a hector and hangs out with the two Suburbians, Heildebrand and Blunderbus, breaking windows, raising hell, but also committing violence against members of the middle and lower classes. This violence represents not the usual dominance of the class that deserves to rule over the satirical butts of inferior classes—as in Shadwell's own *Virtuoso*. It represents unlawful excess on the part of a class that has lost its (natural, moral) superiority.

Sir Charles introduces Heildebrand and Blunderbus to his peers as "honest" and "brave" men "of good Families" (II.213-22)—an appellation that works at once to reveal the opposite but also to suggest Sir Charles's inability to distinguish true worth resulting from birth. These hectors pretend to prey on all classes. Sir Charles invites his comrogues on an excursion: "[W]e will break Windows all the way we go, Kick every Male from a Link-boy to a Lord upwards; Kiss every Female, from the Simpering Lady to the Widemouth Jade that crys Sprats; Swinge Bumbailiffs excessively, and commit filthy outrage, to the astonishment of the *Mobile*" (II.274-79). We see them attack only members of classes lower than lords and ladies, however. Assaulting Gripe does not draw any sympathy for the victim, but assaulting the Citizen and his wife and the three old "Herb-women going to Market" (III.87) and the fiddlers just trying to make an honest living does. And if we have less sympathy for their assaulting the two or three apprentices, who are playing at being hectors themselves, nevertheless we are astonished at the crassness of their relating the incidents of the night, which conclude in a battle with the high constable and his watch, as they return with broken heads:

> *Sir Charles:* [W]e have had a Battle with the *Myrmidons* of St. *Martins,*
>   we have swinged, and are swinged—
> *Blunderbus:* I am sure my Porker is embrued in Blood.
> *Heidelberg:* And mine is stain'd in gore of filthy Peasant. [III.198-201]

This is "filthy outrage" indeed. When the Citizen, portrayed not as a punitive character but as one who pays his taxes and has the right to be outraged, seeks help from the constable, justice is frustrated by the fact that the constable is on the take from Sir Charles. Not even the high constable can take the hectors into custody, for the aristocrats close ranks and beat his watch off. Instead, Shadwell turns them over to the chastisement of Mally's military discipline: "Serjeant take their Names—I shall order them too—I'll teach 'em to roar and bully up and down the Town" (IV.543-45). She reads them the lesson to all such hectors, especially those who have degenerated from their status as knights: "'Sdeath you Dogs, no trifling with me! shall such Rascals as you think it enough to be Drunk, and Swagger, beat Bawds, kick Drawers, squabble with Constables and Watches, break Windows, and triumph in Drunken Brawls and Street-quarrels, and never serve your Countrey? . . . I shall show you there's more than roaring goes to true Valour" (V.315-19, 384-85).

The final piece of poetic justice administered to Sir Charles Swash results from his having squandered his estate: he loses his kept mistress, Chloris, who says to Wildman, the rake who steals her from Sir Charles, "Indeed he has been extravagant, and run out a great part of his Estate; and I hate a man that has run out his Fortune" (V.565-66). Sir Charles's fate underscores that of the other knights in the play. Sir Nicholas Peakgoose's mistress Celia's expense has, along with his own gambling, "broken his Fortune" (V.556). When he triumphs over the conscripted Sir Charles and the hectors who have bilked him, again Mally as woman captain is the agent of satiric punishment:

> *Mrs. Gripe:* How now Sirrah! who are you? a Soldier in no condition is to
>   be laught at, by such an Insect, a Maggot as thou art.
> *Sir Nicholas:* A Maggot! an Insect—I am a Knight, Sir.
> *Mrs. Gripe:* You are a Rascal, Sir! take that—[*Cudgels him.* [V.371-74]

When Sir Nicholas interrupts Celia with her new keeper, the rake Bellamy, she dismisses him with this deep cut: "Get you gone, you impertinent Coxcomb! must you come and interrupt me, when I am talking with a Gentleman; have you no breeding?" (577-79). To Bellamy's description of his and Celia's new deal Sir Nicholas protests, "Hold Sir! not so fast, I forbid the Banes! she's mine! why I have spent half my Estate upon her" (634-35). Indeed, Sir Humphrey has said earlier that Sir Nicholas "starves his Wife and Children" for Celia (I.284). Celia's parting jeer is as harsh— and more legitimately moralistic—than Harriet's to Mrs. Loveit at the end of *The Man of Mode:* "Go! get you home, and live civilly with your Wife; and look after your Children as an honest man should. 'Tis time" (640-41).

In a Restoration comedy, these women would be spouses at the end to the two Town wits, and their rejection of these fools would be seen as a class triumph over nouveaux knights, parvenus with no real "breeding." But in *The Woman-Captain,* the women are whores, not nubile virgins, and the Town wits they match are rakehell whoremasters. One might be tempted to see Chloris and Celia as heroine tricksters, clever courtesans like La Nuche. Indeed, at the beginning, they seem to be the inheritors of the code of constancy, protesting, swearing that they would never be inconstant to their keepers. Chloris says to the courting Wildman, "Oh Lord, I would not be false to Sir *Christopher Swash* for all this earthly good: 'Tis a shame Women should be so false to their Intrigues, as some are; I wonder at their Consciences. What do they think will become of their Souls another day?" (II.142-45). Celia similarly says to the courting Bellamy, "We of our Profession must be as careful of our Credit as Merchants and Bankers should be; if we break with one, we shall ne'r be trusted by another" (162-64). Yet they flirt with and make assignations with Mally as woman captain. So much for their constancy. Mally has the last ironic word on this possible interpretation of the whores: "Good constant Turtles these kept Ladies are, I'll say that for 'em" (V.186-87).

One might be tempted to see them as female folk-tricksters, but Shadwell makes too much fun of them. They are duped by Mally as the woman captain, are attracted to him, courted, and kissed repeatedly. Then they fight over him. Phillis, a third whore, who is also attracted to Mally, scares them off the stage pretending to be a devil. When they flee, they reveal themselves not to be trickster agents in control of their own destiny. They are not in the same league with the successful folk tricksters we have seen. Mally is clearly superior to them at the end when she boasts that she is indeed a woman "but wish my self a Man, for your sakes" (V.665-66).

Nor can we view the union between the whores and the rakehells as the same kind of salubrious union as that between Bevil and Rains or Bruce and Longvil with their aristocratic ladies. For the rakes are as thoroughly discredited as their friend, Sir Humphrey Scattergood (whom they desert as fair-weather friends as soon as his estate is squandered), in their licentious life-styles. They are upstaged by the woman captain and respond not as tricksters in control but as petulant whiners. Wildman laments, "Pox on all these whiffling young Officers! all the Whores run mad after 'em; and a good substantial solid Whoremaster cannot keep one in quiet for 'em" (IV.361-63). They have no illusions about their mistresses, despite their earlier protestations of constancy: watching them flirt with the woman captain, Wildman predicts, "We are like to have very constant Mistresses, if we get 'em" (328). And again, Mally would seem to have the final judgment: she completes her statement about the ladies as constant turtledoves, "And good charitable publick spirited men the Keepers to maintain women, as they wear Perfumes for the use of others" (V.187-88). Whether Dryden wrote the satire on keepers he claimed in the dedication to *The Kind Keeper*, Shadwell did. Bellamy and Wildman come off not as tricksters but dupes themselves. The inconstant whores they get at the end are their just due, their poetic justice.

For *The Woman-Captain* is, like *The Libertine* and *Timon* (but not *Epsom Wells* or *The Virtuoso* or *A True Widow*), antilibertine satire. And their "Company" is satirized not only because it is "lewd" but because of its threat to the political economy of the aristocracy. Sir Humphrey Scattergood's last name is most telling. Finally come into the "Estate" his "Father's Will" kept him from till, it must have been hoped, he had reached an age of real maturity—"four and twenty" (I.11-12)—Sir Humphrey, abetted by Wildman and Bellamy, has speedily begun, as his scandalized old steward phrases it, the "confounding" of that "Estate" (86-87) by mortgaging its "Land and Timber" (71) to the likes of Gripe and his "Extortion" (I.341).[2] A voluptuary descended from Jonson's Sir Epicure Mammon (as critics have long noted), he needs ready cash for his orgies. When he orders the steward to get £1000 for his birthday party, he tells him to let Gripe "have a Mortgage till I cut down Timber to redeem my dirt" (192-93). The land that supports the aristocracy is to him only so much "dirt," the woods that adorn it only so much "Timber" to be turned into the ships that venture to the "Indies" (IV.438) and that also supply the paper on which are written the deeds that convey the wealth from his to the merchant class that outfits the ships and supplies the venture capital. Lawrence Stone has called this kind of ostentatious squandering *the crisis of the aristocracy*, and Shadwell satirizes it.

Sounding like Shadwell's earlier, comic rake heroes, Sir Humphrey, Wildman, and Bellamy disdain those who venture for state "Ambition" or military "Honour" or for metaphysics or mathematics or science or politics—any such vain "shadow"—while ignoring the only substance that matters, "Sense": "[W]e are Lords o'th'world, and enjoy all in it, while they are Slaves" (III.253-77). In defiance of the tradition from Baldesar Castiglione to Sir Philip Sidney, these aristocratic rakes are a satiric parody of Rochester and his followers and even, implicitly, of the king. Witness this song:

> The Kings most faithful Subjects we
> In's Service are not Dull,
> We drink to show our Loyalty
> And make his Coffers full.
> Would all his Subjects drink like us,
> We'd make him richer far,
> More Powerful and more Prosp'rous
> Then all the Eastern Monarchs are[.] [II.401-8]

If these raucous hectors drink the kinds of French wine catalogued by Sir Humphrey and friends in Act I, then they enrich the king by paying fines for drinking forbidden wine (see Slagle's note). Their "Loyalty" is thus ironic. On the other hand, the first two lines possess another meaning, especially when sung in Gripe's house and in the teeth of his Puritanism. They are the king's "most faithful Subjects" in imitating his own riots and orgies. If the king can do it with impunity, why not the rest of aristocracy? Why not all classes? Except, of course, that as in Gay's later *Beggar's Opera*, only the rich, like Sir Charles Swash here, can afford to bribe justice. Witness Sir Humphrey's statement about whores, really about the appellation "whore" itself: when his friends call the kept mistresses of the play whores, he responds, "Fy, fy, Whores! That's a naughty word. They are Ladies; there are no Whores but such as are poor and beat Hemp, and Whipt by Rogues in Blew Coats" (I.268-70). Shadwell satirizes *aristocratic* decadence all the way to the top. These "Lords o'th'-world" have unlimited *droits du seigneur,* it would seem, while the rest of the world, especially those who try to run its government and its enterprise and of course those whose labor sustains the lords' manors, are "Slaves." Thus the motif of constables and watch defeated. Thus the need for Mally's correction.

The standard for correction resides in the play from the start in the figure of the powerless steward, who praises his "good old Master" for the moderation that "increas'd his Wealth" (I.102-3). One key word here is *old;* there is a nostalgia for a former era when moderation built strength and where all was happy in the English countryside: "Many a good *Christmas* has my old Master kept there" (V.77)—another of those feasts when the peasants were treated in the small compensation, as Raymond Williams reminds us, for their backbreaking daily labor. But Shadwell's version of the manor house is not only nostalgic but pastoral. As in Mally's discourse about the liberty of English women, another key word in the steward's discourse is *English:* "[W]hy must your Worship have French Cooks. Methinks my Masters old English Cookmaid, with good store of Parsley and Butter, did very well" (I.159-62). At the same time Shadwell's standard is nostalgic, it is contemporary, smacking of Whiggish patriotism. Sir Humphrey rejects these remonstrations, arguing that his father did well to amass the wealth for him to spend. He rebukes the steward's prudence: "I will revel now with what he left. Choak not me with your Providence with a Pox to you" (I.104-5). Providence here carries not religious but secular meaning: *seeing and planning ahead.* Shadwell's standard carves out a middle ground between aristocratic extravagance and bourgeois abstemiousness: Aristotle's golden mean.

Neither the steward nor Mally corrects Sir Humphrey, however. That is left partly to fate and partly to Mally's dark double, the whore Phillis. The fate operating as a dynamic in the play is *character as fate:* Sir Humphrey's failure to listen to prudential advice and his headlong pursuit of pleasure come back to haunt him. The steward enters in Act V to announce, "I little thought to live to see this day. . . . All your Land in *Essex* is extended by your Creditors. And your Furniture the richest in the County all seiz'd upon" (59-62). The only land he has left has been transferred to Phillis as a settlement upon his kept mistress. The steward announces this part of Sir Humphrey's fate with his characteristic inability to say *lady* or *gentlewoman* or *mistress* anent these women without adding *whore:* "I remember when my old Master purchas'd it, and little thought I should have seen it go out of the Family; and now there is no remedy; for all the Land you had free, you have this day setled upon your Mistress—Whore. [*Aside*" (V.65-68).

Phillis gets the moiety of Sir Humphrey's estate the same way Mally finally gets her settlement—wheedling. Early in the play when Chloris envies Celia's ability to govern her keeper, Phillis turns to Sir Humphrey, cuddles up to him (so I would have her play it), and says fawningly (then turns aside to the audience with an arch look), "I desire not to govern, my Dear; if I have but thy Love, Child, I wish for nothing else—But thy Money. [*Aside*" (I.291-92). At the height of his debauchery Phillis works Sir Humphrey to achieve her wish: "My Dear, I have a Lawyer and Writings ready for that Settlement thou wert pleas'd to promise me, if thou wilt dispatch it now, not that I desire it; but in a case of Mortality: for while thou livest I desire nothing but thee, and when thou art dead 'twill do me little good—for I shall scarce out-live thee. So I am very indifferent, do what thou wilt" (IV.263-68). Her seeming devotion, which is so strong it trammels up logic, overwhelms this Town wit's wits: "No—come my Dear, I'll dispatch it now" (269).

Once Phillis has her settlement, she assumes the airs of the lady of the house and will not tolerate debauchery and the presence of "those little ill-bred Kept things," her sister whores (V.247). Moreover, she claims the house as hers. The dialogue between her and Sir Humphrey is hilarious as Phillis parodies the discourse of the *nouvelles riches:*

> *Sir Humphrey:* How long has it been your House?
> *Phillis:* Since yesterday; and 'tis as much mine, as if it had descended from my Ancestors these 500 years.
> *Sir Humphrey:* To whose bounty do you owe it?
> *Phillis:* To no bounty; I owe it to my own Beauty, and those Charms that made you settle it on me, and my Faith and Constancy has deserv'd it fully. . . . [Y]our Sisters and your Mother shall be welcom to me; provided they give me that respect which is due to me: I intend to visit and keep Company with none but Persons of Quality—
> *Sir Humphrey:* Pray Madam, who is it that has kept you?
> *Phillis:* My Beauty, and my Merit; not your Bounty—
> *Sir Humphrey:* And are not you a Tailor's Daughter?
> *Phillis:* My Fortune makes me of a good Family[.] [225-54]

Twice Phillis insists that her own *merit,* that bourgeois key word, has made her *fortune,* a term that here means both luck and newfound wealth.

The only way Sir Humphrey can "circumvent" (264) Phillis is to make her his lady in earnest, an agreement Phillis obviously accepts because it solidifies her rise in status, even though she thereby surrenders this moiety of Sir Humphrey's estate back to him. To his rakehell comrades who are astonished that he has married his "Wench" (V.588) Sir Humphrey explains and justifies his "proceeding": "I found my self involv'd on a sudden, beyond any other redemption, and therefore chose this, which I hope will set me free. This she-pyrat had rob'd me of what my extravagance had left free, and I have taken Letters of Reprisal, and have gotten my own agen. . . . She is the greatest Fortune I could have gotten, nor do I know why a Man should not fit a Woman that perhaps may last him his life time, and yet draw on a Shoe that he is to wear but two days before he take it" (589-99). Phillis is the greatest fortune available to him because he is estateless. But his rationalizing taking his wench in terms of buying a pair of shoes he has tried out rings as hollow as his friends' wishes for happiness. Earlier he has more honestly appraised his action in an address to the absent Phillis: "I must plague my self to punish thee" (265). In another appraisal, he articulates to the audience the moral lesson in his story: "So—I have parted with most part of my Estate, and Liberty to boot! Oh negligence, and want of thinking" (238-39). The steward has turned out to be Jimminy Cricket. And this fallen Pinocchio must take his punishment without redemption.

For despite Chloris's congratulation—"I wish your Ladiship much Joy; 'tis a great honour to our Function to have one of it so advanced" (V.600-601)—the "she-pyrat" to whom Sir Humphrey is married, this tailor's daughter, is portrayed as neither the witty courtesan La Nuche nor the delightful energy figure Dol Troop. Instead, she is something of an object of satire herself. She too is taken with the woman captain, and at the moment she is protesting like Hamlet's Player Queen to Sir Humphrey, she sends Mally a billet doux seeking an assignation. Arriving for it, she discovers her sister mistresses have similar assignations and goes into denial: "What say They—This must be false—They are conceited! Vain Sluts! I am sure he would meet none but me—I'll rout 'em out of my House" (450-52). Phillis is not so much a successful trickster as a scourge, a "plague," a weapon in Shadwell's satire.[3]

From the beginning of the play Shadwell serves notice that he is writing satire. Like Lear, Sir Humphrey drives truth to kennel when he silences his fool, insisting that fools are out of fashion, even upon the stage. Moreover, "You are a Satyrical Fool, and will give offence." Identifying himself with "*Shakespear*'s Fools," the fool responds, "Indeed this Age is not able to bear Satyr" (I.34-40). His play concludes in poetic justice, with emphasis on the word *justice*. Whether this justice be providential, as it is in most Restoration serious drama—that is, whether the metaphysical realm referred to in Chloris's mock protestation ("What do they think will become of their Souls another day?") or the steward's "godly Meditations" (III.193) or Gripe's fear for the loss of his "Soul" because of his sins against "young Orphans and Comfortless Widows" (IV.141-42) manifests itself in the dynamic of the ending—the ending of the play is quite traditionally moral.[4] All the women in the play have served as scourges against male folly and vice, and most of them have been satirized too. The morality of the old-fashioned steward has been vindicated. And Mally stands out at the end as the One Just Woman—a variation on the satirical tradition of the One Just Man. Her figure will be picked up in comical satires by Southerne and Vanbrugh—*The Wives Excuse* and *The Relapse,* respectively. But here she is portrayed with much more agency, much more control of the situation. Moreover, symbolically the single Mally at the end represents the estate of England, divorced from the decadent aristocracy, ready to be picked up by a descendent of that decent Citizen mocked in the middle of the play, whose hour has come round at last.

Behn's *The Luckey Chance; or, An Alderman's Bargain* (1686) also features tricksters who act as satirical scourges. Belmour, a gentleman nearly out of tragicomic romance, has killed a man in a duel, has had to go into exile to avoid prosecution, and has had to leave behind his beloved and betrothed, Leticia Bredwel. Sir Feeble Fainwou'd, a foolish old City alderman, wants Leticia as his young bride and therefore wants his young rival out of the way, buys his pardon and secrets it, then gives out that Belmour has hanged himself at the Hague. Thinking him dead, Leticia is forced by her small fortune to marry Sir Feeble. Belmour returns the day of the wedding, is unable to prevent it since he is still proscribed, but soon gains access to the Fainwou'ds' Town house disguised as Sir Feeble's nephew Francis and learns from Leticia the truth of her coercion and her continuing constancy. Furthermore, Sir Feeble himself tells his supposed nephew of his vicious plot against Belmour, a rival of "pretty Estate" with whose youth and looks he cannot compete (III.i.37). Sir Feeble entrusts Francis with the secreted pardon, and Belmour sets out to keep the marriage from being consummated until he can liberate Leticia.

Tony Leigh as Sir Feeble may have taken some liberties with the part as Behn wrote it, for she defends herself in her preface against charges of lewdness relating to the moment Sir Feeble chases the waiting women out of the bridal chamber by opening his dressing gown. Perhaps disingenuously Behn writes, "[I]f he do, which is a Jest of his own making, and which I never saw, I hope he has his Cloaths on underneath?" (Pref.,52-53). The stage direction tells the actor to open his gown, but perhaps it was added for publication, perhaps on opening night Leigh had few clothes on underneath (or perhaps he just flashed toward the women *as if* he had nothing on). Howbeit, Belmour/Francis interrupts the consummation with a false message of an urgent meeting of aldermen as the City and indeed the whole country is up in arms. In Sir Feeble's absence Belmour and Leticia make plans to escape. Leticia reads out the lesson of this part of the play, of its poetic justice:

> —Old man forgive me—thou the Agressor art,
> Who rudely forc'd the Hand without the Heart.
> She cannot from the Paths of Honour rove,
> Whose Guide's Religion, and whose End is Love. [III.i.160-63]

Interrupted themselves in their attempted escape, Belmour and Leticia must trick Sir Feeble again. While Sir Feeble prepares for another attempt at consummation and while Leticia prays for deliverance, Belmour appears in their chamber as his own ghost, coat doffed, shirt bloodied. Using religious language, Belmour drives Sir Feeble to confession and repentance. A little like Hamlet with his mother (plus a little of Hamlet's father's ghost), Belmour's ghost admonishes,

> If thou repent'st, renounce her, fly her sight;—
> Shun her bewitching Charms, as thou wouldst Hell;
> Those dark eternal Mansions of the dead—
> Whither I must descend. [V.i.93-96]

Sir Feeble enters the final scene, blathering like Macbeth in the presence of Banquo's ghost. His language still carries heavy religious overtones, as he quotes the ghost: "Hell shall not hold thee—nor vast Mountains cover thee, but I will find thee out—and lash thy filthy Adulterous Carcase" (V.ii.308-9). He sees the ghost, begs it to hide "that bleeding Wound, it chills my Soul!" (314). Then he becomes like King Lear: "Ah Fool, old dull besotted Fool—to think she'd love me—'twas by base means I gain'd her—couzen'd an honest Gentleman—of Fame and Life—" (330-32). Lady Fulbank, playing a comic Cordelia, insists he can make the gentleman amends:

> *Sir Feeble:* Oh wou'd I could, so I gave half my Estate—
> *Lady Ful:* That Penitence attones with him and Heaven. [335-36]

All of this must have been funny stage business, but Belmour's winning back Leticia is different in tone from the typical Town wit's winning the heroine. Belmour and Leticia finally receive Sir Feeble's blessing but only after Belmour has lashed Sir Feeble into recognition of his vice and folly.

Sir Feeble's vice becomes clarified through the subplot concerning Bearjest, Sir Cautious Fulbank's foppish nephew; Bredwel, Leticia's brother, who serves as an apprentice to Sir Cautious; Diana, Sir Feeble's daughter; and Pert, Lady Fulbank's woman. The gist of it is that, like Belmour and Leticia, Bredwel and Diana are precontracted, and Sir Feeble has given his word to Bredwel that he may marry his daughter. But for purposes of economic alliance with Sir Cautious's family, Sir Feeble agrees to give Diana to Bearjest. Bearjest is a boor who cares no more for Diana's inclinations than Sir Feeble does—or did with regard to Leticia's. Moreover, Bearjest is himself precontracted to Pert and breaks his word with her. Bredwel becomes a trickster, courts Diana before Bearjest à la Harcourt, swears he would love her if she were a village maid. Convincing Bearjest that someone else is after Diana and he had better abscond with her, Bredwel and Diana pull a switch, marry each other, and marry Bearjest to the disguised Pert. Pert, in reality a gentlewoman, characterizes what she has done as "a pious Fraud" (V.ii.371) and reveals the precontract. The humbled Sir Feeble grants both couples his blessing. Bredwel attributes the outcome to "what the Pow'rs design'd above" (V.ii.54).

What is at stake here is more than just Behn's typical resistance to enforced marriages. The play satirizes and punishes trothbreakers. Jean A. Coakley in the introduction to her edition of the play reads the play as topical satire, Sir Feeble (as well as his City friends) as a usurper (93-94). Belmour would represent, then, on some level, the legitimate monarch, James Stuart. Behn has satirized the City for its inconstancy. Nevertheless, these two plots are those of tragicomic romance, for as in a Shakespearean tragicomedy, the rightly matched but beleaguered couples finally are married. What makes it useful to call the play a comical satire—or perhaps in this instance a tragicomical satire—is its other plot, particularly its ending.

Unlike the other, romantic couples, Gayman and Julia do not end up together. Like the others, they were precontracted, but Julia appears to have been forced to violate her vows to Gayman and to marry Sir Cautious Fulbank for money. She laments her yielding to force:

> Oh how fatal are forc'd Marriages!
> How many Ruines one such Match pulls on—
> Had I but kept my sacred Vows to *Gayman*
> How happy had I been—how prosperous he!
> Whilst now I languish in a loath'd Embrace,
> Pine out my Life with Age—Consumptious Coughs[.] [I.ii.31-36]

Whatever the intricacies of marital law,[5] Behn has chosen to place Julia in a situation where her remedy is not annulment but adultery. Gayman plies her with gifts till he impoverishes himself, ironically mortgaging his annuity, in a part that is about to yield to the whole, to Sir Cautious. Sir Cautious knows this mortgaging prodigal only by the name of Wasteall, a

name that, like Scattergood, suggests satire on such improvident aristocrats. And while in retribution for Sir Cautious's "unmerciful" treatment
of Gayman (I.ii.109) Julia steals from her husband to redeem her lover,
she insists that the gift be anonymous, for "[t]hat Nicety and Vertue I've
profest, I am resolv'd to keep" (105).

Julia is clear in the terms of her relationship with both husband and
gallant. She admits to Sir Cautious that she loves someone else, even acknowledges when he guesses that it is Gayman. At the same time she
pledges to "love discreetly Sir, love as I ought, love Honestly" and "keep
my Vertue Sir intire" (V.iv.122, 128). Ironically, Sir Cautious has already
bargained her away in an indecent gambling proposal with Gayman and is
even now trying to soften her up to commit adultery "wisely" (132). She
warns him, "There is but one Way Sir to make me hate you; And that
wou'd be tame Suffering" (137-38). To Gayman she has been as down-
right: "[I]f you can afford me a Lease of your Love, / 'Till the Old Gentleman my Husband depart this wicked World, / I'm for the Bargain"
(II.ii.185-87). Having tested his faith to that lease by teasing him into an
assignation with the mystery woman who sends him money—and found it
wanting—Julia makes him confess his infidelity. She seems satisfied with
his honesty, though miffed that he pretends her body was that of an old
and bony woman. We learn later that the assignation was interrupted
before coitus.

In other words, though Julia obviously hopes the old Sir Cautious will
indeed die soon and free her to marry Gayman, adultery is anathema to
her virtue, her sense of self. And while the play obviously satirizes Sir Cautious for being so crass, so parsimonious, so greedy as to sacrifice his wife
for his money, it also satirizes Gayman for being so crass as to enjoy Julia
by stealth. Against the £300 he has lost Sir Cautious wishes he could
wager "nothing" of value in a winner-take-all (IV.569), and Gayman invites Sir Cautious to consider his wife worth nothing inherent. Even
worse, between men, Sir Cautious considers the term cuckold to be "a
Word—an empty Sound—'tis Breath—'tis Air—'tis nothing" (396-97).
Like a typical Cit, Sir Cautious of course fears that Gayman will be so lusty
Julia will know the difference. Indeed, Gayman's "Excess of Love—
betray'd the Cheat" (V.ii.242), and as soon as Julia discovers it, she chases
Gayman out of her bed, railing at him.[6] Protesting as a possessing male,
Gayman insists he "only seiz'd my Right of Love" (230). He is incapable
of understanding her anger that he has virtually raped her, robbed her not
so much of her "Honour" or "Fame" (231-32)—things she cares less
about as the mere "Censures of the Croud" (115)—but of her "Quiet"
(234). She bans him from her sight, intending "never" to see him "more"
(244).

Only when Gayman reveals that Sir Cautious himself sold her to him does she soften her stance and turn her ire on her husband. But not before she asks poignantly, "If he cou'd be so barbarous to expose me, / Could you who lov'd me—be so cruel too!" (266-67). So cruel to expose her as "a base Prostitute, a foul Adulteress" (233) to the world; so cruel to treat her as an object, a gewgaw passed between men. She swears by "sacred" oath "To separate for ever from [Sir Cautious's] Bed" (273-74). At the very end, when Sir Cautious complains to Sir Feeble, the only other character who knows about this alderman's bargain, the chastened Sir Feeble convinces Sir Cautious to accept what has happened as the result of their both being "a couple of old Coxcombs" who have brought poetic justice down upon their own heads (384-85). A chastened Sir Cautious then offers to Gayman, "[I]f I dye Sir—I bequeath my Lady to you—with my whole Estate" (386-87).

This offer would seem to open the door to a comic resolution. Gayman turns to Julia asking her consent. She responds, "No Sir—you do not like me—a canvas Bag of wooden Ladles were a better Bed-fellow" (390-91). She refers to the description Gayman, to decrease Julia's jealousy, made of the woman with whom he had the assignation, which woman was Julia herself. Her comment is arch, a bit of a tease. But her point is to let him know she does not trust him, that he has already failed one test of "Constancy" (394), and his response, like that of Sirs Feeble and Cautious, is one of humiliation: "Cruel Tormentor! oh I cou'd kill my self with Shame and Anger!" (392).

Gayman is not only ashamed but angry with himself, for not only has he transgressed, he may after all have lost Julia. If so, it is because he failed to understand how precious to her was not only her virtue, but, as she explains to Sir Cautious, her "Freedom" and "Humour" (V.112). Her virtue is not traditional: she would cuckold Sir Cautious "if it pleas'd me better than Vertue Sir" (111). In other words, her virtue is not ontological but existential. Like Anouilh's Becket, whose allegiance is not to God but to the honor of God, she upholds an ideal because, in her freedom and individual humor, she identifies with it—better, shapes her identity by means of it. It is an anchor of meaning she chooses more out of aesthetics than ethics. At the end of the play, like the woman captain, she stands out in bas-relief, a scourge of the libertine who failed to appreciate her as a person.

On the eve of the Revolution Durfey had produced another corrective comical satire, *A Fool's Preferment; or, The Three Dukes of Dunstable* (April 1688). Appropriately for its moment in history—just as the aristocracy is about to lose control over at least the apex of the status hierarchy to the rising bourgeoisie—it is a satire on social climbing, a satire aimed not so much this time at the extortions of the City as at the complicity of the Country in its love affair with the Town and the Court. Set in the time of Henry IV, the play begins with the first wannabe, the Country gentleman Cockle-brain, hoping through his wife's gambling to make connections and achieve preferment at Court. His servant Toby pleads, "And shall we never go into the Country agen then, Sir? Will you run out all your Estate here, for this confounded Name of a Courtier?" (I.ii, 25). When Cockle-brain insists how finely the name courtier draws wonder, Toby pertinently replies, "Ay, 'Twill draw your Worship's Land within the walls too, where you may have it, all inclos'd and sure" (25). Metaphoric enclosure within the City walls provides as much a class exclusion as literal enclosure of the commons: the latter excludes the landless, the former the (traditionally) landed. Toby hopes his old uncle, Grub the Country justice, will be able to talk some sense into Cockle-brain; Grub lambastes him, calls him a bankrupt, asks, "What dost thou do at Court but to be ruin'd? Hast reckon'd up thy Income? Dost thou know the value of thy Tenants Sweat and Labour, and thy Expences here?" (25). This is a rare reference to such sweat and labor, all of which is being squandered by an ostentatious aristocracy, maintaining its conspicuous consumption. Things are getting so bad on Cockle-brain's estate that his tenants are running away, and when he asks Toby to sell more land, what his wife, sounding like Sir Humphrey Scattergood, calls "a few dirty Acres" (30), Toby pleads again, "This honest Land, that you are parting with, hath been true to you, and done you loyal Service" (31). His point would seem to mean that the tenants on the land have also done him good service, and as they are probably copyholders and not freeholders, they will be dispossessed.

Grub asks further what good it can do Cockle-brain to bring his wife to Court, where she is liable to beget "a Bastard, Sir, it may be, to inherit your Estate" (26). Hearing she has the steady company of two lords, Grub concludes Cockle-brain is already "a rank Cuckold" (28). Toby decries her lavish living: "And for Eating and Drinking, she's the very Devil, her Belly is a meer Parson's Barn, all your Tenants pay Tyth to't, and yet 'tis never satisfyed" (II.i, 38). But there is no Rabelaisian comic humor here; this is the official discourse of satire.

Durfey provides a vignette that exists to emphasize the positive standard of the satire. Cockle-brain, Grub, and Toby, assisted by the mad Lyonel, a figure for the scourge of satire, drive away the gamblers from Cockle-brain's wife Aurelia, and he orders her to prepare to go down to the Country, where she will rise at "thrifty Hours" (39) and learn good huswifery, where Toby will oversee and pay wages to the good "Workfolks" (43). Dressed in his Country attire, Cockle-brain asks Toby how he looks, and Toby responds in the words of the corrective (nostalgic) standard: "Exceeding well, Sir; Now your Worship looks just like your self; A Man of Means and Credit; so did your wise and famous Ancestors ride up and down to Fairs to cheapen Cattle" (43).

Aurelia has no intention of relinquishing the Town—or her lover Clermont (who has no more love or respect for her than to try to gamble her away like Sir Cautious). So she and her cohorts fool Cockle-brain into thinking the king is jealous that he is leaving, that His Majesty has sent Longoville to knight him. Clermont persuades him to hold out for more than a mere knighthood. Cockle-brain says anyone can be knighted, and he cites instances of meritless promotion (instances Durfey obviously intends as a rebuke): "I have known a Cheese-monger a Knight; a hundred Sniveling, addle-headed Citizens for Cheating, knighted: and Pimps and Cuckolds unnumerable" (46). When Bewford enters with news he has been made a lord, Clermont persuades Cockle-brain to repeat the same strategy, and he responds, "I know a Crook-back'd Fidler call'd a Lord" (47). Longoville enters with news he has been made a marquess (so the previous lordship must have been something less, perhaps that most infamous of ranks, a baronetcy, created by James I precisely to be sold, although that would be an anachronism). But now, only a dukedom will do, so Bewford returns with that offer, and Cockle-brain chooses to be Duke of Dunstable because he likes the sound!

When Toby rides down to the Country to inform Grub that Cockle-brain will not be coming after all, we expect them to be righteously indignant together. Instead, they eschew their former moral high ground and see themselves as fools. Grub will outfit his wife with clothes for Court immediately: "I was a dull Countrey Clod, to let my Nephew rise and get the start before me. . . . I'll trouble my self no more with Sowing and Reaping; but laugh and lye at Ease, let the Weather change as it will" (III.i, 54). Even Toby is dissatisfied with the role of servant, wants to set up for a dukedom himself. Arrived at Court, Grub's wife Phillida opines that their home village Plowden "is such a stinking dunghil to this sweet place" (IV.iii, 72). The Grubs fawn before the Cockle-brains. When Bewford fondles Phillida before his face, then takes her into a private room, the indignant Grub quickly learns he must endure even cuckoldom if he wishes to be preferred.

Because Cockle-brain wants to go down and show off his titles to his tenants, Aurelia decides, "His Grace must be degraded" (V.i, 81). She and her fellow tricksters strip him, award the dukedom of Dunstable to Grub. But Aurelia grows jealous of Phillida because her male cohorts are now enjoying Phillida's favors. So she turns the trick once more, has Grub degraded, and Toby made the third duke. Grub is furious that he has lost the return on his investment of his wife: "What, my Wife lye with a topping Courtier two whole nights, and I no Duke! 'tis impossible?" (87).

Durfey ends the play with a deus ex machina: the Usher of the Black Rod, an agent of the king, informs Toby he is no duke either, orders Aurelia's three tricksters arrested and fined £20,000 apiece for selling the king's honors and dignities, and tells the others they are "such a knot of Fools, that the King, instead of punishing, pities you" (88). The three fools dance together as a demonstration of their foolishness, a public humiliation. The play ends in poetic justice but no comic reconciliation. Grub leaves petulantly, demanding from Cockle-brain the £500 he loaned him and calling his wife "Whore" (89). Cockle-brain will go home and fast for seven years so he can pay back his debts, "recover the Estate I have spent in waiting for preferment, and never so much as look towards old *Sodom* here agen" (89). Aurelia protests she will become "a most Penitent, Obedient Wife, to atone for my past Follies: and no more to heed the senseless Fopperies of the Town, nor the more senseless Fops remaining in it" (90). Cockle-brain accepts her back begrudgingly, "Well—I am forc'd to believe thee: We that are Married, have but small variety of remedy" (90)—that is, though she has cuckolded him, there is no real way to punish her without scandal. Toby will go back "into the Barn, and Thresh agen: there's no Revolution of State there, if the Harvest be but good" and concludes the play thus: "And may no Fool for better Fortune look;/That just from Digging, thinks to be a Duke" (90).

What has been potentially revolutionary is an ambition that trickles down to the lower classes, infecting them with ideas of social climbing, with the philosophy of the Diggers and the Levellers. The play reaffirms status hierarchy by employing tricksters as scourges that are later scourged themselves. In a way, the mad Lyonell, who drifts in and out of the play like Trouble-all in *Bartholomew Fair* and who acts as a scourge on the tricksters and even on Toby at one point, is a malcontent character who figures forth the instability of the times. When his sanity—and his beloved Celia—are returned at the end, the state has been purged, order restored. The chastened lords of manors and justices of the peace have returned to their estates. The barns are once again filled with grain ready to be threshed. The tricksters have scourged and been scourged.[7]

12
Tricksters Get Blown about by the Wind

If some comical satires embody a collective corrective voice, some embody a more menippean jumble of voices that destabilize and subvert the ground on which we might take a stance of judgment. Unlike corrective satire, which underwrites the official discourse of the prevailing ideology, absurdist satire explodes it. When such satire is comical, we are invited to simply throw up our hands and at least chuckle at the failure of our essentializing systems. If dramatic satire is rare, this kind of comical satire is the rarest. Out of all the Restoration comedies between 1660 and 1690 I have read, and I have tried to read them all, I have found only three. One comes at the apex of Restoration drama in 1677, the other two frame the period at its alpha and omega like two ghostly apparitions of Momus.

Durfey's *A Fond Husband; or, The Plotting Sisters* (1677), the most popular and most famous of his early plays, seems radical by comparison to his other, corrective comical satires. From Smith to Hume and Rothstein-Kavenik to Wheatley, I believe critics have misread it as if not the origin, then at least the great springboard for late 1670s sex comedy. Rothstein-Kavenik (206-7) and Payne have it wrong: it is not *The Kind Keeper* that is trying to be the satire, whatever Dryden said to cover himself in the dedication; it is *A Fond Husband*. Wheatley ("Durfey's *A Fond Husband*") thinks the rake/hero Rashley's extravagant rhetoric elevates to the libertine sublime. I agree, but I think that sublime is finally mocked. Rashley is having an affair with Emilia, wife of Peregrine Bubble, in his own house and virtually in his teeth, for part of Rashley's outrageous trick is to narrate their trysts to him pretending they happened with another woman. Ranger, another Town wit, and Emilia's sister-in-law Maria affect the rhetoric of moral outrage. Theirs is primarily religious rhetoric, for they constantly see the devil in the action and Emilia as outrageously "impudent" (a word used over and over), a witch allied with the devils who precede even Eve, that worst of all women. Maria reveals the sociological basis of her concern, as she tells her brother, "Heav'n knows how I have lov'd her, instructed her, and told her the duty of a wife was to obey and be constant; yet all would not do. Therefore I am resolv'd to right my self and you in the discovery; nor shall our race in future times be branded with any spurious offspring" (III.i.193-97).

This economic base of society is underscored in the subplot involving Sir Roger Petulant, a Country squire, and his attempt to marry his nephew Sneak to Bubble's niece, Cordelia. We are never told, but Bubble would appear, despite his aristocratic name Peregrine, to be a wealthy Cit, and this marriage a typical one to replenish gentry estates with City money. But the marriage falls through, for not only does Sneak have a pregnant mistress from Cambridge, Mrs. Snare, he has the pox as well. Durfey stages his exposure in a sweating tub, an ignominious image of aristocratic decadence. Sir Roger rather lamely promises Cordelia another nephew, but no such marriage is contracted by the end of the play. Even if it were, Sneak has provided an unidealized view of the Country, where he has been following his father's footprints among his former mistresses. Sir Roger is satirized for his expansive *droit du seigneur;* he is forced to compromise with his vile nephew. But Sneak, the Cambridge sophomore who would be a Town libertine, is so vile he would bring his syphilitic contamination into his marriage with Cordelia, and Sir Roger intends to have his brother disinherit him.

The ideology of the patrilineal system is destabilized, then, every-where: City husbands cuckolded by Town libertines acting with impudence and impunity, Country *villains* and peasants cuckolded by lords and their sons with equal impunity. Moreover, Cordelia, whose name carries all those positive Shakespearean connotations, spends most of the play fending off the advances of the superannuated Alderman Fumble. It is as if her story is a dark parody of *King Lear,* where France becomes Sneak and Lear becomes the old, deaf lecher Fumble, who cannot keep his paws off of her and who obviously wants her to keep his bed warm until he dies. Cordelia tries to pawn Fumble off on her governess, but her plot—which would have administered some poetic justice—fails.

It is a play of failed plots. The plotting sisters of the subtitle contest for mastery. But Maria, who would seem to have right on her side, and her righteous cohort Ranger never do expose Rashley and Emilia. Part of Durfey's meaning might be that they are not really worthy, that their motivation is contaminated by their own desires. Ranger is jealous that Emilia has chosen Rashley instead of him as an adulterous lover, and he fully intends, à la Manley and Monsieur Thomas, to "enjoy her" (passim). When she turns the tables on him and gets out of a compromising situation by hiding Rashley and accusing Ranger of trying to rape her, we in the audience know if he could, he would do so. On the other hand, Maria is furious that Rashley has thrown her over for Emilia, and she is motivated primarily by envy and concomitant revenge. Of course, the audience's pleasure is heightened by seeing the stately Rebecca Marshall utter the imprecations of heroic drama, as she had in the roles of Dryden's termagants Lyndaraxa and Nourmahal, and most recently, Lee's Roxana in *The Rival Queens*. Perhaps Durfey even intended the roles of the plotting sisters to be played by Rebecca and her sister Anne, both members of the Duke's Company when the play was performed. But it worked even better to have the aging Beck Marshall (this was to be her last play) paired against the young and brilliant emerging talent of Elizabeth Barry. It must have given a special fillip to Maria's envy and rage. This is not a cheerful confrontation, however. Durfey darkens it with Rashley's perverse characterization: "'Twould be excellent sport to hear the two she-wolves bark one at another" (II.ii.26-27).

So the position of satirist-manipulator is undercut for both Ranger and Maria, and the violence of his rapist intentions is matched by Maria's violence in her incredible wish, "Oh that I had thy heart here in my hand! How pleasant were the diet?" (III.i.487-88). Instead, Durfey concludes in an apparent poetic justice on Rashley and Emilia that is not the result of Ranger and Maria's plotting. The adulterers overreach themselves and by accident are finally discovered in flagrante delicto. Their impudence seems to find fitting retribution in Emilia's final loss of wit and glibness, her guilt, and her self-reclusion: "All will not do. O spiteful minute! Taken thus at last? Shame ties my tongue, and absence is most necessary," she says as she runs off never to return on the stage (V.ultima.59-61). The *impudent*, that is literally, the *shameless* has been brought to bear "Shame." Just as we are tempted to anchor meaning here, however, Rashley walks out saying with incredible impudence, "Well, Sir, if I have injur'd you, I wear a sword, Sir,—And so—Farewel" (67-68).

Nevertheless, we grope for grounds for judgment still. The extravagance of the rake is at least exposed, and after all the religious rhetoric of the play, surely its modicum of poetic justice is a sign of providential justice. Then Maria attributes the ending not to the Heaven they have so often invoked but to mere "chance" (83). Moreover, the apparent satire on libertinism is undercut at the end by Ranger's surprising declaration. Not all his efforts have been able to turn Emilia's affection back toward him, so he concludes,

> 'Tis a damn'd thing this wenching, if a man considers seriously on it; and yet 'tis such a damnable age we live in, that, Gad, he that does not follow it is either accounted sordidly unnatural, or ridiculously impotent.—Well, for my part henceforward this shall by my resolution:

> *I'll love for intrest, court for recreation;*
> *Change still a mistriss to be still in fashion.*
> *I'll aid all women in an amorous league;*
> *But from this hour ne'er baulk a love-intrigue.* [86-95]

Durfey has peppered the play with the word "satyr" as if to call attention to what he is doing that is so radically different. But just as Fumble mistakes nonsense songs as "moral satyr" (III.i.402), so do we mistake if we read the play as the "satyr" Bubble wants to write called "A CAUTION FOR CUCKOLDS" (V.v.74-75). Unlike corrective satire, this play blows out from under us any soapbox of righteousness to stand on. Its world is absurd. Ranger's exasperated characterization of Emilia's trickery would seem to apply to the play itself: "Sir, there's nothing of this real" (III.i.108). All the tricksters in the play fail. Except for one: the playwright.

Restoration comedy begins with John Tatham's *The Rump; or, The Mirrour of the Late Times,* acted privately at Dorset Court in February 1660, the same month Monck arrived in London but several months before Charles II was actually restored. The play concludes with no marriages, no joined estates, and not even with any official celebration of the reestablishment of order. It concludes instead with folk justice—the people of London celebrate by eating roasted rumps—but also with a strange folk endurance that extends even to the objects of apparent satire, of discipline and punishment.

The Rump clearly satirizes the Commonwealth, especially the generals in its later stages, when Oliver Cromwell was dead, his son Richard was incompetent to rule, and the army was in a contest for power with the Rump Parliament, which it kept disbanding and reinstating (Hill, 117). The generals are portrayed as vain, ambitious, and unprincipled. One of them justifies the breakup of the Rump that begins the play:

> I lov'd the Father of the Heroicks [Cromwell], while he had a pow'r to do me good, that failing, my reason did direct me, to that Party then prevailing, the fagg end of the parliament. What though I took the Oath of Allegiance as *Oliver,* your Lordship [Lambert], and others did, (without the which I could not have sat there?) yet it Conducing not to our advantage, It was an ill Oath, better broke then kept, and so are all Oaths in the stricter sense, Laws of Nature and of Nations do dispence with matters of Divinity in such a case, for no Man willingly would be an Enemy to himselfe, the very beasts doe by instinct of nature seek for self-preservation, why not Man, who is the Lord of Reason? Oaths, what are they, but Bubbles, that break with their own Emptiness[?] . . . He that

will live in this world, must be endowed with these three rare Qualities;
Dissimulation, Equivocation, and Mental reservation. [I, 8-9]

The various committeemen reveal by their words that they are incapable
of governing. Desborough is more worried about his horse in Smithfield;
Wareston the Scot is a trimmer; Fleetwood is a religious hypocrite, an ambitious fool.[1] When this Committee of Safety attempts to perform the
work of the nation, they worry more about their own perquisites, crack
dirty jokes, blaspheme. When Fleetwood asks where the money is going to
come from for all these perks, Lambert responds, "Pough, my Lord, the
City's big with riches, and near her time I hope to be Deliver'd" (III, 35).

Tatham's sympathies are with this City, whose "Trading is become a
meer Skelliton" (IV, 55), whose apprentices are oppressed and rise up in
arms (clubs), rebelling against their leaders. One of these prentices, who
claims to be the City's champion, proclaims, "Yes, and will spend life and
limbe for *Magna Charta* and a *Free Parliament*" (IV, 39). The Committee orders them home, and the more cowardly prentices are eager to
comply, but the champion demands, "Will you like Cowards forsake your
Petition and have no Answer to't? Rather let us Dye One and All" (40).
He shoots at his oppressors and scatters them, then exhorts the others to
go "Drink the kings health" (42). *Pace* Scott, who sees the play as party
but not royalist satire, they depart shouting, "Viva le roy."

Unfortunately, as Hill reminds us, after the defeat of Lambert by the
advancing army of Monck, Fleetwood and the others capitulated and re-
called the Rump in December 1659, and "[t]he first task Parliament gave
[Monck when he entered London] was to arrest leading members of
London's government and to destroy its defensive gates and chains"
(118). The champion prentice complains, "Was ever such a Rape committed upon a poor She City before? Lay her legs open to the wide world, for
every Rogue to peep in her Breech" (V, 57). Yet he wants not to blame
Monck but Parliament: "Well, On my Conscience he's honest for all this:
The plaguy *Rump* has done this Mischief: Well, Club stand stiff to thy
Master, some body shall suffer for't: I say no more. . . . Well, Ile Warrant
the Souldierie will be honest for all this, and then we'l Sindge the Mag-
gots out of the louzy *Rump*, or else Swindge me" (58). When news arrives
that Monck has taken refuge in the City and they have agreed upon the
election of a free parliament, the champion feels vindicated, and the prentices plan to celebrate.

Before we critics join the general euphoria, however, we would do
well to review the "Argument of the Play" Tatham published as an
epigraph:

> *Fleetwood* is fool'd by *Lambert* to consent
>   To th' pulling out of the *Rump Parliament;*
> Which done, another *Government* they frame
>   In *Embrio,* that wants *Matter* for a *Name.*
>   In brief "By force *Fools* supplant crafty Men,
>   "The Bauble *Exits,* Enter *Knaves* agen.
>   J.T. (italics reversed)]

Who are the "Knaves" who enter again? The Rump, of course. And yet. The champion prentice wants to wreak revenge on these knaves, who are on the verge of being ousted for the last time. But is his trust in the "Souldierie" misplaced? After all, during the prentices' rebellion, the soldiers responded with a mixture of glee, because renewed fighting means more plunder, and with the inherent sadism of armies everywhere. They plan to divvy up the shops and take the prentices into virtual slavery "till they have paid for their Learning" (III, 38). One thinks they should set fire to the City:

> Me thinks I see the Town on fire, and hear the Shrieks and Cryes of Women and Children already; the Rogues running to quench the fire, and we following the slaughter. Here lies one without an Arm, and he cannot hold up a Hand against us; another without a Leg, and he shan't run for't; another without a Nose, hee'l ne're smell us out; another without a Head, and his plotting's spoyl'd: Here lies a rich Courmogeon burnt to Ashes, who rather then he would survive his Treasure, perisheth with his Chests, and leaves his better Angels to wait on Us, you knaves. [38-39]

Here is an apocalyptic note, but with no redeeming metaphysic: the only "Angels" are the coins that survive to attend the soldiers their leader affectionately terms "knaves."

The soldiers are unprincipled too. They do not care which side is right, wish the generals would just duke it out in a ring. After breaking up the Rump at the beginning, they have this extraordinary exchange. One says, "The Nail of providence was in't" (I, 1), and the second answers, "Or the parings rather; no matter which, 'tis done" (2). The soldiers justify their actions according to sheer will-to-power: "[W]hat We did (We did), that was Our Will, and the word of Command lodg'd in Our hilts" (3). Their moral anarchy is mirrored in their metaphysical:

> *1 Soldier:* But, dost thou think there is a Heaven or Hell?
> *2 Soldier:* Why dost thou ask me that question? I am a Souldier, and so art thou, let's ne're trouble our heads about it, a short life, and a merry life I cry, happy Man be his Dole.

3 Soldier: And so say I, while We are here, We are here; when We are gone, We are gone, for better or for worse, for rich or for poor; amongst the good or the bad We shall find room I warrant thee Lad, and our General can expect no more. [3-4]

Will the cycle of fools and knaves be broken by these folk existentialists?

In order to fully appreciate the significance of the soldiers' earthy pragmatism we must analyze the play's subplot (which takes up a good deal of its stage time), the story of the uppity women trying to climb on top. Lady Lambert is furious with her woman Prissilla's failure to address her as your "Highness," the First Lady Presumptive as wife to General Lambert, who is bound to be named the new protector (II, 16). She contrasts her own breeding with that of Mrs. Cromwell, wife of the dead protector, to whom she refers as plain "Joan." Driven to distraction by Lady Lambert, Mrs. Cromwell laments her current state, called by the people "the Commonwealth's Night Mare" (21). Later, after Lambert has fallen to Monck and been imprisoned in the Tower, Mrs. Cromwell triumphs over her rival and defends the memory of her husband: "How durst thou name him but with reverence: He that out-did all Histories of Kings or *Keasors;* was his own Herald, and could give Titles of Honor to the meanest Peasants; made Brewers, Dray-men, Coblers, Tinkers, or any bodie Lords: Such was his power, no Prince ever did the like: Amongst the rest, that precious piece thy Husband was one of his making" (V, 56). Of course, this promiscuous scattering of honors represents a wholesale assault upon status hierarchy, an assault Lady Lambert herself deplores when she puts down the wives of those so raised by Cromwell:

Lady Lambert: I pass by their Dirty breeding. Woman, We say, what Coat of Arms does thy Husband give?
1 Lady: He bears *Argent upon a Bend Gules, three Cuckolds Heads Attyr'd Or.*
Prissilla: Three Cuckolds Heads! Why one is sufficient in all conscience.
1 Lady: 'Tis a Paternal Coat belonging to the Family of the *Wittals.*
Prissilla: It may be they were Founders of *Cuckoldshaven.* . . .
Lady Lambert: 'Tis a wonder with what Impudence those Fellows *Noll* and *Dick* could Knightifie your Husbands! For 'tis a Rule in *Heraldry,* that none can make a Knight but he that is a Knight himself: 'Tis *Zanca Panca's* Case in *Donquixott.* [II, 25]

The wives want to know how her husband can do it then; she maintains bawdily she dubbed him herself. Lady Lambert is so cocksure she invades the meeting of the Committee of Safety and demands to be one of the council: "I have as much right to the place as thou hast, if I am *John Lambert's* Lady and for ought I know my advice may do as well here as thine, for all you perk it so" (III, 35). To her husband she demands her rightful place as "a Free Woman, no Bondslave, Sir" (IV, 43). The implication of all this would seem to be that when political and social hierarchy are destroyed, so is gender hierarchy.

The most delightful character in the play is Prissilla, who is infected by the same climbing disease as her lady and longs to have Trotter, Lambert's secretary, finish his apprenticeship before she will agree to marry him, for she would have his "Wit" more "refin'd" (II, 20). She teases him that if he will return with his lord as a secretary of state, she will admit him to her lip "and something else in a lawfull way" (IV, 45). Left alone on stage, she reveals that she intends to keep Trotter ignorant and illiterate in order to manipulate him better. And concerning his illiteracy, she says puckishly that he obviously hasn't read Aretino or she might have given him more before he left! She then fantasizes herself about being "Ladifi'd" and called madam (46).

When their pretensions are dashed, Lady Lambert laments, "Would we had never known those painted Titles that are so easily washt off" (V, 56). Prissilla herself reads Lady Lambert a similar lesson: assuming a folk wisdom on the occasion of the Lamberts' fall, she mocks Lady Lambert for her pretensions, saying she dreamt the night before "that we have been but Princes in disguise all this while, and that our Vizors are now falling off" (IV, 54). It would appear that this play, subtitled *The Mirrour of the Late Times,* teaches a comic version of the primary lesson of *The Mirrour for Magistrates: sic transit gloria mundi.*

Yet at just this moment in the play, with the Lamberts down, the Committee in chaos, the Rump in danger, and the lessons of Stuart propaganda seemingly so clear, a strange energy takes over the play, an energy emanating primarily from Prissilla. Returning without his laurels, Trotter is berated by Prissilla and wittily describes himself as being "between *Silla* and *Carybdis*"(V, 59)! Silla tongue-lashes him for trying to be a poet and a wit, saying he must have turned his master's head and caused his defeat. She wants to know what trade he will adopt now. He pretends he can teach dancing or even fencing, and gives her a demonstration. This slapstick can hardly be just comic relief, for we are already in a comedy. It continues in the broad farce of the rumproast, where Prissilla dances with a Frenchman, who follows her off to bed. Right in the midst of the prentices' celebratory singing *"Sellingers Round,* We are beginning the World again" (63) and the apparent condign punishment of the members of the Committee, Prissilla reenters as an orange woman and has these remarkable lines: "Fine Civil Oranges, fine Lemmons; fine civil Oranges, fine Lemmons: Me thinks it sounds very well; a pox of her Tailnesse for me [i.e., her Highness Lady Lambert], no matter, ne're repine Wench, thy

Trade's both pleasant and profitable, and if any Gentleman take me up, I am still, Fine civil Oranges, fine Lemmons" (65). "I am still." A comic, lower-class duchess of Malfi. The folk existentialism of the soldiers has come full circle. "[W]hile We are here, We are here; when We are gone, We are gone, for better or for worse, for rich or for poor; amongst the good or the bad, We shall find room I warrant thee Lad." Whatever fools or knaves are in power, the people are immortal, always there—soldiers, prentices, servants. While the generals moralize their endings, Prissilla advises, "Come let's mind our business, words are but wind, Fine civil Oranges, fine Lemmons" (67). Words are but wind, even the words of the play. The Prissillas endure whatever temporary ideology dominates. Like the raped City of London, she is a figure for the estate of England in its folk. And this Third Estate is a trickster, a survivor. Whatever gentleman takes her up, she is herself still, a self that resists the imposition of system.

It is as if, after God's failure to support the right cause in the Glorious Revolution, just concluded at the Battle of the Boyne in the summer of 1690, Dryden availed himself of the traditional story of Amphitryon in his play of that name, produced in October of the same year, in order to depict a universe where the Rhetoric of Order is mere rhetoric, for its regnant deity is not the Logos of Saints John, Augustine, and Thomas Aquinas and the rationalist theologians but the sheer power of Hobbes and the voluntarists. Dryden's Jupiter is supposed to represent the Logos that underwrites the code of word-as-bond, yet he is the arch-perverter of words. He is what Jacques Derrida would call *the dangerous supplement* (*Of Grammatology,* part 2, ch. 2), who supplants by doubling, by duplicity, by the destruction of identity and integrity. And there are, there can be, no bounds to his arbitrary Will to Power.

In a scene added by Dryden to his main sources in Plautus and Molière (see editors' notes, 554) Jupiter's sons, Phoebus and Mercury, comically discuss their father's transgressions (which assault the very principle of patrilinearity ordained to control the transition of power and property and which, of course, have resulted in their own bastardy). Juno has tried to take Jupiter to the "Spiritual Court" over those transgressions, but Jupiter has stood upon his royal "Prerogative" (I.i.24-25). That is, Jupiter holds himself above the law, as Mercury brings home to him, comically and submissively, by inquiring what form he will take to seduce yet another mortal woman, this time Amphitryon's chaste wife, Alcmena: "I was considering into what form your Almighty-ship would be pleas'd to transform your self to night. Whether you wou'd fornicate in the Shape of a Bull, or a Ram, or an Eagle, or a Swan: What Bird or Beast you wou'd please to honour, by transgressing your own Laws, in his likeness; or in

short, whether you wou'd recreate your self in Feathers, or in Leather?"
(73-79). Phoebus more seriously disputes with Jupiter, asking why he
must commit what he himself confesses to be a "Crime" and dissecting
the speciousness of Jupiter's recourse to "the Fates" (88-93). Jupiter is
forced to proclaim,

> Fate is, what I
> By vertue of Omnipotence have made it:
> And pow'r Omnipotent can do no wrong:
> Not to my self, because I will'd it so:
> Nor yet to Men, for what they are is mine.
> This night I will enjoy *Amphitryon*'s Wife:
> For when I made her, I decreed her such
> As I shou'd please to love. I wrong not him
> Whose Wife she is; for I reserv'd my Right,
> To have her while she pleas'd me; that once past,
> She shall be his again. [102-12]

Once again his sons call a spade a spade, the one comically, the other seriously:

> *Mercury:* Here's Omnipotence with a Vengeance, to make a Man a
>   Cuckold, and yet not to do him wrong. . . .
> *Phoebus:* If there be no such thing as right and wrong,
>   Of an Eternal Being, I have done—
>   But if there be— [113-21]

If "pow'r Omnipotent can do no wrong," then there is no such thing
as right or wrong but thinking makes it so, as Hamlet would say. Jupiter
is forced to the last, desperate stratagem of theodicy, cloaking himself in
the incomprehensibility of his providence, which he explains as the good
that will emerge from this evil, the hero Hercules, who "shall redress the
Wrongs of injur'd Mortals, / Shall conquer Monsters, and reform the
World" (126-27). Mercury explodes such theodicy by pointing out that
Jupiter himself made all the monsters and vices Hercules is supposed to
conquer; that is, God himself is the origin of evil. Yet Jupiter's sons—and
all his subjects—are finally forced to submit:

> *Phoebus:* Since Arbitrary Pow'r will hear no Reason, 'tis Wisdom to be
>   silent.—
> *Mercury:* Why that's the Point; this same Arbitrary Power is a knock-
>   down Argument; 'tis but a Word and a Blow; now methinks our
>   Father speaks out like an honest bare-fac'd God, as he is; he lays the
>   stress in the right Place, upon absolute Dominion: I confess if he had

been a Man, he might have been a Tyrant, if his Subjects durst have call'd him to account. [131-38]

That Dryden is glancing at his contemporary situation, as James D. Garrison has ably argued, becomes even more obvious when Jupiter, disguised as Amphitryon, beseeches Alcmena to consider him not her husband but her libertine lover, adding to Molière's similar sentiments (I.iii) the analogy to succession: "In me (my charming Mistris) you behold / A Lover that disdains a Lawful Title; / Such as of Monarchs to successive Thrones" (II.ii.83-85). Right no longer makes might; might makes right. And thus a fortiori all supplanters are justified, those on thrones as well as those in beds. Dryden calls attention to the political implications of the sexual by having Amphitryon complain that Alcmena's favors have been "usurp'd" from him (III.i.294), by directly confronting Jupiter as "base Usurper of my Name, and Bed" (V.i.144; see Garrison, 194), and by using that loaded word again in the epilogue to describe what Jupiter has done, "usurp'd the Husband's name" (13). And when Sosia anachronistically charges others "in the King's name" (IV.i.253), we must ask to whom the appellation refers. There is no king in the play. But if Dryden's world is being reflected, there is no real king there, either, and therefore no one to whom to appeal for justice.

In other details added to the story by Dryden, before Jupiter arrives to usurp Amphitryon's place, Alcmena's clever lady-in-waiting, Phaedra, exacts from her a promise that she be her lady's bedfellow that night. Phaedra insists that Alcmena "swear by *Jupiter*," and when Alcmena asks why, Phaedra explains: "Because he's the greatest: I hate to deal with one of your little baffling Gods that can do nothing, but by permission: but *Jupiter* can swinge you off; if you swear by him, and are forsworn" (I.ii.42-51). In other words, the whole system of word-as-bond, a system that controls not just the estates of men but the royal estate itself, works only if there is an underwriting Word, a Supreme Being that punishes those who break their words—their pledges of allegiance and coronation oaths, their vows of marital fidelity, their promises, their judicial oaths. But Dryden raises the question what happens when God is the trickster and is nothing but power, will, desire?

At one point Jupiter blames his inconstancy of purpose on "Almighty Love . . . Who bows our Necks beneath her brazen Yoke" (III.i.525-27). That is, Jupiter himself is ruled by his desire. So when Alcmena explains that she cannot sleep with the disguised Jupiter because she has given her word to Phaedra, he proclaims in exasperation, "Forswear thy self; for *Jupiter* but laughs / At Lovers Perjuries" (I.ii.146-47). Phaedra complains comically in response, "The more shame for him if he does: there wou'd be a fine God indeed for us Women to worship, if he laughs when our Sweet-hearts cheat us of our Maiden-heads: No, no, *Jupiter* is an honester Gentleman than you make of him" (148-51). But when God is not a gentleman but a libertine himself, Dryden's play forces us to reason, then the binding force of words is lost. Dryden has made one of his lecherous, lawless emperors (as in *Aureng-Zebe* of *Don Sebastian*) into a god who sacrifices everything to his pleasure, including his providence:

> For what's to be a God, but to enjoy?
> Let human-kind their Sovereign's leisure waite;
> Love is, this Night, my great Affair of State:
> Let this one Night, of Providence be void:
> All *Jove*, for once, is on himself employ'd.
> Let unregarded Altars smoke in vain;
> And let my Subjects praise me, or complain. [191-97]

Christian providence implies not only foresight and provision but justice, vindication of the word by the Word, the Logos. In the world of the play, both word and Word are void.[2]

If the law and the Logos do not restrain God himself in his outrageous *droit du seigneur*, then a fortiori lesser figures may have the same license. Despite his comic objections, as in Dryden's sources Mercury himself proceeds by the same law(lessness). Just as Jupiter duplicitously doubles Amphitryon to take away his rights, Mercury doubles Sosia to take away his. Just as Jupiter justifies himself by his power, Mercury dominates Sosia throughout the play by the right of his cudgel. Abetting Jupiter in duping Amphitryon, Mercury comically explains (with the cynical last line added by Dryden to Molière, III.ii.1-8), "This is no very charitable Action of a God, to use him ill, who has never offended me: but my Planet disposes me to Malice: and when we great Persons do but a little Mischief, the World has a good bargain of us" (IV.i.137-40). Again in details added by Dryden, just as Jupiter bribes Phaedra out of her bond with Alcmena, Mercury bribes her into fornication with him. And just as Jupiter makes a mockery of word-as-bond, Mercury threatens Sosia with recalling his "word" of truce and beating him anew (II.i.292-93), and he affects to "pass" his "word" that Gripus will agree to relinquish his pretensions to Phaedra because he, Mercury, carries a sword (V.i.34-36). In a seduction song Mercury articulates the triumphant antitrust code of the play:

> I
> Fair *Iris* I love, and hourly I dye,
> But not for a lip, nor a languishing Eye:

She's fickle and false, and there we agree;
For I am as false, and as fickle as she:
We neither believe what either can say;
And, neither believing, we neither betray.

II
'Tis civil to swear, and say things of course;
We mean not the taking for better for worse.
When present, we love; when absent, agree:
I think not of *Iris,* nor *Iris* of me:
The Legend of Love no Couple can find
So easie to part, or so equally join'd. [IV.i.482-93; italics
reversed]

Like Jupiter and Mercury, Dryden's creation, Phaedra, is more than
willing to be a sexual trickster. Although she appropriates the language of
the traditional code when it is to her advantage—holding Alcmena to her
word in order to gain a bribe or calling Sosia a "perjur'd Villain" because
he fails to produce the bribe his double promised her (III.i.412)—in their
hilarious proviso scene Phaedra answers Mercury's demand that she be
"always constant" to him and "admit no other Lover" with the witty rejoinder, "unless it be a Lover that offers more: and that the Constancy
shall not exceed the Settlement" (V.i.352-55). As opposed to the idealistically constant Alcmena, who is duped by the god who is supposed to
reward that constancy, Phaedra is a figure for inconstancy. She is
"Woman," as Mercury says, "and your minds are so variable, that it's very
hard even for a God to know them" (IV.i.498-99). He describes the
billet-doux hidden in her pocket thus: "full of fraudulence, and equivoca-
tions, and shoeing-horns of Love to him; to promise much, and
mean nothing; to show, over and above, that thou art a mere Woman"
(454-56). As Jupiter in exasperation bribes her to relinquish Alcmena
from her word, he exclaims, "[T]his is a very Woman:/Her Sex is Avarice,
and she, in One,/Is all her Sex" (I.ii.182-85). So woman is a sign of the
radical inconstancy of the world that results from unbridled desire. It is
tempting to speculate that Dryden adds to his sources this misogyny and
its embodiment in Phaedra because of his anger at James II's daughter,
Mary, who was so inconstant as to betray her rather and usurp his throne.
Dryden's variations on the traditional theme darken the implications
of doubling in the story. If the only Absolute is Desire and even God subverts the law by doubling, by a supplementation that is at once a repetition and a supplanting, then integrity and identity are radically threatened,
as is comically played out in the Two Sosias subplot. Sosia's identity has
been supplanted, usurped by Mercury, and he no longer knows who he is

or what name to take. Jupiter and Mercury's doublings have destabilized not only word-as-bond but word-as-name, as unique identity. Expanding on Molière (III.vi), Dryden's Sosia pleads with Mercury, "May it please you, Sir, the Name is big enough for both of us: and we may use it in common, like a Strumpet" (IV.i.374-75). The name that is supposed to fix and hold reality is a whore—unfaithful, inconstant to one identity or meaning, susceptible to endless metonymy. When Dryden's Amphitryon repeats to Sosia twice, "To Repetition, Rogue, to Repetition" (III.i.35-40), he gives us a figure for a world where the Dangerous Supplement destroys societal institutions, from thrones to marital beds to language itself, by denying the possibility of a single, constant state(ment).

When Mercury reveals his divinity to Phaedra in order to complete his seduction and promises to be "secret" and assist her in her petty theft, he justifies himself wittily, "for thou and I were born under the same Planet." Her reply, "And we shall come to the same end too, I'm afraid," indicates a traditional fear of retributive, providential justice. But Phaedra's—and the audience's—expectations of such a justice are not to be fulfilled in the world of this play. Mercury rejoins, "No; no; since thou hast wit enough already to couzin a Judge, thou need'st never fear hanging" (IV.i.471-76). Mercury refers, of course, to Judge Gripus, whom Dryden invents and portrays as corrupted by bribes, sex, and physical threats. Thus when the nobles turn to him to be "Umpire of the Cause" between Jupiter and Amphitryon, we know his corruption frustrates such a charge. His immediate response is to turn to Mercury, who has bullied him, and ask, "On whose side wou'd you please that I shou'd give the Sentence?" (V.i.167-70).

Dryden's real point, however, is not the traditional theme of corrupt human justice. It is that there can be no human when there is no divine justice. When, as Mercury characterizes him, "Our *Jupiter* is a great Comedian; he counterfeits most admirably: sure his Priests have coppy'd their Hypocrisie from their Master" (V.i.129-31); when God himself, because of his omniscience, knows all the right answers to the questions designed to distinguish the true from the false Amphitryon; when the Logos becomes mere self-serving rhetoric, as Jupiter dupes the distraught Alcmena with soothing lies, "Follow no more, that false and foolish Fire, / That wou'd mislead thy Fame to sure destruction!" (262-63); then Amphitryon's desperate pathetic appeals, "Good Gods, how can this be! . . . To this [his sword]—and to the Gods I'll trust my Cause" (246, 276), are absurd. And at the end, Amphitryon and Alcmena are simply silenced by sheer power: making even darker Molière's Jupiter's appeal to the silencing power of his name (III.x), Dryden's Jupiter cynically says,

Look up, *Amphitryon*, and behold above,
Th'Impostour God, the Rival of thy Love:

> In thy own shape, see *Jupiter* appear,
> And let that sight, secure thy jealous fear.
> Disgrace, and Infamy, are turn'd to boast:
> No Fame, in *Jove*'s Concurrence can be lost:
> What he enjoys, he sanctifies from Vice. [393-99]

Desire, when omnipotent, can sanctify whatever means it takes to obtain its end. The witty exchange at the conclusion of the Mercury-Phaedra proviso scene underscores the ramifications:

> *Sosia:* Now I wou'd ask of Madam *Phaedra,* that in case Mr. Heaven
>   there, shou'd be pleas'd to break these Articles, in what Court of Ju-
>   dicature she intends to sue him?
> *Phaedra:* The fool has hit upon't:—Gods, and great Men, are never to be
>   sued; for they can always plead priviledge of Peerage. [V.i.379-84]

Dryden has provided no poetic justice with its underwriting providential justice because he has portrayed God as amoral Desire and Power. Jupiter's promise of a Hercules provides no real consolation, for he too is a figure of Absolute Force, who would bring "Peace" and "Happiness" only by compulsion (V.i.419-21). As Amphitryon and Alcmena "stand mute, and know not how to take it" (V.i.409-10), while the others attempt to congratulate them, Dryden's Mercury adds to Molière's Sosie's injunction to silence (III.x) this strange comment: "Upon the whole matter, if *Amphitryon* takes the favour of *Jupiter* in patience, as from a God, he's a good Heathen" (425-27). On the one hand, the comment frees Dryden from a charge of blasphemy: his Christian audience knows Jupiter is not really God, and only a heathen would justify his abuse of power. But on the other hand, Dryden has portrayed the cosmos as heathen, where there is no recourse against political and sexual usurpers, for God himself is a tyrant and a don juan. Dryden's Sosia, sounding like the Wife of Bath, closes the play with a final expression of the triumph of desire over official discourse:

> For, let the wicked World say what they please,
> The fair Wife makes her Husband live at ease:
> The Lover keeps him too; and but receives,
> Like *Jove*, the remnants that *Amphitryon* leaves:
> 'Tis true, the Lady has enough in store,
> To satisfie those two, and eke, two more:
> In fine, the Man, who weighs the matter fully,
> Wou'd rather be the Cuckold, than the Cully. [437-44]

In other words, in a world without God, there can be no control of desire, and the patriarchal house of cards comes down more ignominiously than Dagon's temple. Dryden must have been angry with God for not intervening. He must have felt like Job when the whirlwind silences him with a display of power, not of reason. But instead of responding like a righteous Phoebus, he chose instead the ludic way of Mercury (god of tricksters) and Sosia, played by those greatest of comic actors of their era, Leigh and Nokes, closing the play with their folk wisdom that turns the defeat of the patriarch into a victory of sorts. If the cuckold can learn to profit from his situation, and be like Shiftwel in *The Life of Mother Shipton*, kept by the keeper too, leaving him merely sloppy seconds with his wife, then he can endure the collapse of systems, delighting in her Rabelaisian copiousness and relinquishing to chance the care of patrimony. Then not so-and-so's son but the Third Estate will inherit the earth, without individual identity after all, just a jumble of random atoms blown about by the wind amidst cosmic laughter.

Thus the endings of a handful of Restoration comedies eschew the closure of comedy and constitute their plays as satires. Some provide at least an implied standard by which the audience is to judge behavior as aberrant. In their corrective satires Durfey and Shadwell locate that standard in a nostalgia for Country values, well-husbanded estates passed on from generation to generation that have not had their heads turned by Town and Court corruption. In *The Luckey Chance* Behn locates her standard in an existential, aesthetic virtue of personal integrity that should not be a token in the estate-building exchanges between men.

This handful of plays might be said to inhabit the right (*recht*) hand. There is another that inhabits the left (*sinister*) hand, eschewing not only closure but standards for judgment. I find it fascinating that the period of Restoration comedy is framed by three such satires, one smack in the middle exposing the absurdity of that comedy's favorite tropes, the other two spanning the period's cusps and taking advantage of the liminal state to expose the amorphous mass which, as Bakhtin says repeatedly in *Rabelais and His World*, crowns and uncrowns, endures all changes of state and system. *The Rump* marks the transition from one failed revolution to a reactionary restoration of the status quo ante; *Amphitryon* marks the transition from failed status quo to revolution. What survives from the first revolution is its leveling truth, the energy of the English folk that transcends hierarchic and hieratic categories. What survives into the next revolution is the seed of a similar energy that will transcend the new era's own bourgeois individualism.

Conclusion

"Aristocratic ideology" names the impulse, operative in a wide diversity of cultures, to conceal the perennial alterations in ruling elites by naturalizing those elites as a static unity of status and virtue, the ongoing "rule of the best." . . . The idea of aristocracy is decisively conceptualized at this time [especially the Restoration] over against the articulation of progressive ideology, and its paradoxical function is to mediate the persistence of a category whose impermanence is signaled by the vary fact that only now need it be conceptualized as such. This is not to suggest, however, that status values—like deference and paternalistic care—that we commonly associate with aristocratic social relations lose their force in the early modern period. On the contrary, they undergo the more elaborate sort of "theatricalization" that is likely to occur whenever social convention is raised to the level of self-conscious practice. [McKeon 169]

In this book I have tried to demonstrate just such a "theatricalization" of aristocratic ideology in Restoration comedy—a process that attempts to affirm persistence even as it acknowledges impermanence. Restoration comedy both underwrites and undercuts the ideology of English late-feudal aristocracy. It underwrites it by socializing the great energy of its rebellious gay-couple tricksters into marriages that build estates and by disciplining its class enemies through in-your-face, often sexual aggression. It also underwrites indirectly by satirizing the decadence of its own class, its falling away from old standards, its treatment of women. Restoration comedy undercuts by trickery that reveals seams in its supposedly seamless garment and that creates spaces in the margins for the dispossessed, whose disruptive energy it celebrates.

At its most radical Restoration comedy's playwrights explode the hierarchical systems of late-feudal patriarchy into random atoms of desire. How company playwrights—aspiring bourgeois, gentry, even courtiers—could be so subversive or could get away with it boggles the mind. Yet Shakespeare and Jonson and Middleton and Brome could. Perhaps one way to look at the folk-subversive strain of Restoration comedy is to see it as a persistence of something Elizabethan. Indeed, it would seem no accident that the strain is most prevalent in the 1660s, when older plays and older playwrights attempted to bridge the Interregnum. Perhaps, as Lévi-Strauss might suggest, the strain represents the persistent reminder of the chthonic itself (Cope's daemonic). Whatever its origin, it cries out for inclusion in our histories of Restoration comedy, Restoration drama, Restoration culture.

Restoration comedy, then, reveals even as it attempts to conceal the fluidity of class and status. It reveals the economic base of its honor culture, a base that often required transfusions of new money conveyed from places as far away as the Indies through the conduit of the daughters of the Citizens it trashes most violently at the moment of virtual capitulation. It reveals the lack of any real unity of status and virtue (birth and worth), and any real unity, solidarity of class. It reveals the faces and the voices of at least some of the dispossessed. And it does so through the creation of some of world comedy's greatest tricksters and greatest satiric butts. But this supernova is the sign of the death of a galaxy, blazing most brightly even as it dies, and signaling the creation of a new galaxy, a new ideological paradigm.

By 1691 Restoration comedy as I have described it is essentially over, existing in the repertoire but not birthing new examples. A new paradigm takes its place, incorporating some earlier tropes, like that of the younger brother trickster in Farquhar's *The Beaux' Stratagem* (1707) or the One Just Woman in the comical satires of Southerne (*The Wives Excuse* [1691]) and Vanbrugh (*The Relapse* [1696]). But as Braverman has most recently and most cogently argued ("Rake's Progress," 156-63), the Restoration rake becomes bifurcated into rakish villain and *honnête homme,* as in William Congreve's *The Double Dealer* (1693) or *The Way of the World* (1700). A variation off Braverman's model is that the rake becomes bifurcated into an effete beau who ends up defeated, as in Mary Pix's play of that title (1700; see my "Dramatic Shifts"), and into the good-natured man of feeling, as in Pix's play or Farquhar's. And the new subject of comical satire becomes bourgeois capitalism and its rapacity as in John Gay's *The Beggar's Opera* and Henry Fielding's *The Author's Farce* (1728 and 1730, respectively; see my "Critique of Capitalism"). The comedies of Shadwell—starting in 1681 with *The Lancashire Witches* and moving through *The Squire of Alsatia* (1688) and *Bury Fair* (1689) to *The Amorous Bigotte* and *The Scowrers* (both 1690) and finally to *The Volunteers* (1692)—most clearly mark this paradigm shift, peopled as they are with heroes and heroines and patriarchs and prodigal sons so essentially good-natured and benevolent as to create that new form of comedy called *sentimental,* in which the aristocratic yields to the bourgeois family romance, articulated most famously in Sir Richard Steele's *The Conscious Lovers* (1722; see my "Shifting Tropes," 215-19).

Let me examine briefly one example of this new comedy, coming as it does virtually simultaneously with *Amphitryon* around that pivotal time of the Battle of the Boyne and written not by the later, already known as pro-Whiggish Shadwell but, surprisingly, by the later, supposedly still pro-Tory Crowne. *The English Frier; or, The Town Sparks* (March 1690) virulently attacks Catholic priests who, like James II's infamous Jesuit adviser Father Edward Petre, meddle in affairs of state to the detriment of the English Constitution. In that sense it is a stridently anti-Jacobite play, produced for clear purposes of propaganda just before the Revolution's climactic battle. Lord Wiseman speaks for all wise Englishmen who know what is best for them: "'[T]is very honourable to pay reverence to our princes, and all obedience to their lawful commands; but I am very unwilling to pay respect to priests and fryers that abuse the Court and nation" (I.125-28).

Lord Stately and Lady Pinch-gut, representatives of the still powerful Catholic families of the aristocracy, must be shown the error of their ways through the breaking of their slavish devotion to the Court and through the exposure of the hypocrisy of Father Finicall. Finicall maneuvers Sir Thomas Credulous to will his entire estate to his wife, Lady Pinch-gut, who in turn will bequeath it to the Catholic church. Sir Thomas is an important Cit who sniffs out Finicall's hypocrisy, so he feigns conversion and compliance until he can stage a scene of exposure, which is of course a sexual scene, where Finicall, à la Tartuffe, pursues the maid Pansy. The implication is that just as Finicall seduces a supposed naïf so does the church seduce a naive country and threaten to steal its estate.

Before the scene of entrapment, Finicall is made a bishop (as James had wanted to make Father Petre) and tyrannizes over Stately, gloating that he and his fellow peers had already relinquished control by easing the laws on Catholics, that "the Court have their sence from us" (IV.336-37). Stately responds (with no self-awareness from Crowne about the damning implications of the analogy), "And their nonsense too: what base slaves are we, we are slaves to slaves: ecclesiastical blackes, but not half so honest or usefull as the blackes we have from Guinney" (338-41). The English peerage were in danger before the Revolution of becoming slaves to priests who are themselves slaves to Rome. Indeed, foreplay to Finicall's seduction of Pansy takes the form of a long rehearsal of the evil machinations of Rome and her priests, their worldwide conspiracy. Draped over her, he is finally taken prisoner by an appropriate alliance of self-reasserting aristocrats and Cits, an alliance that mirrors the oligarchy that emerged from the Revolution.

Crowne's successful play is more than just topical anti-Jacobite propaganda.[1] It also embodies an emergent, oppositional, bourgeois ideology—that is, an ideology that cloaks the new oligarchy in what we have come to call a middle-class ethos. The male protagonist of the play, like Shadwell's

Belfond, Jr. and Congreve's Mirabel, is an already reformed rake who will not marry his mistress Airy but will take care of her: "I love you, and wish more good to you than you do to your self. I wish you honesty, which you care not for. I have committed a fault with you; to make you amends, and keep you out o' temptation, I allow you two hundred pounds a year. Use me how you will, it shall be continued to you, provided you do no harm to your self by a vitious course o' life" (I.449-55). The moralizing strikes the different note. Airy's wit is the only refreshing throwback to Harriet, Hellena, Hillaria, Lady Fancy, Sir Anthony Love. Indeed, she is the only sympathetic trickster in the play, maneuvering Wiseman so that she might be able to keep him. But she is reduced to the role of a minor character, a cast mistress who will be pawned off on a rake no more worthy than Congreve's Fainall. Wiseman sounds positively priggish about her, as he generalizes misogynistically: "That ever such a potent and belov'd queen as Beauty shou'd have such a weak counseller as woman" (460-61). Indeed, Wiseman looks not backward to Dorimant or the Restoration trickster but forward to Darcy in *Pride and Prejudice*.

Laura marks the advent of the *heroine* who must be reclaimed—from her coquetry. She is the avatar of Millamant, Bellinda: "[W]here is the woman that would not be thought the top beauty of the world? . . . The hour of marriage ends the female reign" (III.ii.30-31, 158). But Laura lacks the discretion to avoid the company of the Restoration rake, Young Ranter, who has degenerated into a scowrer and eventually directly assaults Laura and tries to rape her. Wiseman lectures her concerning this dangerous coquetry: "Madam I wooe you not so much to me, as to your self; value your self; you have much excellence, do not spread it up and down till it be slight as leaf-gold, nor guild every clock with your favours; you take a pride to conquer wretches I scorn to beat" (IV.i.176-81). When Wiseman catches Laura and Young Ranter in what appears to be flagrante delicto, he inflates lecture to sermon: "[L]adies are discourteous to themselves, who take liberties discretion will not allow, though innocency may. Madam, though you be innocent, your reputation will suffer, and all your excellence be lost. Your beauty, like the feild [*sic*] of an outlaw that endures no government, is condemn'd never to be sowed: no ill man can attain you, no wise and good man dares" (V.ii.140-46).

Here we can see that the concerns of Revolutionary comedy remain superficially the same as those of Restoration comedy. Not to put too fine a point on it, Wiseman compares Laura to a field to be plowed and sown—as long as it remains within patriarchal government, and that includes preserving reputation. Comedies still need to put the right couple together for the good of estates so that both estate and couple will bear fruit. But it is the woman's energy that must be socialized. The chastened

Laura finally reforms: "I am now sensible of my folly, and henceforward my Lord, I will receive your love as it deserves" (V.ii.185-86). Moreover, Wiseman concludes the play with a perfect contrast with *The Man of Mode*, insisting that he and his friend Bellmour have access to the upper-class plowing fields while wild men like Young Ranter have not: "In those sweet bosomes, we admission finde, / Whence you wild braves are shut like blasting-winde" (V.iii.351-52). That enormously attractive energy of the Dorimants is precluded from scattering the grain gathered in the barn of the new order.

Moreover, the play moralizes about class. Lord Stately, like Steele's Sir John Bevil, exudes class snobbery. He looks down his nose at the Bellmour who courts his daughter Julia: "[Y]ou have a good estate, and are of a very good family for a commoner" (II.ii.13-14). Wiseman again reads the lesson: "This fool makes the whole business o' greatness to be foppery and impertinence" (20-21). Later, Sir Thomas Credulous, that Cit from supposedly a lower class, corrects his better, Lord Stately: "Because he's above the common rank o' men, he thinks he must be above the common sence, and humanity" (V.iii.54-55). When Old Ranter protests what good blood his son has in his body, Julia ripostes: "So has a pig, wou'd he had some good manners, and good sence" (IV.i.104-5). When he protests they are from as good a family as any in England, Julia's response heralds the new bourgeois ethos of merit as measured in conduct: "No the families that ha' manners in 'em are better families" (109-110). Perhaps it might be said that the *comedy of manners* begins not in 1668 with Etherege's *She Wou'd if She Cou'd* but in 1690 with *The English Frier*. The label then might acquire some precision as referring to comedy of the bourgeois family romance from late Shadwell and Crowne through late Sheridan.

The critical tradition of addressing Restoration comedy as a *comedy of manners* was a bourgeois construction, created to demonstrate *taste*, the status symbol that has served since Addison as a sign the bourgeoisie merited its new position as dominant class. It was a tradition that homogenized Restoration comedy, obscuring objectionable elements (*The Country-Wife* was included in neither major anthology of the mid-twentieth century, *The Plain Dealer* only reluctantly) and indulging our bourgeois fantasy idols of the cultured (if reformed) gentleman and the witty but chaste gentlewoman. Restoration comedy was thus Austenized. The "Restoration comedies" anthologized and performed as classics have tended to be in this century, especially in America, Congreve's *The Way of the World*, Farquhar's *The Beaux' Stratagem*, Goldsmith's *She Stoops to Conquer*, and Sheridan's *The Rivals* or *The School for Scandal*—each of which is rather clean and decorous, none of which is a Restoration comedy.

The heroic efforts of Hume and his mentor Scouten, of Rothstein and his protégeé Kavenik, of Staves and Pearson (all of whose scholarship I honor even as I may disagree with particular interpretations) to redirect our attention to plays Nicoll and Smith and Leo Hughes wrote about but which were neglected by post-World War II critics in the main, who focused on only Wycherley and Etherege before Congreve, have not proved as fruitful as they must have wished, for criticism continues to focus on the Big Three. Several of the revisionist critics I mentioned in the Preface and have cited throughout have made valuable contributions but mostly to the study of these canonical writers, occasionally expanded to include Dryden, Behn, Shadwell, Southerne, Otway, Sedley, even Durfey. But what about the social comedies of Rhodes, St. Serfe, Orrery, Crowne, Southland, New-castle, Arrowsmith, Betterton, Belon, Fane, Caryll, Rawlins, Porter, Ravenscroft, Carlile, or the anonymous author of the wonderful *Mr. Turbulent* (not to mention plays loosely attributed to Behn but virtually ignored)? And the subversive comedies of Tatham, Cowley, Robert and James Howard, Buckingham, Wilson, Lacy, Thompson, Dover, Head, Tate, Duffet, Newcastle, Ravenscroft, Porter, and perhaps Behn again, or the anonymous author of *The Mistaken Husband*? Tidy studies of Restoration comedy have swept these untidy excrescences under the rug.[2] But while the comedies of the canonical can be very powerful, I submit that these almost totally neglected plays, especially the folk-subversive comedies and comical satires, have a democratic élan vital that both demands our attention and commands our respect.

Notes

Introduction

1. Ideology is a vexed concept. Relying on Bakhtin and Voloshinov/Bakhtin, as well as Althusser and Saussure, Jameson employs a definition that I find enabling for my purposes in this book: "For Marxism . . . the very content of a class ideology is relational, in the sense that its 'values' are always actively in situation with respect to the opposing class, and defined against the latter: normally, a ruling class ideology will explore various strategies of the *legitimation* of its own power position, while an oppositional culture or ideology will, often in covert and disguised strategies, seek to contest and to undermine the dominant 'value system'" (84). Each text is a *parole* in the *langue* of class discourse and enters into a dialogic relationship between classes (84-85). In order to see, to analyze the class dynamics of an apparently naturalized and universalized hegemonic discourse or *langue*, Jameson argues, we need to identify its units or "*ideologemes*" (87). I have preferred the Bakhtinian phrase *official discourse* over the Saussurian and the rhetorical term *tropes* over the rather awkward *ideologemes*. In Part 1 I shall examine "ruling class ideology" as it manifests itself in what I call *social comedy*. In Parts 2 and 3 I shall examine not so much "oppositional culture or ideology" as subversions, breakdowns of "ruling class ideology" from within. In the Conclusion, I shall glance at "oppositional ideology" as it emerges around the time of the Glorious Revolution.

2. I am aware that the concept of class, especially vis-à-vis status, is vexed in this period. For students of literature McKeon's monumental book on the novel has most thoroughly and most conveniently surveyed this vexation (*Origins*, ch. 4). Throughout this study I use the terms *class* and *status* without a great deal of precision, reflecting their interpenetration in scholarly discourse, an interpenetration McKeon takes as a sign of dialectical instability both then and now.

3. Dates are of first performance as nearly as we, with the great help of *The London Stage* and Hume's additions and corrections, can tell. Smith adjudges the Willmore-Hellena subplot of Behn's *Rover* to be an example of what he calls "cynical" comedy because he views Willmore as dominating Hellena (94). Hellena seems to me very much to hold her own, refusing to be a slave either to him or to her own biology and socializing Willmore into marriage.

4. Throughout I capitalize such words as Cavalier, Cit(y), Country, Town,

and Suburbs as proper references to not so much persons and places as sites of power in continuous relation and tension to one another in a culture war that is an extension of the English Civil War.

5. *The Century of Revolution*. Throughout this study, I unapologetically rely on this standard Leftist general history of the period, which, at least to my knowledge, has yet to be supplanted.

6. Plays with line numbers are cited by act, scene (where scene divisions are noted and clear), and line(s), separated by periods. Otherwise, as in this citation, page numbers (or sometimes signature numbers where pagination is absent or totally irregular) are given after commas.

7. Hume, Corman, and Payne have all analyzed the problematics of taking Restoration authors (and critics, too, for that matter) at face value in their generic distinctions.

8. I could have picked *Marriage A-la-Mode* as an example, but having treated Restoration tragicomedy elsewhere ("Ideology"), I am trying, insofar as I am able, to avoid that genre in this book, however difficult it is to draw hard generic lines, especially in plays that are themselves of a *mixt way*. Let me loosely call tragicomedies plays that are *essentially* (itself not an ontological but heuristic term) romances with high, serious plots bordering on tragedy (including murders, rapes, usurpations, and the like either real or threatened), however they may be mixed with low plots that include satire and farce. That means excluding several plays not only Dryden but Nicoll and others have identified as comedies. See the bibliography at the end of "Ideology," to which I would add the following plays: Abraham Bailey's *The Spightful Lady*, Behn's *The Dutch Lover* and *The Town-Fop*, John Bulteel's *The Amorous Gallant*, John Corye's *The Generous Enemies*, Sir William Davenant's *The Law against Lovers* and *The Rivals*, Thomas Duffet's *The Spanish Rogue*, Thomas Durfey's *The Banditti* and *The Commonwealth of Women*, Alexander Greene's *The Politician Cheated*, John Leanerd's *The Counterfeits* and *The Country Innocence*, and Edward Howard's *Six Days Adventure*. Other plays (Behn's *The Revenge*, the duke of Buckingham's *The Chances*, Thomas Duffet's *The Amorous Old-woman*, James Howard's *All Mistaken*, John Lacy's *Sir Hercules Buffoon*, Lewis Maidwell's *The Loving Enemies*, Edward Ravenscroft's *The English Lawyer*, even Cowley's *The Cutter of Coleman Street*) probably also belong in the same category, but I will be treating at least aspects of them that are so germane to this study as to defy exclusion. Again, let me stress my position that genres are both historical and critical categories *with no fixed boundaries*. It may make traditionalists more comfortable to substitute the word *mode* for *genre* and *subgenre* throughout my argument.

I also exclude from this study burlesques (Buckingham's *The Rehearsal*; Duffett's *The Empress of Morocco*, *The Mock-Tempest*, and *Psyche Debauched*), potpourri plays (Davenant's *Play-house To Be Let*), pure farces (Thomas Otway's *The Cheats of Scapin*, Ravenscroft's *Scaramouch*, Edward Howard's *The Man of Newmarket*, Behn's *The Emperor of the Moon*, and William Mountfort's *The Life and Death of Doctor Faustus*); plays that are essentially translations or close adaptations (Richard Flecknoe's *Demoiselles a la Mode*, the anonymous *The Feign'd Astrologer* and *The Liar*; Ravenscroft's *The Citizen Turn'd Gentleman*, Shadwell's *The Miser*, Matthew

Medbourne's *Tartuffe*); and plays written before 1660 and performed virtually unchanged (Thomas Killigrew's *The Parson's Wedding*, the duke of Newcastle's *The Country Captain*). But alas, I have no *fixed* definiton of these categories either and may instead be perceived to transgress them.

In an effort to steer between the Scylla of pedantry and the Charybdis of insouciance I offer in my bibliography a list of editions of Restoration comedies cited and a list of editions of Restoration tragicomedies treated. In the interests of completeness, the former includes all the plays that I consider original Restoration comedies and that I have cited in the text or notes; in the interests of brevity, the latter includes only those other plays that I have actually treated in some detail in the text or notes and does not include plays simply mentioned in passing, like those in the above paragraphs, tragedies, the later comedies of Shadwell (because I consider such sentimental comedies to belong in the category of bourgeois tragicomic romance), or the Revolutionary comedies of the 1690s. I also do not glut the bibliography with classic nondramatic works available in multiple editions.

9. See Braverman, "Rake's Progress," for the only recent treatment of this dimension of Restoration comedy in general (though he himself treats very few plays). Whenever appropriate, I shall cite other secondary treatments of contending over estates (including the estate of England) in individual plays. My choice to cite only criticism apposite to my argument should not be interpreted as contempt for other excellent criticism of Restoration comedy, especially by previous generations of scholars, but rather as my attempt not to distract my readers by constant comparisons between apples and oranges.

Recently, Hinnant has argued that the conspicuous sexual consumption of Restoration rake/heroes "is linked by a perception of equivalences of value among people, services, and objects to short-term liaisons as finite relationships between individuals [that is, the emerging consumer culture]. Even marriages that eventually issue forth from these liaisons do not completely destroy the link with the original conception of expenditure, which continues to exist as a shadow over the long-term prospects of such marriages" (79). Although I find this reading extremely provocative, I remain convinced that the cultural work social comedy performs is fundamentally conservative, socializing rakes into marriages that are linked with estates. In order to distinguish Restoration from earlier social comedy, Hinnant maintains that "Restoration comedy exalts marriages based on free consent and . . . the negotiations for these marriages take place without any consideration of money" (81). The generalization is simply empirically not true. Moreover, one of the "equivalences" Hinnant tries to maintain supposedly obtains between Dorimant and the lawyer Medley compares him to: "[B]ehind the obvious differences, one can detect in Medley's admiration for Dorimant a recognition that the energy and enterprise of the rake-hero is strangely consonant with that of the eminent solicitor" (81). Hinnant's thesis invites him to stress those similarities, mine to stress those differences: it is precisely the similarities between contending oligarchies that necessitate Restoration comedy's need to (re)establish class differences. I stress also the differences between Hinnant's thesis and mine not out of disrespect but, on the contrary, out of respect for its seriousness and out of a conviction that criticism advances dialectically.

10. See *Revels*, 166-67. In his isolation of the aristocratic virtues of *generosity*, *liberality*, and *courage* (if not *plain-dealing* and *love* as well), Schneider is on the brink of seeing extended class warfare as central to Restoration comedy: "It continues the Cavalier side of the Civil War by attacking not just Puritans but the Puritan economic philosophy. . . . [O]n night after night, the Puritans were exposed to contempt and laughter on the stage, now not casually as before the Rebellion, but with a vengeance" (40-41). But Schneider qualifies: "Class conflict in the Civil War may have contributed to the prejudice against trade in Restoration comedy, but its antecedents are considerably more ancient and honorable. . . . If class warfare were rigorously carried on in Restoration comedy, all gentry ought to be liberal in the management of wealth" (49-51). Schneider fails to distinguish between Town and Country as sites of power; he also fails to note that the apparent avarice of gentry who are blocking agents in this comedy has to do with the necessity of building and maintaining estates. But his use of the term "honorable" is most telling: if one can cite Cicero as an authority for the virtue of *liberality* (49), then one can by implication, free Restoration ideology from *dishonorable* roots—and, by implication, a criticism that might expose the "universal" values critics are attracted to in Restoration comedy as socially constructed and associated with Stuart aristocratic, antidemocratic ideology.

11. Staves, whose reading of the play is generally on target (*Players' Scepters*, 203-7), has a problem with Careless's request for that oath. Once we focus on the play as class warfare, Careless's desperate wish-fulfillment becomes intelligible.

12. Scouten (in *Revels*, 167-70), Hume (111-16), and Backsheider (56-62) have all been disturbed by the ending of the play—the former two because it does not fit a more romantic model for comedy wherein all are united at the end in comic resolution, the latter because the king himself does not appear on the stage as a deus ex machina. The king's absence, Backscheider incredibly asserts, "suggests the crumbling of the Stuart conception of the power of the sovereign. This play goes beyond questioning the king as the supreme power and symbol of the nation [as she interprets other entertainments doing] to finding dubious his power to unite and mediate" (62). I should like to know by what possible logic one could draw that inference from the ending of this play. To Scouten and Hume I would only ask why comedy cannot represent the triumph of one ideology over another, even in an aggressive fashion. To me there is no doubt that the play celebrates the restoration of Stuart hegemony and its concomitant ideology. And just as it rubs the Days' so also it rubs the commonwealthsmen's faces in their class triumph.

13. See esp. Derek Hughes and Markley, *Two-Edg'd Weapons* (121-37). Whereas both view the discursive code as failing, I view it as being tested in the fires of irony and holding. Whereas Markley sees the absence of the traditional hymeneal celebration at the end of the play as an absence of closure signifying that traditional stylistic possibilities were simply no longer viable for Etherege, I see the deferral of actual marriage at the end of *The Man of Mode* or of *She Wou'd If She Cou'd* (1668) as being no more of an undercutting of the usual function of such marriages at the end of comedy (so well articulated by Markley, 135-36) than

the deferred marriages of Shakespeare's *Love's Labours Lost* or, say, of Shadwell's *Virtuoso* (1676). I agree that these ironic social comedies cast a skeptical eye on idealism, but the social function of the eventual marriage remains the same.

14. In one of the rare positive images of the Country gentleman, Sir Robert Howard and the duke of Buckingham reverse the satire but underscore the same economy in the play of that title (written for performance in winter 1669 but banned), where the eponymous hero, Sir Richard Plainbred, whom Hume and Scouten describe in the dramatis personae as "An exemplary country gentleman, wise and witty, who detests city fashions and believes in old-fashioned country virtues," engages in the following significant dialogue with his former servant Trim concerning Country versus Town:

> *Sir Richard:* I do abhorr a place, where the most estimed crafts are cheat-
> ing; and the most admirable policy word-breaking; where most
> people spend all they have, and some more than theyr own. Greatnes
> is now to be judg'd by outside, and interest chang'd for grandeur.
> Your Countrymen scarce know theyr Landlords, and are grown too
> poor to care for 'em. Fy upon't, Trim, in former times we liv'd by one
> another, and now we live upon one another.
>
> *Trim:* Sir I cannot but remember, when I was but a stripling, how your
> honest Tenants and neighbors would rejoyce, to shew their good
> wills; here Sir is nothing but 'Your servant', and a mouth made.
> [V.400-412]

Sir Richard's nostalgia for a relationship of mutual benefit is part of the fiction of the Country that Williams throughout his study demonstrates as masking its harsh reality, harsh for those countrymen, most of whom were the landless upon whose backs rested the wealth of those landlords.

In the Howard/Buckingham play, Sir Richard is in town to consolidate estates after his brother's death, "whose faire estate now joyn'd to his makes his daughters the richest heires, that ever the West of England brag'd of. . . . [T]heir land reaches to the sea, and their Royalty of fishing to the Ocean" (I.210-12; 248-49). And by the end of the play, these heiresses are married to the appropri-ately named Country wits (not an oxymoron in this play) Worthy and Lovetruth, both heirs themselves to "good estats and good names" (I.i.382-86) and both good potential husbands in the two senses of the term:

> *Lovetruth:* We wil save our Estats, and spend our revenues.
> *Worthy:* And leave posterity an easy example. [II.i.519-20]

The closing embrace of this social comedy reinforces not only the moral of hus-bandry but also the continuation of the late feudal economy. Blessing the united lovers, Sir Richard proclaims,

> For my self, Worthy, and Lovetruth, we'l to the Countrey with our wifes;
> where we'l cheerfully spend what we have, and wast nothing that our

Ancestors left us; We'l not expose our content to noise, nor our fortunes to crowds; we'l doe good to all, that desire, and hurt to none that deserve it; we'l love our King, and be true to our Countrey, wish all well[.] [V.537-43]

The above description from the dramatis personae is, as in most plays, printed in italics. Here as elsewhere I have omitted such italics, as I have all those marking entire passages, such as songs, prologues, epilogues, and closing tags. In other words, I retain original italics only when they mark an internal contrast of some kind.

15. A portion is that part of her parents' (usually her father's) estate a woman brings with her into marriage. Our modern "dowry" is a misnomer for this period. "Dower" was the ancient lifetime right of a woman to one-third of her husband's land after his death. "Jointure" was a substitute provision for dower, written into the marriage settlement. For these and other terms concerning marriages and estates used throughout this study, consult Staves, *Married Women's Separate Property*, glossary.

16. See Armistead's annotations for this repeated opinion.

17. Corman too sees no reason to doubt the movement toward marriage at the end (23-24). Kunz reads the play, à la Smith (though Smith does not like this play and thinks it is a forerunner of what he calls "cynical comedy" [see ch. 4]), as moving toward the union of the gay couples (1:113-36).

18. Using Richard Levin, Corman distinguishes dimensions of *Epsom Wells* according to the four causes of Aristotle. He writes concerning the material cause, "Material unity is achieved most effectively in *Epsom-Wells* by the fact that all the characters, as visitors to the spa, are involved in the same basic round of activity, focusing especially on the daily visit to the Wells with which the play opens. Shadwell is thus able to introduce his characters in a single place where they might reasonably be expected to meet and mix, very much in the tradition of *Bartholomew Fair*, though because the social range is more limited, this social world is even more unified" (25). Corman is onto something, though he does not read out of this material causality its sociopolitical implications. Weingrod Sandor, in her reading of the setting of the play as "a site where opposites meet," sees finally only a reaffirmation of "the established order" (34), missing, it seems to me, despite the inclusion of Williams's *The Country and the City* in her bibliography, the implications of her earlier announced thesis that the setting of the play "mediates between those who possess and those who lack elite status" (9). She misses especially the obfuscated interdependence of Country, Town, and City analyzed below.

1. Nubile Tricksters Land Their Men

1. In "Romantic Love and Social Necessities" Wheatley revisits the topic of enforced marriage in Restoration comedy in the light of recent social history and corrects the older thesis that these plays generally celebrate romantic love and oppose marriages of convenience. Wheatley rightly notes the essential conser-

vatism of most Restoration comedy in insisting on the social necessity of marriages based upon economic prudence, even as it examines and celebrates freedom of choice. Following his mentor, Rothstein, Wheatley describes this ambivalence as a compromise formation. Although as the fabric of my argument unfolds it will become obvious that I disagree with some details of Wheatley's fine readings of individual plays (most notably of Betterton's *Amorous Widow*), I am in essential agreement and welcome his insights.

Stone sees marriage historically moving away from strict patriarchal control toward freedom of choice, but he notes two intermediate positions: one where parents choose mates, children essentially obey parents, but reserve a right of veto that they may exercise only once or twice; and another where children choose mates, "on the understanding that [the choice] will be made from a family of more or less equal financial and status position, with the parents retaining the right of veto" (271). The trend Stone marks is a gradual one over time (from the reestablishment of a stricter patriarchal control in the first half of the seventeenth century to its considerable relaxation by the end of the eighteenth), and one cannot identify these intermediate positions with periods of time in between but only with individual cases and circumstances (see esp. ch. 7). Stone glances at Restoration comedy, as well as the eighteenth-century novel, for evidence of this shift in attitude, evidence he finds "[a]s early as 1668" in the resistance to enforced marriage in Sedley's tragicomedy, *The Mulberry Garden* (277). We will find such evidence from the inception of Restoration comedy, but what I find most interesting about Stone's examples from this comedy is that he cites complaints by both Ravenscroft's Hillaria and Behn's Julia, Lady Fulbank (from *The Luckey Chance* [1686]), without noting that Hillaria wants not only freedom of choice but equal freedom of promiscuity after marriage (see above, intro.), while Julia insists on her chastity even though married to a man she contemns and betrayed by him to an unwitting copulation with her lover (see below, ch. 11). The vast majority of Restoration comedies are conservative, allowing choice only within prescribed status limits and punishing female sexual promiscuity before and after marriage. A small but potent minority are subversive, like Ravenscroft's play and like those analyzed in Part 2 below. Restoration comedy thus does provide corroboration for Stone's thesis (especially for the second of those two intermediate positons), though he missed the truly radical nature of one of his own examples.

For a tougher look at the economic realities of marriage for women in this period, one that tempers Stone's optimism about any steady progress toward *companionate marriages*, see Staves, *Married Women's Separate Property*.

2. For an excellent Foucauldian reading of the failure of patriarchal strategies of containment and surveillance in this play, see Velissariou.

3. Cf. Rothstein and Kavenik, who note this appropriation (168-69) but state the case too strongly for what they call *moraliste comedy:* "The increasing freedom for women in plays, coupled with a general social weakening of the norm of marriage, progressively strained what one might call the 'ritual plan' of the plays, their standard reaffirmation of the social order" (170). On the contrary, throughout the Restoration period, what I call *social comedy* continues to reaffirm that order by granting women more freedom to choose—within the confines of

aristocratic political economy. What I call *subversive comedy* makes sense only by playing off this continuing tradition. For example, Rothstein and Kavenik are quite right about the subversiveness of "the clever servant Rose" (171) of Payne's *The Morning Ramble; or, The Town-Humours* (1672), who dons breeches to win the amoral rake Townlove. The fact that Townlove takes Rose as his mistress and not his wife is, first of all, an anomaly in these breeches parts plays, and second, actually an underwriting of status hierarchy: she is not of the right class to be made a wife. So the play frustrates the normal expectation of gay-couple comedy and thus subverts the Williamsesque sense of an ending (the production of estates and heirs), but only half-heartedly: the Muchlands get their desired mates and will be "secure . . . in the knowledge of their own Children" (II.i, 14), which security, as Townlove himself admits (this is him talking), is the reason for possessiveness in sexual relations.

4. Sir Marmaduke's reference to the "Prince" against which religion teaches people to rebel works across the grain of the rest of the irony in the passage: Mariana's religious resistance is, of course, a good thing; Dissenters' resistance against their lawful king a bad. Lacy's royalism winks through the arras.

5. See Hill's several chapters on economics.

6. Spencer appreciates the trickery of the women in this play, trickery into which they are forced not only by their circumstances but also by their "subordinate position" (97). Although affirming the play's reinscription of patriarchy, Spencer insists Behn gives the maximum amount of expression to "female desire" and "female action" (100).

7. In addition to plays already treated, see also Porter's *The Carnival,* Sir William Killigrew's *Pandora,* and Southland's *Love a la Mode* (all 1663, all featuring male as well as female tricksters).

8. In Etherege's *She Wou'd if She Cou'd* (1668), a play with slight trickery on the part of the witty heroines, who escape their guardian parents to troll for lovers in the park, then test their constancy, Courtall assures his fellow rake Freeman that their witty women will not really care that they have failed the test of constancy: "Never fear it; whatsoever women say, I am sure they seldom think the worse of a man, for running at all, 'tis a sign of youth and high mettal, and makes them rather piquee, who shall tame him" (III.i.102-5). Their women are aware exactly how the game is played: Ariana says to them, "I know you wou'd think it as great a Scandal to be thought to have an inclination for Marriage, as we shou'd to be believ'd willing to take our freedom without it" (V.i.454-57). Courtall rejects Gatty's playful accusation that such men "seldom mortgage your persons without it be to redeem your Estates" by insisting he and Freeman have not mortgaged their quite real estates, but the final language of courtship between them reveals the nature of their necessary agreement:

> *Gatty:* These Gentlemen have found it so convenient lying in Lodgings, they'l hardly venture on the trouble of taking a House of their own.
> *Courtall:* A pretty Country-seat, Madam, with a handsom parcel of Land, and other necessaries belonging to't, may tempt us; but for a Town-Tenement that has but one poor conveniency, we are resolv'd we'll never deal. [V.i.485-500]

They will indeed get their Country-seat with land and other necessities—like maids of various kinds to siphon off their surplus energy as they exercise their *droit du cuissage* with impunity. As with Dorimant's willingness to go on a Lenten pilgrimage to the Country, their willingness to wear their own penitential suits, as it were (like the one Lady Cockwood makes Sir Oliver wear when he has had a night of debauchery), and to defer the immediate gratification of their sexual desires for the nubile tricksters signals (*pace* Markley) a period of detoxification from an overdose of broken promises. It is not language but action that reaffirms comedy's enactment of social necessity.

9. In "Female Rebels and Patriarchal Paradigms" I analyzed the character of Angellica Bianca and her failure to escape the subculture of the sexual surplus.

10. Another nubile trickster play worth mentioning if not analyzing is Ravenscroft's *The Wrangling Lovers; or, The Invisible Mistress* (1676), where the mistress of the subtitle is something of a trickster trying to help her brother gain a woman and herself a man, but she engenders nothing but those Spanish intrigue mistakes of the night, often resulting in duels between men, until at last good sense wins out and the proper women gain the proper men, complete with blessings and fortunes.

2. Mature Women Tricksters Man Their Land

1. For an analysis of what women could own and how much control they could have over estates, see Staves, *Married Women's Separate Property.*

3. Eligible Male Tricksters Get into the Deed

1. N.B. that Orrery's modern editor has numbered lines consecutively through acts despite scene changes.

2. Apparently Orrery had produced his other, less entertaining comedy, *Mr. Anthony,* in the same year. It is worth noting that Pedagogue, Mr. Anthony's tutor, constantly reminds him of his father's threat to "subvert the Order of Law and Nature, and make your Fathers younger Son your eldest Brother" (I.i. 159-61). To nominate primogeniture as the "Order" not only of "Law" but of "Nature" is very much in the interest of Stuart ideology.

A play similar to Orrery's *Guzman* because a male trickster not only gains a witty woman who redeems the ravages of his estate but also gains a foolish but rich husband for his equally impecunious sister to manage is the unacted, unpublished *The Frolicks; or, The Lawyer Cheated,* written by Elizabeth Polwhele and dated 1671 by Milhous and Hume, who have rescued the play from oblivion in a modern edition.

3. Regents editors Nicolson and Rodes' quotation marks around this closing tag are impertinent. The original is in italics.

4. Markley has brilliantly analyzed the ideological ambiguities of this play in "Masculine Sexuality and Feminine Desire" (131-37), and I hesitate to offer a supplement. But I think he ignores some of the motivation for the concluding unions, motivations that, at least in the instance of Wilding and Charlot, may make ideological coherence after all.

5. The desire for such verisimilitude, with its accompanying sympathy for the women of the play as if they were real persons, drives Hersey's misreading in his introduction to his critical edition (82-118). Hersey's edition is unreliable, dropping whole lines. For a better reading, which nevertheless still focuses primarily on character analysis, see Copeland.

4. SOME TRICKSTERS GET TRICKED

1. Though I admire the sophistication of his ideological reading of this play, Flores sees more negotiation between classes than I do. That is, while the fluidity among classes is recognized in Restoration comedy, hegemonic ideology usually (and relentlessly) attempts to discipline parvenus. See the section on punitive elements below (ch. 6).

2. Wycherley's *Love in a Wood; or, S[t] James's Park* (1671) belongs in this group of plays, although most of the trickster/tricked (Wycherley's own metaphor is crossbiting) motif occurs among the *punitive* and not the *sympathetic* characters. Among the latter, it could be argued that the sexual trickster Ranger, who refuses to settle down to Lydia, gets tricked. Lydia follows him on an evening ramble in St. James's Park, and the consequences bring Ranger close to deadly rivalry with his fellow Cavalier Valentine (though of the Town, known more for his sword than his wit) over Valentine's beloved Christina, to whom Lydia indirectly causes Ranger to be attracted. So Lydia is an inept trickster, and she is completely outclassed in trickery by her lower-class counterparts, Mrs. Joyner and Mrs. Crossbite (see ch. 10).

3. Durfey's Townly in *Sir Barnaby Whigg; or, No Wit Like a Womans* (1681) is another trickster who seems to overstep the bounds of trickery between Town wits. Although Townly has had a modicum of success cuckolding Country and Sea fools, he goes too far when he informs Gratiana, who has been *très dangereuse* in granting her love to the reforming rake Wilding, that not he but Wilding is Livia's (the wife of the sea captain Porpuss) lover. Wilding defends himself against Gratiana's anger by making Townly confess he lied: "A Pox on my Lying tongue, it will be my ruine one time or other" (V.ii, 62). The play concludes with Wilding, who has just recently inherited an estate himself, socialized into marriage with Gratiana, "Lord *Lofty*'s Daughter, a rich Heiress . . . and a vast fortune" (I, 9). But if this trickster Townly is ultimately tricked, it is more by his own overreaching. No boisterous, brazen Cavalier Cit-cuckolder at the end, he escapes two angry husbands with the threat of violence if caught again.

4. *Mr. Turbulent*'s Fairlove's sympathetic treatment of the bourgeois couples who walk in Moor-fields—"Men and their Wives ordinarily walk here together very lovingly" (I, 4)—strikes an anomalous note but is (*pace* Rothstein and Kavenik, 252) only one swallow and does not make a summer. On the other hand,

they are right to point to the wrens nesting in Shadwell's *The Lancashire Witches, and Tegue o Divelly The Irish-Priest* (1681), which I have treated in "Shifting Tropes" as a protosentimental play—a genre I take to be the equivalent of bourgeois tragicomedy (215-19).

5. TOWN TRICKSTERS TUP THEIR RIVALS' WOMEN

1. Braverman, "Libertines and Parasites," argues provocatively that "the major libertine comedies of the mid-1670s express the inability of an aristocratic social body to perpetuate itself. . . . [T]he courtier-rake exercises . . . power of seduction to compensate for his obsolescence in the gentry world of marital exchange, where his evident illegitimacy suggests that he can sustain but cannot reproduce the proto-heroic idiom he represents. Despite his reputation, however, his power is social rather than political, his unparalleled potency restricted to the private sphere because it is acutely limited in the public domain" (78). Although I admire Braverman's interpretation, I differ with him in seeing the cuckolding libertine as still potent in the public sphere of class warfare.

2. John Dover's *The Mall* (1674) features the cuckolding of an "old impotent Letcher" (I.i, 2), Mr. Easy, who is later identified as "an old decripped Miser" (II.ii [misnumbered iii], 24) and who is forced by the libertine Lovechange to accept wife swapping; less is made of his Cit status, which remains implicit in the single appellation "Miser." Nevertheless, Easy's nervous, nearly hysterical acceptance of his status as cuckold anticipates Nokes's and Leigh's grand portrayals of similar roles in plays of the later 1670s. Other plays that might seem to demand treatment here—Wycherley's *The Country-Wife* and Durfey's *A Fond Husband*—I treat in chs 7 and 12, respectively.

3. Rothstein and Kavenik make much of this lack of consummation in their building a case for Molière-influenced comedies of the late 1660s and 1670s as "compromise-formations" (120-26). Strangely, like most critics of Restoration comedy, they remain preoccupied with issues of morality and completely neglect the class conflict in this and other plays. Sir Peter Pride and his lady are perhaps as much the butt of the satire as Brittle. They rank no higher than baronet (with the usual possibility that the title was purchased), and they have foolishly traded their daughter for money. Both the Prides and the Brittles are the victims of the surplus sexual energy of the dominant aristocratic group in these plays, Town wits.

4. Rothstein and Kavenik (170-71) object to Payne's characterization of the play as conservative (in her introduction to the Augustan Reprint Society's facsimile edition). I agree with the point they make—that the play is less orthodox finally than the tragicomedy *Marriage A-la-Mode*—but it is nevertheless conservative in my sense of plays that underwrite Cavalier dominance, albeit less idealistically than heroic and tragicomic romances.

5. Here is a clear case where Braverman's reading of the 1670s libertine through the lenses of Michel Serres' theory of the parasite ("Libertines and Parasites") applies in one sense (Sir Generall gets something for nothing) but not in another (he seems to me not a relatively impotent figure consigned to the social

sphere but a warrior in class conflict, albeit a conflict transferred to the drawing room). Braverman's reading of this figure as the "noise" or static in a transitional stage between aristocratic and bourgeois ethoi conforms to a developmental model requiring an early stage of fullness, a middle stage of emptiness, and a final stage of fullness with different content. Some of the best critics of Restoration drama read it according to such a model (Brown; Staves, *Players' Scepters*). I prefer the model of the paradigm shift.

6. Dryden's *The Spanish Fryar; or, The Double Discovery* (1680) features a comic subplot with all the trappings of Cavalier Cit-cuckolding—old, impotent Cit banker intimidated by the friar for fear of being excommunicated and therefore made incapable of collecting debts; beautiful young wife who hates her slavery and longs for delivery; lusty Cavalier youth who longs to deliver the wife into his bed and who constantly threatens the Cit husband with his sword and his fists—but one of the discoveries at the end is that these adulterous lovers are siblings. Incest remains a far stronger taboo than adultery, so the cuckolding is never consummated. Nathaniel Lee's *The Princess of Cleve* (performed after the 1680 death of Rochester, to which it alludes, and probably before the end of 1682) features a comic subplot in which two bourgeois pretenders to wit try to ape the sexual mores of their betters only to be cuckolded in their faces and even shot at by Cavaliers. The Cavaliers' phallic dominance is both literal and figured in the pistol that is later alluded to by the wives who force the Cits into passive submission. So the Cit-cuckolding serves as an episode in the festering class warfare. But the play focuses on intraclass Rochestrian cuckolding as the rakish duke de Nemours aims at—and will apparently get—the Princess of Cleve over her husband's dead body. It does not just celebrate class dominance but at the same time undercuts it through relentless, ubiquitous satire. Moreover, given the death of the Prince of Cleve, the high social position of most of the characters, and the seriousness of the action between them, the play is more a tragical than a comical satire (at least, not to be facetious, a tragicomical satire). For a reading of its sense of an ending as satire, see my "Poetical Injustice," 28-36.

7. Munns believes that the king and the Cavaliers are portrayed as impotent in this play and concludes, "There is little to choose between the representatives of cavalier ease or city politics. The whig is dished, but the loyal tories—the impotent pimp Sir Jolly and the unemployed soldiers who must trade their military might for sexual performance—do not add up to a striking alternative" (77). Although I admire Munns's approach to Otway generally, I think she misses the ideological implications of the cuckolding in the play and the significance of Beaugard's assertion at the end, demanding that Sir Davy treat his wife as Beaugard's mistress. Otway portrays a world where worth goes unrewarded, but he still insists on that worth as he takes out his artistic revenge on the Cits and parvenus—and indeed rewards his Cavaliers with the women and money they clearly deserve. For another excellent if brief recent reading of this play, see Cordner, xv-xxii.

8. For treatments of Behn's *The False Count;, or, A New Way to Play an Old Game* and *The Luckey Chance; or, An Alderman's Bargain* see below, chs. 9 and

11, respectively. Both involve Cit-cuckolding but are dominated by other subversive and satirical concerns.

9. *Pace* Hume, who maintains that the play "is rollicking good fun with no ulterior point whatever" and who denies that the play is political because it was performed annually on the Lord Mayor's Day for years (355). Hume's protégé, Harwood, follows suit (87-88), despite flirting with a sociopolitical reading of the play along class lines (97), a reading he dismisses by baldly asserting, "no political or theological metaphors seem very probable constructs by which the play can be understood beyond its literal dimension" (97), by which "literal dimension" he means that the play is simply a farce that delights in sex for sex's sake.

With regard to audience response: The fact that the play was performed for the next century, especially on the Lord Mayor's Day for half of it, rather than denying the play's power relations, seems to me to underscore the aggressive nature of performing such plays in the teeth of middle-class audiences, who during the Exclusion Crisis apparently sat there and took it and even laughed and enjoyed it and perhaps even internalized it, like the cuckolded Cits portrayed by Nokes and Leigh. After 1688 Whigs could afford to indulge themselves; besides, an audience always considers itself superior to objects of satire, even when of their class or group. Like Swift's tennis players, they deftly stroke the ball into someone else's court. Moreover, one of the Town wits (as in Behn's *False Count,* performed in the same season) is identified in the dramatis personae as a "young merchant." Perhaps Behn and Ravenscroft were still throwing sops to the Whigs during the Exclusion Crisis (as Owen argues anent the early part of the crisis, but curiously neglecting, though she discusses *The Roundheads,* either of these plays of the later part). Loveday's being identified with the merchant class indicates the behind-the-ideology fluidity we have noted elsewhere in Restoration comedy. As the richer merchants literally moved into the Town, as well as in a few instances like this figuratively, those merchants in the audience could look down their noses at the pettier bourgeoisie.

10. Markley, "Masculine Sexuality and Feminine Desire," 125-31; Kubek, "Night Mares." The articles complement each other's political readings, but Kubek's goes on to argue that women are put back in their places in the aristocratic order and disallowed any real feminist political liberation (cf. Harwood, 97). Owen also discusses the sexual politics of the play (41-42), briefly and not so interestingly as Kubek and Markley.

11. Backscheider suggests that Sir Charles's union with Philipa also represents an appeal for healing the Cavalier-Cit rift (256 n. 98). Perhaps, but the play is so stridently anti-Cit that the union more probably would seem to symbolize dominance and submission.

12. Cf. Crowne's *Regulus* and my article on it.

13. I am obviously in complete disagreement with Staves's reading of this play as undercutting aristocratic ideology (*Players' Scepters,* 235-39) as I am in general with her reading of the function of marriage (and sex) in Restoration comedy. The "debauchery" of 1670s comedy, for example, seems to me anything but "meaningless" (168).

6. Satiric Butts Get Disciplined

1. Markley (*Two-Edg'd Weapons*, 140-50) argues that the verbal wit fails to adequately distinguish wits from witwouds in this play. Moreover, the Town wits seem no better able than the Cits to discern true from false. But again, perhaps action adequately discriminates: Not only does Vincent attack Dapperwit for the betrayal of friendship inherent in his backbiting, he continually manifests friendship for both Valentine and Christina and does everything he can to resolve their differences. Although Valentine is foolishly jealous and hotheaded, it is from an excess of aristocratic passion often portrayed as endemic to gentry youth. While Ranger has more than his share of sexual energy, that too is an aristocratic excess. By the end of the play both men are socialized into marriage with nubile gentry women. Through the distribution of rewards and punishments, Wycherley clearly differentiates between sympathetic and punitive characters. Moreover, even with regard to language, Wycherley does not portray Ranger or Vincent frittering away a critical opportunity searching for a simile.

2. I shall return to the Mistresses Joyner and Crossbite in ch. 10.

3. Seven great comedies were produced that year: aside from *Tunbridge Wells* they were Behn's *Sir Patient Fancy*, Leanerd's *The Rambling Justice*, Shadwell's *A True Widow*, Dryden's *The Kind Keeper*, Durfey's *Trick for Trick*, and Otway's *Friendship in Fashion*. The runner-up year 1676 had six: Etherege's *The Man of Mode*, Shadwell's *The Virtuoso*, Rawlins's *Tom Essence*, Durfey's *Madam Fickle* and *The Fool Turn'd Critick*, and Wycherley's *The Plain Dealer*. I know "great" is a problematic and perhaps idiosyncratic term, but I cannot imagine either company not delighting in the production of this baker's dozen. Of them, however, according to Corman (13), only Etherege's and Wycherley's plays entered the repertoire.

4. In a minor though delightful touch, the playwright has even Grin Squeak, the projector, incarcerated: Lucy concludes he is mad too, for his estate is entirely paper with no land. The dawning age of paper money and paper securities, just over the horizon, is portrayed in anticipation as sheer chaos.

5. Virulent, punitive anti-Cit satire surfaces again a few years later at another crucial moment in these culture wars as Charles approached death and James approached the throne. The anonymous *The Rampant Alderman; or, News from the Exchange* (fall 1684?) portrays the title character as a hypocritical, disloyal cabalist of the Good Old Cause. When asked whether he would jump for the King, the alderman answers, "The King of *England*, no not I: I'de not Jump over a Straw for him. For a certain Duke, that shall be nameless [that is, Monmouth], I could Jump, tho the Joynt-Stool were as high as the Exchange" (II, 13). He affects the noble Cordelia, and when he has her trapped and she threatens to force her way out, he delights in the prospect of some S & M, B & D, claims he is hot, tries to take out his penis to show her, but it eludes him! The Town wits come to her rescue, and he fears "they have got the Tokens of my Manhood in a Cleft Stick already" (III.i, 22). Indeed, he is threatened with castration throughout in quite specific, crude language—clearly a political weapon in these wars. Rover: "[L]et's go and contrive how to Supplant this Old Fusty Alderman; for if he intends to Cut up my Sister like a young Virgin Pullet, by this Light, I'll cut him like an Old

Capon; he shall be as bare as the Eunuchs in the Grand Signior's *Seraglio*. I'll see what the Alderman has in his Purse for once"; Wilding: "I think he may spare the Jewels in it, for any good his Worship will do with 'em. But prithee *Jack*, Is not this he that was always voting Mischief against the King, and speaking Treason in the Common Council?" (I.i, 4). The delightful French chevalier La Bounce concludes this motif: "You shall not have one Stone to tro ata de Dog, nor Arm, nor Leg to stand upon, you Poltroon" (III.ii, 25). This play bills itself as "A Farce" on the title page, has only the three acts of farce. It is a perfect example of how *entertainment* serves ideology, no matter how apparently trivial or nonsensical.

7. TOWN TRICKSTERS TUP EACH OTHER'S WOMEN

1. Markley briefly but insightfully glances at this aspect of the play: "[Horner's] role represents a potentially devastating assault on patriarchal ideology. Horner becomes a random variable in equations of patrilineal power; he could conceivably father most of the heirs to property in his end of the town" (*Two Edg'd Weapons*, 164). His end of the Town, symbolically at least, is the West End, the upper-class end, near the Court. His threat is not to Moor-fields but St. James.

2. I am indebted to Sedgwick's insights, first published anent this play in "Sexualism and the Citizen of the World." Although I am intrigued by Weber's (*Rake-Hero*, 53-69) and Burke's ("Alterity") provocative arguments that *The Country-Wife* envisions communities of freedom or alternative possibilities of sexual relations, I agree more with Pat Gill (54-75) that the play's joke is at the expense of women and that patriarchy is alive and well at the end.

3. Cohen has analyzed this and other dangers inherent in the play: "[T]he possiblility of calamity is an omnipresent feature of [the lives of these aristocratic men and women] as long as duplicity and contradiction determine the ideological formations of social existence" (2). That is, everyone in the play knows that the system relies on lies to keep plastering over the cracks of its supposed idealism in order to preserve male control.

4. See Thompson, 88-91; Weber, *Rake-Hero*, 65-69.

5. Laura Brown rightly sees that the "satiric subject" of *The Country-Wife* is "its author's own class" (49). She proceeds immediately, however, to quote Sparkish's complaint about the satirizing of knights on the stage. As we have seen, most of these knights—like Sir Jaspar, Sir Martin Mar-all, Sir Simon Addleplot, Sir Formal Trifle—are nouveaux knights, parvenus affecting but not possessing the breeding of real aristocrats. Aside from this minor quibble, I find Brown's general argument of her chapter on "Dramatic Social Satire" (ch. 2) very sophisticated: that mature Restoration comedy expresses a disjunctive ambiguity between moral and social aspects as it both celebrates and satirizes libertine Town wits. What rings especially provocative in her analysis is the suggestion that Restoration libertinism was an act of defiance "from an ideological vantage point outside an increasingly capitalist society and reflecting the discontent of a class whose partial exclusion from traditional routes to wealth, power, and prerogative provides it with a critical perspective upon that society. For this reason, libertinism is inevitably viewed as a

threat and ultimately repudiated, even by the Restoration libertine himself" (42). The reason libertinism is such a threat, Brown argues, is that it is radically anarchic and in an important sense has a great deal in common with left-wing mid-century radicalism (41-42). Brown sees even this mature comedy as finally conservative, unable to resolve the ideological contradictions and choosing to reinforce the status quo. I agree that it is conservative, and I agree that Wycherley's last two great plays remain disjunctive. While I disagree with some of Brown's readings of serious plays and while I want to employ more categories than just satire for mature Restoration comedy, I see Brown's as one of the most important books on Restoration drama of my generation, and in this chapter I find a great deal of compatibility. I hope my readings might be viewed as complementary to hers.

6. Munns takes me to task for calling Beaugard the real atheist of the play (Munns 86; Canfield, "Thomas Otway," 168), but I meant it in this larger, metaphorical sense. We both read this play as "subversive" of traditional, aristocratic official discourse (Munns, 93). And Munns has employed a metaphor similar to mine: "The political ideal of the seamless body politic, its parts reflecting and reinforcing the whole, is celebrated in the dedication and repudiated in the play" (90). Munns is interested in the new, conservative, proto-Burkean (my term) bourgeois fabric Otway creates in its place. I am more interested in Otway's aggressive pulling apart of the seams.

7. Wheatley ("Defense") sees the play as conservative, reinforcing traditional structures not because they are essentially true but because they keep order. My difference with him has to do with my sense of the play's emphasis on the subversion of that order.

8. For another good new reading of *The Plain Dealer,* see Bacon; however, he seems to miss the point that Wycherley portrays the widow as an uppity woman. While Bacon concedes that "Wycherley does not break completely with patriarchal values" (439), he implies that "the playwright approves" the widow's "feminine self-assertion" (436) in this play as well as that of the women of quality in *The Country-Wife.* For an important empirical analysis of the stereotype of the voracious widow from Restoration comedy, see Todd.

9. In calling Manly's aggressive revenge against Olivia a form of rape, I am in agreement with Pat Gill's response (81-82) to Bode's objection to the use of the term.

10. Pat Gill has one of the best recent readings of *The Plain Dealer* (75-96). Though it does not so directly address the economic ideological issues that concern me (and Braverman and Burke), her reading corroborates mine concerning the aggressive put-down of uppity women and the restoration of Manly and his version of patriarchal hegemony: "Part of the reason that *The Plain Dealer* was so popular with contemporary audiences (especially other dramatists) and that Wycherley was affectionately referred to as 'Manly' Wycherley or the 'Plain-Dealer' may have been that this was truly a Restoration play. It restored—with irony insufficient to the attractiveness of the vision—a lost world: new, bourgeois, foppish values had to make way for old, manly traditions, and rich young virgins were shown to prefer it that way. The rhetoric of manipulation (legal, sexual, and social) becomes once more a masculine province" (95). I would only quibble that the

irony of what Brown would call the disjunctive elements of the play is indeed sufficient to call its nostalgic resolution into question.

11. One notes that Lady Squeamish is the cousin of Sir Noble, whose father was an alderman who purchased a Country estate, of which Sir Noble is the heir as elder brother. She could therefore be a City woman. Still, she might be of much higher status.

12. Munns has an excellent reading of this play in terms of the absence of any transcendence and the dominance of bourgeois economic metaphors for human (power) relations (62-70). I offer my reading from the perspective of tricksters and estates as complementary to hers.

8. NAUGHTY HEROINE TRICKSTERS GET AWAY WITH IT

1. See Williams on the elasticity of traditions and their power to co-opt potentially revolutionary formations (*Marxism and Literature*, ch. 7). For a response to feminist criticism concerning female rebels in Restoration drama, see my "Female Rebels and Patriarchal Paradigms." Pearson in her excellent *Prostituted Muse*, published in the same year as "Female Rebels," independently corroborates my argument: "In the Restoration . . . [male] comic writers were creating powerful, brilliant and strong-minded heroines: such heroines, though, are rarely too disturbing to male insecurities since they ultimately surrender themselves to the male and the 'natural' order of male domination" (54); further, "The most radical alternative open to the heroine is simply to choose the husband she wants" (51). Pearson acknowledges that male authors did attempt to present supposedly transgressive heroines of various kinds, but she insists that these transgressors really underwrite patriarchy: "In the presentation of gender, most drama of the Restoration and early eighteenth century is the most seductive species of conservative propaganda: that which seems to offer opportunities for radical change. . . . [V]alues of stability and order . . . are ultimately reinstated, the more firmly because of the vigour and attractiveness of the subdued opposition" (83). For example, Pearson interprets the apparent transgressiveness of the eponymous heroines of Shadwell's *The Woman-Captain* (1679), who through a vigorous transvestite ruse obtains a separation from an oppressive husband, and Sedley's *Bellamira; or, The Mistress* (1687), who through her wiles delightfully eschews convention and obtains security as a kept woman, to be compromised by patriarchal patterns in the subplots, the one undercutting the whole notion of an independent woman in command (108), the other implicating Bellamira and her sister whores in the patriarchal cover-up of rape (99). It is the purpose of this chapter, however, to show some of the limitations of Pearson's and my own earlier generalizations. And while I agree about *Bellamira,* for a different interpretation of Shadwell's play see below, ch. 11.

2. Munns fails to respond to this point in her otherwise fine reading of the play (61-70).

3. See Pearson, ch. 1. Pioneering studies were also written by Gagen and McDonald, though their perspectives kept them from either analyzing in detail or appreciating the significance of these more subversive women tricksters. Staves (*Players' Scepters,* ch. 3) came a lot closer.

4. Plays that Pearson (166-67) finds growing increasingly dark without, it seems to me, appreciating their comic subversiveness. However witty, Juliana in Arrowsmith's *The Reformation* remains subservient to Pisauro in their con artist team.

5. *Pace* Gallagher, Julia is more an existential heroine than a trickster. See ch. 11, for my treatment of the play as corrective comical satire.

6. Wittmore's confusion over the basket supposedly containing Sir Patient's hoard but containing at the end Sir Credulous Easy seems cleared up when Maundy announces that she has sent the basket with the money to Wittmore's lodgings (V.664): there must be two baskets. If not, Lucia and Wittmore are indeed denied any triumph but the trick. Since Maundy's comment is in no way qualified, however, I believe that the trick is Behn's on the audience.

7. See "Masculine Sexuality and Feminine Desire" (119-25) as well as Markley and Rothenberg.

8. For sympathetic readings of *The Second Part of the Rover* and Willmore and La Nuche's movement to the margins, see Hutner (111-18) and Taetzsch, who writes, "How like a 1960's 'relationship' this sounds—one in which two idealistic young people decide to live together without benefit of marriage in order to love each other freely outside their cultural ideology"—though she problematizes their future happiness (36). Markley, with typically profound insight, sees that "Willmore's exile from his country and from his estate paradoxically frees him from the immediate demands of patrilineal ideology—to marry and to father heirs," but recognizes that the ending of the play is nostalgic and offers no alternative "sociopolitical program" ("Masculine Sexuality and Feminine Desire," 120, 124-25). For a reading of the play as satire on libertinism—a mistaken reading in my opinion—see Owen (40-41).

9. A play Pearson curiously fails to treat.

10. Pearson, who sees the subversiveness of this play (52), correctly disputes Hume about the open-endedness of the comic plot's ending (Pearson, 268 n. 30).

11. *Gay Couple*, 58. As far as we now know, Smith had the dates and consequently the priority between the two plays wrong. See Hume, 253 and n.

12. Pearson acknowledges that at the end of the play Sir Anthony/Lucia "seems set on a life of independent freebooting, a radical if not readily imitable alternative to a conventional female role." Southerne is one of those rare playwrights, according to Pearson, who treats women "with compassion." Yet even here, her praise is qualified: "It would be quite misleading, however, to see her as a feminist hero. . . . A real female community is visibly missing from the world of *Sir Anthony Love,* and without the support of such a community, women must choose to be victims or to prey on each other." She sees the tricksters' ruses throughout the play as "sinister" (116-17).

13. Since I first gave this reading in a lecture at the American Society for Eighteenth-Century Studies in Pittsburgh in April 1991, Helen Drougge has published her article on female sexuality in Southerne's comedies, including *Sir Anthony Love*. Independently, we both arrived at an appreciative reading of the radical nature of Sir Anthony's subversion of the patriarchal system and its carnivalesque *jouissance*. I am happy for the corroboration and for the shared interest in this all-too-neglected play.

14. Southerne's play, a considerable success, would seem to qualify Wheatley's contention that "[b]y 1687 in the theater, whatever the practice was in society, it was no longer possible to stage profitably new plays that endorsed marriages that were made for social and economic reasons. . . . Romantic love, once a liberal conception, had become the new orthodoxy" ("Romantic Love and Social Necessities," 67).

9. MALE FOLK TRICKSTERS ERUPT FROM BELOW

1. These folk trickster-figures are potent presences in the alpha and omega of my study, Tatham's *The Rump* (February 1660) and Dryden's *Amphitryon* (October 1690), both of which I treat below as absurdist comical satires (ch. 12).

2. For an appreciative treatment of Teg, see Hume, 113-14.

3. Foster, 111. Foster also says in a note, "The Irish population of *c.* 1650 is hard to estimate. It had certainly dropped; 34,000 soldiers emigrated, and others were conscripted or sold abroad. 'Slave-hunts' certainly happened, though their extent has been exaggerated; there were possibly 12,000 Irish in the West Indies by the late 1660s" (107 n. xix).

4. Wilson's *The Projectors* has a similar Jonsonian energy, but I shall treat it briefly in ch. 11 below.

5. Published in 1663. Title page says, "Acted privately, with general Applause."

6. See Shinagel's introduction to the modern edition of *The English Rogue,* as well as the early chapters themselves.

7. Unlike *The Committee, Hic et Ubique* is not kind to the Irish. Collonel Kiltory does just that, chasing "the very spawn of rebellion" over mountain and bog, those Irish rebels who killed Head's own father in 1641. Patrick, Kil-tory's servant, is portrayed as the stereotypical superstitious and cowardly Irishman, though he has one moment of subversion: discovering someone "putting the great fuck upon my weef" (an act of colonial dominance, at least symbolically), he falls out of the loft onto them and sticks his pitchfork in the perpetrator's ass, telling him "to stay dere til I fetch the Cunt—stable" (I.vi, 18). But when he asks Kil-tory to help, he is kicked off the stage.

Another marginal(ized) comedy perhaps worth mentioning is Robert Neville's *The Poor Scholar,* a collegiate effort perhaps acted but certainly not in London, where it was published in 1662. It is a social comedy wherein student wits successfully rebel against their patriarchal superegos and marry the women of their choice. But there are some interesting bits of subversive energy that if they come not from the folk, at least come from that special subculture of collegiate humor. The maid Uperephania advises her charge against marriage:

> Well, Madam, be advis'd by me, ne're marry if you're wise: these men (when once marri'd) are alwaies licking their wives lips, and by too frequent breathing on those Red Roses, make 'um at last as blew as their

own noses in a winter morning. Consider, That for a few drams of Bestial pleasure, you must be wrack't to a confession that you have been at your sport, by the untollerable Pangs of Child-bed: your body will once in nine months, be unjoynted, after you have been glu'd unto a man: these men (like Tinkers) will stop up one Hole in us, but make three for't, by weakning our bodies: they'l go abroad and drink o'th best, and vex their wives at home, till they are drunk with their own tears. We women are the ships in which men sail i'th Ocean of this world; they'l leap into us willingly at first, and come aboard, but when we leak, by reason of th'infirmities of age, they'l let us sink and perish, and leap as fast out of us: ne're trust, 'um Mistriss [*sic*]. [IV.v, sigF4v]

Meanwhile, there is this earthy courtship between one of the student rebels, Aphobos, and his mistress, Anaiskuntia (!):

> *Aphobos:* Come my *Anaiskuntia,* when shall we make a conjunction Copulative? What will't always be nibbling at my Bait, and never take it in?
> *Anais:* Your hook appears too much, Sir, to make me tast the Bait; I'm afraid you come upon the catch, onely to try whether I'le bite or no; and if I do, you'l onely tear open my mouth, make it bleed, and then leave me. [IV.vi, sig G1r]

Finally, Neville provides the main student protagonist, Eugenes Junior, with this quite remarkable soliloquy, in which the student trickster figure moves from sophomoric bawdry to heroic energy:

> What would they have made me live immur'd, and cag'd up in my chamber? This was (like a Nun that has had a Clap) to be buried alive in a Coffin of a larger Volume, must I have walkt up and down in my Chamber like a pale Ghost, and (as't were b[y] Magick Charmes) be limited and confin'd to walk no further? I'le make 'um know, that it would prove as easie, to manacle Omnipotence, or confine a Spirit, as me; although I could not, like *Dadalus,* make me wings, and take my flight out of my cage, yet I could file a Bar, and break my passage out o'th'chamber window, they should not have left me an eye of light, had they intended to secure my person, I can creep th'rough a window, eat Iron Bars thorough like *Aquafortis,* break th'rough the gaping jaws of danger, for to obtain the sight of my dear *Morphe;* had they dispersed serpents teeth, and sown 'um in my way, and (*Cadmus* like) made them to spring up armed men, I'de have encountrer'd with 'um all[.] [V.i, sigG1v]

    8. I obviously disagree with Hume, who reads M. Raggou as the object of "anti-French satire" (244).

    9. Lacy has two other folk-subversive comedies from the 1660s. In *Sauny the Scott; or, The Taming of the Shrew* (1667) and *The Dumb Lady; or, The Farriar*

Made Physician (1669), Lacy revisited some of these themes and tropes. The title character in the first is full of folk ebullience and punctuates the play with his robust, scatological highland humor. But the really subversive work of the play lies in its egalitarianism: Sauny refuses to doff his hat to his betters and often defies his master, as when he refuses to obey Petruchio in restraining Margaret the shrew: "S'breed Sir, stay her yer sen, but hear ye Sir, an her tale gea as fast as her tang, Gud ye ha meet with a Whupster, Sir" (II, 11). More strikingly, the Town wit Winlove says to his clever servant Tranio, "[T]ho' our Bloods give me Precedency (that I count Chance) My Love has made us Equal, and I have found a frank return in thee" (I, 1).

In the second play, the farrier Drench's wife makes a mockery of patrilineal genealogy, informing him the first child is his, the rest hers; when he threatens to kill the four bastards, she responds with folk wisdom: but are not man and wife one flesh, says she, "and then are not your children mine, and mine yours, Mr. *Drench?*" And he: "Faith, I doubt this argument is the general security that mankind has to warrant their off-springs Legitimate" (I, 6). Throughout Drench articulates a bawdy folk antimorality that pervades the play, high plot as well as low. He maintains he has so much impudence that "if ever impudence come to be worship'd as a Deity, they'l set me upon pedestal for their god" (V, 66). Immediately afterward, as Drench's words linger in the play's echo chamber, Gernette, the morose father and guardian of Olinda, sullenly says to the victorious Leander, "[T]hou art a pretty fellow, I confes, but the most impudent and audacious Villain, to marry my Child against my will, and before my face too" (V, 81). Drench has earlier propounded the doctrine of impudence: "[S]ome men rail at impudence, and speak it vitious, when the Jest is, they that rail most at it, make most use on't: 'tis doubtless the greatest blessing in the world, and most men do their business by it" (III, 29). Trickster impudence is the great leveler.

In Howard and Buckingham's social comedy *The Country Gentleman*, also a product of the late 1660s, the central satire of the play on Sir Cautious and Sir Gravity, in which Sir Cautious is seated on a swivel chair so he can rotate between papers on two surrounding desks, however much it may have been aimed at Buckingham's enemies in particular, is aimed *ideologically* at the new man of power in London with his fingers on events in "what part of the world you please" (III.i.77). The picture drawn is ostensibly that of a foolish solipsist but is in reality that of the colonial manager. Sir Richard's posture (cited in the intro. n. 14)—and Howard and Buckingham's satire—belie the interimplication of the Country and the City. The barber Trim's rise in status at home mirrors the meteoric rise of the West Indian merchants, from Old Peregrine to Heathcliff, and thus reflects the status instability—or perhaps better, flexibility—that was always already there but is now exacerbated by the new political economy.

Carrying us into the 1680s is one more intervening play with a disruptive folk element, the tragicomedy *The Revenge; or, A Match in Newgate* (1680), probably by Aphra Behn. The high plot(s) would seem to reaffirm status hierarchy, but the low plot tends to reduce everyone to the same common denominator. The play opens with the vintner Dashit lamenting his loss of silver plate to one Trickwel, whom he characterizes as a Jesuit in disguise "sent from beyond Sea to ruine honest Citizens" (I.31-32). Trickwel is an outrageously cheeky trickster, who disguises himself again and again to mercilessly persecute Dashit—for the sheer pleasure it seems at first. Till we learn Trickwel is no Jesuit. He is a former squire, whose land was siphoned off by Dashit: Trickwel complains to Wellman that Dashit "cozen'd me of an Estate of some two hundred a year, with his damn'd Reckonings, and then who but honourable Mr. *Trickwell,* the noble Squire, and soforth, till he had got all my Land in Mortgage; then took the forfeiture, and turn'd me out of doors" (I.177-81). Thus the *revenge* of the play's title refers to low as well as high plot.

Dashit gets money to buy new plate; Trickwel disguises himself as a barber, lathers him up, entrances him with stories of monsters and popery, then steals the money. Disguised as a peddler, Trickwel infiltrates Dashit's society, learns he sends new plate, this time a bowl, home to his wife. Like Brer Rabbit, Trickwel beats Dashit home in another disguise, fools his wife into accepting a salmon supposedly sent for a feast, then tricks her out of the bowl, ostensibly so Dashit can emblazon it with his arms. To top it all, Trickwel returns in the midst of Dashit's fit at being duped again and tricks Mrs. Dashit out of the salmon!

The point of all this trickery would seem to be that Trickwel is a Town wit, a superior trickster, taking out his revenge upon a cheating parvenu who has and deserves no coat of arms. And we expect him to triumph in the end, regaining his estate. Indeed, Trickwel manages to get Dashit thrown into Newgate and visits disguised as a parson, picking pockets right and left and promising Dashit he will comfort his widow after he is hanged. Tending to his own estate, Dashit gives his wife Trickwell's estate papers with instructions for her to take them to the lawyer for forfeiture. But Trickwel picks her pocket too, and Dashit is forced to accept the loss in order to be freed.

Trickwel does not unite with some witty woman, however. Instead, he is forced to marry his co-con artist, Mrs. Dunwel. Although he is included in the final comic embrace, his slide down the status ladder has not been reversed. Indeed, at one point he has pursued Corina, the whore of the high plot, attempting to buy her favors with the silver bowl he stole and insisting that his vices betrayed him to lose the estate of an erstwhile gentleman. She asks if he believes the lover of the high-class Wellman could fall so low as to receive such a rascal to her arms. He responds, and this cuts subversively deep: "If I were there, you'd finde but little difference; and possibly the next they entertain may fail to pay this price I offer ye. This Raskal and that beautious haughtie thing, bating the Sex, differ but very little. I live by Brauls, by rapine, and by Spoils, in Fears, Vexations, Dangers, so do you; I eat when I can get a fool to treat me, and you can do no more" (IV.167-71). The common denominator is survival.

The leveling implications of the play come home most radically in the concluding scene. The playwright has added an apparently gratuitous extra plot. In Newgate one Shamock teaches the other prisoners how to beg. His woman Nan has gotten herself arrested and condemned so she can take a turn at Tyburn with her man, has even bespoken a coffin that will hold them both. The atmosphere is that of folk gallows humor, as the condemned couple engage in a very funny discussion of the coffin, which is unfortunately lined with pitch. They complain they will stick to it and will not fit together—Nan proposes lying on her arm! As she is preoccupied, Trickwell picks her pocket and she can not pay the joiner. But the joiner generously gives them the coffin on credit (one thinks of Céline's great title, *Mort à crédit*). The final, weird twist is that when Nan gets a reprieve, she is furious, insists on dying with her husband, and is led out with him disconsolate.

This wholly separate plot added in the last part of Act V threatens to take over the mood of the ending. Nan represents a folk parody of Marinda's idealistic love. As in a split-plot tragicomedy, the lower plot comments on and redefines the idealism of the higher plot in terms of not just pragmatism, as in *Marriage A-la-Mode*, but a kind of leveling that finally celebrates folk resilience. Shamock and Nan are figuratively grouped at the end with Trickwell and Mrs. Dunwell as tricksters who, win or lose, inhabit an atmosphere Bakhtin describes as "steeped in 'merry time,' time which kills and gives birth" (*Rabelais and His World*, 211). The ending of the play rejoices in such merry time, subverting its own official discourse of tragicomedy.

10. For the similarity to Gay's *Beggar's Opera* see Hume (298) and Kephart.

11. Leigh's role of Guiliom as false count was anticipated signally by Underhill's role as Merryman the falconer who disguises himself as the Viscount Sans-terre in Betterton's *The Amorous Widow*. Merryman abets his master Cunningham's effort to obtain Philadelphia by drawing off the widow Lady Laycock. The name *sans-terre* is a delightful touch, indicating Merryman's landless status. Unlike Guiliom, Merryman abandons marriage to the widow and thus never moves up. Whether Betterton modified his play in the version we possess (though acted by 1670, not published till 1710) in the light of Congreve's *The Way of the World* (1700) or whether Congreve purloined Betterton's plot wholesale I do not know, but Merryman obviously resembles Mirabel's servant who masquerades as Sir Rowland to draw off Lady Wishfort, another superannuated amorous widow.

Underhill created another memorable lower-class character who takes on the airs and rhetoric of his betters, Circumstancio of Lewis Maidwell's tragicomedy *The Loving Enemies* (1680). His speech in the pillory sounds again like a Restoration W.C. Fields:

Ah how dark and erroneous are the sentiments of the unphilosophick, which proceed from want of definition and distinction, they suppose this Pillory to be *malum verum*, which we that have been better taught know to be but *malum apparens*, no wise man can suffer ill; for how insignificant is *malum poenae*, when the essence of a man is free from *malum culpae!* Oh what consolation do I find in Metaphysicks! I will assure you Auditors, neither candid, nor gentle, that I value not this Pillory nor its Pilloreity. [II.i, 14]

At the end Circumstancio refuses to marry the old maid Nuarcha—"Ask the performance of any Command rather than this Entreaty of necessitous Conjunction Copulative" (V, 70)—and he closes the curtain on the concluding romantic marriages: "The Learned observe that the mind of man in great Passions of Joy and Grief cannot curiously attend the Eloquence of Speaking. *Ergo,* I will defer my complemental Entertainment, till I have woven my Thoughts into an Epithalamium" (V, 72).

Another memorable lower-class energy figure is Cupes the book-crier in Ravenscroft's tragicomedy *The English Lawyer* (1677), who paints himself as resourceful as tricksters from Jonson's Mosca to Behn's Guiliom: "No, don't doubt me for any trick, shape, or device: I have been almost of all Professions. I was a strowling Player in *France;* Pimp and Bravo to a Courtezan, at *Venice;* a counterfeit Creeple, at *Naples;* servant to a Mountebank, at *Florence;* a Muliteer, at *Rome;* a Vintner's Accountant, at *Thoulouse.* In *Holland,* I carrry'd about an Ape, in the habit of a Cardinal. Then I went to *England,* where I was first a Sow-gelder in the Countrey; afterwards, I was an under-Butler, or Wash-pot in the Inns of Court, among the Lawyers: For some misdemeanours I fled the Countrey, went to *Geneva,* where I got to be a Vestry-man; not liking the Profession, I came running away with the Church-Bibles, the Childrens Psalters, Testaments and Catechises, which I sold to the *Hugonots* here. With the gain hereof any my Wives Portion, I set up this beggarly Profession of Pamphleteer" (II, 15).

12. Neither as good nor as radical a play, Tate's subsequent *Cuckolds-Haven; or, An Alderman No Conjurer* (1685) features a pair of tricksters, the wonderfully named Sir Petronell Flash and Quick-silver (another name for Mercury). From an alderman, a usurer, and a lawyer who traffic in the estates of the nobility, they steal money, wives, and an uppity daughter who in her inordinate desire for quality resembles Behn's Isabella. Though he is apparently the son of a tradesman and a gentlewoman, Quick-silver operates in the play as a prentice who affects the style of a gentleman and eschews "Labour" as a "Curse" (I.i, 3): "*footra* for dull Preferments of the City. I will to Court" (I.ii, 7). Like Head's Peregrine, he articulates the parasite's ethic: "Trades to live withal? No, I say, still let him that has Wit, live by his Wit; and he that has none, let him be a Tradesman" (II.ii, 17).

Thomas Jevon's *The Devil of a Wife; or, A Comical Transformation* (1686) also features, like *A Duke and No Duke,* a transformation of identities, in which a shrewish Cit-wife of a noble Country gentleman (the similarity to the Howard-Buckingham character of the name is not incidental, for this Sir Richard is portrayed as positively as the former) is tamed by being switched with a cobbler's wife and receiving appropriate beatings and humiliation. Her middle-class parsimoniousness is contrasted with the upper-class liberality of her husband, and a fiddler's comment about the joylessness of Sir Richard's hall can be read as a reminder, poignant in 1686, of what happened to the estate of England during one Puritan tyrannical reign. But the play is not just a comedy satirizing Puritan ungenerosity and hypocrisy (the lady has a chaplain named Noddy, who is stereotypically hypocritical and is administered a folk justice at the end as the servants beat him as if he were on a blacksmith's anvil), with a warning about the dangers of Country gentlemen marrying City wives to repair their estates. The comedian Jevon has created in his role of Jobson the cobbler a refreshingly crude Rabelaisian commoner, who not only administers discipline to the uppity wife (at the end of the play, when set up by Sir Richard with £500, Jobson promises not to beat his real wife again, and the lady forgives him for his beatings of her) but embodies a rollicking "true English heart" and considers "Drunkenness as the best part of the Liberty of the Subject" (I, 6). More important, Jevon creates in Jobson's wife Nell a peasant woman who exceeds Sir Richard's lady in a *natural* gentility: good temper, kind words, respect for servants and their holidays, real (Anglican) piety, *proper* deference toward her husband. Of course the cultural-constructedness of all this, serving to naturalize the feudal, patriarchal power relations, marks the play as not truly subversive but reactionary. Sir Richard's boast that "it has always been the Custome of my House to give my Servants Liberty in this Season, and all my Country Neighbours used to meet, and with their innocent Sports divert themselves" (8-9), in the face of his wife's antipastoralism, is another romanticizing of the harsh reality of Country life and lord-peasant relations.

10. FEMALE FOLK TRICKSTERS CLIMB ON TOP

1. Cohen interprets Lucy, like all clever servant tricksters, as an agent of "social conservatism" because she and they "do not seem to desire the kind of social change that would reward the likes of them and place them in control of the moral and intellectual nincompoops to whom they are obliged to defer. Instead, they help to sustain the inequity of their own positions. In so accepting and perpetuating their own inferior status, characters like Lucy are made to conform to an essentially conservative construction of a world where merit and ability are subordinated to birth and acquired social position" (13-14). Cohen seems to want such clever servants to be agents of (bourgeois) revolution. But they are tropes in a discourse that allows them at best parasite status, feeding off a system their playwright, at least in this instance, has revealed to be the lies Cohen has so well underscored in this fine article. Other clever servants in Restoration comedy marry up in the hierarchy, a movement that has overtones of bourgeois social mobility for the meritorious. But it is Richardson's Pamela who transcends the class barrier most signally as part of that finally triumphant bourgeois ethos.

Dover's *The Mall; or, The Modish Lovers* (1674) features several clever women servants, the wittiest and most mischievous being Peg. She is an excellent spy, eavesdropping on others' plots and foiling them in the interest of her mistress, Mrs. Easy, who has been forced into a marriage because neither she nor her gallant, Lovechange, could afford marriage together (although now she is doubly sorry, for Lovechange has come into money after all). She praises Mrs. Easy's wit in substituting Courtwell for Lovechange with Mrs. Woodbee: "Oh th Wit of Woman! [*sic*] Madam, I adore your contrivance" (II.ii [misnumbered iii], 28). But Peg is the prime agent in this sisterhood of subversion. Mrs. Easy leaves her in her clothes to fool her husband: "Ile trust thy management of the business, and thy Wit to deceive the old Man"—even as far as trusting her "Maiden-head" in bed with him, where it would remain "without danger." Peg's reply reveals her irrepressible puckishness: "I think [so], for any great massacre he has made of yours" (III.ii, 28-29). Hume's summary of the scene is misleading: "Peg (dressed as Mrs.

Easy while the lady gallivants) is bedded by Mr. Easy in that role—undressed on stage and hauled off, helpless" (298). Peg is far from helpless: she douses the light; Mrs. Easy, back from her assignation, resubstitutes for her in bed; Peg returns with a light, allowing Mrs. Easy to triumph over Mr. Easy, threatening divorce. When Peg sues for a reward, Mrs. Easy proclaims, "Thou, dear *Peg*, are Loves Matchivil, and deserv'st a Statue rear'd to thy memory for all honest discreet Maids to worship" (III.i, 38). The key word "honest" has been subversively reinterpreted, and the suggestion is that a typical resourceful and witty aristocratic woman, when abetted by a machiavellian woman servant, can successfully rebel against the hegemonic patriarchal code. Though the ending brings together in marriage another woman who has played a breeches part and her (temporarily) unfaithful lover (Camilla/Perigreen and Courtwell) and another romantic couple (Grace and Amorous), it also divorces the Easys and Woodbee and Lovechange in a fantasy of wife swapping. Easy's concluding tag implies that "Religion, and her Hosts of Vertues" no longer provide an adequate structure for the patriarchal superego to resist either the "pow'r of Love" (that is, unbridled desire) or the power of the new "gods Almighty," Easy's—or anyone's—"Guinneys" (V, 71). If the play be a Cit-cuckolding comedy (see above, ch. 5, n. 2), the agency is far less that of a Town wit or his witty woman than it is that of the women of the servant class.

2. Porter's *The French Conjurer* features another delightful such parasite. Sabina is identified in the dramatis personae as "servant to Claudio," but she is really a bawd, a Spanish procuress in the tradition of La Celestina, the most famous bawd in European literature, and her part of the play is positively Boccaccian. If Claudio's cuckolding of the goldsmith Cit, Pedro, makes this play fundamentally social comedy underwriting the ideology of the Cavalier as naturally dominant, Sabina's energy nevertheless demands separate consideration. She is so wittily attractive in the opening dialogue with Claudio that he comments aside to the audience, "This is the nimblest little Bawd I ever met with: Most of her profession are such heavie bundles of filth, that the very sight of the nauseous Caterer is enough to spoil a mans appetite to the Venison" (I, 3). Claudio is so taken with Sabina's plot to provide him access to the Cit's wife he promises her gold, and she responds, "Then fear not commanding what woman you please. Those Embassadours from *Peru* and *Mexico* negotiate more Love-affairs, than all the Ministers of *Cupid* put together" (I, 8). Sabina is a folk agent of subversion in that she subverts genealogy by supplanting Pedro's potential male heir with one of Claudio's. Like La Celestina, Sabina represents the marginal agent who provides for the surplus sexual energy of the ruling elite. Unlike La Celestina, Sabina suffers no poetic justice. If the play ends with one romantic couple marrying after overcoming blocking obstacles (Clorinia and Dorido), it also ends with one aggressive couple delighting in the illegitimate animal energy of adulterous sex even as they enact class dominance. This latter couple is abetted by a witty and attractive woman parasite, who, we trust, is amply rewarded for her services by those other, more consequential Spanish ambassadors from America.

3. Hume makes this same connection, arguing that the parts of Don John and 2 Cons were played by Charles Hart and Nell Gwyn, the actors who had es-

tablished the trope of the gay couple in Dryden's *Secret Love* and James Howard's *All Mistaken* (254).

4. Curiously, Pearson sees humanizing and issues of sexual inequality and injustice in this play, but only with regard to Pleasancet, the feisty but chaste heroine who lands Woodall in the end (50). In her section on prostitutes, she does not mention the play or any of these others I treat in this section (93-94).

5. Behn treats Lucetta, the lower-class whore in her social comedy *The Rover*, with sympathy too, but she is ultimately a less successful, less subversive trickster, for she is controlled by her pimp Sancho. If Aldo is a pimp, he is more benevolent, a compromiser, and Tricksy really does not need him for her final trick. Defoe will replace the benevolent father pimp with Mother Midnight.

6. A late example of this subversion of class is Behn's eponymous heroine of the comitragedy *The Widow Ranter; or, The History of Bacon in Virginia* (1689), the tobacco-smoking, swearing, hard-drinking, transported woman bully, who marries up into transplanted gentry.

7. For the biographical information, see Bernbaum, 1. For her playing herself, see Bernbaum, 2 and 26, where he cites Pepys and Genest as his authorities (n. 3).

8. How Hume can see the concluding dance of Cicco and Strega as "sardonic brutality" is beyond me (298).

PART 3 INTRODUCTION

1. Zimbardo treats virtually all 1670s comedies as satires in *A Mirror to Nature*, ch. 4; in a series of recent articles, she has begun to treat virtually all Restoration literature as what I call absurdist satire, referential to nothing. For Brown, see *English Dramatic Form*, ch. 2.

2. See my reading of the play in "Poetical Injustice," 23-28.

3. Other examples from the 1670s include Shadwell's *Timon of Athens* and all of Otway's other tragedies. For the latter, see my "Thomas Otway." For extended readings of *The Princess of Cleve* and *Venice Preserv'd*, see my "Poetical Injustice," 28-36, and *Word as Bond*, 300-310, respectively.

II. TRICKSTERS SCOURGE AND GET SCOURGED

1. Wheatley, "Durfey's Adaptations," also sees the ending, in contrast with Fletcher's, as problematic, certainly unconventional, and with no closure.

2. Alssid sees Sir Humphrey's father as having been too restrictive, thereby producing the opposite from his desired result (87). Perhaps, but Scattergood Senior is not the antithesis to Sir Humphrey, Gripe is. I think Alssid reads too much of *The Squire of Alsatia*, where such an educational theme is undeniable, back into *The Woman-Captain*.

3. Alssid correctly associates Phillis with a satirical "leveling" theme (87), but Pearson reads Phillis's role as scourge too misogynistically, as if she represents "the

dangers to men and to male order when women are allowed to take control" (108). Sir Humphrey blames his own lack of prudence rather than Phillis's greed.

4. Hume assesses this play as "little more than a straight farce . . . definitely light-weight" (333). Rothstein and Kavenik assert that "*The Woman-Captain* makes no moral point" (232). Wheatley sees its morality as "merely prudential" and interprets the courting of the woman captain by the whores thus: "[I]n a strictly materialist, hedonist, and prudentialist moral world, the unnatural becomes the natural" (*Without God*, 140). I think once we view the play as a satire, these misreadings evaporate. One final note: the repeated kisses between the women could possibly be interpreted as suggesting that only a world *between women* can truly transcend the evils of patriarchy. But then, like lesbian pornography in magazines for men, those kisses, designed by a male playwright, may only have been intended as titillation *between men*.

5. Coakley has done a nice job of interpreting the play in the light of these intricacies (91-94). See also Nadler for a good review of these materials anent another Behn play, the tragicomedy *The Town Fop*.

6. Gallagher's argument about this play is based on an interpretation that Julia is concealing how much she enjoyed the difference. Such a reading may enhance Gallagher's portrait of Behn as masked playwright, but it trivializes Julia's entire stance in the play with regard to her personal virtue. As the woman who has confessed even to her husband her love for a gallant, she is not the type to be "hiding" anything (41). But at least Gallagher does not trivialize the entire play, as does Hume: "For the most part, *The Lucky Chance* is a cheerful city marriage farce, full of tricks, intrigue, and mock ghosts" (369).

7. Wheatley, "Durfey's Adaptations," notes that Durfey has altered Fletcher's ending in order to give the play a different, conservative moral—though he does not discuss the play as a satire per se. Hume sees the "repentance" and "morality" at the end as "exaggerated" and "ridiculous" (371). Perhaps Aurelia's conversion is unconvincing, but that does not discredit the morality as ridiculous, especially if one adjusts the generic frame. Viewed as a satire, the play's morality has been there all along and the poetic justice of the ending marks vice and folly as scourged.

12. Tricksters Get Blown about by the Wind

1. In the "second impression" of the play in 1661, Tatham made an imperfect transition from *à clef* names for these generals (e.g. Bertlam for Lambert). For clarity's sake, I have simply used the historical names supplied in the 1661 edition.

2. Garrison reads the play as portraying a world void of justice and faith. As such, our readings dovetail, though I hope mine comes in at an angle sufficiently different to supplement his. See also Milhous and Hume's appreciative reading of the play as satire (ch. 7), following Garrison. For recent interpretations that read out further political implications, see Bywaters, 56-74 (who, in identifying Phaedra and not Alcmena with England itself, misses an opportunity) and Cordner xxxi-xl.

Conclusion

1. Staves treats Crowne's play as merely "anti-Catholic" (*Players Scepters*, 92) and thus misses an opportunity to interpret its oppositional, bourgeois ideology. On the other hand, she nicely treats some of the tropes of that ideology as they come to dominate Shadwell's later plays (308-13). Smith long ago cited these plays as signs of something new (ch. 6), the seeds of which he saw in earlier drama (ch. 5). The benevolence he sees in earlier characters, however, seems to me to be a sign of aristocratic generosity. Shadwell's or Crowne's sermonizing man of sense seems a figure in a different tapestry.

2. To their credit Schneider, Corman, and Burns have not entirely done so. Burns's and my approach differ so much, however, that I have had no occasion to cite him throughout. He steadfastly eschews sociological interpretation, to the extent that he denies political meaning even to a play like Crowne's *City Politiques*, which he calls "no more political than *Duck Soup*" (104)!

Bibliography

EDITIONS OF RESTORATION COMEDIES CITED

Anonymous. *The Counterfeit Bridegroom; or, The Defeated Widow*. London, 1677.
———. *The Factious Citizen; or, The Melancholy Visioner*. London, 1685. [Originally, *Mr. Turbulent; or, The Melanchollicks* 1682.]
———. *Knavery in All Trades; or, The Coffee-House*. London, 1664.
———. *The Mistaken Husband*. London, 1675.
———. *The Rampant Alderman; or, News from the Exchange*. London, 1685.
———. *The Woman Turn'd Bully*. London, 1675.
[Arrowsmith, Joseph.] *The Reformation*. 1673. Intro. Deborah C. Payne. Augustan Reprint Society, 237-38. Los Angeles: Clark Library, 1986.
Behn, Aphra. *The City Heiress; or, Sir Timothy Treat-All*. *The Works of Aphra Behn*, 7:1-77. Ed. Janet Todd. Vols. 5-7: *The Plays*. Columbus: Ohio State Univ. Press, 1996.
[———]. *The Debauchee; or, The Credulous Cuckold*. *Works*, 5:387-443.
———. *The False Count; or, A New Way to Play an Old Game*. *Works*, 6:299-356.
———. *The Feign'd Curtizans; or, A Nights Intrigue*. *Works*, 6:83-159.
———. *The Luckey Chance; or, An Alderman's Bargain*. *Works*, 7:209-84.
———. *The Roundheads; or, The Good Old Cause*. *Works*, 6:357-424.
———. *The Rover; or, The Banish't Cavaliers*. *Works*, 5:447-521.
———. *The Second Part of the Rover*. *Works*, 6:223-98.
———. *Sir Patient Fancy*. *Works*, 6:1-81.
B[elon], P[eter]. *The Mock-Duellist; or, The French Vallet*. London, 1675.
Betterton, Thomas. *The Amorous Widow; or, The Wanton Wife . . . Now First Printed from the Original Copy*. Appended to Charles Gildon, *The Life of Mr. Thomas Betterton, the Late Eminent Tragedian*. 1710. Reprint with a new preface by Arthur Freeman. Eighteenth-century Shakespeare, no. 4. Gen. ed. Arthur Freeman. London: Frank Cass, 1970.
Carlile, James. *The Fortune-Hunters; or, Two Fools Well Met*. London, 1689.
Caryll, John. *Sir Salomon; or, The Cautious Coxcomb*. London, 1671.
Crowne, John. *City Politiques*. Ed. John Harold Wilson. Lincoln: Bison–Univ. of Nebraska Press, 1967.
———. *The Country Wit*. *The Comedies of John Crowne: A Critical Edition*, 1-158. Ed. B.J. McMullin. The Renaissance Imagination. Gen. ed. Stephen Orgel. New York: Garland, 1984.
———. *The English Frier; or, The Town Sparks*. *Comedies*, 481-616.
———. *Sir Courtly Nice; or, It Cannot Be*. *Comedies*, 331-480.

D[over], J[ohn]. *The Mall; or, The Modish Lovers.* London, 1674.

Dryden, John. *Amphitryon; or, The Two Sosias. The Works of John Dryden.* California edition, 5:221-318. Ed. Earl Miner, George R. Guffey, and Franklin B. Zimmerman. Berkeley and Los Angeles: Univ. of California Press, 1976.

———. *The Assignation; or, Love in a Nunnery.* California edition, 11:317-415. Ed. John Loftis, David Stuart Rodes, and Vinton A. Dearing. Berkeley and Los Angeles: Univ. of California Press, 1978.

———. *An Evening's Love; or, The Mock-Astrologer.* California edition, 10:195-314. Ed. Maximillian E. Novak and George Guffey. Berkeley and Los Angeles: Univ. of California Press, 1970.

———. *The Kind Keeper; or, Mr. Limberham.* California edition, 14:1-95. Ed. Vinton Dearing and Alan Roper. Berkeley and Los Angeles: Univ. of California Press, 1992.

———. *Sir Martin Mar-all; or, The Feigned Innocence.* California edition, 9:205-89. Ed. John Loftis and Vinton A. Dearing. Berkeley and Los Angeles: Univ. of California Press, 1966.

———. *The Wild Gallant.* California edition, 8:1-91. Ed. John Harrington Smith, Dougald MacMillan, and Vinton A. Dearing. Berkeley and Los Angeles: Univ. of California Press, 1965.

Durfey, Thomas. *A Fond Husband; or, The Plotting Sisters. Two Comedies by Thomas D'Urfey,* 145-259. Ed. Jack A. Vaughn. Rutherford, N.J.: Fairleigh Dickinson Univ. Press, 1976.

———. *The Fool Turn'd Critick.* London, 1678.

———. *A Fool's Preferment; or, The Three Dukes of Dunstable.* Part 2 of *A Study of the Plays of Thomas D'Urfey with a Reprint of "A Fool's Preferment."* Ed. Robert Stanley Forsythe. *Western Reserve University Bulletins (Literary Section Supplements)* 19, n. 5 (May 1916) and 20, n. 5 (1917).

———. *Madam Fickle; or, The Witty False One. Two Comedies,* 34-143.

———. *The Royalist.* London, 1682.

———. *Sir Barnaby Whigg; or, No Wit Like a Womans.* London, 1681.

———. *Squire Oldsapp; or, The Night-Adventurers.* London, 1679.

———. *Trick for Trick; or, The Debauch'd Hypocrite.* London, 1678.

———. *The Virtuous Wife; or, Good Luck at Last.* London, 1680.

Etherege, Sir George. *The Man of Mode[; or, Sir Fopling Flutter].* Ed. W.B. Carnochan. Regents Restoration Drama Series. Lincoln: Bison–Univ. of Nebraska Press, 1966.

———. *She Wou'd if She Cou'd. The Dramatic Works of Sir George Etherege,* 2:89-179. Ed. H.F.B. Brett-Smith. 2 vols. 1927. Reprint. St. Clair Shores, Mich.: Scholarly Press, 1971.

Fane, Francis. *Love in the Dark; or, The Man of Bus'ness.* [London], 1675.

Head, Richard. *Hic et Ubique; or, The Humors of Dublin.* London, 1663.

Howard, James. *The English Mounsieur.* 1674. Intro. Robert D. Hume. Augustan Reprint Society, nos. 182-183. Los Angeles: Clark Library, 1977.

Howard, Sir Robert. *The Committee. Four New Plays,* 67-134. London, 1665.

———. Howard, Sir Robert, and George Villiers, second duke of Buckingham. *The Country Gentleman: A "Lost Play" and Its Background.* Ed. Arthur H. Scouten and Robert D. Hume. Philadelphia: Univ. of Pennsylvania Press, 1976.

[Jevon, Thomas.] *The Devil of a Wife; or, A Comical Transformation.* London, 1686.

Killigrew, Sir William. *Pandora.* London, 1664.

Lacy, John. *The Dumb Lady; or, The Farriar Made Physician.* London, 1672.

———. *The Old Troop; or, Monsieur Raggou.* London, [1672].

———. *Sauny the Scott; or, The Taming of the Shrew.* . . . *[N]ever before printed.* London, 1698.

[Leanerd, John.] *The Rambling Justice; or, The Jealous Husbands. With the Humours of Sir John Twiford.* London, 1678.

Nevil[l]e, Robert. *The Poor Scholar.* London, 1662.

Newcastle, William Cavendish, duke of. *The Humorous Lovers.* London, 1677.

———. *The Triumphant Widow; or, The Medley of Humours.* London, 1677.

Orrery, Roger Boyle, earl of. *Mr. Anthony. The Dramatic Works of Roger Boyle, Earl of Orrery,* 2:514-84. Ed. William Smith Clark II. 2 vols. Cambridge, Mass.: Harvard Univ. Press, 1937.

———. *Guzman. Dramatic Works.* 1:437-513.

Otway, Thomas. *The Atheist; or, The Second Part of the Souldiers Fortune. The Works of Thomas Otway,* 2:291-399. Ed. J.C. Ghosh. 2 vols. 1932. Reprint. Oxford: Clarendon, 1968.

———. *Friendship in Fashion. Works,* 1:331-432.

———. *The Souldiers Fortune. Works,* 2:89-196.

[Payne, Henry Neville.] *The Morning Ramble; or, The Town-Humours.* London, 1673.

Polwhele, Elizabeth. *The Frolicks; or, The Lawyer Cheated (1671).* Ed. Judith Milhous and Robert D. Hume. Ithaca, N.Y.: Cornell Univ. Press, 1977.

Porter, Thomas. *The Carnival.* London, 1664.

———. *The French Conjurer.* London, 1678.

[———]. *A Witty Combat; or, The Female Victor.* London, 1663.

Ravenscroft, Edward. *The Careless Lovers. Edward Ravenscroft's "The Careless Lovers" and "The Canterbury Guests": A Critical Old-Spelling Edition,* 1-209. Ed. Edmund S. Henry. Satire and Sense. Gen. ed. Stephen Orgel. New York: Garland, 1987.

———. *Dame Dobson; or, The Cunning Woman.* London, 1684.

———. *The London Cuckolds.* 1682. *Restoration Comedy,* 2:435-551. Ed. A. Norman Jeffares. 4 vols. London: Folio, 1974.

———. *The Wrangling Lovers; or, The Invisible Mistress.* London, 1677.

[Rawlins, Tom]. *Tom Essence; or, The Modish Wife.* London, 1677.

[———]. *Tunbridge Wells; or, A Days Courtship.* London, 1678.

[Revet, Edward]. *The Town Shifts; or, The Suburb-Justice.* London, 1671.

[Rhodes, Richard.] *Flora's Vagaries.* London, 1670.

Sedley, Sir Charles. *Bellamira; or, The Mistress. The Poetical and Dramatic Works of Sir Charles Sedley,* 2:1-97. Ed. V[ivian] de Sola Pinto. 2 vols. London: Constable, 1928.

St. Serfe [Sydserff, Sir] Thomas. *Tarugo's Wiles; or, The Coffee-House.* London, 1668.

Shadwell, Thomas. *Epsom Wells. The Complete Works of Thomas Shadwell,* 2:

95-182. Ed. Montague Summers. 5 vols. 1927. Reprint. New York: Benjamin Blom, 1968.

———. *The Humorists. Complete Works,* 1:175-255.

———. *The Sullen Lovers; or, The Impertinents. Complete Works,* 1:1-92.

———. *A True Widow. Complete Works.* 3:277-363.

———. *The Virtuoso.* Ed. Marjorie Hope Nicolson and David Stuart Rodes. Regents Restoration Drama Series. Lincoln: Bison–Univ. of Nebraska Press, 1966.

———. *The Woman-Captain. Thomas Shadwell's "The Woman Captain": A Critical Old-Spelling Edition.* Ed. Judith Bailey Slagle. Intro. Jack M. Armistead. The Renaissance Imagination. Gen. ed. Stephen Orgel. New York: Garland, 1993.

Southerne, Thomas. *Sir Anthony Love; or, The Rambling Lady. The Works of Thomas Southerne,* 1:157-257. Ed. Robert Jordan and Harold Love. 2 vols. Oxford: Clarendon, 1988.

[Southland, Thomas.] *Love a la Mode.* London, 1663.

Tate, N[ahum]. *Cuckolds-Haven; or, An Alderman No Conjurer.* London, 1685.

———. *A Duke and No Duke.* London, 1685.

Tatham, J[ohn]. *The Rump; or, The Mirrour of the Late Times.* London, 1660.

———. *The Rump; or, The Mirrour of the Late Times.* Second Impression, Newly Corrected, with Additions. London, 1661.

T[hom(p)son], T[homas]. *The English Rogue.* London, 1668.

———. *The Life of Mother Shipton* London: n.d.

Wilson, John. *The Cheats.* London, 1664.

———. *The Projectors.* London, 1664.

Wycherley, William. *The Country-Wife. The Complete Plays of William Wycherley,* 251-371. Ed. Gerald Weales. Garden City, N.Y.: Anchor-Doubleday, 1966.

———. *The Gentleman Dancing-Master. Complete Plays,* 125-249.

———. *Love in a Wood; or, St James's Park. Complete Plays,* 1-124.

———. *The Plain Dealer. Complete Plays,* 373-534.

EDITIONS OF RESTORATION TRAGICOMEDIES TREATED

[Behn, Aphra]. *The Revenge; or, A Match in Newgate. Works,* 6:161-222.

———. *The Widow Ranter; or, The History of Bacon in Virginia. Works,* 7:285-354.

[Buckingham, George Villiers, duke of.] *The Chances.* London, 1682.

Cowley, Abraham. *A Critical Edition of Abraham Cowley's "Cutter of Coleman Street."* Ed. Darlene Johnson Gravett. The Renaissance Imagination. Gen. ed. Stephen Orgel. New York: Garland, 1987.

Dryden, John. *Marriage A-la-Mode.* California edition, 11:219-316. Ed. John Loftis, David Stuart Rodes, Vinton A. Dearing et al. Berkeley and Los Angeles: Univ. of California Press, 1978.

———. *The Spanish Fryar, or, The Double Discovery.* California edition, 14:97-203.

Ed. Vinton Dearing and Alan Roper. Berkeley and Los Angeles: Univ. of California Press, 1992.

[Duffett, Thomas.] *The Amorous Old-woman; or, 'Tis Well If It Take.* London, 1674.

Howard, James. *All Mistaken; or, The Mad Couple.* London, 1672.

Lacy, John. *Sir Hercules Buffoon; or, The Poetical Squire.* London, 1684.

Lee, Nathaniel. *The Princess of Cleve. The Works of Nathaniel Lee,* 2:147-227. Ed. Thomas B. Stroup and Arthur L. Cooke. 2 vols. 1955. Reprint. Metuchen, N.J.: Scarecrow, 1968.

Maidwell, L[ewis]. *The Loving Enemies.* London, 1680.

Ravenscroft, Edward. *The English Lawyer.* London, 1678.

OTHER WORKS TREATED

Adams, Percy G. "What Happened in Olivia's Bedroom? Or Ambiguity in *The Plain-Dealer.*" *Essays in Honor of Esmond Marilla,* 174-87. Ed. Thomas Austin Kirby and William John Oliver. Baton Rouge: Louisiana State Univ. Press, 1971.

Alssid, Michael. *Thomas Shadwell.* Twayne's English Authors Series 50. New York: Twayne, 1967.

Armistead, J.M. *Four Restoration Playwrights: A Reference Guide to Thomas Shadwell, Aphra Behn, Nathaniel Lee, and Thomas Otway.* Boston: G.K. Hall, 1984.

Backscheider, Paula R. *Spectacular Politics: Theatrical Power and Mass Culture in Early Modern England.* Baltimore: Johns Hopkins Univ. Press, 1993.

Bacon, Jon Lance. "Wives, Widows, and Writings in Restoration Comedy." *Studies in English Literature* 31 (1991): 427-43.

Bakhtin, Mikhail. *Problems of Dostoevsky's Poetics.* Ed. and trans. Caryl Emerson. Intro. Wayne C. Booth. Theory of History and Literature, 8. Minneapolis: Univ. of Minnesota Press, 1984.

———. *Rabelais and His World.* Trans. Hélène Iswolsky. 1968. Reprint. Bloomington: Indiana Univ. Press, 1984.

Beebee, Thomas O. *The Ideology of Genre: A Comparative Study of Generic Instability.* University Park: Pennsylvania State Univ. Press, 1994.

Bernbaum, Ernest. *The Mary Carleton Narratives 1663-1673: A Missing Chapter in the History of the English Novel.* Cambridge, Mass.: Harvard Univ. Press, 1914.

Bode, Robert F. "A Rape and No Rape: Olivia's Bedroom Revisited." *Restoration: Studies in English Literary Culture, 1660-1700* 12 (1988): 80-86.

Braverman, Richard. "Libertines and Parasites." *Restoration: Studies in English Literary Culture, 1660-1700* 11 (1987): 73-86.

———. "The Rake's Progress Revisited: Politics and Comedy in the Restoration." In *Cultural Readings of Restoration and Eighteenth-Century Theater,* ed. J. Douglas Canfield and Deborah C. Payne, 141-68. Athens: Univ. of Georgia Press, 1995.

Brown, Laura. *English Dramatic Form, 1660-1760: An Essay in Generic History.* New Haven, Conn.: Yale Univ. Press, 1981.

Burke, Helen. "'Law-suits,' 'Love-suits,' and the Family Property in Wycherley's *The Plain Dealer.*" In *Cultural Readings of Restoration and Eighteenth-Century Theater,* ed. J. Douglas Canfield and Deborah C. Payne, 89-113. Athens: Univ. of Georgia Press, 1995.

———. "Wycherley's 'Tendentious Joke': The Discourse of Alterity in *The Country Wife.*" *The Eighteenth Century: Theory and Interpretation* 29 (1988): 227-41.

Burns, Edward. *Restoration Comedy: Crises of Desire and Identity.* London: Macmillan, 1987.

Bywaters, David. *Dryden in Revolutionary England.* Berkeley and Los Angeles: Univ. of California Press, 1991.

Campbell, Oscar James. *Comicall Satyre and Shakespeare's Troilus and Cressida.* San Marino, Calif.: Huntington Library and Art Gallery, 1938.

Canfield, J. Douglas. "The Critique of Capitalism and the Retreat into Art in Gay's *Beggar's Opera* and Fielding's *Author's Farce.*" In *Cutting Edges: Postmodern Critical Essays on Eighteenth-Century Satire,* ed. James E. Gill, 320-34. Knoxville: Univ. of Tennessee Press,1995.

———. "Dramatic Shifts: Writing an Ideological History of Late Stuart Drama." *Restoration and 18th Century Theatre Research* 2d ser., 6 (1991): 1-9.

———. "Female Rebels and Patriarchal Paradigms in Some Neoclassical Works." *Studies in Eighteenth-Century Culture* 18 (1988): 153-66.

———. "The Ideology of Restoration Tragicomedy." *ELH: A Journal of English Literary History* 51 (1984): 447-64.

———. "Poetical Injustice in Some Neglected Masterpieces of Restoration Drama." In *Rhetorics of Order/Ordering Rhetorics in English Neoclassical Literature,* ed. Canfield and J. Paul Hunter, 23-45. Newark: Univ. of Delaware Press, 1989.

———. "*Regulus* and *Cleomenes* and 1688: From Royalism to Self-Reliance." In *English Culture at the End of the Seventeenth Century,* ed. Robert P. Maccubin and David F. Morrill. Special issue of *Eighteenth-Century Life* 12 (1988): 67-75.

———. "Royalism's Last Dramatic Stand: English Political Tragedy, 1679-1689." *Studies in Philology* 82 (1985): 234-63.

———. "Shifting Tropes of Ideology in English Serious Drama, Late Stuart to Early Georgian." In *Cultural Readings of Restoration and Eighteenth-Century Theater,* ed. Canfield and Deborah C. Payne, 195-227. Athens: Univ. of Georgia Press, 1995.

———. "The Significance of the Restoration Rhymed Heroic Play." *Eighteenth-Century Studies* 13 (1979): 49-62.

———. "Thomas Otway." In *Dictionary of Literary Biography,* vol. 80, *Restoration and Eighteenth-Century Dramatists, First Series,* ed. Paula Backscheider, 146-71. Detroit: Bruccoli Clark Layman–Gale, 1989.

———. *Word as Bond in English Literature from the Middle Ages to the Restoration.* Philadelphia: Univ. of Pennsylvania Press, 1989.

———, and Deborah C. Payne, eds. *Cultural Readings of Restoration and Eighteenth-Century Theater.* Athens: Univ. of Georgia Press, 1995.

Coakley, Jean A, ed. *Aphra Behn's "The Luckey Chance" (1687): A Critical Edition.* Satire and Sense. Gen. ed. Stephen Orgel. New York: Garland, 1987.

Cohen, Derek. "*The Country Wife* and Social Danger." *Restoration and 18th Century Theatre Research* 2d ser., 10 (1995): 1-14.

Coleman, Anthony. "Shadwell's 'Country Hero.'" *Notes & Queries* 216 (1971): 459-60.

Connery, Brian A., and Kirk Combe, eds. *Theorizing Satire: Essays in Literary Criticism.* New York: St. Martin's Press, 1995.

Cope, Jackson I. *Dramaturgy of the Daemonic: Studies in Antigeneric Theater from Ruzante to Grimaldi.* Baltimore: Johns Hopkins Univ. Press, 1984.

Copeland, Nancy. "'Who Can . . . Her Own Wish Deny?': Female Conduct and Politics in Aphra Behn's *The City Heiress.*" *Restoration and 18th Century Theatre Research* 2d ser., 8 (1993): 27-49.

Cordner, Michael. Introduction to *Four Restoration Marriage Plays,* ed. Cordner with Ronald Clayton. Oxford: Oxford Univ. Press, 1995.

Corman, Brian. *Genre and Generic Change in English Comedy, 1660-1710.* Toronto: Univ. of Toronto Press, 1993.

Derrida, Jacques. *Of Grammatology.* Trans. Gayatri Chakravorty Spivak. Baltimore: Johns Hopkins Univ. Press, 1976.

Drakulic, Slavenka. "The Rape of Bosnia-Herzegovina." *Arizona Daily Star,* 16 December 1992, A17. Copyright *New York Times.*

Flores, Stephan. "Negotiating Cultural Prerogatives in Dryden's *Secret Love* and *Sir Martin Mar-all.*" *Papers on Language and Literature* 29 (1993): 170-96.

Forsythe, Robert Stanley. *A Study of the Plays of Thomas D'Urfey with a Reprint of "A Fool's Preferment."* 2 parts. *Western Reserve University Bulletins (Literary Section Supplements)* 19, n. 5 (May 1916) and 20, n. 5 (1917).

Foster, R.F. *Modern Ireland, 1600-1972.* Harmondsworth, England: Allen Lane-Penguin, 1988.

Foucault, Michel. *Discipline and Punish: The Birth of the Prison.* Trans. Alan Sheridan. 1977. Reprint. New York: Vintage, 1979.

———. *Power/Knowledge: Selected Interviews and Other Writings, 1972-1977.* Ed. Colin Gordon. Trans. Colin Gordon, Leo Marshall, John Mepham, and Kate Soper. New York: Pantheon, 1980.

Freehafer, John. "The Formation of the London Patent Companies in 1660." *Theatre Notebook* 20 (1965): 6-30.

Gagen, Jean Elisabeth. *The New Woman: Her Emergence in English Drama 1600-1730.* New York: Twayne, 1954.

Gallagher, Catherine. "Who was that masked woman? The prostitute and the playwright in the comedies of Aphra Behn." In *Last Laughs: Perspectives on Women and Comedy,* ed. Regina Barreca. Special issue of *Women's Studies* 15 (1988): 23-42.

Garrison, James D. "Dryden and the Birth of Hercules." *Studies in Philology* 77 (1980): 180-201.

Gill, James E., ed. *Cutting Edges: Postmodern Critical Essays on Eighteenth-Century Satire*. Tennessee Studies in Literature 37. Knoxville: Univ. of Tennessee Press, 1995.

Gill, Pat. *Interpreting Ladies: Women, Wit, and Morality in the Restoration Comedy of Manners*. Athens: Univ. of Georgia Press, 1994.

Griffin, Dustin. *Satire: A Critical Reintroduction*. Lexington: Univ. Press of Kentucky, 1994.

Gutleben, Christian. "English Academic Satire from the Middle Ages to Postmodernism: Distinguishing the Comic from the Satiric." In *Theorizing Satire: Essays in Literary Criticism*, ed. Brian A. Connery and Kirke Combe, 133-47. New York: St. Martin's Press, 1995.

Harwood, John T. *Critics, Values, and Restoration Comedy*. Carbondale: Southern Illinois Univ. Press, 1982.

Hersey, William R., ed. *A Critical Old-Spelling Edition of Aphra Behn's The City Heiress*. Satire and Sense. Gen. ed. Stephen Orgel. New York: Garland, 1987.

Hill, Christopher. *The Century of Revolution, 1603-1714*. The Norton Library History of England. New York: Norton, 1961.

Hinnant, Charles H. "Pleasure and the Political Economy of Consumption in Restoration Comedy." *Restoration: Studies in English Literary Culture, 1660-1700* 19 (1995): 77-87.

Holland, Peter. *The Ornament of Action: Text and Performance in Restoration Comedy*. Cambridge: Cambridge Univ. Press, 1979.

Homer. *The Iliad of Homer*. Trans. Richmond Lattimore. 1951. Reprint. Chicago: Phoenix–Univ. of Chicago Press, 1961.

Hughes, Derek. "Play and Passion in *The Man of Mode*." *Comparative Drama* 15 (1981): 231-57.

Hughes, Leo. *A Century of English Farce*. Princeton: Princeton Univ. Press, 1956.

Hume, Robert D. *The Development of English Drama in the Late Seventeenth Century*. Oxford: Clarendon, 1976.

Hutner, Heidi. "Revisioning the Female Body: Aphra Behn's *The Rover*, Parts I and II." In *Rereading Aphra Behn: History, Theory, and Criticism*, ed. Hutner, 102-20. Charlottesville: Univ. Press of Virginia, 1993.

———, ed. *Rereading Aphra Behn: History, Theory, and Criticism*. Charlottesville: Univ. Press of Virginia, 1993.

Jameson, Fredric. *The Political Unconscious: Narrative as a Socially Symbolic Act*. Ithaca, N.Y.: Cornell Univ. Press, 1981.

Jordan, Robert. "The Extravagant Rake in Restoration Comedy." In *Restoration Literature: Critical Approaches*, ed. Harold Love, 69-90. London: Methuen, 1972.

Kephart, Carolyn. "An Unnoticed Forerunner of 'The Beggar's Opera.'" *Music and Letters* 61 (1980): 266-71.

Kernan, Alvin B. *The Cankered Muse*. Yale Studies in English 142. New Haven, Conn.: Yale Univ. Press, 1959.

———. *The Plot of Satire*. New Haven, Conn.: Yale Univ. Press, 1965.

Kubek, Elizabeth Bennett. "Night Mares of the Commonwealth: Royalist Passion and Female Ambition in Aphra Behn's *The Roundheads.*" *Restoration: Studies in English Literary Culture, 1660-1700* 17 (1993): 88-103.

Kuhn, Thomas. *The Structure of Scientific Revolutions.* 2d ed. Chicago: Univ. of Chicago Press, 1970.

Kunz, Don R. *The Drama of Thomas Shadwell.* Salzburg Studies in English Literature: Poetic Drama 16. 2 vols. Salzburg: Institut für Englische Sprache und Literatur, Universität Salzburg, 1972.

Lévi-Strauss, Claude. "The Structural Study of Myth." Trans. Claire Jacobson. 1963. Reprinted in *European Literary Theory and Practice: From Existential Phenomenology to Structuralism,* ed. Vernon W. Gras, 289-316. New York: Delta-Dell, 1973.

Markley, Robert. "'Be impudent, be saucy, forward, bold, touzing, and leud': The Politics of Masculine Sexuality and Feminine Desire in Behn's Tory Comedies." In *Cultural Readings of Restoration and Eighteenth-Century Theater,* ed. J. Douglas Canfield and Deborah C. Payne, 114-40. Athens: Univ. of Georgia Press, 1995.

———. *Two-Edg'd Weapons: Style and Ideology in the Comedies of Etherege, Wycherley, and Congreve.* Oxford: Clarendon, 1988.

———, and Molly Rothenberg. "Contestations of Nature: Aphra Behn's 'The Golden Age' and the Sexualizing of Politics." In *Rereading Aphra Behn: History, Theory, and Criticism,* ed. Heidi Hutner, 301-21. Charlottesville: Univ. Press of Virginia, 1993.

McDonald, Margaret Lamb. *The Independent Woman in the Restoration Comedy of Manners.* Salzburg Studies in English Literature: Poetic Drama and Poetic Theory 32. Ed. James Hogg. Salzburg: Institut für Englische Sprache und Literatur, Universität Salzburg, 1976.

McKeon, Michael. *The Origins of the English Novel 1600-1740.* Baltimore: Johns Hopkins Univ. Press, 1987.

Milhous, Judith, and Robert D. Hume *Producible Interpretations: Eight English Plays 1675-1707.* Carbondale: Southern Illinois Univ. Press, 1985.

Munns, Jessica. *Restoration Politics and Drama: The Plays of Thomas Otway, 1675-1683.* Newark: Univ. of Delaware Press, 1995.

Nadler, Sheryl. "Aphra Behn's Conflicted View of Marriage in *The Town Fop.*" *Restoration and 18th Century Theatre Research* 2d ser. 9 (1994): 34-50.

Nicoll, Allardyce. *A History of English Drama, 1660-1900.* Vol. 1, *Restoration Drama, 1660-1700.* 4th ed. Cambridge: Cambridge Univ. Press, 1952.

Nixon, Cheryl L. "Creating the Text of Guardianship: 12 Car. II.c.24 and *Cutter of Coleman Street.*" *Restoration: Studies in English Literary Culture, 1660-1700* 19 (1995): 1-28.

Novak, Maximillian E. "Margery Pinchwife's 'London Disease': Restoration Comedy and the Libertine Offensive of the 1670's." In *Studies in Restoration and Eighteenth-Century Drama,* ed. C.R. Kropf. Special issue of *Studies in the Literary Imagination* 10 (1977): 1-23.

Owen, Susan J. "'Suspect my loyalty when I lose my virtue': Sexual Politics and Party in Aphra Behn's Plays of the Exclusion Crisis, 1678-83." *Restoration:*

Studies in English Literary Culture, 1660-1700 18 (1994): 37-47.

Payne, Deborah C. "Comedy, Satire, or Farce? Or the Generic Difficulties of Restoration Dramatic Satire." In *Cutting Edges: Postmodern Critical Essays on Eighteenth-Century Satire*, ed. James E. Gill, 1-22. Knoxville: Univ. of Tennessee Press, 1995.

Pearson, Jacqueline. *The Prostituted Muse: Images of Women & Women Dramatists 1642-1737.* London: Harvester, 1988.

Perkinson, Richard H. "Topographical Comedy in the Seventeenth Century." *ELH: A Journal of English Literary History* 3 (1936): 270-90.

The Revels History of Drama in English. Vol. 5, *1660-1750.* Ed. John Loftis, Richard Southern, Marion Jones, and A.H. Scouten. London: Methuen, 1976.

Rothstein, Eric, and Frances M. Kavenik. *The Designs of Carolean Comedy.* Carbondale: Southern Illinois Univ. Press, 1988.

Rubin, Gayle. "The Traffic in Women: Notes on the 'Political Economy' of Sex." In *Toward an Anthropology of Women,* ed. Rayna R. Reiter, 157-210. New York: Monthly Review Press, 1975.

Schneider, Ben Ross, Jr. *The Ethos of Restoration Comedy.* Urbana: Univ. of Illinois Press, 1971.

Scott, Virgil Joseph. "A Reinterpretation of John Tatham's *The Rump: or The Mirrour of the Late Times.*" Philological Quarterly 24 (1945): 114-18.

Sedgwick, Eve Kosofsky. *Between Men: English Literature and Male Homosocial Desire.* New York: Columbia Univ. Press, 1985.

———. "Sexualism and the Citizen of the World: Wycherley, Sterne, and Male Homosocial Desire." *Critical Inquiry* 11 (1984): 226-45.

Shinagel, Michael. Introduction to *The English Rogue,* by Richard Head. Boston: New Frontiers, 1961.

Smith, John Harrington. *The Gay Couple in Restoration Comedy.* Cambridge, Mass.: Harvard Univ. Press, 1948.

Spencer, Jane. "'Deceit, Dissembling, all that's Woman': Comic Plot and Female Action in *The Feigned Courtesans.*" In *Rereading Aphra Behn: History, Theory, and Criticism,* ed. Heidi Hutner, 86-101. Charlottesville: Univ. Press of Virginia, 1993.

Stallybrass, Peter, and Allon White. *The Politics and Poetics of Transgression.* London: Methuen; Ithaca, N.Y.: Cornell Univ. Press, 1986.

Staves, Susan. *Married Women's Separate Property in England, 1660-1833.* Cambridge, Mass.: Harvard Univ. Press, 1990.

———. *Players' Scepters: Fictions of Authority in the Restoration.* Lincoln: Univ. of Nebraska Press, 1979.

Stone, Lawrence. *The Family, Sex and Marriage in England 1500-1800.* New York: Harper and Row, 1977.

Taetzsch, Lynne. "Romantic Love Replaces Kinship Exchange in Aphra Behn's Restoration Drama." *Restoration: Studies in English Literary Culture, 1660-1700* 17 (1993): 30-38.

Thompson, James. *Language in Wycherley's Plays: Seventeenth-Century Language Theory and Drama.* University: Univ. of Alabama Press, 1984.

Todd, Barbara J. "The remarrying widow: a stereotype reconsidered." In *Women in English Society 1500-1800,* ed. Mary Prior. London: Methuen, 1985.

Velissariou, Aspasia. "Patriarchal Tactics of Control and Female Desire in Wycherley's *The Gentleman Dancing-Master* and *The Country Wife.*" *Texas Studies in Literature and Language* 37 (1995): 115-26.

Weber, Harold. "Carolinean Sexuality and the Restoration Stage: Reconstructing the Royal Phallus in *Sodom.*" In *Cultural Readings of Restoration and Eighteenth-Century Theater,* ed. J. Douglas Canfield and Deborah C. Payne, 67-88. Athens: Univ. of Georgia Press, 1995.

———. *Paper Bullets: Print and Kingship during the Reign of Charles II.* Lexington: Univ. Press of Kentucky, 1995.

———. *The Restoration Rake-Hero: Transformations in Sexual Understanding in Seventeenth-Century England.* Madison: Univ. of Wisconsin Press, 1986.

Weingrod Sandor, Louise E. "Spa Drama from Shadwell to Sheridan." Ph.D. diss., Brandeis University, 1988.

Wheatley, Christopher J. "'But speak every thing in its Nature': Influence and Ethics in Durfey's Adaptations of Fletcher." *Journal of English and Germanic Philology* (forthcoming).

———. "The Defense of the *Status Quo* and Otway's *The Atheist.*" *Restoration and 18th Century Theatre Research* 2d ser. 4 (1989): 14-30.

———. "Romantic Love and Social Necessities: Reconsidering Justifications for Marriage in Restoration Comedy." *Restoration: Studies in English Literary Culture, 1660-1700* 14 (1990): 58-70.

———. "Thomas Durfey's *A Fond Husband,* Sex Comedies of the Late 1670s and Early 1680s and the Comic Sublime." *Studies in Philology* 90 (1993): 371-90.

———. *Without God or Reason: The Plays of Thomas Shadwell and Secular Ethics in the Restoration.* Lewisburg, Pa.: Bucknell Univ. Press, 1993.

Williams, Raymond. *The Country and the City.* New York: Oxford Univ. Press, 1973.

———. *Marxism and Literature.* New York: Oxford Univ. Press, 1977.

Zimbardo, Rose. "At Zero Point: Discourse, Politics, and Satire in Restoration England." *ELH: A Journal of English Literary History* 59 (1992): 785-98.

———. *A Mirror to Nature: Transformations in Drama and Aesthetics 1660-1732.* Lexington: Univ. Press of Kentucky, 1986.

———. "The Semiotics of Restoration Satire." In *Cutting Edges: Postmodern Critical Essays on Eighteenth-Century Satire,* ed. James E. Gill, 24-42. Knoxville: Univ. of Tennessee Press, 1995.

Index

Note: Bold indicates substantive treatement of plays.

Index of Characters

Index

DATE DUE			